Reflections on Ethics and Responsibility

Zachary J. Goldberg
Editor

Reflections on Ethics and Responsibility

Essays in Honor of Peter A. French

Springer

Editor
Zachary J. Goldberg
Ludwig-Maximilians-Universität Munich
Munich, Germany

ISBN 978-3-319-50357-8 ISBN 978-3-319-50359-2 (eBook)
DOI 10.1007/978-3-319-50359-2

Library of Congress Control Number: 2016963699

Printed on acid-free paper

This Springer imprint is published by Springer Nature
The registered company is Springer International Publishing AG
The registered company address is: Gewerbestrasse 11, 6330 Cham, Switzerland

To my parents, Harold and Nancy

Foreword

Peter French was my senior colleague at the University of Minnesota, Morris, from 1974 through 1981. In December 1973, Peter was conducting interviews at an APA Eastern Division Meeting. It was my one and only interview; I was there to practice, to see if I could land an interview. I hoped to be finished with my Ph.D. in time for the following year's convention. Peter and I hit it off. I don't remember details, but I do remember thinking that he seemed genuinely interested. And then I got a call-back.

Just a few months before, one of my CUNY Professors had commented to my wife at a department party that I would probably get a job at a small school in some no-place in the Midwest. Barbara laughed—repressing a shiver—and thought: I'm a New Yorker; no way we are going to no-place in the Midwest.

The University of Minnesota, Morris was 3.5 h west/southwest of Minneapolis-St. Paul, 50 miles from the South Dakota border. The population was 3,500; 5,000 when school was in session. There were more people on our block in Manhattan. The largest structure on Main St. was a grain elevator. The one movie house still had love seats, and the floors were sticky.

But it was my first interview, my first shot at a life in philosophy, and I relished the opportunity. I arrived during a break in what I would come to see as the relentless Minnesota winter, an actual thaw, the sun shining and warm. The college was inviting, a small but attractive campus with actual flesh and blood students. My potential colleagues: Peter was a well-informed analytic philosopher, on top of the goings-on in ethics and political philosophy (and generally in contemporary philosophy); Ted Uehling was a historian of philosophy with special interest in Kant. A real Kantian, you might say. And I was introduced to a variety of other faculty members from other disciplines, all or most of whom seemed intellectually serious. And the position was offered to me!

The philosophy team of three at UMM was not a department but a discipline in the Division of the Humanities. Despite its size there was a great deal going on in Philosophy. Under Peter's influence, an unusual number of outside speakers, including philosophers of note, were coming to campus to give colloquia. Moreover, a journal had just been started in which the papers were to be published, *Midwest*

Studies in Philosophy. My first year on campus coincided with the first year of publication. I had fallen into something unusual.

The journal—I'm morally certain it was Peter's idea—did not start with a bang. Our Division Head approached it by asking us what were the conditions for failure. The University Press was not interested. An APA colleague said to me, upon hearing of our venture, "Just what we need: another journal."

With no real institutional funding we somehow found funds—I can't remember how but there is no question that it was Peter's initiative—to publish a limited first annual issue. I was to organize the second annual issue—its topic was philosophy of language—and I succeeded in getting Kripke, Donnellan, Quine, and Davidson to contribute and soon the University of Minnesota Press was very interested. In 2017 we are still publishing our journal, now with Wiley-Blackwell.

Peter was a fine teacher, popular but not a popularizer. He was also a gifted writer. I read some of his early papers and was impressed. He was also generous with his time, reviewing critically my own writing. I have worked long and hard on my writing, and at this point many years later I take great pleasure in it. Peter was a definite influence, improving the clarity of my writing, attending to issues of style and concision. As I think about it, he was much more of an influence on my writing than were my teachers in graduate school. It is something for which I have always been grateful.

Peter was ambitious for our quasi-department, ambitious in the best sense. Our colloquium program was probably superior to that of many of the best graduate programs in the country. That sounds ridiculous, but it was true. Among the speakers over the next few years were Donald Davidson (at least twice), David Kaplan, Hector-Neri Casteneda, John Perry, Alvin Goldman, Fred Dretske, Alvin Plantinga, and John Searle. Our philosophical guests provided a seminar for our majors and then a general lecture to the campus. We won a fellowship (I wrote the proposal under Peter's tutelage) that allowed us to bring J. L. Mackie to UMM from Oxford, and for an entire quarter. We ran a "Philosophy for Children" program during multiple summers; we were training elementary school teachers to teach philosophy to their students. And we were learning a great deal in the process.

We taught large lower division courses but also specialized seminars, my own in the philosophy of language, Peter's in ethics and political philosophy, Ted's in history. David Kaplan addressed my seminar (I believe it was on Kripke's *Naming and* Necessity) and commented that at UCLA there would not be an undergraduate class on such advanced material; it would be taught only in graduate seminars. But we had very bright students and such was the ethos of philosophy at UMM. And Peter was the driving force. It is a rare pleasure to be able to tell the UMM Philosophy story, especially in the context of a volume in Peter's honor.

University of California, Riverside
Riverside, CA, USA

Howard Wettstein

Contents

List of Contributors

Maike Albertzart Humboldt University, Berlin, Germany

Carlos Gómez-Jara Díez Universidad Autónoma de Madrid, Madrid, Spain

John Martin Fischer University of California, Riverside, Riverside, CA, USA

Peter A. French Arizona State University, Tempe, AZ, USA

Zachary J. Goldberg Ludwig-Maximilians-Universität Munich, Munich, Germany

Ishtiyaque Haji University of Calgary, Calgary, AB, Canada

Virginia Held CUNY Graduate Center, New York, NY, USA

Tracy Isaacs Western University, London, Canada

Andrew C. Khoury Arizona State University, Tempe, AZ, USA

Michael McKenna University of Arizona, Tucson, AZ, USA

Benjamin Mitchell-Yellin Sam Houston State University, Huntsville, TX, USA

William J. Morgan University of Southern California, Los Angeles, CA, USA

Deborah Tollefsen University of Memphis, Memphis, TN, USA

Margaret Urban Walker Marquette University, Milwaukee, WI, USA

Howard Wettstein University of California, Riverside, Riverside, CA, USA

Leo Zaibert Union College, Schenectady, NY, USA

Editor's Introduction

Peter A. French's intellectual contributions to a wide spectrum of philosophical discussions have made him an influential figure in the fields of metaethics, normative ethics, applied ethics, as well as legal and political philosophy. He is perhaps best known for his original work focusing on the identification and exploration of the scope and nature of the moral responsibility and agency of individuals and collectives. Despite the abstruse character that is inherent to such philosophical issues, French reliably relates his conceptual discoveries to actual events, real social and cultural practices, as well as literature and film. This immediacy renders French's scholarship vital and accessible to a wide variety of audiences, highly relevant for current moral and political debates, and essential for thinking about pressing questions of individual and collective moral responsibility and agency. For all of these reasons, this Festschrift honors the work of Peter French.

French's international reputation in moral philosophy and normative and applied ethics is built upon his extensive and insightful body of work. (See the French Bibliography in this volume for a complete list of publications). As a single author, co-author, or editor he has contributed 61 books to the philosophical literature, some of which have been translated into multiple languages. He has published scores of articles in the major philosophical and legal journals and reviews, many of which have been anthologized. His publications have had a great influence in normative and applied ethics and have helped establish and sustain these fields as abiding and substantive challenges for both students and professional researchers. Spanning more than 30 years, his writings on collective responsibility continue to shape topics in ethics, applied ethics, and legal theory.

French's impact on philosophical discussion and the profession of philosophy does not end with his own contributions. He is senior editor of *Midwest Studies in Philosophy*, was the General Editor of the *Issues in Contemporary Ethics* series, and was the Editor of the *Journal of Social Philosophy* for 16 years. In 2002, French was appointed to the Board of Officers of the American Philosophical Association. The APA *Newsletter on Philosophy and Law* dedicated an issue to him in 2008 in recognition of his impact on the area of moral philosophy.

Beyond his roles as philosopher, colleague, and contributor to the profession, Peter French is a teacher. Several contributors to this volume, including myself, were fortunate enough to be his student, either in graduate school or in an NEH seminar. French's dedication to his students is unsurpassed. His intellectual excitement for philosophy is undeniable, and he effortlessly imparts this enthusiasm to his students and colleagues.

The current volume is comprised of 14 critical expositions of French's views on ethics and responsibility spanning his entire body of work. The essays in this book offer new and unique philosophical positions, while exploring, expanding and responding to those of French. The present essays have been selected due to their collective breadth and variety in grappling with the abundant themes appearing throughout French's work, as well as their individual depth and corresponding ability to enhance the philosophical literature concerning their respective topics. The goal of this volume is to present chapters that directly confront and philosophically analyze French's most influential theories and arguments, but also to include chapters by authors who seek to broaden some of French's original insights. An additional highlight of this volume is the concluding piece written by French, which provides both a new philosophical analysis as well as some reflection on his earlier work and its influence.

Andrew Khoury builds on French's work concerning different kinds of moral responsibility and characterizes eight types of responsibility ascription. Khoury distinguishes not only between individual and collective agents and actions, but also between responsibility attributed to an agent at the time of the action and subsequent to the action. These distinctions help demonstrate that responsibility attributed to an agent over time requires psychological or attitudinal connectedness on the part of the responsible agent. Khoury's analysis provides a framework for understanding when and which responsibility ascriptions are appropriate.

Maike Albertzart's essay challenges French's account of corporate moral responsibility. Although she agrees with French's insight that a corporation's internal decision-making (CID) structure validates its status as an intentional, rational agent, Albertzart argues that such groups fail to be appropriate subjects of moral responsibility. Relying on a Kantian conception of autonomy, she argues that group agents fail to fulfill the necessary conditions of autonomous agency because they lack the ability to choose the principles that are definitive of their wills. She concludes that individuals bear moral responsibility for the actions of group agents.

The theme of Carlos Gómez-Jara's essay is the influence that French's work on corporate responsibility has had in the field of corporate criminal liability. French's arguments regarding a corporation's CID not only explain the manner in which corporations can exercise agency, but also provide the conceptual framework for holding corporations liable for lack of compliance with legal strictures. Gómez-Jara explains how French's theory of corporate moral responsibility agrees with prominent theories and practices of corporate legal responsibility.

Virginia Held's essay considers the suitability of French's work on collective responsibility for dealing with entrenched problems of ethnic conflict and violence. Insofar as most of these conflicts involve groups, only a theory of group agency and collective/corporate responsibility is applicable to them. She demonstrates the multiple ways in which French's work coheres with the ethics of care and why such approaches are superior to alternative methods familiar in the history of moral and political philosophy.

Michael McKenna undertakes an analysis of French's view that moral responsibility amounts to nothing more than a collection of practices. French's deflationary account explicitly eschews appeals to metaphysical facts in favor of attending to those practices that constitute our moral lives. Although McKenna resists some of French's assertions regarding our responsibility practices, he strives to show that French's insights are nevertheless consistent with his own conversational theory of moral responsibility.

Ishtiyaque Haji's contribution focuses on French's frequent reliance throughout his work on Frankfurt-style cases and their conclusion that individuals can be morally responsible for what they have done even if they lack the ability to do otherwise. Haji entertains a possible objection to this conclusion. He suggests that one might think that blameworthiness requires moral impermissibility, which in turn requires avoidability. Appealing to French's work concerning the supererogatory and his portrayal of the complexity of the moral landscape, Haji demonstrates that an individual can be blameworthy for permissible acts, thereby rejecting the proposed objection to Frankfurt examples.

In her chapter, "Responsibility, Obligation, and Climate Change" Tracy Isaacs explores French's analysis of the responsibility of "inactive fictive groups" in the context of climate change. She resists French's claim that for practical purposes we ought to focus on actually existing entities and argues in favor of paying more heed to putative groups. Isaacs contends that a coordinated effort to transform putative groups into effective collective agents can make a positive contribution to global problems in general, and climate change in particular.

William J. Morgan concentrates on French's influential work in the field of intercollegiate sports ethics. He argues that although French's diagnosis of the ethical issues belonging to intercollegiate sports is apt, French's proposed solution to these problems only raises additional ethical complications. Morgan identifies commercialization at any level to be problematic for the goals and successful practices of the university, and argues for a halt to the intrusion of the market into university affairs.

Deborah Tollefsen focuses on French's work on moral innocence and challenges his claim that the loss of moral innocence yields a knowledge of moral concepts. Although Tollefsen agrees with French that the loss of moral innocence is a necessary condition of responsible moral agency and membership in the moral community, she argues that it provides knowledge of human vulnerability rather than a robust conceptual understanding of good and evil. The former is more fundamental than the latter, and losing one's moral innocence provides one with this requisite knowledge.

In his essay, "Evil and a Worthwhile Life", Zachary J. Goldberg examines French's account of moral evil and his claim that it ought to be understood as a human action that jeopardizes another's aspirations to live a worthwhile life. Although Goldberg finds French's account of moral evil to be correct, he contends that French's subsequent argument for what makes a life worthwhile is too demanding. In order to salvage French's definition of evil, Goldberg distinguishes worthwhile lives from meaningful, valuable, significant, and good lives. He concludes that French's account of evil is correct if we understand a worthwhile life as one that is worth the time and effort of the individual whose life it is.

Margaret Urban Walker investigates whether there is a responsibility to remember mass violence and grave atrocity, and on whom this responsibility falls. To answer these questions she explores French's suggestion that collective memories can render communities morally challenged. Walker argues that states, most obviously democratic ones, and some nonstate actors have a duty to foster accurate collective memory and to remember historical injustice. She seeks to confront some of the challenges raised by French's account by thinking of the pursuit of accurate historical memory as a civic virtue.

The theme of Leo Zaibert's chapter is French's philosophical analysis of vengeance and its moral justifiability. He poses a dilemma for French's theory arguing that either French does not adequately distinguish vengeance from punishment, or that vengeance is not as virtuous as he claims. Addressing the first horn of the dilemma, Zaibert suggests a way of distinguishing between punishment and vengeance that differs from French's account. Turning to the second issue, Zaibert calls attention to the avenger's supposed imperviousness to the suffering she inflicts—a trait that is difficult to interpret as a virtue.

John Martin Fischer and Benjamin Mitchell-Yellin address French's philosophical analysis of the significance of death in Westerns. Although French draws a contrast between the worldview of "westerners", who believe that death is necessary for meaningfulness in life, and that of "easterners", who are committed to a religious immortality, Fischer and Mitchell-Yellin suggest a third alternative. They argue in support of the desire for secular immortality and in so doing try to defeat Bernard Williams' well-known skeptical view that immortality entails boredom.

This volume concludes with a contribution from Peter French. French discusses cases in which persons' moral beliefs do not match their behavior. Referred to in the philosophical literature as alief/belief discordance, French offers an original explanation of this phenomenon with support from both the story of Huckleberry Finn and the life of Thomas Jefferson as illustrative examples. French proposes that what he calls "prizings", a variety of what Harry Frankfurt called cares and similar in some ways to Hume's description of passions, may explain why individuals can sincerely hold certain moral beliefs while exhibiting behavior that transgresses those beliefs. This analysis supports the conclusion that individuals' volitional attitudes may be more important than their moral beliefs for ascriptions of moral praise or blame. The chapter ends with an enlightening clarification of French's account of corporate moral personhood and its (lack of) connection to the Supreme Court decision in *Citizens United*.

A final word is due regarding the composition of this volume. I am delighted to have had the honor to serve as editor. However, this publication would not have been possible without the enthusiastic participation of all of the authors, as well as the support of the editorial staff. I am grateful to all who contributed to the completion of this project.

Individual and Collective Responsibility

Andrew C. Khoury

Introduction

Like most philosophically interesting notions, attributions of responsibility and blame are far from straightforward. This is due, in part, to the fact that there are a number of different senses of such notions to which one might appeal. For example, Peter French argues that the following claim is not necessarily inconsistent:

> Charles Manson is to blame for the Tate/LaBianca murders, but he cannot be blamed, even though we do blame him (1976, 43).

Roughly, the first occurrence of "blame" functions to make a purely causal claim, the last refers to our actual emotional responses, and the second concerns whether such responses are warranted. It is worth carefully distinguishing amongst these senses. But even when we are focused on a particular sense of responsibility or blame, such as the extent to which blaming attitudes are warranted, there are still a variety of notions that we may have in mind when making a responsibility attribution. My task in this chapter is to draw three distinctions that are applicable when discussing moral responsibility, in terms of blameworthiness and praiseworthiness, in the context of both individuals and collectives. Peter French's work on responsibility is deserving of its influence and the claims developed and defended here, as will become evident, owe much to this important work.

The three binary distinctions drawn give rise to eight types of responsibility attribution. I will discuss each type in turn, but given the wide scope of the topic what I will say about each must be fairly brief. My chief purpose, then, is more that of the surveyor than that of the architect, though I will attempt to do some theory building.

A.C. Khoury (✉)
Arizona State University, Tempe, AZ, USA
e-mail: andrew.khoury@asu.edu

Z.J. Goldberg (ed.), *Reflections on Ethics and Responsibility*,
DOI 10.1007/978-3-319-50359-2_1

The sense of responsibility with which I will be concerned is that of moral responsibility. By moral responsibility, I mean the extent to which one is blameworthy or praiseworthy. As noted above, this sense of responsibility should be distinguished from mere causal responsibility (e.g. "the rain is responsible for ruining your shoes") as well as the question of whether a given agent is actually held responsible by anyone (e.g. "the electorate held him responsible for the scandal"). It should also be distinguished from legal responsibility (e.g. "she was found responsible for misconduct") and responsibility in the sense of duty or obligation (e.g. "it is his responsibility to watch the children"). The sense of responsibility that I will be discussing is the sense in which being responsible is a matter of being an apt target of the reactive attitudes such as guilt, resentment, and indignation on the one hand and (certain forms of) pride, gratitude, and approbation on the other.[1] One important feature of this sense of responsibility is that it admits of degrees. One can, for example, be more or less blameworthy or more or less praiseworthy.

Three Distinctions

An attribution of moral responsibility, in the intended sense, typically has the following form (or readily submits to such a form):

> Subject S is morally responsible (i.e. blameworthy or praiseworthy) to degree *d* for object O.

Such attributions involve a three-place predicate relating a subject and object to some degree or other.[2] Much attention has been directed at such attributions in the individual context. These are contexts in which both the subject is an individual agent and the object is an individual action (or the consequence of some individual action).

In the latter half of the twentieth century, and owing, in part, to the great harms that occurred during WWII and the Vietnam War, some theorists turned their attention to responsibility in a collective context. For example, French argued that there are certain kinds of actions that can only be committed by collectives, not individuals:

> There is, of course, a class of predicates that just cannot be true of individuals, that can only be true of collectives. Examples are abundant, and surely include "disbanded" (most uses of), "lost the football game", "elected a president", and "passed an amendment." (1998, 37)

What French was suggesting is that, in addition to individual actions, there is a large and significant class of actions (and corresponding consequences) that can only be brought about collectively. French argued further that not only are there

---

[1] See Strawson (1962).

[2] See French (1976, 443–444). He argues that blame is a two-place predicate (e.g. "We blame X for Y"). Insofar as one can be more or less blameworthy for a given object, responsibility in the sense of blameworthiness or praiseworthiness is (at least) a three-place predicate.

collective actions, but there are also collective agents that are not straightforwardly reducible to individual agents.[3] For now, simply note the conceptual possibility that in a responsibility attribution of the form "subject S is responsible to degree *d* for object O," the subject may be an individual or a collective agent and the object may be an individual action (or consequence) or a collective action (or consequence).[4] I am not now making a claim about the truth or falsity of such attributions, I mean only to set them out for subsequent discussion.

In addition to the distinctions concerning subject and object there is another distinction that concerns the temporal dimension of a responsibility attribution. Sometimes we attribute moral responsibility for an action to an agent at the time of the action, what I call *synchronic responsibility*. At other times we attribute responsibility for an action to an agent at some time after the action has occurred, what I call *diachronic responsibility*.[5] More precisely, synchronic responsibility concerns the extent to which an agent at time t_1 is responsible for an action that occurs at t_1. Diachronic responsibility concerns the extent to which an agent at some later time t_2 is responsible for an action that occurred at t_1.[6] Synchronic responsibility involves the responsibility of an agent at the time of action, while diachronic responsibility involves the responsibility of an agent at some time after the action occurs.

We have, then, three binary distinctions concerning attributions of moral responsibility, understood as the extent to which an agent is blameworthy or praiseworthy:

(a) **Subject**: Individual agent or collective agent.
(b) **Object**: Individual action or collective action.
(c) **Temporality**: Synchronic or diachronic.

Taken together these three distinctions yield eight different types of moral responsibility attribution. These are represented in Table 1. "S" denotes the subject, "O" denotes the object, and the subscript denotes individual (i) or collective (c). I discuss these types of responsibility attribution below.[7]

---

[3]See French (1984).

[4]For ease of expression I'll speak of the object as being an action rather than an action or consequence, but the disjunction should be taken as implied.

[5]See Khoury (2013); also see Matheson (2014) who uses the language of synchronic and diachronic ownership.

[6]The point here is that moral responsibility needs to be indexed to time. The manner in which I've placed the temporal index here naturally accords with a four-dimensionalist ontology; the subject of a responsibility attribution is an agent *at a time* rather than an agent *simpliciter*. But this is not the only option, and nothing in what follows requires the adoption of four-dimensionalism. For example, one might instead hold that moral responsibility is a four-place rather than three-place predicate relating subject, object, degree, and time. Or one might hold that instantiation itself is a temporal relation or appeal to a temporal sentential operator. Which account one prefers will depend on one's favored solution to the problem of temporary intrinsics (see Lewis 1986, 203–205).

[7]Note that on this conception the distinction between individual responsibility and collective responsibility is wholly accounted for in terms of the relata of the moral responsibility relation.

Table 1 Types of moral responsibility attribution

Type	Subject	Object	Temporality	Formal structure
1	Individual	Individual	Synchronic	S_i at t_1 is morally responsible to degree *d* for O_i at t_1
2	Individual	Individual	Diachronic	S_i at t_2 is morally responsible to degree *d* for O_i at t_1
3	Collective	Collective	Synchronic	S_c at t_1 is morally responsible to degree *d* for O_c at t_1
4	Collective	Collective	Diachronic	S_c at t_2 is morally responsible to degree *d* for O_c at t_1
5	Individual	Collective	Synchronic	S_i at t_1 is morally responsible to degree *d* for O_c at t_1
6	Individual	Collective	Diachronic	S_i at t_2 is morally responsible to degree *d* for O_c at t_1
7	Collective	Individual	Synchronic	S_c at t_1 is morally responsible to degree *d* for O_i at t_1
8	Collective	Individual	Diachronic	S_c at t_2 is morally responsible to degree *d* for O_i at t_1

Type 1

Attributions of Type 1, individual synchronic responsibility for individual action, are familiar (though not necessarily under that description). In such attributions a claim is made about the extent to which an individual is responsible for an individual action at the time the act occurs. For example, suppose that Red has committed murder at time t_1. An attribution of Type 1 makes a claim about the extent to which Red at t_1 is blameworthy for his murderous action that occurs at t_1.

The debate between compatibilists and incompatibilists about causal determinism and moral responsibility is best understood, I think, as a debate most fundamentally about the conditions of Type 1 attributions of moral responsibility. Incompatibilists argue that the truth of Type 1 attributions is incompatible with determinism while compatibilists deny this. There are many accounts of Type 1 in the literature and much of the debate has concerned the kind of control that is required for the truth of such attributions. Some argue that this type of responsibility requires agent-causal freedom, others argue that it is simply a matter of the proper alignment amongst one's desires, while others argue that it is a matter of being properly responsive to reasons.[8] For now let us note that while much of the debate has focused on the control condition, all plausible accounts will admit that there are conditions relating to the agent's beliefs and desires at the time of action.[9]

Alternatively, one might attempt to account for the distinction, not in terms of distinct relata, but in terms of distinct relations as May (1987), chapter 4 appears to hold.

[8]See, for example, O'Connor (2000), Frankfurt (1971), and Fischer and Ravizza (1998).

[9]For example, it is widely acknowledged that there is an epistemic condition on responsibility.

This is simply the rather trivial claim that whether and the extent to which an (individual) agent is (synchronically) blameworthy or praiseworthy for an action is partly determined by the beliefs and desires from which she acted. For example, if Red met the proper control condition with respect to his killing of the victim, then his Type 1 blameworthiness will be largely a matter of his beliefs about what he was doing and the quality and content of the values and desires that moved him to act.

Type 2

Attributions of Type 2, individual diachronic responsibility for individual action, are common in our lives though less commonly discussed explicitly in the literature. An attribution of Type 2 involves making a claim about the extent to which an individual at a later time is responsible for some action that occurred at an earlier time.[10] For example, suppose that Red has committed murder at time t_1. An attribution of Type 2 makes a claim about the extent to which Red at some later time t_2 is blameworthy for his murderous action at t_1.

If an individual's diachronic responsibility for an individual action (Type 2) was always equivalent to that individual's synchronic responsibility for that individual action (Type 1), then this would be a distinction without a difference. For example, many theorists explicitly or implicitly believe that diachronic responsibility is a straightforward matter of personal identity.[11] According to this view, diachronic responsibility does not come apart from synchronic responsibility so long as personal identity holds; if an individual at t_1 is blameworthy to degree *d* for some action that occurs at t_1, then some individual at t_2 is blameworthy to degree *d* for the action that occurred at t_1 if and only if the agent at t_2 is personally identical to the agent at t_1.

I have argued elsewhere that personal identity is neither necessary nor sufficient for individual diachronic responsibility.[12] For present purposes, let me briefly review those arguments. To see that personal identity is not necessary consider the following case. Suppose that Bonnie has robbed a bank at time t_1 and suppose that she is blameworthy for doing so to some degree *d*. Now imagine that in order to confuse the police Bonnie freely and knowingly decides to undergo a fission operation. This operation involves removing her brain from her skull, separating the left and right hemispheres, and placing them into two new brainless bodies. Call

[10]Note that the debate in the literature about whether responsibility is essentially historical is a debate most fundamentally about the proper conditions of Type 1 attributions. It is not directly a debate about the conditions of Type 2.

[11]Locke, for example, appears to endorse this view: "In this personal identity is founded all the right and justice of reward and punishment" (1694, 46). Many others have agreed.

[12]See Khoury (2013) where I develop the distinction between individual synchronic and diachronic responsibility for individual action in more detail. Also see Shoemaker (2012) and Matheson (2014).

the person resulting from Bonnie's left brain hemisphere Lonnie, and the person resulting from Bonnie's right brain hemisphere Ronnie. Suppose further that each brain hemisphere is a functional duplicate of the other such that both Lonnie and Ronnie awake from the operation with Bonnie's (quasi-) memories, personality traits, and all other psychological characteristics. Each are, at time t_2, delighted at the success of the operation and the subsequent police confusion and begin to devise their next nefarious activity. I have only sketched the details of the example, but insofar as we imagine such a case vividly I think it is intuitively compelling to think that both Lonnie and Ronnie at t_2 are blameworthy to degree *d* for the robbery that occurred at t_1. For example, it would seem very natural to think that Lonnie is fully blameworthy for the earlier action in an alternate scenario in which the right brain hemisphere is tossed into the garbage rather than implanted into a brainless body. And if so, there doesn't seem to be good reason to deny that Lonnie is blameworthy in the scenario in which Ronnie is present as well. It is hard to see how a fact extrinsic to Lonnie, such as whether Ronnie exists or not, could affect Lonnie's blameworthiness for the earlier action.[13] If both Lonnie and Ronnie are blameworthy to degree *d* for the earlier robbery, then personal identity is not necessary for individual diachronic responsibility for individual action. This is because both Lonnie and Ronnie are diachronically responsible for the earlier action but both cannot be personally identical with Bonnie. This is because personal identity is a transitive relation. Thus, if Lonnie is personally identical to Bonnie, and Bonnie is personally identical to Ronnie, then Lonnie is personally identical to Ronnie. But this is impossible; Lonnie and Ronnie are not one and the same. Thus, personal identity is not necessary for individual diachronic responsibility for individual action.[14]

We do not, of course, interact with the products of fission in our daily lives (though perhaps we will at some point in the future). What is more significant to the world with which we are acquainted is the fact that personal identity is not sufficient for individual diachronic responsibility for individual action. Return to the case of Red who committed a murder at time t_1. Suppose that the Red of our example is Ellis Boyd 'Red' Redding (played by Morgan Freeman) from the 1994 film *The Shawshank Redemption*. In the film Red is incarcerated in the Shawshank Penitentiary for an act of murder that he committed when he was a teenager.

[13]As Parfit asks in relation to the question of survival in such cases, "How could a double success be a failure?" (1984, 256).

[14]One might object to this claim by appealing to four-dimensionalism. According to the objection, prior to the fission operation there were actually two distinct but overlapping space-time worms occupying the Bonnie body. While this move might help one resist the fission cases as counterexamples to the claim that personal identity is necessary for diachronic responsibility, one will still be forced to deal with further counterexamples. This is because four-dimensionalism, as such, does not provide an account of the relation that unifies two person-stages as stages of the same space-time worm. The four-dimensionalist must appeal to some account of the unity relation, whether it be psychological or biological, and there are then further counterexamples to the necessity claim given those particular accounts. See Shoemaker (2012).

But the film takes place decades later when Red is an aging man. The kind and gentle character that we are confronted with in the film shows no semblance to any collection of beliefs or values that could lead one to commit murder. Rather, Red strikes us as one of the most decent characters in the film. I claim that given what he is like at that later time, Red the old man (at t_2) is (at least) less blameworthy for the murder than is Red the teenager (at t_1). His blameworthiness has diminished given the psychological changes that he has undergone over that time.[15] If so, then personal identity is not sufficient for individual diachronic responsibility for individual action on the natural assumption that Red at t_2 is personally identical to Red at t_1.[16]

What, then, is the relation that underlies attributions of individual diachronic responsibility for individual action, if not personal identity? The reason that Lonnie and Ronnie, intuitively, are diachronically blameworthy for the robbery appears to have to do with the fact that their intentional attitudes are relevantly related to the intentional attitudes of Bonnie that gave rise to the robbery. Both Lonnie and Ronnie possess, identify with, and endorse the very same attitudes that led Bonnie to commit the crime. And the reason that Red at t_2 seems less (or not) blameworthy for the murder at t_1 is that his intentional attitudes at t_2 are not relevantly related to the intentional attitudes of Red at t_1 that gave rise to the murder. Rather than being about personal identity, individual diachronic responsibility is, I suggest, a matter of *psychological connectedness*. Two states are psychologically connected when there is both a causal and similarity relation between them. For example, a memory is psychologically connected to some experience when the experience causes the memory (in the right way), and the memory is of that earlier experience (that is, they share intentional content). The same is true of other intentional attitudes such as beliefs and desires. A desire at a time is psychologically connected to a desire at a later time to the extent that there is an appropriate causal and content relationship between them. To speak roughly, this is simply the way in which intentional attitudes persist across time.[17]

Psychological connectedness needs to be distinguished from psychological continuity. Psychological continuity is the ancestral relation of psychological connectedness. This means that psychological continuity is made up of overlapping

[15]One might object that Red at t_2 is just as blameworthy for the murder as is Red at t_1, it is simply that it is less appropriate to overtly blame Red at t_2 than Red at t_1. I agree that it would be less appropriate to overtly blame him at t_2 than at t_1, but I believe that the best explanation of this judgment is simply that he is less blameworthy at t_2 than at t_1. See Khoury (2013, 737–738, 744). Also see Khoury and Matheson ms.

[16]Note that Red at t_2 is personally identical with Red at t_1 on the two most popular accounts of personal identity: the psychological criterion and the biological criterion.

[17]See Parfit (1984, 204–207). The qualification is needed because persistence will hold only when connectedness holds uniquely (i.e. one-one, not one-many). But because whether this relation holds uniquely or not is arbitrary, psychological connectedness captures "what matters" in the persistence of psychological states.

chains of (strong[18]) psychological connectedness. An important implication of this is that psychological continuity is a binary and transitive relation and, for that reason, does not entail the existence of any particular distinctive psychological features, while psychological connectedness is not transitive and does entail the existence of particular distinctive psychological features. For example, I am now psychologically continuous with my 2 year old self but I am not now (very) psychologically connected with my 2 year old self. Myself at 3 years old remembered the experiences of myself at 2 years old, myself at 4 years old remembered the experiences of myself at 3 years old and so on. Because there are these overlapping chains of direct psychological connections (e.g. memory, belief, and desire), I am now psychologically continuous with myself at 2 years old. But there are few, if any, direct psychological connections between my current self and myself at 2 years old. I do not now, for example, remember any experiences of myself at 2 years old.

On the account that I defend, individual diachronic responsibility for individual action is directly sensitive to psychological connectedness with the intentional attitudes that gave rise to the action in question.[19] Suppose that at t_1 some agent commits some bad action because of some criticizable collection of intentional attitudes and is therefore blameworthy to degree *d* at t_1 for the action. If the agent at some later time t_2 is maximally psychologically connected to those intentional attitudes that gave rise to the action, then the agent is, at t_2, blameworthy to that same degree *d* for the earlier action. If the agent at t_2 is psychologically connected to the motivations that gave rise to the action at t_1 only to a small degree, then the agent at t_2 is only blameworthy for the earlier action to a small degree. This is, I take it, the case with Red from *The Shawshank Redemption*.

Type 3

Responsibility attributions of Type 3 involve attributing synchronic responsibility to a collective agent for some collective action. For example, to say that British Petroleum at t_1 is blameworthy for acting negligently at t_1 is to make an attribution of Type 3. Various accounts of Type 3 attributions have been put forward. For example, eliminativists claim that talk of collective agency is either in error or else merely

[18]Parfit (1984, 206) defines strong psychological connectedness as *enough* connections to ensure that identity holds day to day, on a revised Lockean view of personal identity. Strong connectedness, then, is a non-scalar binary relation unlike psychological connectedness *simpliciter*. Appeal to overlapping chains of strong connectedness (i.e. psychological continuity) is necessary in order to craft an account of personal identity from the notion of psychological connectedness. This is because personal identity is a form of numerical identity and so must have the logic of numerical identity (e.g. it must be non-scalar and transitive), but psychological connectedness does not have the appropriate logic (e.g. it is scalar and intransitive).

[19]See Khoury (2013), and Khoury and Matheson ms.

shorthand for talk of individual agency.[20] On this conception, presumably, Type 3 attributions are either false or else merely a handy device to refer to a set of Type 1 or Type 2 attributions.

Other theorists reject this form of eliminativism. French, for example, has influentially argued that Type 3 attributions are not always reducible to Type 1 or 2 attributions.[21] Rather, a collective can be functionally structured in such a way that grounds attributions of moral responsibility, in part, because that functional organization can ground attributions of intention. Appealing to a Davidsonian conception of action, some event counts as an action only if there is a true description of that event under which it is intentional.[22] French argues that a corporation's internal decision structure (its CID Structure), which consists of a flowchart delineating the hierarchical roles of the individual members and a set of rules that specifies the conditions under which a corporate decision has been made, grounds these corporate intentional descriptions. They ground the identification of the corporate reasons for which the corporation acts and which may not coincide with the individual reasons for which the individual members act.

Christian List and Philip Pettit have recently rigorously defended the idea of collective moral agency along similar functionalist lines.[23] They argue first, that it can make good sense to adopt what Daniel Dennett has called "the intentional stance" towards some collectives. Adopting this stance towards an entity involves attributing intentional attitudes, such as beliefs and desires, towards the entity as a means of explaining its behavior.[24] For example, just as attributing such attitudes can prove indispensable in explaining the behavior of humans, so too can it prove indispensable when explaining the behavior of some collectives. It is relatively uncontroversial that collectives can be organized in such a way that they can form beliefs about the way the world is, desires concerning how they want the world to be, and that they can act on the basis of those beliefs so as to realize those desires. For example, a given collective may hold a vote to decide whether it, qua collective, will endorse some proposition or seek to realize some goal. None of this is particularly surprising.

What is surprising is that ensuring that a collective has consistent intentional attitudes gives rise to autonomy at the level of the collective.[25] If a collective is to count as an agent it must minimize the possibility that it has inconsistent beliefs and desires, otherwise it could not act so as to realize its desires on the basis of its beliefs thereby undermining the very possibility of agency. In order to guarantee this minimal condition of agency, List and Pettit argue, a minimally complex collective that holds attitudes on logically related propositions must be organized in such a way

---

[20] This language comes from List and Pettit (2011).

[21] See French (1984, 1998).

[22] See Davidson (1980).

[23] See Pettit (2007) and List and Pettit (2011).

[24] See Dennett (1987).

[25] See Pettit (2007) and List and Pettit (2011).

that gives rise to the possibility that the collective has an attitude that is not shared by *any* of its members. List and Pettit argue further that since collectives can consider and endorse propositions with moral content (because their individual members can bring these propositions up for consideration) and because collectives can then control what they do on the basis of their collectively endorsed attitudes, collectives can meet the conditions of moral agency. Of particular note is the possibility that a collective is morally responsible in a way that none of its members are (say, because the collective endorses a morally objectionable proposition that is not held by any of its members).

The basic idea of accounts of this kind, which are best understood as accounts of Type 3 (collective synchronic responsibility for collective action), is that collectives can count as moral agents because they have and can freely act upon intentional attitudes such as beliefs and desires, and these attitudes can have moral content. A collective's synchronic responsibility for a collective action is determined in large part, just as is an individual's synchronic responsibility for an individual action, by the attitudes expressed by the agent in the action.[26] At this point, I merely want to note my sympathies with accounts in this spirit and discuss the other types of responsibility with this analysis in hand.

Type 4

A responsibility attribution of Type 4 attributes to a collective diachronic responsibility for a collective action. For example, to say that British Petroleum is now blameworthy for its past negligent actions that led to the Gulf oil spill is to make an attribution of Type 4.

Just as it is rather natural, but mistaken, to think that individual diachronic responsibility for individual action is a matter of personal identity, one might similarly think that collective diachronic responsibility for collective action is a matter of collective identity, understood as a form of numerical identity.[27] On this view, collective identity is both necessary and sufficient for diachronic collective

[26] I take it that one of the primary insights of Strawson's (1962) landmark essay is that this is what moral responsibility is most fundamentally about. Silver (2002, 2005) and Tollefsen (2003) have defended a Strawsonian approach to collective responsibility according to which appropriate collectives can be the proper target of the reactive attitudes. Recently, Björnsson and Hess (2016) have argued that appropriate collectives can also be the proper *bearers* of the reactive attitudes. In my view the Strawsonian approach is complementary to, rather than an alternative to, the functionalist approaches of French and List and Pettit.

[27] Janna Thomson appears to invoke this view when she says: "They [properly organized collectives] ought to act responsibly, and when they do wrong they ought to make recompense. Since these collectives persist through time and, in many cases, through the generations, so, it seems, do their responsibilities" (2006, 158; also see her remarks on 159–160). Abdel-Nour endorses the claim that identity is necessary and sufficient for both individual and (arguably) collective diachronic responsibility: "No matter when the agent's role as cause of a bad state of affairs is

responsibility for collective action. If a collective at t_1 is blameworthy to some degree for some collective action that occurs at t_1, then some collective at a later time t_2 is blameworthy to that same degree for that very action if and only if the latter is numerically the same collective as the former. If this view were true, then the distinction between Type 3 and Type 4 would be a distinction without a difference. But this view is mistaken. Collective numerical identity is neither necessary nor sufficient for collective diachronic responsibility for collective action.

First, for reasons parallel to the above argument that personal numerical identity is not necessary for individual diachronic responsibility for individual action (Type 2), collective numerical identity is not necessary for collective diachronic responsibility for collective action (Type 4). Imagine that a terrorist organization O carries out an attack X at time t_1. Imagine that the organization is structured in such a way that it meets the conditions of collective synchronic responsibility, such as those outlined in the previous section, and hence, is blameworthy to some degree *d* for its attack at time t_1. Now imagine that in the subsequent confusion and chaos following the attack, the members of the terrorist organization O are separated into two groups. Call the resulting groups O1 and O2. Each half, suppose, reasonably believes that it is all that remains of O and that the others have perished. This is, in effect, a case of collective fission. Suppose that at a later time t_2 O1 and O2 continue on as before, exemplifying the same organizational structure as O, and pursuing the same goals in accordance with the same policies and so on. Suppose that, at t_2, both continue to fully reflectively endorse the attack X which occurred at t_1. Insofar as we imagine such a case vividly, I think it is intuitively compelling to think that both O1 and O2 at t_2 are blameworthy to degree *d* for the attack X which occurred at t_1. For example, it would seem very natural to hold that O1 at t_2 is blameworthy for the attack X in a similar case in which O2 does in fact perish (if one is not skeptical, in general, of Type 4 attributions). It is hard to see how a fact extrinsic to O1, such as O2's survival or death, could affect O1's responsibility for X. But if both O1 and O2 are blameworthy for the earlier attack, then collective numerical identity cannot be necessary for collective diachronic responsibility for collective action. Both O1 and O2 are diachronically responsible for the attack but both O1 and O2 cannot be numerically identical with O, for this would imply that O1 and O2 are numerically identical with each other which is absurd; they are not one and the same, they are two independent systems of belief and desire.[28] Hence, identity is not necessary for collective diachronic responsibility for collective action.[29]

And for reasons parallel to the above argument that personal numerical identity is not sufficient for individual diachronic responsibility for individual action (Type 2), similarly collective numerical identity is not sufficient for collective diachronic

---

discovered or established, this discovery incurs a responsibility on her merely by virtue of her identity with the agent who performed the deed" (2003, 697). Also see Van den Beld (2002).

[28] This language comes from List and Pettit (2011, 34).

[29] One might appeal to four-dimensionalism in order to attempt to resist this counterexample. The same remarks apply in the collective context as do in the individual context. See note 14.

responsibility for collective action (Type 4). Imagine that at time t_1 a car manufacturer M intentionally acts so as to deceive a national regulatory agency as well as its customers, by installing defeat software in its vehicles that cheats on emissions tests. Suppose that the actions of the car manufacturer ground an attribution of Type 3, collective synchronic responsibility for its collective action A: *M's freely and knowingly cheating on emissions tests.* Now suppose that 50 (or 500 or 5000) years have passed. Imagine that during that time M altered its organizational structure and policies that gave rise to the earlier emissions cheating, made sincere public apologies for doing so, and offered proportional restitution to those affected. Imagine that now, at t_2, M voluntarily meets environmental regulations much more stringent than those required by law and is widely recognized to set the bar for environmentally friendly vehicles in the automotive industry. Suppose that M at t_2 shares none of the intentional attitudes of M at t_1 that gave rise to the past action A. Insofar as we imagine such a case vividly, I think it is intuitively compelling to think that M at t_2 is (at least) less blameworthy for A than is M at t_1. That is, M's blameworthiness for A has diminished with the passage of time in virtue of the changes it has undergone. If so, then identity is not sufficient for collective diachronic responsibility for collective action (Type 4), on the assumption that M at t_2 is numerically identical with M at t_1.[30]

I suggest that the same relation that grounds individual diachronic responsibility for individual action (Type 2) grounds collective diachronic responsibility for collective action (Type 4). The reason that O1 and O2 at t_2 are blameworthy for the earlier action committed by O at t_1 is because both O1 and O2 are fully connected to the intentional attitudes that led to the earlier attack. And the reason that M at t_2 is less blameworthy for A than is M at t_1, is because M at t_2 is no longer connected to the intentional attitudes that gave rise to A. Recall that the relevant notion of psychological connectedness, what might be better referred to in

[30]The plausibility of this claim depends, in part, on the correct account of collective numerical identity. Suppose that the correct account appeals to, as do the most popular accounts of personal numerical identity, some form of continuity such as psychological or attitudinal continuity, or some form of physical continuity. Continuity is a relation that is non-scalar and transitive, as it must be if it is to play the appropriate role in an account of numerical identity (which is non-scalar and transitive). Though these logical features of the continuity relation allow it to play the appropriate role in an account of numerical identity, they entail the possibility that continuity can hold in the absence of any "direct connections" whatsoever. That is, continuity is a relation that is made up of overlapping chains of some other underlying relation. There can be overlapping chains of that underlying relation over some duration (and so continuity) even if there are no direct chains of that underlying relation over that duration (and so no direct connections). If the correct account of collective numerical identity looks something like, for example, Parfit's Psychological Criterion (1984, 207), then it will be possible that a collective at one time is numerically identical with a collective at another time even though they share no attitudes whatsoever. For example, it would be possible for a collective at t_1 that is an attitudinal and functional duplicate of the Nazi SS to be uniquely continuous with, and for that reason numerically identical with, an attitudinal and functional duplicate of Oxfam at a later time t_2. It is in light of such cases that the claim that collective numerical identity is sufficient for diachronic responsibility is most difficult to sustain. On this point in the individual context see Khoury and Matheson ms.

this context simply as attitudinal connectedness, concerns (what matters in[31]) the persistence of intentional attitudes across time. The picture I am defending is this: When an agent acts it does so on the basis of a collection of intentional attitudes, for example beliefs and desires.[32] An agent's synchronic responsibility, whether individual (Type 1) or collective (Type 3), is largely a matter of the moral quality of these attitudes. And an agent's diachronic responsibility, whether individual (Type 2) or collective (Type 4), is largely a matter of (what matters in) the persistence of those attitudes.[33] Attitudinal connectedness is the proper way to understand (what matters in) the persistence of intentional attitudes, hence, attitudinal connectedness is the relation that grounds ascriptions of diachronic responsibility.

Various accounts of Type 4 have been put forward (particularly in the context of national responsibility for historic injustice). I think that the above account commands a great deal of intuitive appeal. But another reason to prefer this account over rivals concerns theoretical parsimony. The fact that we can explain both individual diachronic responsibility for individual action (Type 2) and collective diachronic responsibility for collective action (Type 4) on a single theoretical model is a mark in its favor.

Types 5–8

I will discuss attributions of Types 5–8 together because they share an important feature. All these attributions involve an asymmetry between subject and object. That is, while attributions of Types 1–4 all involve either individual responsibility for individual action (whether synchronic or diachronic), or collective responsibility for collective action (whether synchronic or diachronic), attributions of Types 5–8 involve a contrast between subject and object. They involve either individual responsibility for collective action (whether synchronic or diachronic), or collective responsibility for individual action (whether synchronic or diachronic).

One might attempt to develop an account of Types 5–8 that takes its cue from the above analysis of Types 2 and 4. The notion of attitudinal (or psychological) connectedness, it was argued, grounds ascriptions of Types 2 and 4. An individual is morally responsible for some individual action in the past to the extent that the individual is connected to those intentional attitudes that gave rise to the action. Similarly, a collective is morally responsible for some past collective act to the extent that it is connected to those intentional attitudes that gave rise to the past

[31] See note 17.

[32] I speak of beliefs and desires for the sake of simplicity. We may need to include reference to other intentional attitudes, notably plans and concerns. See Bratman (1987) and Frankfurt (1982).

[33] Notice that this formulation allows for the possibility that there are additional requirements. For example, one might wish to hold that diachronic responsibility requires that the agent in some way freely chooses to continue to have the relevant attitudes.

collective action. (Recall that attitudinal states are connected, in this way, to the extent that there exists a proper causal and similarity relation between them.)

In a similar vein, one might argue that an individual member of a collective is synchronically or diachronically responsible for an act of the collective (Type 5 or 6) to the extent that the individual is connected, in this way, to the attitudes that gave rise to the collective act. Suppose that a racist organization collectively acts to cause harm. On the view being suggested, a member of the organization may be responsible for that very collective act to the extent that she is connected to the attitudes that led to the action.

To put it another way, recall the general account of Type 3, collective synchronic responsibility for collective action, discussed above. Collectives can be organized in such a way that it makes sense to adopt the intentional stance towards them. We can then explain collective actions by attributing intentional attitudes to the collective such as beliefs and desires. And these intentional attitudes may have moral content that grounds attributions of Type 3 (and [what matters in] the persistence of which grounds attributions of Type 4). That is, collectives can act with a morally evaluable quality of will. The view being currently considered suggests that an individual can be responsible for a collective act to the extent that her individual quality of will is relevantly connected to the collective quality of will. This could occur either synchronically (Type 5) or diachronically (Type 6).

Suppose that an individual member of an appropriately structured racist organization votes in favor of pursuing certain racist policies that the organization then adopts and acts upon. On this view, the individual is responsible for the collective act to the extent that her quality of will is similar and properly causally related to the collective quality of will that gave rise to the collective act.[34] Similarly, an individual may be diachronically responsible for a past collective act to the extent that the individual is connected to the past collective quality of will.[35]

The prime advantage of this view is that it has the potential to offer a subtle account of the way that responsibility for collective acts distributes to individual members. It allows that the responsibility of members is not necessarily on a par,

[34] According to this view, if an individual member votes against that policy of collective action then she may not be responsible for that particular collective action because she is not relevantly connected to the collective's "springs of action." It should be emphasized, however, that this in no way implies that there is nothing else for which the individual is responsible (e.g. her becoming a member).

[35] There are a number of accounts in a similar general spirit. For example, Abdel-Nour (2003) argues that an agent can be properly connected to the past action of another (and arguably of a past collective like a nation) via the emotion of pride, and that this grounds attributions of responsibility. According to Abdel-Nour, "when there is national pride, there is national responsibility" (713). May (1992) argues that one can be responsible for the acts of a distinct agent in virtue of sharing the relevant attitudes that gave rise to the act.

but tracks their relation to the morally relevant features of the collective.[36] A similar account might be given for attributions of Types 7 and 8.

This is just a brief sketch in broad strokes and a fully developed account would need to address further questions. For example, in what way is the causal direction relevant? An individual may be attitudinally connected to a collective will because the individual's attitudes are, in part, a cause of the collective will (e.g. by means of voting). Alternatively, an individual may be attitudinally connected to a collective will because the collective's attitudes are a cause of some of the individual's relevant attitudes (e.g. by means of indoctrination). There may be other possible ways in which an individual's attitudes may be related to the collective attitudes in a way that grounds these types of responsibility attribution. For example, one might appeal to the supervenience relation that holds between the collective attitudes and the individual attitudes.[37] Furthermore, it seems that there may be important distinctions to be made amongst the relevant attitudes. Collective action involves sets of collective belief and desire. It may be that some of those beliefs and desires (or some combination of them) are morally innocuous while others are not. Thus, it appears to matter for responsibility to which collective attitudes in particular the individual is connected even holding fixed the collective action and the degree of the connection.[38]

While I am inclined to think that an account along the general lines suggested above is the most promising account of the truth of attributions of Types 5–8, I am hesitant to endorse the view that such attributions are possibly true. Notice that all plausible accounts of Types 5–8, including the above, will share a general structural feature, namely, that they make use of what we can call a *tracing strategy*. This strategy involves "tracing" from the object of the responsibility attribution to some distinct property of the subject that is thought to ground the responsibility attribution.[39] For example, on some accounts of Types 5 and 6 an individual can

---

[36]Contrast with, for example, David Silver's (2002) account. While he helpfully frames the issue of Type 6 attributions as one concerning an individual's proper ownership of past collective action, his positive account of this ownership seems to imply that there are no differences amongst members with respect to their responsibility for a collective act. This is because, on his account, one owns the past actions of a collective of which one is a member, simply in virtue of the fact that one is a full-fledged member of that collective. But, arguably, it is implausible that all members of a collective are all equally responsible for the past acts of the collective. Some, for example, may reflectively endorse (i.e. be attitudinally connected to) the attitudes that gave rise to the past action to a greater extent than others, and this seems morally relevant.

[37]One can accept that collective attitudes supervene on individual attitudes without accepting that a collective's attitude towards a proposition supervenes on the attitudes of its individual members with respect to that very proposition. See List and Pettit (2011, 64–73). It's worth noting that the relevant supervenience relation may not be a form of attitudinal connectedness, as defined here, insofar as the latter but not the former involves a causal relation.

[38]The same issue arises in the case of individual diachronic responsibility for individual action (Type 2).

[39]The notion of tracing is familiar in the literature on free will and moral responsibility in the individual context. Many theorists believe that an appeal to tracing is necessary in order to explain

be responsible for a collective act only if we can trace from the collective act to an appropriate participatory intention.[40] Other accounts hold that we must be able to trace back to an appropriate attitude or an act of identification.[41]

All such accounts involve specifying some distinctive basis on which the subject is morally responsible for the object.[42] And on each of these accounts, because the basis and object are ontologically independent the relation between them is contingent such that the basis and object can come apart.[43] And this feature, in turn, entails a form of moral luck.

Suppose, for example, that the given account holds that an individual subject S_i is blameworthy for collective act O_c on the basis of some individual property P of S_i. Because P (whether it be a participatory intention, a faulty attitude, an act of identification, or whatever) is ontologically independent from (and for that reason, only contingently related to) O_c, we can imagine an alternate scenario in which S_i has P but O_c does not occur. On the given account, there is a difference in S_i's blameworthiness across the two scenarios despite the fact that there is, by hypothesis, *no difference* with respect to the basis of S_i's blameworthiness across the two scenarios. S_i is blameworthy for O_c in the first scenario but not in the second (because it does not occur). But whether O_c occurs or not is a matter independent of the basis on which S_i is held responsible. This result is as implausible, by my lights,

---

a range of cases of moral responsibility such as drunk driving cases. For example, suppose that an agent freely and knowingly becomes inebriated at a party and subsequently drives home and kills a pedestrian. Stipulate that the agent lacks the control required for moral responsibility at the time of the accident. But, intuitively, the agent is responsible for killing the pedestrian. Many think that we can properly explain the agent's responsibility only if we trace back from the control-deficient event (the killing of the pedestrian) to some non-control-deficient event (e.g. the agent's getting drunk). See, for example, Fischer and Ravizza (1998), and Fischer and Tognazinni (2009). Some theorists have raised problems for tracing and offered alternative accounts. See Vargas (2005), Khoury (2012), King (2014), Shabo (2015), and Agule (2016).

[40] See Kutz (2000).

[41] See May (1992) and Abdel Nour (2003).

[42] Kutz (2000, 122) makes explicit the distinction between object and basis.

[43] This is true with respect to the actual above accounts referenced. Here is a sketch of an argument for the general claim that this relation must be contingent. Note first, that no plausible basis of an individual's responsibility for a collective act, such as her own individual contribution, will itself be sufficient for the occurrence of the collective act. This is because collective action is only possible in the context of the contributions of multiple individuals (i.e. a collective).

Secondly, one can argue that no particular individual contribution is itself necessary for the collective act by appealing to the multiple realizability of collective action (see List and Pettit 2011, chapter 3). French noted early on that certain kinds of collectives, what he called conglomerates, could be multiply realized: "The existence of a conglomerate is compatible with a varying membership. A change in the specific persons associated in a conglomerate does not entail a corresponding change in the identity of the conglomerate" (1998, 44). And it is not implausible to hold that collective action is also multiply realizable such that the actual contribution of any particular member could be fulfilled by another individual. If so, then the actual contribution of any particular member won't be necessary for the occurrence of the collective action. Assessing the extent to which collective action is multiply realizable in this way would require a full account of the individuation of collective action.

as the claim that the mere presence of a bird in the path of one's bullet can lessen one's blameworthiness in the context of a murder attempt.

Types 5–8, then, entail a form of moral luck that is relevantly similar to resultant (or consequential or outcome) moral luck.[44] Because the basis and object are ontologically independent, facts independent of the basis (such as whether the relevant object occurs) can affect the agent's blameworthiness. Two agents may have exactly the same properties that constitute the relevant basis, but they may be blameworthy for different objects in virtue of facts external to the basis. And this is a form of moral luck. One's blameworthiness can be affected by things other than that in virtue of which the agent is blameworthy. The only way to rule out the possibility of this form of moral luck is to hold that the possible objects of an agent's responsibility cannot be ontologically independent from the relevant basis of responsibility.[45] This, in turn, entails denying the possible truth of Types 5–8 insofar as the object of these responsibility attributions (e.g. a collective act) is ontologically independent of any plausible basis of the attribution (e.g. the individual's own acts).

These anti-moral-luck considerations underlie the claim with which H.D. Lewis began his famous attack on collective responsibility: "If I were asked to put forward an ethical principle which I considered to be especially certain, it would be that no one can be responsible, in the properly ethical sense, for the conduct of another" (1948, 3). Lewis thought this entailed the rejection of collective responsibility altogether because he did not seriously consider the possibility that collectives could be bona fide agents in their own right. But Types 3 and 4, which involve collective responsibility for collective action, do not run afoul of the above principle. Types 5–8, however, do. They all involve an agent's responsibility for the conduct of another agent.[46] For this reason I remain skeptical of the possibility of the truth of such attributions.[47] However, intuitions about moral luck are by no means univocal and I do not expect this objection to gain traction with those not antecedently wary of resultant moral luck. To those who do not see the acceptance of this form of moral luck as a theoretical cost to be avoided, I offer the above account of these forms of responsibility attribution that appeals to attitudinal connectedness.

Before closing I want to briefly consider an objection. I have raised a skeptical worry concerning the possibility of the truth of Types 5–8. These forms of responsibility attribution involve tracing from the object of the attribution to an ontologically independent basis of the attribution. For this reason such attributions give rise to a form of moral luck which, according to the worry, should be rejected. One might object that my own account of Type 2 (individual diachronic responsibility for individual action) and Type 4 (collective diachronic responsibility for collective

---

[44] See, for example, Williams (1981) and Nagel (1979). Also see Zimmerman (2002).

[45] I defend this claim, in slightly different terms and in relation to individual responsibility, in Khoury (2012).

[46] Or more carefully, for the conduct of an agent with which the former is not relevantly continuous.

[47] French (2016) has recently raised an objection in a sympathetic spirit against particular accounts of complicity.

action) similarly involves tracing and so entails the same form of moral luck. For an attribution of Type 2 or 4 to be grounded we must be able to appropriately trace back from the time to which responsibility is attributed to the time at which the relevant action occurred.

In response, Types 2 and 4 are not relevantly analogous to Types 5–8. With respect to Types 5–8 we must trace back from something that is ontologically independent of the basis (namely, the object) to the relevant basis. It is this structural feature that gives rise to moral luck. But this structural feature is not present in attributions of Types 2 and 4. This is because Types 2 and 4 do not involve tracing back from something that is ontologically independent of the basis to the basis. Rather, these types of responsibility attribution concern, as it were, (what matters in) *the very persistence* of the relevant basis. In this way the objection can be resisted.

In slightly different terms, I accept the principle that we can only be responsible *for* those things that *are* the bearers of responsibility relevant value: in my view, willings that have particular qualities. The most plausible account of types 5–8 involves tracing from something external to the subject's willing to that subject's willing. This entails a form of moral luck. But Types 2 and 4 don't involve tracing back from something external to the willing. They involve (what matters in) the very persistence of the relevant willing.[48]

Conclusion

Peter French's work on individual and collective responsibility has been agenda setting. Building on some of this work, in this chapter I drew attention to three distinctions that arise in the context of individual and collective moral responsibility: subject, object, and temporality. These three binary distinctions give rise to eight types of responsibility attribution. I discussed these various types of responsibility attribution, suggesting that collective responsibility across time can be understood on the model of individual responsibility across time. I considered the possibility that attributions that involve an asymmetry between subject and object can be understood along similar lines, but raised a skeptical concern that such attributions give rise to a form of moral luck. My primary goal, however, has not so much been to defend a particular account of any of these eight types of responsibility attribution,

[48]I should reemphasize, too, that my skepticism only concerns responsibility construed as blameworthiness or praiseworthiness. It is plausible that individuals may have duties or obligations in light of the actions committed by the groups of which they are members. And so it is plausible, *in this distinct sense*, that individuals can be responsible for (i.e. have a duty to respond to) collective harms. See Radzik (2001).

but rather to simply set them out clearly in the hope of gaining some limited degree of clarity in the murky landscape of individual and collective responsibility. A landscape which would be all the murkier without French's work.[49]

References

Abdel-Nour, Farid. 2003. National responsibility. *Political Theory* 31(5): 693–719.

Agule, Craig. 2016. Resisting tracing's siren song. *Journal of Ethics and Social Philosophy* 10(1): 1–24.

Björnsson, Gunnar, and Kendy Hess. 2016. Corporate crocodile tears? On the reactive attitudes of corporate agents. *Philosophy and Phenomenological Research*. doi:10.1111/phpr.12260:1-26.

Bratman, Michael. 1987. *Intention, plans, and practical reason*. Cambridge, MA: Harvard University Press.

Davidson, Donald. 1980. *Essays on actions and events*. Oxford: Oxford University Press.

Dennett, Daniel. 1987. *The intentional stance*. Cambridge, MA: MIT Press.

Fischer, John Martin, and Mark Ravizza. 1998. *Responsibility and control: A theory of moral responsibility*. New York: Cambridge University Press.

Fischer, John Martin, and Neal Tognazzini. 2009. The truth about tracing. *Noûs* 43(3): 531–556.

Frankfurt, Harry. 1971. Freedom of the will and the concept of a person. *Journal of Philosophy* 68(1): 5–20.

———. 1982. The importance of what we care about. *Synthese* 53(2): 257–252.

French, Peter. 1976. Senses of blame. *Southern Journal of Philosophy* 14(4): 443–452.

———. 1984. *Collective and corporate responsibility*. New York: Columbia University Press.

———. 1998. *Individual and collective responsibility*. Rochester: Shenkman.

———. 2016. Complicity: That moral monster, troubling matters. *Criminal Law and Philosophy* 10(3): 575–589.

Khoury, Andrew. 2012. Responsibility, tracing, and consequences. *Canadian Journal of Philosophy* 42(3/4): 187–207.

———. 2013. Synchronic and diachronic responsibility. *Philosophical Studies* 165(3): 735–752.

Khoury, Andrew and Benjamin Matheson. n.d. "Is Blameworthiness Forever?" unpublished manuscript.

King, Matt. 2014. Traction without tracing: A solution for control-based accounts of moral responsibility. *European Journal of Philosophy* 22(3): 463–482.

Kutz, Christopher. 2000. *Complicity: Ethics and law for a collective age*. New York: Cambridge University Press.

Lewis, H.D. 1948. Collective responsibility. *Philosophy* 23(84): 3–18.

Lewis, David. 1986. *On the plurality of worlds*. Oxford: Blackwell.

List, Christian, and Philip Pettit. 2011. *Group agency: The possibility, design, and status of corporate agents*. Oxford: Oxford University Press.

Locke, John. 1694. Of identity and diversity. In *Essay concerning human understanding*. Reprinted in Perry 2008, pp. 33–52. Berkeley: University of California Press.

Matheson, Benjamin. 2014. Compatibilism and personal identity. *Philosophical Studies* 170(2): 317–334.

[49]A distant ancestor of this piece was a chapter in my doctoral dissertation of which Peter French was the director. Peter is well known for his writings, but he is also a devoted teacher and mentor and I thank him for his continued support through the years. I also thank Zachary Goldberg for inviting me to contribute to this volume and for comments on the manuscript, and Benjamin Matheson for helpful discussion and comments.

May, Larry. 1987. *The morality of groups*. Notre Dame: University of Notre Dame Press.
———. 1992. *Sharing Responsibility*. Chicago: The University of Chicago Press.
Nagel, Thomas. 1979. *Mortal questions*. New York: Cambridge University Press.
O'Connor, Timothy. 2000. *Persons and causes: The metaphysics of free will*. New York: Oxford University Press.
Parfit, Derek. 1984. *Reasons and persons*. Oxford: Oxford University Press.
Perry, John. 2008. *Personal identity*. Berkeley: University of California Press.
Pettit, Philip. 2007. Responsibility incorporated. *Ethics* 117(2): 171–201.
Radzik, Linda. 2001. Collective responsibility and duties to respond. *Social Theory and Practice* 27(3): 455–471.
Shabo, Seth. 2015. More trouble with tracing. *Erkenntnis* 80(5): 987–1011.
Shoemaker, David. 2012. Responsibility without identity. *Harvard Review of Philosophy* 18(1): 109–132.
Silver, David. 2002. Collective responsibility and the ownership of actions. *Public Affairs Quarterly* 16(3): 287–304.
———. 2005. A Strawsonian defense of corporate moral responsibility. *American Philosophical Quarterly* 42(4): 279–293.
Strawson, P.F. 1962. Freedom and resentment. *Proceedings of the British Academy* 48: 1–25.
Thompson, Janna. 2006. Collective responsibility for historic injustice. *Midwest Studies in Philosophy* 30: 154–167.
Tollefsen, Deborah. 2003. Participant reactive attitudes and collective responsibility. *Philosophical Explorations* 6(3): 218–235.
Van den Beld, Ton. 2002. Can collective responsibility for perpetrated evil persist over generations? *Ethical Theory and Moral Practice* 5(2): 181–200.
Vargas, Manuel. 2005. The trouble with tracing. *Midwest Studies in Philosophy* 29(1): 269–291.
Williams, Bernard. 1981. *Moral luck*. Cambridge: Cambridge University Press.
Zimmerman, Michael. 2002. Taking luck seriously. *Journal of Philosophy* 99(11): 43–576.

Monsters and Their Makers: Group Agency Without Moral Agency

Maike Albertzart

> *The bank is something else than men. It happens that every man in a bank hates what the bank does, and yet the bank does it. The bank is something more than men, I tell you. It's the monster. Men made it, but they can't control it.*
>
> (Steinbeck 2000, 35–36)

Introduction

Groups can, and often do, cause damage: a herd of stampeding cattle might injure a dog walker; an angry crowd of protesters might trample down a park's flowerbeds; and a company's lax safety regulations might lead to a disastrous oil spill. Cases of the first kind are tragic, but neither the group nor its individual members are appropriate objects of moral blame. Matters are different when the damage is the result of intentional human actions, as in the second and third cases. In the second case one might hold the protesters individually responsible for the damage done to the park. However, if each individual has a viable excuse for her or his behavior – say, that panic broke out and that there was no choice but to keep running forward – there seems to be no one left to be held responsible for the damage.[1] By contrast, cases like the third appear to offer an alternative locus of moral responsibility: the group itself. This chapter is concerned with such organized groups. It is concerned with the kind of groups Steinbeck describes in the epigraph above: banks and companies which appear to constitute agents distinct from their members. Experience shows that such groups easily spiral out of control. They

---

The title is based on Peter French's article, "Monsters and Their Makers". (French 1972).

[1]Some authors claim that even mere aggregate collectives can be held morally responsible. See Held (1970), May (1992), and Killoren and Williams (2013). However, these authors are in the minority and I will not discuss their position here.

M. Albertzart (✉)
Humboldt University, Berlin, Germany
e-mail: maike.albertzart@philosophie.hu-berlin.de

Z.J. Goldberg (ed.), *Reflections on Ethics and Responsibility*,
DOI 10.1007/978-3-319-50359-2_2

have the power to cause grave damage for which the individual members of the respective groups often apparently lack moral responsibility. According to Peter French, groups can and should be held morally responsible in such cases.

In a series of highly influential books and articles French has championed the possibility of, and the need for, corporate moral responsibility. For over three decades he has argued that corporations and other organized group can constitute group agents that are appropriate subjects of moral responsibility. Opponents of this view usually argue against the possibility of group responsibility by denying groups the status of intentional, rational agents (see e.g. Narveson 2002; Velasquez 2004).[2] A group's capacity for intentional, rational action and its capacity for moral action are widely assumed to rise and fall together.[3] By contrast, I will argue that although groups can form intentional, rational agents, they fail to be appropriate subjects of moral responsibility. The chapter is divided into three parts. The first part outlines French's account of corporate intentionality and moral agency. In the second part I will argue, contra French, that although groups can form intentional, rational agents, they fail to be appropriate subjects of moral responsibility. Following Kant, I will show that group agents lack the kind of autonomy that is constitutive of moral agency. French has challenged moral theorists to "give up the seventeenth-century conceit and admit that the social world in which ethics must be relevant has more than humans in it" (French 1995, 35). He rightly points out that group agents are now the dominant members of the social system and that we cannot afford to ignore them in our moral deliberations (French 1995, 13). However, as I will show in the final part of the chapter, this does not necessarily require treating them as morally responsible. Building on some of French's own work, I will argue that it can be appropriate to assign individual group members moral responsibility for the actions and character of group agents. If group agents spiral out of control and become "monsters" we are morally responsible for the harm they cause and, if necessary, to reform or extinguish them.

French's Account of Corporate Agency and Moral Agency

Groups often treated as agents in public discourse include political groups like political parties, governments and states; commercial entities like firms and corporations; as well as cultural and religious organizations like universities and churches. However, the fact that we speak of, and treat, such groups as agents does not mean that they actually possess the status of agents. It could be that our talk of group agency is best understood as being metaphorical, or as a useful fiction, or, if taken

[2]For an exception see Haney (2004) and Hedahl (2013).

[3]Most defenders of group responsibility hold that if a group can act intentionally and rationally, it can be regarded as a moral agent. See e.g. May (1987), Gilbert (2000), Arnold (2006), Tuomela (2007), and O'Madagain (2012).

literally, as simply misguided (see e.g. Quinton 1975). In order to establish whether groups can constitute agents, one first has to lay down the relevant conditions for agency. According to French, agents are characterized by the following three capacities:

1. *Intentionality*: Agents have the ability to act intentionally. To say that something acts intentionally is to say that it has purposes, plans, goals, and interests that motivate some of its behavior (see French 1995, 10).
2. *Rationality*: Agents have the ability to make rational decisions and to consider rational arguments regarding their intentions, in particular arguments about the ways to realize their long- and short-term interests (see French 1995, 12).
3. *Responsive adjustment*: Agents have the ability to respond to criticism by altering their intentions and patterns of behavior (see French 1995, 12).

French argues that some organized groups possess these capacities: they exhibit intentionality that is not reducible to the intentions of the individual members of the group, their intentions can be rational, and they can respond to criticism by altering their intentions and patterns of behavior (see French 2011, 214). Such groups have an established way by which they construct plans, make decisions, and convert them into actions: a CID (Corporate Internal Decision) structure. The CID structure is "the personnel organization for the exercise of the corporation's power with respect to its ventures" (French 1984, 41). It enables groups to act in the manner of agents. The intentionality of such group agents, that is, their purposes, plans, and interests, are constituted by its established corporate goals (see French 1984, 45). These corporate goals are channeled and enacted through its CID structure. CID structures consist of two central elements. First, they exhibit an organizational or responsibility flowchart that delineates stations and levels within the corporate power structure. And second, CID structures contain rules that reveal how to recognize plans and decisions that are organizational ones and not simply personal decisions or intentions of the humans who occupy the positions identified on the flow chart (see French 1984, 41; French 2011, 217). The primary function of the CID structure is to draw experiences from various levels of the corporation into a decision-making and ratification process (see French 1984, 41). It is designed to ensure that the concatenated intentions and actions of the individual group members will achieve the group's designated purposes. As French puts it, a CID structure "*incorporates* acts of biological persons" (French 1984, 41–42). It "subordinates and synthesizes the intentions, desires, and actions of various human persons [. . .] into an organizational action" (French 2011, 217). The purposes, plans, goals, and interests of group agents can, and often do, differ from those that motivate the human persons who occupy positions in the CID structure (French 2011, 218). However, using the group's CID structure we can describe the concerted actions of those individual human beings as corporate actions done with a corporate intention to execute an organizational plan or as part of such a plan. When an action performed by a bona fide member of a group is an implementation of its policy, and accords with its procedural rules, then it is proper to describe the act as done for corporate purposes or to advance corporate plans, goals or interests, even if the group member's intentions in performing the action differ from those of the group (see French 2011, 218). It is in this sense that the intentionality of the group agent is not reducible to the intentions of the individual members of the group. French's model of a CID structure also helps to explain how situations of the kind described by Steinbeck can come about: since the intentions of a group agent might differ from the intentions of the group's members, it can happen that every employee in a bank hates what the bank does, and yet the bank does it.

In addition to the ability to act intentionally, CID structures provide groups with mechanisms for rational decision-making over time. Interestingly, in contrast to individual human agents, group agents are actually protected from certain failures of rationality. According to French, group agents "have decision structures constructed, unlike human minds, to focus their actions on and to maintain a virtually unswerving commitment to specific long-term goals and plans" (French 1995, 47). As a result, they do not suffer from weakness of will. Of course, this does not mean that group agents are always successful in reaching their goals and pursuing their plans. But, as French points out, "[b]ad judgment, even outright stupidity, is not weakness of will" (French 1995, 47).

Moreover, French argues that the nature of CID structures also enables groups to fulfill the third characteristic of agency, that is, responsive adjustment. He points out that organizations, if they are to survive for very long, have to be "capable of making rational nonprogrammed decisions directed to the satisfaction of their interests" (French 1995, 33). The organizational policies of such groups "must be somewhat flexible" so that they can respond to unexpected circumstances (French 2011, 219). According to French, successful CID structures build in that capacity and encourage "some reactive, responsive, discriminatory elements with respect to policies" (French 2011, 219). He claims that this capacity for nonprogrammed responsive decision-making is sufficient for the ability to respond to criticism by altering intentions and patterns of behavior.

French's account rests on a broadly functionalist conception of agency, although French very rarely uses functionalist vocabulary. What renders French's conception of agency functionalist is that mental states are defined and identified solely by their causal roles. Something qualifies as a belief or intention, for example, because it fulfills the causal roles of a belief or an intention. Since these causal roles are multiply realizable, the possibility of agency is not limited to certain entities, such as human and non-human animals. Representational states, for example, do not presuppose a specific biological sensory apparatus. Functionalism is, therefore, predestined to serve as a background theory for accounts of group agency. Indeed, it seems necessary to accept some form of functionalism in the theory of mind in order to be open to the possibility of group agency, and I will presuppose it here. Given a functionalist account of the mental, one cannot argue against the possibility of group agency by pointing out that groups are simply not the kinds of entities which could possess a mind and thus form intentions. Manuel Velasquez, for example, asserts that "[c]orporate policies and procedures [. . .] cannot serve as corporate minds for the simple reason that they are not minds: they do not form intentions" (Velasquez 2004, 120). Similarly, John Searle insists that "consciousness is in individual minds, in individual brains" (Searle 1990, 406). Raimo Tuomela argues that "[p]ersons have (biological) bodies and perform bodily actions in contrast to collectives", and that groups can be said to intend to act only in a "somewhat metaphorical" sense (Tuomela 1984, 145). These claims are begging the question against functionalism: something qualifies as a mental state because it fulfills the causal roles of this mental state. If a group manifests the purposes, activities and capacities that define a given mental state, then it can be said to possess this mental state. French's model of a CID structure helps to explain how groups can come to function as agents. They can exhibit intentionality, rationality, and the capacity to alter their behavior in the light of reasons. Given a functionalist conception of agency, it is plausible to understand certain groups as agents distinct from their members.

However, for French, intentionality, rationality, and responsive adjustment are not only individually necessary and jointly sufficient criteria for agency, they also qualify their bearers as moral agents, and hence as subjects of moral responsibility. French especially stresses the importance of responsive adjustment for moral agency and it is on this capacity that I wish to focus. He writes

> Ethics requires of its subjects the capacity to respond. Of course, it is especially concerned with the entity's capability for effective response to moral criticism, as well as the ability to alter offensive behavior, and react to unanticipated outcomes. (French 1995, 34)

According to French, the ability to respond to moral criticism thus derives from the capacity for responsive adjustment. Since group agents possess the latter they also possess the former and it, therefore, makes sense to hold group agents morally responsible "in terms of both their actions and their characters" (French 2011, 221). I agree that in order to be a proper target of moral evaluation an agent has to be capable of responding to moral criticism which, in turn, presupposes the ability to alter one's actions, plans and policies. However, although most group agents are, as French rightly points out, more than merely mechanical in the way they interact with other agents and respond to various issues, their responsive capacity is severely limited. This limitation is not only a matter of degree. There is a fundamental difference between group agents and normal adult human beings. As I will argue in the next section, group agents lack a certain kind of autonomy that is necessary for the ability to respond to moral criticism.

Moral Agency and Autonomy

In order to illuminate the difference between group agents and normal adult human beings it is helpful to look at Kant's conception of agency and autonomy. In the *Metaphysics of Morals* Kant identifies the ability to act with the faculty of desire, that is "the faculty to be, by means of one's representations, the cause of the objects of these representations" (Kant 1996c, 6:211). Thus understood, Kant's conception of action is compatible with a broadly functionalist conception presupposed by French and other defenders of group agency. According to Kant, every action starts with an incentive, where an incentive is the "subjective ground of desire", that is, a motivationally loaded representation of an object (Kant 1996a, 4:427). An agent is subject to an incentive when she is aware of the features of some object that make the object appealing to her (Korsgaard 2009, 104–105). Incentives do not directly cause an agent's movements. They work in conjunction with principles, which determine the agent's responses to the incentives. Since Kant focuses on human action, he does not explicate what kind of principles guide the actions of non-human agents. At this point Christine Korsgaard's account of the distinction between animal action and the actions of normal, adult human beings proves illuminating.

Korsgaard argues that in the case of non-human animals the principles in question are the animal's instincts. For an animal with the instincts of a cat, for example, a mouse is an occasion to give chase. In the human case the principles in question are a person's normative principles. A person's principles determine what she counts as a reason. For example, for a person whose principle it is to help those in need, the fact that another person is suffering appears as a reason to help. As Korsgaard emphasizes, all actions are necessarily autonomous. There is a difference between actions and mere movements. When a cat chases a mouse, for example, that is not something that happens to the cat, but something that the cat does. If an agent acts she is the author of her movements. An agent is the author of her movements when those movements are caused by the agent operating as a unit and not by some alien force that is working in or on the agent. However, although all actions are necessarily autonomous, there is an important difference between non-human action and the actions of normal, adult human beings. The movements of non-human animals are autonomous when they are governed by their instincts. An animal's instincts constitute its nature. When an animal is governed by its instincts, its movements spring from its nature and are thus caused by the animal operating as a unit. Understood in this first sense, to be autonomous is to be governed by the principles of one's own causality, principles that are definitive of one's will. All agents are autonomous in this first sense. Normal adult human beings are capable of a second, deeper sense of autonomy. They are capable to *choose* the principles that are definitive of their will. We choose our maxims (see Korsgaard 2009, 82–108).[4]

The fact that we, unlike other agents, are capable of choosing the content of our principles is what constitutes our status as *moral* agents. It is what makes us morally responsible for our actions. We are not only agents but also persons. According to Kant, a person "is a subject whose actions can be *imputed* to him. [. . .] [A] person is subject to no other laws than those he gives to himself (either alone or at least along with others)" (Kant 1996c, 6:223).

Group agents do not qualify as persons. Like non-human animals, they lack the ability to choose the principles of their own causality. Group agents fail to be autonomous in the second sense, because they are created for specific purposes and

[4]Since the capacity of being governed by the principles of one's own causality as well as the capacity to choose the principles that are definite of one will could at least in principle be spelled out in functionalist terms, this conception of autonomy is compatible with the functionalism presupposed in the first part of the chapter.

these purposes determine the principles of their willing, that is, their organizational structure. The designated purpose of a group agent determines its CID structure and thus its judgments, intentions, and actions. A group agent is autonomous *in the first sense* if its judgments, intentions, and actions are in accordance with its organizational structure. Any mental states and actions that fall outside this structure are not caused by the group agent operating as a unit. They are not the mental states and actions of the group agent. As French himself emphasizes, "[i]f members act in ways that violate organizational policy, their acts are no longer organizational" (French 2011, 219). Not all actions performed *within* a group are actions performed *by* the group. A group agent's mental states and actions are constituted by its organizational structure, which, in turn, has to be enacted by its members. Any actions that are not sanctioned by the CID structure are not actions of the group agent.

While substantial changes to a group agent's CID structure are possible, these changes will always have to be the result of alien forces working in or on the agent. Thus, substantial changes to a group agent's CID structure cannot be initiated by the group agent itself. In this respect group agents resemble complex robots. Like complex robots, group agents might be capable of adapting to their environment and acquiring new skills, but substantial modifications of their organizational designs can be achieved only by external forces. Accordingly, group agents cannot be held morally responsible either for failing to initiate such changes, or for any actions that flow from their potential design faults. The inability of group agents to substantially change their CID structure fundamentally limits their capacity for responsive adjustment. Certain reasons will be inaccessible to group agents because their CID structures lack the appropriate processes of recognizing such reasons.

In this context it is important to distinguish between the ability to *respond* and the ability to *react* to moral criticism. Many non-moral agents can react to moral criticism because they can react to rewards and punishments. Dogs, for example, can be trained to behave in non-aggressive and helpful ways. Similarly, well-functioning corporations will react to economic rewards and punishments and can, therefore, be 'trained' to follow certain standards of behavior. Consumer boycotts and the threat of lower sales figures, for example, might lead a corporation to adopt higher environmental standards or better working conditions for its employees. In such cases the group agent reacts to moral criticism because it is designed to respond to economic reasons, but it does not respond to moral criticism in the sense of responding to moral reasons. Group agents can only recognize and respond to reasons which are sanctioned by its designated purpose and which are inscribed in its CID structure.

At this point one might object that while business corporations are unable to respond to moral reasons, non-for-profit organizations might be designed to do so. However, the crucial point is that group agents of all kinds will have to be specifically designed to respond to moral reasons and that they will thus only be able to respond to those moral reasons they have been designed to recognize. Group agents can neither be held morally responsible for adopting an insufficient set of moral reasons nor for failing to recognize moral reasons they have not been designed to recognize. They also cannot be held responsible for responding to a moral reason if their CID structures preclude the required changes in intentions and patterns of behavior. Such failures of responsive adjustment will be due to the specific CID structure of the group agent, that is, to its specific character. In contrast to normal adult human beings, it is not appropriate to morally criticize group agents for such character flaws. While moral agents are at least in principle capable of altering their character – or, in Kantian terms, the principles of their willing – group agents are unable to undertake such changes. They are unable to choose the principles that are definitive of their will, and hence unable to determine what kind of reasons they recognize and treat as moral reasons.

This is not to say that group agents are unable to make any changes at all to their organizational policies. As I pointed out in the previous section, it is plausible to assume that group agents have to be able to make some rational nonprogrammed decisions in order to satisfy their interests and survive over time. However, while the CID structures of successful group agents have to be somewhat flexible, the basic policies are unchangeable. In this context the examples French offers for possible nonprogrammed decisions are telling. He explains that the most obvious cases in which corporations evidence rational nonprogrammed decision-making are in new product and service development. While adherence to established procedures is normally required, the development process cannot really be routinized since there are usually too many variables (see French 1995, 33). Other examples for nonprogrammed decision-making include the relocation of plants, the selection of new board members and the acquiring of properties (see French 1995, 34). Moreover, French himself remarks

> The policies of an organization seem to be inviolate. The basic ones generally are; indeed, they have to be for reasons of maintaining organizational identity. In that respect, they are unlike policies adopted by individual human. You could adopt a policy of honesty, but you may occasionally violate that policy by lying. When you lie it is still you lying. If members act in ways that violate organizational policy, their acts are no longer organizational. (French 2011, 219)

Why is it that normal adult human beings can adopt a policy of honesty, occasionally violate that policy by lying and still act autonomously, whereas group agents cannot? I suggest that the answer lies in the fact that group agents can act autonomously in the sense of being governed by the principles of their willing, but are incapable of autonomy understood as the ability to choose the principles that are definitive of their will. Any flexibility that group agents might possess with regard to their organizational policies has to be built into their CID structures. If group members act in ways that violate the group's principles, these actions fail to qualify as autonomous actions of the group agent because they are not governed by the principles that are definitive of the group agent's will, that is, its CID structure. Since group agents lack autonomous control over their CID structures, they cannot change their policies at will. In the case of group agents violations of organizational policies therefore mean that it is not the group agent itself who acts. By contrast, normal adult human beings can adopt a policy of honesty, occasionally violate that policy by lying, and still act autonomously because they can choose a principle that provides them with a reason to lie. Such a principle might be immoral, but it is nevertheless the principle of the agent and it licenses her to treat a certain incentive as a reason to lie. The lie qualifies as the agent's action because it is governed by her principles. She can change the principles that determine her reasons for actions because she possesses autonomy in the second, deeper sense.

The fact that group agents lack autonomy understood as the ability to choose the principles that are definitive of their will also helps to explain why they cannot exhibit weakness of will. As I pointed out in the first part of the chapter, according to French, group agents do not suffer from weakness of will because their CID structures ensure a virtually unswerving commitment to specific long-term goals and plans. Weakness of will is a complex phenomenon and this is not the place to attempt an in-depth analysis. However, I suggest that the distinction between two forms of autonomy offers a way of understanding how agents, who are capable of weakness of will, can act freely and intentionally against their better judgment. Such agents act against their better judgment because their action violates one or more of the principles that are definitive of their will. At the same time such agents act freely and intentionally because they act on a maxim, that is, on a subjective principle of their willing. Yet, the agent does not deem these principles to be good principles. The principles will often be ad hoc and conflict with the agent's long-term plans. For example, she might choose to adopt a principle of personal advantage that license her to treat a certain incentive as a reason to lie, even though her better judgment tells her to adhere to her principle of honesty (see Kant 1996a, 4:423). Group agents are incapable of such acts of weakness of will because they cannot adopt principles of action that are in conflict with their CID structure. If a group agent violates the principles of its CID structure the resulting action is no longer the action of the group agent. As French puts it

> [The] CID structure not only forms the personality of the corporation, it determines its identity as well. It is constitutive of the corporation in every major way. A corporation simply is that particular one because it has that particular CID structure. (French 1995, 35)

Similarly, my plans and normative principles enable me to remain the agent I am even after every molecule in my body has been changed. Yet, despite this similarity, there is an important difference between the principles that constitute our identity over time and those of group agents. In the case of group agents autonomous action and identity is an all or nothing matter. In the case of normal adult human beings loss of agency is more a matter of degree. While some defeasibility and violations of principles is to be expected in normal adult human beings, frequent violations of, and contradictions between, an agent's principles might lead us to diagnose the agent with weakness of will or other forms of irrationality, and constant, rapid changes of plans, policies and plans will make it difficult to interpret the agent's movements as her actions at all. I suggest that it is for this reason that, as French remarks, "within the CID structure, most of the puzzles of identity that plague our thinking about human persons never arise" (French 1995, 35–36).

It is worth pointing out that the objection against the moral responsibility of group agents developed above is distinct from an objection discussed in the literature (see Haji 2006; List and Pettit 2011; Hess 2014). The concern found there is that group agents necessarily lack autonomy because their action must always originate in their members: a group agent cannot act without some of its members acting. If we assume further that individuals are in control of anything they do in acting for a group and that one and the same action cannot be subject both to the control of a group agent and to the control of one or more individuals, we seem forced to conclude that group agents cannot be in control of what they do; such control always rests exclusively with the individuals who act for the group (see List and Pettit 2011, 160). Moreover, critics argue that group agents can only deliberate by means of their members deliberating and, therefore, lack the capacity for responsive adjustment that necessary for moral responsibility (see Haji 2006). However, the autonomy that these authors are concerned with is autonomy in the first and not the second sense. French's model of CID structures helps to explain how groups can possess this form of autonomy even though their actions always necessarily originate in the actions of their members. As I pointed out in the first part of the chapter, the intentions of group agents can, and often do, differ from those of its individual members. In such cases the same event can be described both as an individual action performed for individual reasons and as the action of a group agent done for organizational reasons. CID structures make it possible to describe what is happening as actions of a group agent, and not just as the actions of a specific group member. It is due to these two levels of description that one and the same action can be viewed as being subject both to the control of a group agent and to the control of one or more individuals.[5] In addition, the model of CID structures shows how group agents can develop their own processes of deliberation. Of course, these processes of deliberation require the participation of individual agents in order to produce results, but the judgments or intentions resulting from these processes are not necessarily identical with the judgments or intentions of the participating individual agents: they originate in the CID structures of the group agent and not the individual decisions of its individual members.

The objection against the possibility of group responsibility brought forward in this section rests on a concern about autonomy understood in the second and not in the first sense. While group agents are capable of autonomy in the first sense, they lack the second, deeper form of autonomy that is constitutive of moral agency. Group agents are created for specific purposes and these purposes determine their CID Structure, which, in turn, determines their actions, plans and policies. They fail to be appropriate subjects of moral responsibility because they lack the ability to choose the principles that are definitive of their will.

This conclusion might seem disturbing. It seems to imply a highly problematic conception of corporate responsibility according to which group agents appear to exist in a complete moral void where – to use Milton Friedman's words – "there is one and only one social responsibility of business – to use its resources and engage in activities designed to increase its profits" (Friedman 1962, 133). I will

[5] For List and Pettit's solution to the problem see List and Pettit (2011, 161–163).

address this worry in the next section. However, before doing so it is worth pointing out the advantages of denying group agents the status of moral agents. In his earlier work French characterized corporations not only as moral agents, but also as moral persons that should have "whatever privileges, rights and duties as are, in the normal course of affairs, accorded to all members of the moral community" (French 1984, 32; see also French 1979). Yet to afford corporations an equal right to, say, assistance when in need or to political participation seems counter-intuitive and highly dangerous. It would endow already over-powerful agents with even more powers. Most defenders of group responsibility agree that any moral claims group agents might have on us should be purely derivative. That is, they will be claims that the group's members or any other individual human agents have on us (see List and Pettit 2011, 170–185).[6] However, once we assign group agents the status of moral agents it is difficult to justify their treatment as second-rate moral agents with duties but without rights.[7] By contrast, according to the Kantian conception of moral agency advocated here, group agents have neither rights nor duties because they do not qualify as moral agents. A moral agent is "by virtue of the autonomy of his freedom" an end in itself (Kant 1996b, 5:87). Group agents cannot constitute moral agents because they are unable to set the principles of their own willing. They are mere things, where a thing "is that to which nothing can be imputed" (Kant 1996c, 6:223).

Moral Responsibility for Group Agents

Proponents of group responsibility are especially concerned about cases where a group agent causes serious harm, but where none of its members are morally at fault for this harm.[8] They believe that a failure to assign group agents the status of moral agents would lead to a deficit of responsibility in such cases. The assignment of moral responsibility to group agents is thus thought to be necessary in order to fill the gap in responsibility which seems to arise when a group's members cannot be held individually responsible for a harm caused by the group. In this context French claims that "[i]f an ethical theory systematically cannot address the organization offender qua organization offender, then it will be impotent with respect to minimizing a great deal of underserved harm, and [...] a failure in ethics" (French 2011, 213). However, it is important to note that in many cases the assignment of group responsibility will be either – even by French's own standards – unwarranted or superfluous. Consider the following case. A group causes grave

[6]For an exception see Graham (2001).

[7]For an attempt see Hess (2013) and List and Pettit (2011).

[8]It is important to emphasize that this is a concern about moral responsibility and not about legal responsibility. Equally, my argument is an argument about moral and not about legal responsibility. Nothing I have said in this chapter is meant to deny the legal responsibility of group agents.

harm because some of its members act wrongly. Assume further that each of those individuals has a viable excuse for their actions. Say, they are under great personal stress or ill. If the individual group members' wrong actions imply actions that go beyond or against their designated roles within the group, then these actions will not qualify as actions performed by the group agent and any ascription of group responsibility will thus be unwarranted. As pointed out earlier, not all actions performed within a group are actions performed by the group. Any actions that fall outside the CID structure are not actions of the group agent and, consequently, not something the group agent can be held responsible for. If, on the other hand, an individual group member's wrong action is performed in accordance with the group's organizational structure and could have been prevented by changing this structure, then any assignment of group responsibility will be either superfluous or, again, unwarranted. In cases where the group's members had the obligation and ability to make the necessary changes to the organizational structure, at least some members can be held responsible for a failure to do so and there is thus no need to hold the group agent morally responsible. In cases where the group's members were jointly unable to initiate the necessary changes, the group agent will inherit this inability and thus fail to be morally responsible. Although the intentionality of group agents is not reducible to the intentions of their individual members, the members' "bodily movements are necessary for the organization to act" (French 2011, 218). Thus, if the group's members are unable to perform the necessary movements, the group agent will be unable to act and accordingly cannot be held responsible for this inaction.

This notwithstanding there seem to be cases where group agents cause grave harm and where none of its members can be held fully individually morally responsible for this harm. To dismiss such cases as mere misfortunes seems to be wrong. It is unfortunate if a storm destroys the harvest or a herd of stampeding cattle injures a dog walker, but if a group agent like BP causes an oil spill the suggestion that it is just one of these unfortunate things seems to ring false (see Wolf 1985, 274). I suggest that the reason why this rings false is that business corporations and other group agents are human creations. As with other things we create or use, we are liable for the damage group agents might cause. Although French does not discuss the possibility of moral responsibility *for* group agents, his work is highly illuminating in this context. In *Corporate Ethics* he points out that the principals who formed the early business corporations in the US and Western Europe did so for their own rational reasons, that is, for personal gain. It certainly was not their plan to radically transform society. However, French goes on to wonder if they might not see themselves as in something of the dilemma of the scientist in Mary Wollstonecraft Shelly's novel *Frankenstein*:

> After all, Frankenstein did not set about to make a monster to terrorize the world. His plan in manufacturing the monster was, depending on the version of the story [...], to further the ends of science, to prove that he was the greatest scientist of his time, to gain personal glory. But he did create a monster that was soon out of his control. (French 1995, 18)

French is quick to add that he does not mean to suggest that the corporate structured world is monstrous (see French 1995, 18). But many will disagree and it is thus worth pursuing his analogy. In a paper entitled "Monsters and their Makers" French points out that Frankenstein's monster is not to be held morally responsible for its actions:

> One could say, "The monster was to blame for the young girl's death," much as the fog might be to blame for the collision of two ships. 'Blame' here would mean 'cause' or 'one of the causes' and not blameworthiness of the sort occasioned by sub-standard behavior. (French 1972, 14)

By contrast, Frankenstein is morally responsible for the acts of the monster he created, regardless of his potentially good intentions (see French 1972, 14; see also French 2011). French writes:

> Despite the fact that the scientist has no control over the monster, despite the fact that he had only good intentions at its creation, I think the townsfolk are justified in holding him morally blameworthy for the monster's deeds. He should have expected dire consequences to occur when he created a monster. (French 2011, 237)

I suggest that the same holds true with regard to group agents. The moral responsibility in question is prospective as well as retrospective. We have prospective moral responsibility for group agents because group agents are powerful, and potentially dangerous, means created to serve our purposes. We have a moral duty to manage those means responsibly. Moreover, it can be appropriate to assign group members retrospective moral responsibility for a harm caused by a group, even though none of the members are morally at fault for the harm. Group members can be responsible for a group agent like parents are for the actions of their underage children or a dog owner for the actions of her dog. If group agents spiral out of control and become "monsters" we are morally responsible for the harm they cause.

French emphasizes that blame can be vicarious (French 2011, 236). He argues that parents, for example, are to blame for their children's delinquency when their parenthood has not been up to the quality to be expected (French 1972, 10). Thus, moral blame is appropriate if a person's performances or character fail to reach a certain standard (French 1972, 10). However, while there are certainly many cases of harm caused by group agents where vicarious blame is called for, vicarious blame is not the only form of retrospective responsibility that is relevant with regard to group agents. Moral responsibility does not need to be linked to blame. This is clear in the case of prospective responsibility, but it also holds true with regard to retrospective responsibility. Retrospective moral responsibility is not limited to cases where a group's members (or other individuals linked with the group agent) fail to reach a certain standard. We can be morally responsible for a harm caused by things we created or use, even if we took all possible precautions in doing so. Similarly, parents can be responsible for the damage caused by the actions of their underage children, even if their parenting has been exemplary. While vicarious blame would be inappropriate in such cases, individual agents can nevertheless be morally liable for the harm caused. They have duties of reparation. In contrast to moral responsibility understood as blame, assignment of this form of moral responsibility is appropriate even if the individual in question could not have foreseen or prevented the harm caused by the non-moral agent or thing for which she is responsible. The moral responsibility in question does not stem from a prior moral failing of the individual, but from the special relationship that connects her to the non-moral agent or thing in question. In the case of group agents the connection might be one of creation, ownership, participation or use. The plausibility of moral responsibility for group agents is reinforced by the fact that our relationships with them are normally voluntary. Moreover, most individuals profit from their ownership, membership and use of group agents. However, while it is relatively easy to see why individuals can be held morally responsible for group agents, it proves difficult to specify the individual retrospective and prospective responsibilities in question because they can differ from group agent to group agent and from individual to individual. For example, individual moral responsibility for group agents will usually differ depending on whether we are dealing with a strictly hierarchical structured group agent or a group agent with more democratic decision structures. Furthermore, it is plausible to assume that an individual's moral responsibility for a group agent does not only depend on the nature of her relationship with the agent, but also partly on her ability to repair a damage done by the group agent and to initiate change within it. Accordingly, a CEO's responsibility for a corporation, for example, will differ from that of an employee working in the production line, which again will differ from that of a consumer of the corporation's goods and services. Finally, what differs in these cases is not only the degree of responsibility, but also the content of the responsibilities. For example, a consumer might have a duty to inform herself about the companies she uses and, if necessary, boycott them, but it is very unlikely that she will acquire duties of reparation through her usage.

According to French, there is very little likelihood that individual human beings will ever again regain the status they once held in society and he adds that "[p]erhaps that is not something to mourn" (French 1995, 18). Group agents certainly have powers which individual human agents lack and, if used correctly, we can greatly profit from these powers. However, the power of moral agency is not among them and it is, therefore, paramount that group agents remain within our control.

References

Arnold, Denis G. 2006. Corporate moral agency. *Midwest Studies in Philosophy* 30: 279–291.

French, Peter. 1972. Monsters and their makers. In *Individual and collective responsibility. Massacre at My Lai*, ed. Peter French, 1–15. Cambridge, MA: Schenkman.

———. 1979. The corporation as moral person. *American Philosophical Quarterly* 16: 207–215.

———. 1984. *Collective and corporate responsibility*. New York: Columbia University Press.

———. 1995. *Corporate ethics*. Orlando: Harcourt Brace.

———. 2011. *War and moral dissonance*. Cambridge: Cambridge University Press.

Friedman, Milton. 1962. *Capitalism and freedom*. 2002 ed. Chicago: University of Chicago Press.

Gilbert, Margaret. 2000. *Sociality and responsibility: New essays in plural subject theory*. Lanham: Rowman and Littlefield.

Graham, Keith. 2001. The moral significance of collective entities. *Inquiry* 44: 21–41.

Haji, Ishtiyaque. 2006. On the ultimate responsibility of collectives. *Midwest Studies in Philosophy* 30: 292–308.

Haney, Mitchell R. 2004. Corporate loss of innocence for the sake of accountability. *Journal of Social Philosophy* 35: 391–412.

Hedahl, Marcus. 2013. The collective fallacy: The possibility of irreducibly collective actions without corresponding collective moral responsibility. *Philosophy of the Social Sciences*: 283–300.

Held, Virginia. 1970. Can a random collection of individuals be morally responsible? *Journal of Philosophy* 67: 471–481.

Hess, Kendy M. 2013. "If you tickle us . . . ": How corporations can be moral agents without being persons. *Journal of Value Inquiry* 47: 319–335.

———. 2014. The free will of corporations (and other collectives). *Philosophical Studies* 168: 241–260.

Kant, Immanuel. 1996a. Groundwork of the metaphysics of morals. In *Immanuel Kant. Practical philosophy*, ed. Mary J. Gregor. Cambridge: Cambridge University Press. (Immanuel Kant. 1903–11. Grundlegung der Metaphysik der Sitten. In Kants Schriften, ed. Preußische Akademie der Wissenschaften, vol 4. Berlin: Walter de Gruyter.)

———. 1996b. Critique of practical reason. In *Immanuel Kant. Practical philosophy*, ed. Mary J. Gregor. Cambridge: Cambridge University Press. (Immanuel Kant. 1908/13. Kritik der praktischen Vernunft. In Kants Schriften, ed. Preußische Akademie der Wissenschaften, vol 5. Berlin: Walter de Gruyter.)

———. 1996c. The metaphysics of morals. In *Immanuel Kant. Practical philosophy*, ed. Mary J. Gregor. Cambridge: Cambridge University Press. (Immanuel Kant. 1907–14. Die Metaphysik der Sitten. In Kants Schriften, ed. Preußische Akademie der Wissenschaften, vol 6. Berlin: Walter de Gruyter.)

Killoren, David, and Bekka Williams. 2013. Group agency and overdetermination. *Ethical Theory and Moral Practice* 16: 295–307.

Korsgaard, Christine M. 2009. *Self-constitution. agency, identity, and integrity*. Oxford: Oxford University Press.

List, Christian, and Philip Petitt. 2011. *Group agency. The possibility, design, and status of corporate agents*. Oxford: Oxford University Press.

May, Larry. 1987. *The morality of groups: Collective responsibility, group-based harm, and corporate rights*. Notre Dame: University of Notre Dame Press.

———. 1992. *Sharing responsibility*. Chicago: The University of Chicago Press.

Narveson. Jan. 2002. Collective responsibility. *The Journal of Ethics* 6: 179–198.

O'Madagain, Cathal. 2012. Group agents: Persons, mobs, or zombies? *International Journal of Philosophical Studies* 20: 271–287.

Quinton, Anthony. 1975. Social objects. *Proceedings of the Aristotelian Society* 76: 1–27.

Searle, John. 1990. Collective intentions and actions. In *Intentions in communication*, ed. Philip R. Cohen, Jerry Morgan, and Martha E. Pollack, 401–415. Cambridge, MA: MIT Press.

Steinbeck, John. 2000 (first published 1939). *The grapes of wrath*. London: Penguin.

Tuomela, Raimo. 1984. *A theory of social action*. Dordrecht: Reidel Publishing.

———. 2007. *The philosophy of sociality: The shared point of view*. Oxford: Oxford University Press.

Velasquez, Manuel G. 2004. Why corporations are not morally responsible for anything they do. In *Contemporary issues in business ethics*, ed. Joseph R. DesJardins and John J. McCall, 114–125. Belmont: Wadsworth.

Wolf, Susan. 1985. The legal and moral responsibility of organizations. *Nomos* 27: 267–286.

French's Influence on the Modern Discussion of Corporate Criminal Liability: The Case of Corporate Citizenship and Corporate Compliance

Carlos Gómez-Jara Díez

Introduction

For a criminal law theorist and practitioner, corporate criminal liability provides a very distinct opportunity. Not only is it one of the few really worldwide debates in the area of criminal law, but also it is a subject matter in which philosophical considerations play a key role. For an outsider it should be extremely interesting to see how in the same essay, black-letter law arguments in various jurisdictions are raised together with citations of renowned philosophers. If you then add to the mix the repercussions in the all-mighty corporate world, the result is quite distinctive compared to traditional fields of criminal law. To make things even more interesting, there are few areas of criminal law in which the polarization of supporters and detractors of a specific theory is more palpable.

The question of *if* and *how* corporations should be punished is a fascinating subject. Criminal law is an anthropocentric system of rules based, accordingly, on the conduct of human beings i.e., natural persons. However, since its inception, there has been an attempt to extend the scope of criminal law to certain organizations. Conventional wisdom has varied greatly throughout centuries, and what was considered as a given in some epochs, was later considered as the opposite. Up until the late eighteenth century, the basic principle was *univeristas delinquere potest*. Citing a relatively unknown dissertation (Malblanc 1793), Feuerbach (1818, § 28) initiated a path that ultimately led in continental Europe to the aphorism *societas delinquere non potest*.[1] In the Anglo-American world, the conventional

[1]For a interesting comparative law perspective, see Dubber (2013).

C.G.-J. Díez (✉)
Universidad Autónoma de Madrid, Madrid, Spain
e-mail: cgj@corporatedefense.es

Z.J. Goldberg (ed.), *Reflections on Ethics and Responsibility*,
DOI 10.1007/978-3-319-50359-2_3

authority for the ban on corporate criminal liability is attributed by Blackstone to Lord Chief Justice John Holt in 1701: "A corporation is not indictable but the particular members of it are".[2] Baron Thurlow is often quoted to have said in the early 1700s: "Did you ever expect a corporation to have a conscience when it has no soul to be damned, and no body to be kicked? And by God, it ought to have both!" (Wilberforce 1783, iii App)[3]

In the twentieth century, conventional wisdom experienced, again, a major shift. In 1909 the US Supreme court applied a civil law principle to criminal law: the *respondeat superior* doctrine, commonly used in civil law cases, was used to hold a corporation criminally liable. In the last quarter of that same century, European legislations began to acknowledge corporate criminal liability.[4] Probably, the consolidation of the "society of organizations" (Perrow 1989), played a significant role in the overall acknowledgement that corporations are to be held criminally liable.

The first decade of the twenty-first century has shown some contradictory tendencies. Some theorists have labeled the American tradition as a century-old "mistake" (Hasnas 2009), while more and more legislations worldwide introduced corporate criminal liability provisions. Put bluntly: at the time where legal theory questioned the wisdom of holding corporations criminally liable, more legal systems were introducing such provisions. It seemed as if criminal theory was detached from criminal policy. What seemed obvious to some, seemed unreasonable to others.

In the face of such debate, one trend was quite revealing: if a legal system introduced corporate criminal liability, then the criminal liability of the corporation ought to be based on some kind of corporate conduct. Here, corporate compliance began to play a major role. Compliance programs were the only real defense against corporate criminal liability. This was not self-evident, nor easy to prove. The first step was undertaken by the Organizational Sentencing Guidelines that considered as a mitigating factor at sentencing (i.e., not at trial) the implementation of an effective compliance program. The second step came with the Principles of Federal Prosecutions of Business Organizations, where "the existence and effectiveness of the corporation's pre-existing compliance program" was a factor to be considered in determining whether to charge a corporation (United States Attorneys' Manual, Principles of Federal Prosecution of Business Organizations 1999, Title 9–28.000, 28.300). Other legal systems such as those in Switzerland (Pieth and Ivory 2011a,

[2]Anonymous, 88 Eng. Rep. 1518 (K.B. 1701). However, almost a hundred years before that statement, in the case of Sutton's Hospital [77 Eng. Rep. 960, 973 (K.B. 1612)] the following statement was noted: corporations "cannot commit treason, nor be outlawed, nor excommunicate, for they have no souls, neither can they appear in person, but by attorney".

[3]Interestingly enough, the actual quote seems to be "Corporations have neither bodies to be punished nor souls to be condemned; they therefore do as they like". Therefore, if punishment is not equaled to bodily punishment or soul condemnation, the potential punishment of corporations could be argued.

[4]For a recent account see the contributions in Pieth, Mark and Radha Ivory eds, (2011b) and Gobert and Pascal (2011).

33–35), Italy (De Maglie 2011), Chile (Salvo 2011), or Spain (Gómez-Jara 2010) – just to name a few[5] – quickly followed suit.

It is probably a fair statement to note that, currently, the *legal* debate is not so much focused on "if" corporations should be punished, but on "how" they should be punished. The *philosophical* debate though is all the more relevant because the answer to the "if" question conditions to a great extent the "how". To answer the "if" question, one must carefully look into the meaning of criminal sanctions. What does it mean to impose criminal (as opposed to civil or administrative) sanctions? Here the expressive function of criminal procedure and criminal punishment plays a great role.

It would seem unfair to impose *criminal* law sanctions to corporations on the basis of *civil* law principles. And precisely that is what has been ongoing for decades not only in the US system of corporate criminal liability, but in other European legal systems. Given the peculiar nature of corporations and the use of *monetary* penalties as the common criminal sanction against corporations, the standards of corporate criminal liability have drifted away from the traditional principles of criminal law. What would be unthinkable in terms of individual criminal liability is commonplace in corporate criminal liability.

Imagine a natural person (NP1) acting on behalf of another natural person (NP2). If NP1 commits fraud acting on behalf of NP2, would the court automatically consider that NP2 is guilty? Or would the court order an inquiry into NP2's participation in those facts? Wouldn't the court inquire if NP1's action was ordered, instigated, or somehow inspired by NP2? Wouldn't the court direct the jury to consider whether NP2 had some kind of knowledge of what NP1 was doing? It is likely that NP2 would not be found guilty without some investigation into what NP2 could have done to prevent NP1's criminal acts, or an investigation into what NP2 knew or should have known about NP1's acts. All of this should also hold if instead of NP2 and NP1, we talk about a corporation and an employee. The basic principles of criminal law should not change simply because an actor is a corporation.

It is here that Peter French's contributions are so noteworthy. First, French's analysis of the CID Structure focuses on genuine corporate wrongdoing – as opposed to individual wrongdoing. Instead of asking "what has a representative done on behalf of the corporation" i.e., a civil law question, French asks "what was the CID Structure of the corporation itself" i.e., a criminal law question. As we shall see, the modern legislative account for French's formula has taken the shape of corporate compliance programs. True, the current international tendency towards compliance management systems – instead of compliance programs – has a bigger scope than just the CID Structure. But the essence of French's argument is clearly present.

Second, and probably even more interesting, French's views on corporations as members of the moral community are not far off from the current debate

[5]See the contributions Pieth, Mark and Radha Ivory eds. (2011a). Gobert and Pascal (2011). See also Corporate Culture as a Basis for the Criminal Liability of Corporations (2008).

on corporate citizenship and how it affects corporate criminal liability. Quite the opposite. Corporate criminal liability means that corporations are treated as relevant members of society. Imposing criminal sanctions on a person (whether natural or legal) means that a distinct type of freedom is assigned to those persons. Imposing criminal sanctions to persons without such recognition, deprives criminal sanctions from its original meaning, and from the very essence that enables us to distinguish criminal sanctions from civil or administrative sanctions.

As we shall see, both issues are closely intertwined. For criminal law to remain true to its very own nature, corporate criminal liability can only be imposed on (legal) persons for whom a certain degree of freedom is recognized (independent of the freedom recognized for natural persons acting on their behalf). Precisely such recognition of freedom is what makes them members of the moral community. Consequently, assessing whether or not to impose a criminal sanction must take into consideration how the corporation has exercised its legally recognized freedom. Here, the CID Structure plays a significant role.

Going back to our example with natural persons: imagine a natural person NP1 acting on behalf of a natural person NP2 with diminished capacity i.e., no degree of freedom relevant to criminal law is recognized.[6] Could a criminal sanction be imposed on NP2 because of the actions of NP1 on his/her behalf? The response is clearly no. Only to the extent that a certain degree of freedom is recognized for NP2, and only to the extent that NP2 has ordered /instructed/permitted the actions of NP1, can NP2 be subject to criminal liability. These bedrock principles of criminal law should not go unnoticed when addressing corporate criminal liability. As we shall see, French's position honors both of them.

Our analysis will be developed more from a legal perspective rather than philosophical perspective. Given that corporate criminal liability is already a world-wide phenomenon introduced in many legislations, what does it mean that a corporation is criminally liable?[7] The response is that corporate criminal liability recognizes that corporations are members of the moral community. This raises the second issue to address: in order for corporate criminal liability to be consistent with the bedrock

[6]Persons with diminished capacity are what French et al. (1992), term as "moral patients". "This category would include young children, the mentally impaired, animal, even trees and other parts of the natural environment." The key here is to note how criminal law deals with such "moral patients" when "full-fledged members of the moral community" act on their behalf: the legal systems does not impose a criminal sanction on those moral patients, but on the full-fledged member of the moral community. Therefore, if criminal law imposes criminal sanctions on corporations, it is not treating corporations as moral patients, but as full-fledged members of the moral community.

[7]As French himself acknowledged in French (1984), Preface, X: at the time "The burden of proof should fall on the revisionist, on those of us who would argue that corporations should be admitted to full-membership in the moral community." However, given that most there has been an expansion of legislation introducing corporate criminal liability, it is fair to reverse the burden of proof: if corporate criminal liability is related to being considered a full-fledged member of the moral community, and corporate criminal liability is a world-wide phenomenon, the "contra-revisionists" should have the burden of proof and therefore explain why corporate criminal liability is a century-old mistake. See, consequently, Hasnas (2009).

principles of criminal law, which corporate factors – as opposed to individual factors – are to be assed for imposing a criminal sanction on a corporation? The answer to this question is that those corporate factors are embedded in the corporation's compliance programs.

Corporate Criminal Liability and the Moral Community: The Rise of Corporate Citizenship

At the inception of his theory, Peter French considered certain type of corporations i.e., conglomerates,[8] were to be considered as moral persons and therefore members of the moral community (French 1979, 207). As he later explained, he proposed an "innovative application of [old moral] principles to the corporation treated as itself a full-fledged moral person. My work has focused on both that anchor and course" (French 1984, Preface, XII). The main argument for French's conclusion that corporations were to be considered as full-fledged members of the moral community was that corporations were intentional actors.

Now, the current legal and political landscape has greatly evolved over the past decades. What could have been considered in the 1980's as "American exceptionalism" – only the US had an active system of corporate criminal liability – is nowadays relatively commonplace. Many jurisdictions have introduced this type of legislation and it is being enforced more often than not. Interestingly enough, another trend is quite noticeable in recent years. Corporations are being increasingly granted fundamental rights and therefore increasingly recognized – at least from a legal perspective – as full-fledged members of the moral community.

In this regard the evolution of two interrelated debates provide valuable insights into the modern discussion of corporate criminal liability. The first debate deals with corporate citizenship; the second, with the expressive function of criminal law. It would certainly surpass the reasonable limits of this contribution to refer to the various positions regarding those debates, but I strongly believe that it pays to note some basic trends and link them with French's reasoning. The reason for conducting such an approach is that French's assertions on corporate intentionality and its importance for full-fledged membership of the moral community nicely dovetail with modern discussions on the expressive function of criminal law and its relationship to corporate citizenship.

---

[8]Javier Cigüela has recently coined the term "Meta-Subject" to refer to French's "conglomerates". See Cigüela (forthcoming).

The intimate connection between citizenship and criminal law can hardly be questioned.[9] Regardless of important distinctions to be introduced into the relationship between those two concepts,[10] the bulk of the argument, dating back to the Enlightenment, resorts to the fact that the criminal law system is legitimate to the extent that the persons upon which punishment is sought have been able to participate in the conformation of those set of rules i.e., they are citizens. Consequently, by imposing criminal punishment on a person, the state is recognizing in such person a certain degree of citizenship.[11]

The modern account of this approach has been provided by the theorists of the expressive function of criminal law[12] and more importantly by legal theorists interested in exploring the social meaning of imposing criminal law sanctions.[13] Especially noteworthy is the contribution of Lawrence Friedman, connecting the possibility of a corporation expressing its views of society in the public square with the possibility of suffering the imposition of a criminal sanction.

> A corporation thus can be considered as similarly situated to an individual for purposes of the expressive rationale if it has a discrete identity within a community and expressive potential – that is if ... a corporation objectively can be viewed as having an identity apart from its owners, managers, and employees to which expressive conduct can be ascribed.... The modern corporation also can be substantively distinguished from its owners, managers and employees by its capacity to express independent moral judgments in the discourse of the public square, and so to participate in the process of creating and defining social norms. (Friedman 2000, 846)

According to Friedman, this capacity derives, in the US discussion, "from the Supreme Court's discussion in *First National Bank of Boston vs. Belloti* (435 U.S. 765, 1978)" (Friedman 2000, 849). In his well-argued opinion, "*Bellotti* thus implicitly acknowledges that the voice with which the corporation speaks in the public square represents an interest distinct from that of the individuals, or groups of individuals, who manage or work for the corporation. The Court recognized, in other words, the capacity of the corporation to express unique viewpoints, attitudes and moral judgments" (Friedman 2000, 851). Therefore, and closely related to the corporate citizenship discussion: "Though the corporation *qua* corporation cannot vote, *Bellotti* validates its community identity by sanctioning

[9]For a recent overall account of this connection see Pawlik (2012) and Pawlik (2004) (an interesting English review of this book is found in Kaiser 2006). Modern accounts noting various perspectives in Duff (2013), Dubber (2010), and Ramsay (2006). For a broader perspective see Farmer (2014).

[10]See Dubber (2010).

[11]Not surprisingly, some jurisdictions distinguish between citizens (in broad terms) and aliens in order to adequate the State's response to their actions. For instance, certain jurisdictions contain rules substituting prison sanctions for deportation in case of crimes perpetrated by aliens. Other jurisdictions, such as the US, "diminish" the citizenship status of convicted felons by way of systematically depriving them of their voting rights, which leaves them in a "permanent state of second class citizenship" (Fletcher 2006).

[12]For an overview, see Adler (2000).

[13]Friedman (2000). See also Kahan (1998) and Buell (2006).

corporate contributions to 'what counts in democracy': discussion and debate about a community's problems, fears and hopes, including determinations about that conduct which should be deemed laudable, and that conduct which should be condemned. Corporations, like individual members of a community, participate in the process of creating and defining social norms, and in so doing distinguish themselves from those individuals" (Friedman 2000, 852). "Because corporations satisfy the conception of the wrongdoer contemplated by the expressive rationale, cases in which the government secures a criminal conviction of a corporation can be viewed as the effectuation of expressive retribution, just as in cases involving individual defendants" (Friedman 2000, 852–853).

As Dan M. Kahan noted:

> Just as crimes by natural persons denigrate societal values, so do corporate crimes. Members of the public show that they feel this way, for example, when they complain that corporations put profits ahead of the interests of workers, consumers, or the environment. Punishing corporations, just like punishing natural persons, is also understood to be the right way for society to repudiate the false valuations that their crimes express. Criminal liability "sends the message" that people matter more than profits and reaffirms the value of those who were sacrificed to "corporate greed." (Kahan 1998, 618–19)

Therefore, there is bidirectional relationship between corporate citizenship – understood as the possibility to participate in the process of creating and defining social norms – and corporate criminal liability. From a social meaning perspective, imposing a criminal sanction on a corporation means acknowledging that the corporation is member of society that participates in the "process of creating and defining social norms" i.e., a full-fledged member of the moral community in French's terminology. Coincidently, recognizing the capacity of corporations to participate in the "process of creating and defining social norms" acknowledges the soundness of corporate criminal liability.

CID Structure, Compliance Programs and Compliance Management Systems: Focusing on Corporate Wrongdoing, Not on Individual Wrongdoing

Against this backdrop it seems reasonable to conclude that it makes sense to hold corporations criminally accountable. However, to the same extent that it is important to identify the distinct corporate *persona* upon which the criminal sanction is imposed, it is equally important to identify the distinct corporate wrongdoing for which the corporation is held criminally accountable. In this sense, if a corporation would be criminally sanctioned for the individual wrongdoing, the distinct meaning of criminal law would be lost. It is of the essence to properly differentiate between corporate wrongdoing/corporate punishment and individual wrongdoing/individual punishment.

It is precisely at this point that French's contributions regarding the nature of corporate wrongdoing come especially into play. To understand this nature it should be noted that French distinguishes between aggregates and conglomerates (French 1984, 1–18; French et al. 1992, 15–18). Essentially, conglomerates are different from aggregates in that they have (i) internal decision making procedures, (ii) stricter control of the conduct standards, and (iii) role assumption by individuals. Conglomerates possess a distinct identity that cannot be reduced to the identity of its members. Ascribing responsibility to a conglomerate cannot be reduced to ascribing responsibility to the individuals associated with the conglomerate (French 1984, 163).

Out of these three elements, it is the first one that draws special attention. According to French, the components of the corporation's internal decision structure (CID Structure) consist of the corporation's flowchart and procedural and recognition rules (French 1979, 212; 1984, 52; 1986, 37). Every corporation has an established way by which it makes decisions and converts them into actions, a CID Structure. CID Structures have two elements crucial to our understanding of how intentionally acting corporations emerge at certain levels of the description of events: (1) an organizational flow chart that delineates stations and levels within the corporation; and (2) rules that reveal how to recognize decisions that are corporate ones and not simply personal decisions of the humans who occupy the positions identified on the flow chart. These rules are typically embedded, whether explicitly or implicitly, in statements of corporate policy. In French's words,

> The organizational rules distinguish players, clarify their rank, and map out the interwoven lines of responsibility within the corporation. They give us the grammar of corporate decision-making. Policy procedure rules provide its logic. When the corporate act is consistent with an instantiation or an implementation of established corporate policy, then it is proper to describe it as having been done for corporate reasons, as having been caused by a corporate desire coupled with a corporate belief and so, in other words, as corporate intentional. (French 1984, 44)[14]

The distinct elements of the corporate structure that French identified decades ago have been developed over time. Noteworthy is that those elements have been gradually incorporated into the now well-known compliance programs. Not surprisingly in a 1996 contribution French noted that corporate integrity is based on a "... compliance system, and an active ethics officer plugged into the CID Structure in a significant way" (French 1996, 153). This is all the more relevant as compliance programs are now considered as the bulk of corporate criminal liability.

Compliance programs entered the corporate criminal liability landscape in 1991 with the Organizational Sentencing Guidelines in the US system of Federal Criminal

[14]Explanatory: "A CID Structure subordinates and synthesizes the intentions and actions of various human persons (and even the behavior of machines) into a corporate action. What I mean by that is that the CID Structure not only organizes the various human beings in the system into a decision-making and acting entity, it makes it possible for us and those within the structure to describe what is happening as corporate. In the absence of the structure, the various activities of the humans and machines would be utterly unintelligible".

Law.[15] The fact that a corporation could significantly reduce the criminal sanction if it had in place an effective compliance program triggered a palpable response in the corporate world. Corporations were eager to implement compliance programs in order to mitigate their potential criminal responsibility (Kaplan et al. 1998). When in 1999 the US Attorneys Office considered effective compliance programs as a factor to be considered by prosecutors to make the decision whether or not to charge the corporation,[16] their importance became paramount.[17]

In the first stages of the twenty first century, compliance programs were the only real possibility of a corporation to avoid criminal liability; not only in the US, but worldwide (Pieth and Ivory 2011b; Gobert and Pascal 2011). Consequently, corporate wrongdoing has been increasingly conceived as a lack of corporate compliance programs or, at least, as a defective implementation of those corporate compliance programs. In a nutshell: if a corporation had in place, at the time of the relevant events, an effective compliance program, then there was no corporate wrongdoing, and criminal liability could only be ascribed to the individuals – not to the corporation.

This initial assumption has evolved, from a legal perspective, into the notion that the target of corporate punishment is aimed at blaming the corporate culture/policy/procedures.[18] From a criminal law perspective, corporations are to be blamed – and consequently punished – for a distinct corporate wrongdoing. Perhaps a way to describe this differentiation is to distinguish between the *individual offense* (that derives in individual criminal liability) and the *corporate offense* (that results in corporate criminal liability).

Interestingly enough, a parallel development has been taking place in the compliance world. For some time now, there have been international efforts at standardizing compliance programs. As a result, the trend has moved away from the formalistic i.e., checklist approach, connotation of the term "programs" and has adopted a management-system approach. As Richard S. Gruner and Louis M. Brown noted two decades ago: "Viewed as management systems, law compliance programs are examples of performance quality management systems or 'quality systems.'"[19] The recently enacted standard *ISO 19600 – Compliance Management*

[15]US Sentencing Commission, US Sentencing Guidelines, Chapter 8 (1991). See Paula Desio, Deputy General Counsel, US Sentencing Commission, An Overview of the Organizational Guidelines, [available at: http://www.ussc.gov/sites/default/files/pdf/training/organizational-guidelines/ORGOVERVIEW.pdf].

[16]See Principles of Federal Prosecution of Business Organizations (June 1999). Attorney General Eric Holder.

[17]See Gruner (2005) and Orland (2004).

[18]See from various perspectives Bucy (1991), Laufer (1994), Lederman (2000), Quaid (1998), and Moore (1992). See generally Laufer (2006).

[19]See Gruner and Brown (1996). "For purposes of corporate law compliance programs, high quality performance is performance that meets the stated or implied demands of various laws. A "quality system" aimed at maximizing law compliance is comprised of organizational structures, assigned responsibilities, procedures, processes, and resources that a corporation or other organi-

Systems. Guidelines –[20] represents the foundational standardization of this type of management systems and offers the fundamental guidelines to properly apprehend their meaning and scope.

For our discussion, one of the key features of compliance management systems is the special emphasis placed in the compliance culture of the corporation. It could be well argued that the goal of these Compliance Management Systems is to establish a compliance culture as part of the organizational culture. Actually, the very concept of compliance is closely related to corporate culture. As the ISO 19600 notes "Compliance is an outcome of an organization meeting its obligations, and is made sustainable embedding it in the culture of an organization". Not surprisingly, the ISO 19.600 Guidelines devote a specific chapter to "Compliance Culture" (ISO 19.600. 7.3.2.2.) and specifically acknowledge that "organizations that want to be successful in the long term should maintain a culture of integrity and law-abidance".

From this perspective, the distinct *corporate offense* can be properly assessed by looking into the functioning of the Compliance Management System of the corporation. These management systems do not only delineate the organizational rules and procedures of the company i.e., the CID Structure, but actually serve as a basis for evaluating the degree of law-abiding behavior of the corporation. If the corporation has an adequate compliance culture, then it can be considered as a "Good Corporate Citizen" and, therefore, should not be subject to corporate punishment for the acts of its directors, officers and/or employees. Conversely, if the corporation lacks an adequate compliance culture, then it makes perfect sense to blame the corporation for its corporate wrongdoing.[21]

By way of linking the *corporate offense* to the Compliance Management System of the corporation two complementary goals are achieved: first, the expressive function of criminal law is linked distinctively to "corporate": we blame the corporation for not having an adequate compliance culture; second, we offer the corporation a distinct (affirmative[22]) *corporate defense*: if the corporation proves that it had an adequate compliance culture, then it should not be subject to *corporate punishment*, regardless of the individual offense.

zation devotes to the pursuit of law compliance. These corporate resources should be applied to ensure that corporate employees act lawfully in carrying out tasks as corporate agents" (752).

[20]http://www.iso.org/iso/home/store/catalogue_tc/catalogue_detail.htm?csnumber=62342. See generally Bleker and Hortensius (2014).

[21]See generally Gómez-Jara (2011).

[22]Podgor (2007) (noting the urgency for an affirmative defense based on corporate compliance programs); Weismann and Newman (2007) and Gruner and Brown (1996) (due diligence test for corporate criminal liability; Walsh and Pyrich (1995)).

What Has Systems Theory to Do with It?

The arguments laid out so far are based on a certain reading of Peter French's work and the late developments in the field of corporate criminal liability. However, French himself has noted the compatibility of these arguments with a certain approach on the basis of the so-called autopoietic i.e., self-produced systems theory.[23] This should come as no surprise, as a number of academics in Europe use this theory in their assessments of corporate criminal liability.[24]

From a philosophical point of view, the autopoietic social systems theory[25] is based on a epistemological theory known as (operative) *constructivism.*[26] These theories purport to explain how certain social systems achieve an internal degree of complexity until they become systems that are capable of self-reproduction. The output of those self-reproductive systems (in this case, corporate organizations) *may have* and sometimes *has had* a significant impact on legal structures.

Although a thorough explanation of systems theory lies outside the purpose of this paper, it suffices to note that, according to this theory, business organizations, human beings, and the legal system are all considered to be autopoietic i.e., self-producing systems. An autopoietic system is a system that is capable of reproducing itself. The difference between the different systems lies in the different ways in which they can achieve self-reproduction. Thus, corporate entities self-reproduce by way of corporate decisions, human beings self-reproduce by thought processes, whereas the legal system self-reproduces by way of legal communication.[27] In the corporate context, it is fair to say that some corporations tend to develop an internal complexity over time that ends up making them capable of self-organization and self-governance. Hence, it is not only logical, but also necessary to acknowledge that corporations often achieve a certain control over their own sphere of influence.[28]

For the last 20 years Gunther Teubner has conducted major research on the requirements for a corporation to become a so-called high-order self-producing system.[29] As Teubner puts it: the corporation leaves the "diminished capacity" stage by way of a hypercyclical link between the self-referential qualities of the organizational system, i.e. a double self-referentiality (Teubner 1988b, 43). To word it differently: over time, there is an accumulation of self-referential

---

[23]See French (2011, 272–273).

[24]See among others Bottke (1997, 1995), Heine (1995), Lampe (1994), Lütolf (1997), and Rotsch (1998); Schünemann has adopted as a "bedrock principle the theory of autopoietic systems" (Schünemann 1996, 132); Schünemann contends that "the only theory available to justify a true corporate criminal law is systems theory" (Schünemann 1999, 230).

[25]See Luhmann (1996). For an outstanding introduction to this social theory, see Rasch (2000).

[26]On operative constructivism, see Luhmann (2002).

[27]See Luhmann (2008) and Teubner (1993a). For the specifics on organizations as autopoietic systems, see Luhmann (2000).

[28]See in Bottke (1995, 48–63), Heine (1998, 217).

[29]See Teubner (1993a, 28, b, 1988a, b).

cycles in business corporations that end up in a hypercycle linking all of them together. In that precise moment the corporate actor emerges as a high order autopoiyetic system.[30] Those self-referential circles start their processes in four different domains: the system's limit, the system's structure, the system's elements, and the system's identity.[31] The limit is provided by corporate membership; the structure embodies the final/conditional corporate decision premises; the elements, i.e. the basal operations that enable the system's autopoiesis, are constituted by corporate decisions[32]; and finally, the system's identity is reflected in the corporate identity. Therefore, when corporate identity is hypercyclically linked to corporate decisions, and corporate rules determine corporate membership, a corporate actor emerges as a reality different from each and every underlying psychological system. It achieves a self-organization capacity that exceeds the organizational capacity of any of its members.[33]

This systems-theory approach seems perfectly consistent with Peter French's approach. The key lies in the acknowledgement that corporations have a certain degree of autonomy. For corporate criminal liability to be consistent with the general principles of criminal law it must tackle on that distinctive corporate autonomy. The sharp edge of criminal law acquires profound social meaning when corporate criminal liability focuses on the corporate (not individual) offense, and corporate punishment is suffered by non law-abiding corporations that are blamed for lacking an adequate compliance culture. Consequently, if corporations can avoid corporate criminal liability by showing they had an adequate compliance culture, a clear incentive for implementing effective Compliance Management Systems will be in place. This sound rationale seems to be more consistent from a theoretical point of view and more effective from a policy perspective.

Conclusion

When Peter French wrote his first piece on this topic in 1979, compliance and corporate citizenship were subject matters on the eve of development. From an absolutely different perspective, Peter French advanced some of the findings that, with time, reached considerable consensus in the legal world. Although still a heavily debated topic in the philosophical and legal academy, corporate criminal liability in the twenty first century is closely related to both compliance and corporate citizenship. Every single day, corporations are subject to criminal investigations

[30]Explaining that an autopoietic social system is "a system of actions/communications that reproduces itself by constantly producing from the network of its elements as new communications/actions" (Teubner 1988a).

[31]See the explanatory graphic in Teubner (1988b, 115).

[32]On corporate decision as a basis for organizational systems, see Teubner (1989).

[33]See Teubner (1988a, 140).

and/or proceedings in which compliance plays a great role; by the same token, corporations are increasingly recognized as (distinct) citizens that participate in the public square.

It took centuries for the system of criminal law to adapt to the idiosyncrasies and complexities of the human mind; it will probably take centuries for the system to adapt to the idiosyncrasies and complexities of the corporate organization. All in all, we are probably witnessing the first stages of this adaptation. But, to be sure, it seems like an unstoppable trend.

Visionaries like Peter French normally share some common traits: sharp analysis and logical development. Their initial findings are initially subject to heavy criticism. It is only time that rewards their fortitude.

Laudatio

While conducting the research for my Ph.D on corporate criminal liability I came across Peter French's book "Collective and Corporate Responsibility" (French 1984). This did not come as a surprise, as French's work was constantly cited in essays concerning corporate criminal liability. What did surprise me, was the clarity and, at the same time, profoundness of French's arguments. Even more surprisingly was the fact that his theory had extremely practical implications. It rapidly reminded me of Kant's short essay "On the Common Saying: That May Be True in Theory, but It Is of No Use in Practice" (Kant 1996), and confirmed my agreement with Kurt Lewin's statement "there is nothing more practical than a good theory" (Lewin 1952, 169).

Probably out of naiveté, I sent him a short essay on "Corporations as Victims of Mismanagement" (Gómez-Jara 2008) not having real expectations that such a great philosopher would take the time from his busy schedule to actually read a work authored by an unknown Spanish Ph.D student. Christmas came to me early in August of 2011 when I read French's book *War and Moral Dissonance*. Not only had he read the short essay, but commented on it and was "grateful" to me in the "Acknowledgements". This was totally unexpected. Why would a great philosopher of the twentieth and twenty-first century read and comment on an essay by some unknown and irrelevant student? I could not resist the temptation to meet him and exchange ideas in person.

My trip to Arizona State University was more than worthwhile. I was able to warmly discuss before lunch, during lunch, and after lunch such a breadth of interesting topics that when I came back home I could not write down fast enough the many insights on various subjects that our conversations produced. From then on, we exchanged works and ideas, resulting, at least from my side, in valuable arguments to support some key concepts. Without a doubt, I was the one who benefited more from this relationship.

References

Adler, Matthew D. 2000. Expressive theories of law: A skeptical overview. *University of Pennsylvania Law Review* 148: 1363–1501.

Bleker, Sylvie, and Dirk Hortensius. 2014. ISO 19600: The development of a global standard on compliance management, Business Compliance 2.

Bottke, Wilfried. 1995. *Assoziationsprävention: Zur heutigen Diskussion der Strafzwecke*. Berlin: Duncker & Humblot.

———. 1997. Standortvorteil Wirtschaftskriminalrecht: Müssen Unternehmen "strafmündig" werden? Bermerkungen zum Stand des Wirtschaftskriminalrechts in der Bundesrepublik Deutschland. Wistra: 241–253.

Bucy, Pamela. 1991. Corporate Ethos: A standard for imposing corporate criminal liability. *Minnesota Law Review* 75: 1095.

Buell, Samuel W. 2006. The blaming function of entity criminal liability. *Indiana Law Journal* 81: 473–537.

Cigüela, Javier. Collective organizations as meta-subjects. *Zeitschrift für Internationale Strafrechtsdogmatik* (forthcoming).

De Maglie, Cristina. 2011. Italy. In *European developments in corporate Criminal Liability*, ed. James Gobert and Ana-Maria Pascal, 252. London: Springer.

Dubber, Markus D. 2010. Citizenship and penal law. *New Criminal Law Review* 13: 190–215.

———. 2013. The comparative history and theory of corporate criminal liability. *New Criminal Law Review* 16: 203–240.

Duff, R.A. 2013. Responsibility, citizenship and criminal law. In *Philosophical foundations of criminal law*, ed. R.A. Duff and Stuart Green. Oxford: Oxford University Press.

Farmer, Lindsay. 2014. *Making the modern criminal law: Criminalization and civil order*. Oxford: Oxford University Press.

Feuerbach, Paul Anselm. 1818. *Lehrbuch des gemeinen in Deuschtland gültigen peinlichen Rechts*. 6th ed. Gießen: Heyer.

Fletcher, George P. 2006. Political theory and criminal law. *Criminal Justice Ethics* 25: 18–38.

French, Peter A. 1979. The corporation as a moral person. *American Philosophical Quarterly* 16: 207–215.

———. 1984. *Collective and corporate responsibility*. New York: Columbia University Press.

———. 1986. Principles of responsibility, shame and the corporation. In *Shame, guilt and corporate responsibility*, ed. Hugh Curtler. New York: Haven Publications.

———. 1996. Integrity, intentions, and corporations. *American Business Law Journal* 34: 141–156.

———. 2011. *War and moral dissonance*. Cambridge: Cambridge University Press.

French, Peter A., Jeffrey Nesteruk, and David T. Risser. 1992. *Corporations in the moral community*. New York: Holt, Rinehart, and Winston.

Friedman, Lawrence. 2000. In defense of corporate criminal liability. *Harvard Journal for Law & Public Policy* 12: 833.

Gobert, James, and Ana-Maria Pascal, eds. 2011. *European developments in corporate criminal liability*. London: Springer.

Gómez-Jara, Carlos. 2008. Corporations as victims of mismanagement: Beyond the shareholder vs. *Directors Debate, PACE Law Review* 28: 795–813.

———. 2010. *Fundamentos modernos de la responsabilidad penal de las personas jurídicas*. Madrid: BdF.

———. 2011. Corporate culpability as a limit to the overcriminalization of corporate criminal liability: The interplay between corporate compliance, self-regulation and corporate citizenship. *New Criminal Law Review* 14: 78.

Gruner, Richard. 2005. *Corporate criminal liability and prevention*. New York: Law Journal Press.

Gruner, Richard S., and Louis M. Brown. 1996. Organizational justice: Recognizing and rewarding the good citizen corporation. *Journal of Corporate Law* 21: 731.

Hasnas, John. 2009. The centenary of a mistake: One hundred years of corporate criminal liability. *American Criminal Law Review* 46: 1329.

Heine, Günter. 1995. *Die Strafrechtliche Verantwortlichkeit von Unternehmen*. Baden-Baden: Nomos.

Heine, Gunter. 1998. New developments in corporate criminal liability in Europe: Can Europeans learn from the American experience – or Viceversa? *Saint Louis-Warsaw Transatlantic Law Journal* 4: 173.

Kahan, Dan M. 1998. Social meaning and the economic analysis of crime. *Journal of Legal Studies* 27: 609–622.

Kaiser, Hanno F. 2006. The three dimensions of freedom, crime, and punishment. *Buffalo Criminal Law Review* 9: 691.

Kant, Immanuel. 1996. *Practical philosophy* (ed. and trans. Mary J. Gregor). Cambridge: Cambridge University Press.

Kaplan, Jeffrey M., Joseph E. Murphy, and Winthrop Swenson. 1998. *Compliance programs and the corporate sentencing guidelines: Preventing criminal and civil liability*. New York: West Publishers.

Lampe, Ernst J. 1994. Systemsunrecht und Unrechtssysteme. *Zeitschrift für die gesamte Strafrechtswissenschaft* 106: 690.

Laufer, William S. 1994. Corporate bodies and guilty minds. *Emory Law Journal* 43: 648–730.

———. 2006. Corporate bodies and guilty minds. *The failure of corporate criminal. Liability*. Chicago: University of Chicago Press.

Lederman, Eli. 2000. Models for imposing corporate criminal liability: From adaptation and imitation toward aggregation and the search of self-identity. *Buffalo Criminal Law Review* 4: 641–708.

Lewin, Kurt. 1952. In *Field theory in social science: Selected theoretical papers by Kurt Lewin*, ed. Dorwin Cartwright. New York: Harper & Brothers.

Luhmann, Niklas. 1996. *Social Systems*. Trans. John Bednarz & Dirk Baecker. Stanford: Stanford University Press.

———. 2000. *Organisation und Entscheidung*. Opladen: Westdeutscher Verlag.

———. 2002. *Theories of distinction: Redescribing the descriptions of modernity*. Stanford: Stanford University Press.

———. 2008. *Law as a social system*. Oxford: Oxford University Press.

Lütolf, Sandra-Hilda. 1997. *Strafbarkeit der juristischen Person*. Zürich: Duncker & Humblot.

Malblanc, Julius Friedrich. 1793. *observationes quaedam ad delicta universitatum spectantes*, Erlangen.

Moore, Jennifer. 1992. Corporate culpability under the federal sentencing guidelines. *Arizona Law Review* 34: 743.

Orland, Leonard. 2004. *Corporate criminal liability. Regulation and compliance*. New York: Aspen Publishers.

Pawlik, Michael. 2004. *Person, Subjekt, Bürger.: Zur Legitimation von Strafe*. Berlin: Duncker & Humblot.

Pawlik, Michael. 2012. *Das Unrecht des Bürgers: Grundlinien der Allgemeinen Verbrechenslehre*. Tübingen: Mohr Siebeck.

Perrow, Charles. 1989. A society of organizations. In *Kultur und Gesellschaft*, ed. Max Haller, Hans Joachim Hofmann-Nowotny & Wolfgang Zapf. Frankfurt/New York: Campus.

Pieth, Mark, and Radha Ivory, eds. 2011a. *Corporate criminal liability. Emergence, convergence, and risk*. New York: Springer.

Pieth, Mark & Radha Ivory, 2011b. Emergence and convergence: Corporate criminal liability principles in overview. In *Corporate criminal liability. Emergence, convergence, and risk*, ed. Mark Pieth & Radha Ivory, p. 35. New York: Springer.

Podgor, Ellen P. 2007. A new corporate world mandates a "Good Faith" affirmative defense. *American Criminal Law Review* 44: 1537.

Quaid, Jennifer A. 1998. The assessment of corporate criminal liability on the basis of corporate identity: An analysis. *McGill Law Journal* 43: 67–114.

Ramsay, P. 2006. The responsible subject as citizen: Democracy and the welfare state. *Modern Law Review* 69: 29–58.

Rasch, William. 2000. *Niklas Luhmann's mdernity: The paradoxes of differentiation*. Stanford: Stanford University Press.

Rotsch, Thomas. 1998. *Individuelle Haftung in Großunternehmen*. Baden-Baden: Nomos.

Salvo, Nelly. 2011. Principales aspectos de la Nueva Ley de Responsabilidad penal de las Personas Jurídicas en Chile (Ley N° 20.393). In *Corporate criminal liability. Emergence, convergence, and risk*, ed. Mark Pieth & Radha Ivory, p. 289. New York: Springer.

Schünemann, Bernd. 1996. Art. 4: Maßnahmen gengen Unternehmen. In *Deutsche Wiedervereinigung III Unternehmenskriminalität*. München: heymanns.

———. 1999. Criticising the notion of a genuine criminal law against legal entities. In *Criminal responsibility of collective and legal entities*. Freiburg: Iuscrim.

Teubner, Gunther. 1988a. Enterprise corporatism. New industrial policy and the "Essence" of the legal person. *American Journal of Comparative Law* 36: 130–155.

———. 1988b). Hypercycle in law and organization: The relationship between self-observation, self-constitution and autopoiesis. In *European yearbook in the sociology of law*, ed. Alberto Febrajjo. Milan: Giuffrè: 43–70.

———. 1989. How the law thinks: Toward a constructivist epistemology of law. *Law & Society Review* 23: 727–758.

———. 1993a. *Law as an autopoietic system*. Oxford: Blackwell Publishers.

———. 1993b. The many-headed hydra: Networks as higher-order collective actors. In *Corporate control and accountability. Changing structures and the dynamics of regulation*, ed. Joseph McCahery, Sol Piciotto, and Colin Scott. Oxford: Clarendon Press.

Walsh, Charles J., and Alissa Pyrich. 1995. Corporate compliance programs as a shield to criminal liability: Can a corporation save its soul? *Rutgers Law review* 47: 605–689.

Weismann, Andrew, and David Newman. 2007. Rethinking criminal corporate liability. *Indiana Law Journal* 82: 411–451.

Wilberforce, William. Life of Thurlow, 1783.

Ethnic Conflict and the Ethics of Care

Virginia Held

Groups and Individuals

The Middle East is a cauldron of conflict and violence. Among the primary causes are ethnic antagonisms: versus Shia, versus Sunni, versus Alawite, versus Kurd, versus Yazidi, versus Houthi, and so on. When efforts are made to bring the ethnic groups of an existing state together to counter a threat from violent extremists, such efforts often fall apart along ethnic lines. Comparisons are sometimes made to the Balkans, and the conflicts that tore apart the former Yugoslavia and its region in the 1990s. Those conflicts were also ignited by ethnic antagonisms, which continue, though at a muted level. Elsewhere in the world, numerous violent conflicts are fueled by ethnic hatreds and resentments: in China with the Uighurs, in Myanmar with the Rohingha, in South Sudan with the Dinka, the Nuer, and the Shilluk, and so on, and on.

The examples are too numerous and too deadly to ignore. Yet they are not well understood or dealt with by our dominant political, legal, and moral theories. The latter are too individualistic and too voluntaristic to take account adequately of ethnic loyalties and conflicts. Actual persons are not born nor do they actually become Lockean men hypothetically contracting with their fellow men to establish governments and citizenships. They are rarely Rawlsian free and equal rational individuals imagining the political and legal entities to which they could voluntarily agree to belong. They are usually not looking to be guided by the moral theories that have grown with and are compatible with these prevailing views of the liberal tradition.

V. Held (✉)
CUNY Graduate Center, New York, NY, USA
e-mail: vheld@gc.cuny.edu

Z.J. Goldberg (ed.), *Reflections on Ethics and Responsibility*,
DOI 10.1007/978-3-319-50359-2_4

Human persons are born into groups, with ties of family, of language, of shared histories, of association, built into their senses of self. They are enmeshed in social relationships. They form new families, and new ties, within and across social groups. Human persons require years and years of care merely to survive. To develop into grown persons, they have had years and years of social influence and education and formation in some groups or other, and these groups are often primarily ethnic groups. Persons remain in relationships with social groups. Yet our dominant political and legal and moral theories have virtually nothing to say about such groups and can barely recognize their existence. Peter French's understanding of groups and collectivities is more promising for considering them.

Philosophers who deal only with ideal justice risk being irrelevant. National boundaries, ethnic or racial divisions and fortunes, seem as arbitrary as any other particularity to be discounted in delineating the requirements of ideal justice. From the perspective of ideal justice, arguments for anything less demanding than cosmopolitan egalitarianism are very hard to sustain. And so for the world as it is, divided into regional and national and ethnic and religious and other groups, ideal justice may seem to have little to offer.

The liberal individualism that overwhelmingly dominates political and legal and moral theory in the U.S. and U.K. asks us to put aside all divisive identifications and to think like rational individuals contracting with other individuals for our own interests, and agreeing on certain restraints. But identities run far deeper than individual interests or abstract norms. Ethnic and other identities tie us to others, to our families, our groups, our fellow members of various groups. They cannot be dismissed as merely part of the tribal past that modern law and states and moralities are to overcome.

Standard normative political theories merely assume the existence of the states for which they offer their recommendations about rights, obligations, interests, preferences, and values. The boundaries and group inclusions of states are merely posited, not discussed. Yet almost all actual states, with their borders, and inclusions and exclusions of groups, did not come into existence through plebiscites and voluntary agreements. They came to exist through violence, force, coercion, domination, and deception. Some are small and weak, others huge and in possession of enough power to destroy all human life in vast regions. Analogies between international relations and the imagined contractual relations between hypothetically free and equal citizens are particularly questionable.

To understand the normative recommendations appropriate for large numbers of the most pressing problems of our times we badly need to understand ethnic groups and the responsibilities of such groups and their members, and the responsibilities of nonmembers towards them.

While liberal individualism and its associated moral theories of Kantian ethics, utilitarianism, and most of virtue theory are not very suitable for dealing with major global problems such as those of climate change and the environment, or of global poverty, or of group conflicts and migrations, a newer moral theory, the ethics of care, is much more promising. I will discuss it later in this essay.

Liberal individualism remains suitable for many of the much narrower questions of the legal and political structures of society to be recommended once their boundaries and group inclusions have been determined. The ethics of care is more capable of addressing the broader issues of the environment, of global poverty, of international interactions, *and* of group need and conflict, along with the more personal issues of family and small group relations. It is more reliably supportive of nonviolent solutions and the building of trust. It encompasses the narrower theory appropriate for legal and political matters.

Peter French and Responsibility

Peter French has been one of the few contemporary philosophers whose views allow us to make sense of groups and group responsibility. He has written perceptively about groups, and the persons in them. He understands that for a group to have the power to do something, it is not satisfactory to simply suppose that each of the members of the group has the power to do it (French 1992, 71). "To have power... in a group," he writes, "is to possess the dispositional property of being able, if one wants, under certain conditions, to move a group to action or inaction" (71). Sometimes a person will have a specific capacity to address a need, as when a doctor might lead a group effort to treat some injured fellow victims of a natural disaster. At other times, it may be unclear how the group, and the persons in it, can act. "A person has a moral responsibility," French writes, "to understand the station he or she occupies in society at large and in more restricted groups" (78). The notion of 'station' may not be the best way to think of this position, which may be changeable and unclear, but it will serve. "People may not know their individual powers, and have had no way of finding out about them," he continues. "Still, there is a rational person test that can be applied. Simply, any rational person in the circumstances should recognize the reasonable course of action and try to communicate it to the group. If the person is unable to persuade the group or enough of the members to create the critical mass to accomplish the task, at least the person has tried . . . " (78).

French has also written about "fictive groups" and whether they can be thought responsible for important global social problems such as poverty and climate change. "Moral theory," he writes, "should not abandon the global matters, even if they seem unmanageable to the favored subject of Western moralists, the isolated individual actor" (79). He examines various possible fictive groups, and cites Larry May's conception of "loosely structured groups" (May 1990). French considers how, even if they are not responsible for having caused world hunger, "the affluent of the world," or "the world's thirty richest people" might be responsible for the failure to overcome or alleviate it. He concludes that in addressing "great social problems" it might be best to focus on "already existing entities that have the resources and the power to effect the changes we think morality recommends" (French 1992, 84) and that can and should be held responsible, entities such as states and corporations.

French is especially known for writing persuasively about corporate responsibility, and how corporations and corporation-like structures such as states, can act and should be held responsible (French 1984, 1991). Writing about the environment, he argues that to deal with the enormous problems involved "in a responsible and effective fashion, we must be prepared to dynamite some of the most cherished and firmly placed cornerstones of the political liberalism that has dominated Western academic discussion of moral philosophy for centuries" (French 1992, 96–97). Atomistic individualism cannot handle such problems as our responsibilities to future generations, along with many other issues. We must be able to deal with the responsibility of corporation-like entities that have internal decision structures and that "manifest intentionality and make decisions, have rights and duties in law, carry on nonlegal relationships.... They are historical entities with births, lives, and deaths. They flourish and decline, succeed and fail" (100). We must be able to assign responsibility for the protection of the "springs, forests, and waterways" of our planet to such collective entities as states and corporations (101).

French focuses especially on "ascriptions" of responsibility, for purposes of blame, punishment, retaliation, and compensation. He argues that "the ascription of responsibility, no matter how complex internally, ultimately depends for its sense on [our] practices," practices such as punishment and the assessment of compensation owed (19). Citing the example of the *Exxon Valdez* oil spill, he writes: "Exxon was assessed the financial burden of compensating the state of Alaska as well as those whose livelihoods depend on the wildlife in Prince William Sound..." (18). He points out that "the practice of holding people responsible for things that happen, hence the concept of responsibility itself, depends for its sense on the purpose or ends to which we put it: the practices in which it is integral and which also depend on it" (19). He notes that some philosophers emphasize punishment, that utilitarians often focus on compensation, while Aristotle is especially concerned with character. He concludes that "responsibility ascription cannot be eliminated as long as we would sustain a stable moral community" (28). And he shows why we should often ascribe responsibility to such collectivities as corporation-like entities.

Philip Pettit is another philosopher who argues for the responsibility of corporations. He shows that corporations are "conversable agents," systems that self-interpret and commit themselves as agents (Pettit 2016). Some other corporate organizations are clubs, religious institutions, universities, voluntary associations, political parties, and political states. Corporations have decision-making structures, they act in pursuit of purposes, they have authorized spokespersons to speak in their name. They are thus conversable agents and entities fit to be held responsible.

Taking Responsibility

I agree that we need practices of ascribing responsibility. Some skeptics doubt that responsibility ascriptions can ever really be justified. If, for instance, those who act wrongly always do so involuntarily, or out of ignorance, or if no one can ever do other than they do because, as causal determinism may be thought to imply, it is impossible, then our standard practices of ascribing responsibility are undermined. Most of us, however, regard at least some of our practices of holding persons responsible to be essential to social life. Persons must be held accountable for at least a range of their actions. There are very good reasons, as well, to extend practices of ascribing responsibility to various collective entities.

We can, however, shift the focus of our attention from *holding* people and collective entities responsible for purposes of blame or punishment to recommending that they *take* responsibility for various actions that ought to be done (Held 2002; for a related view see Young 2006). This is especially relevant in addressing large-scale social problems. Even when it may be unclear that collectivities should be held accountable for various problems for purposes of blame, it may be entirely clear that they ought to take responsibility for addressing such problems because the problems need to be dealt with and they have the capacity to deal with them. Problems such as global poverty and climate change are good examples.

Consider how the wealthy countries of the world ought to take responsibility for alleviating global poverty. Understanding the history of colonialism, of slavery, of capitalist exploitation, and what these did to the societies from which slaves were seized, resources extracted, and institutions destroyed, one should hesitate to conclude that the rich nations are *not* responsible for the poverty and misery of the developing world. One might plausibly assign responsibility to them and demand compensation. But even if the developed countries, and especially their current populations, are thought not directly responsible for *causing* the problems, as can also be argued, they should not be thought exempt from responsibility. They should *take* responsibility because the need is overwhelming and they are in a position to respond to it. Doing so is eminently feasible. Thomas Pogge, a leading scholar dealing with global poverty, has calculated that if it had been distributed more fairly, only *half* of what the top one-twentieth of people in the world have *gained* in wealth over the past decades of globalization would have been sufficient to raise the world's poor to an adequate standard of living (Pogge 2001, 2011).

Ethnic Groups and Responsibility

Ethnic groups are rarely organized in the form of corporate organizations. Modern states are almost all multi-ethnic, though one group may be dominant. Ethnic groups are not, however, mere random assortments of persons. Ethnic groups have an identity as groups and some continuity over time. Their members have some shared characteristics such as ancestry, religion, language, habitation on specific territory, or at least shared history. They are capable of a variety of actions (Poole 1999; Kovac 2001, 2006).

It is much less clear than in the case of corporate entities that ethnic groups should be held responsible for actions taken or not taken by their members, though it is often persuasive to assign responsibility even to relatively unorganized groups when they have inflicted serious harms. It is even more clear that members can *take* responsibility *as members* (Held 2002). They can consider themselves spokespersons. If an event occurs, such as the bombing of a market frequented by members of one ethnic group and the members of another group are suspected, if no members of the suspected group come forward to contest the charges, if the charges are untrue, or to disavow the violence, or to call for such acts to not be repeated, the group might be judged to be condoning such violence. Members can take responsibility for trying to guide the group against violence.

Larry May argues that a practice in which people see themselves as sharing responsibility, for various harms caused by or occurring within their communities, will decrease the harms that groups bring about (May 1992). We can ask of people that they change their attitudes when such attitudes contribute to causing harm. He examines racist attitudes, arguing that even if group members do not themselves participate in acts of racist violence, if they have racist attitudes they may well contribute to the greater probability that harm will be done. "One's attitudes often are as important to the increased likelihood of harm in a community," he argues, "as one's overt behavior" (May 37). Persuasive accounts show how a climate of hatred can contribute to violent actions being taken, as when attitudes among various Israelis may have contributed to the assassination of Yitzhak Rabin in 1995 as he sought peace with the Palestinians (Ephron 2015).

Such discussion is highly relevant to the ethnic hatred that so often fuels ethnic conflict. We can ask of ethnic groups that they curb the hatred that promotes violence against other groups, and ask of members that they take responsibility for the attitudes they and their groups hold or condone. A practice in which more people take responsibility for what the groups of which they are members bring about will be a morally better practice.

Individual and Group Responsibility

When we hold organized groups responsible, little follows about the responsibilities of any individual members. How individuals may or may not be responsible depends on their positions and actions and inactions within the group. Peter French's discussion of the internal decision structures of corporations (CID Structure), for instance, reminds us how some groups structure their power (French 1991). The leader or leaders of a state or a corporation may make decisions that lead to actions for which a citizen or worker may have little or no responsibility. In unorganized groups such as most ethnic groups, individual responsibility may be hard to assign and group responsibility even harder. There are, however, good reasons to consider that ethnic groups may sometimes be responsible for various events: such groups are not mere arbitrary assortments of individual persons, and those in them can and often ought to act *as members* (Held 2002). But as with organized groups, we cannot draw conclusions about individual responsibility from what we may conclude about the responsibility of the group. Nor should it be thought that a whole group is at fault when a small number of its members do something egregious.

Assigning responsibility to a group is a practice that can be put to morally bad as well as good uses. Many writers have assailed collective responsibility as wrongly blaming innocent individuals for the crimes and misdeeds of other members of the groups to which they happen to belong (see e.g. Lewis 1991; Cushman and Mestrovic 1996). Or, blaming the group is sometimes misused as an excuse, as when individual members blame the corporate entity or group and fail to acknowledge their own responsibility for what has been done or not done. And praising or blaming a group as a whole for the deeds of a few of its members is a well-known and popular mistake of inference.

These, however, are misuses of the concept of group responsibility. They depend on a mistaken inference from group responsibility to individual responsibility, or the reverse. One should never simply *infer* that because a group did x, all the members of the group did x, or that a group did x because some individual members did x. The judgments must be arrived at on their own merits. That one should not infer from the group to the individual, or the reverse, holds whether the group is an organized collectivity such as a corporation or a state, or an unorganized collectivity such as an ethnic group. Determinations of what groups have done and what individual members have done should always be ascertained on grounds of the relevant facts and judgments about each, rather than by inference from the collectivity to the member, or the member to the collectivity (Isaacs 2011).

Peter French is well aware of the reasons we might reject notions of the responsibility of groups. "Clearly the concept of collective responsibility," he wrote early in his career, "is not without difficulties, and the weight of those difficulties may be such to persuade us that it is not a helpful moral notion . . ." (French 1972, 10–11). But he went on to make good sense of how collective entities can and should be thought responsible. While I do not share his view that corporations are "full-fledged moral persons," (French 1991) he has shown convincingly, I believe, how corporations can make decisions, and can act, and why they should be held to be responsible. Such views can be extended in appropriate ways to other collective entities, and we can come to understand why there are better reasons to accept various notions of group responsibility than to reject them. Dealing with many of the most important problems facing us requires that we do so.

When we avoid misuses of assigning responsibility, we can see the good moral reasons to be able to hold corporations and states responsible, and also to sometimes assign responsibility to unorganized collectivities such as ethnic groups. Most of us already recognize the good moral reasons to hold individual persons responsible. There are even stronger reasons, moral and other, for such groups and the individuals in them to *take* responsibility for the actions and inactions of such groups.

The ethics of care offers the kind of moral theory that can make good sense of these claims, that can show how moral responsibility ought to be assigned to groups and persons, and taken by them. It can also offer persuasive recommendations on how groups, both organized and unorganized, ought to act.

The Ethics of Care

The ethics of care arose in the last decades of the twentieth century when, under feminist impulses to rethink much inquiry, attention began to be directed toward the work and practices of mothering and caregiving, activities that had been almost totally neglected by philosophers and political and legal theorists engaged in moral inquiry. The philosopher Sara Ruddick examined the thinking involved in practices of mothering, the philosopher Nel Noddings explored the phenomenological aspects of caring for children and others, and the psychologist Carol Gilligan studied the kind of moral reasoning often engaged in by girls and women, but seldom by boys and men, when confronted with a moral problem (Ruddick 1980, 1989; Noddings 1984; Gilligan 1982). Gradually, many moral philosophers and political theorists developed a new, alternative moral theory, the ethics of care, to challenge the dominant normative approaches of Kantian ethics, utilitarianism, and virtue theory (Held 2006), and to challenge the assumptions with which they and traditional liberal political theory had been built.

Care ethics has by now become significantly influential, as can be seen by the inclusion of chapters presenting its perspective in such volumes as *The Routledge Handbook of Global Ethics* (Moellendorf and Widdows 2015); *Philosophical Foundations of Human Rights* (Cruft et al. 2015); and the *Oxford Handbook of Distributive Justice* (Olsaretti 2016). The continuing publication of important new volumes further developing the ethics of care is additional evidence (Barnes 2012; Engster and Hamington 2015; Miller 2012; Tronto 2013). The apparent growth of interest in care in the first decades of the twenty first century resembles the growth of interest in human rights that occurred in the last quarter of the twentieth century, an interest that has become enormously influential both in theory and in practice.

The ethics of care has developed beyond its earliest focus to recognize that the perspective of the recipient of care is fully as important as that of the provider of care in understanding what care recommends. It has become even more clearly than in its first formulations a comprehensive moral approach applicable to political and global issues and not only to those of the contexts of family and friendship where it originated.

The moral considerations apparent in the existing practices of care that were newly attended to, and that are ascertainable even more clearly in care as we can understand that it ought to be practiced, are very different from those of traditional moral theories (Gilligan 1982; Noddings 1984; Ruddick 1980, 1989). Gradually, over the last several decades, the moral approach or theory known as the ethics of care or care ethics has developed to make explicit this alternative view and to explore its implications (Bowden 1997; Bubeck 1995; Engster 2007; Held 1993, 2006; Kittay 1999; Sevenhuijsen 1998; Slote 2007, 2013; Tronto 1993, 2013). Its values may be most evident in personal relations among family members and friends, in such practices as caring for children and others who are dependent. However, its values of empathetic concern, of meeting people's needs with sensitivity and effectiveness, and of cultivating trust, can be seen to be highly relevant to human activities and relations far beyond the household.

The implications of the ethics of care are being explored for human relations everywhere and of all kinds. The rigid separation of public and private that has so distorted our views of the moralities appropriate for each is being superseded, as we recognize how care and its values are central to human well-being everywhere. Exploring the implications of attending to care is transforming issues of political, social, and international life and security. And we are beginning to understand how our theories and practices need to change (Held 2006; Kittay 1999; Sevenhuijsen 1998). We should consider, for instance, how to conceptualize a caring society (Harrington 1999; Noddings 2002), and what the implications of a care approach may be for international relations and global concerns (Held 2011; Mahon and Robinson 2011; Robinson 1999, 2011).

When attention started first to be paid to the practices of mothering and other caring activities, the more standard questions of justice were applied, newly, to this kind of activity. Questions were raised about whether it is fair that women are assigned such a large proportion of this necessary work, and about why so much of this work is unpaid or poorly paid. Applying theories of justice to the labor of care can show how unfairly distributed are opportunities to be well cared for. They suggest that governments ought to be far more involved than they have been in assuring that persons needing care, of whatever kind, receive it, and that social arrangements are in place and capable of providing it (Engster 2007). And they suggest that those wanting to care for their own families should not be required by economic necessity to be care workers for others in wealthy countries far from their homes (Mahon and Robinson 2011).

Attention to care can also lead, however, to a deeper inquiry, an inquiry into the gender bias built into political and moral theory itself, and not only into how it has been applied. It can lead to a questioning of the near complete focus of theory on justice and rights and universal principles. The dominant moral approaches have been built on the concerns of men in public life and have overlooked the experience of women in the caring activities essential to life. When we do focus on care work, we can become aware of the values incorporated into this work, and how they can be used to evaluate existing practices. We can see how existing practices ought to be improved and how the values of care ought to be extended to other practices and relations in society.

Central among the values of care are responsiveness to need, sensitivity, empathetic awareness, and the fostering of trust. These values are very different from the rational consent to abstract principles of duty, or maximization of utility, or even cultivation of individual virtuous dispositions, of the dominant moral theories. Yet we can understand how urgent and compelling they are for the care that is so essential to human life, and how suitable such values would be if extended to other areas of human interaction than the contexts of family and friendship.

In contexts of care, we appreciate the value of such emotions as empathy and concern for others in enabling us to understand what we ought to do. In contrast, the traditional and prevailing moral theories are rationalistic theories that ask us to reject our emotions as we recognize what reason demands. The emotions considered are those such as anger, aggressiveness, and blind selfishness, which can be seen as threats to morality. On the view of the prevailing theories, although some emotions can sometimes aid us in carrying out our duties, we ought, in determining what we ought to do, to look only to rational understanding.

Utilitarianism's conception of reason as instrumental and calculative is significantly different from Kantian conceptions of reason as able to reveal the universally valid norms to which all persons ought to assent. But both views are the basis for rationalistic moral theories advocating reliance on a single overarching universal principle for moral guidance: the Categorical Imperative or the Principle of Utility. Virtue theory focuses on the good person rather than the right action, but it also is individualistic, seeing persons as fundamentally separate and independent. It appraises the dispositions of individuals rather than the values central to care among interdependent persons. And conceptions of which dispositions are virtuous and how the virtues ought to be understood turn out to be heavily dependent on cultural attitudes and traditions that are often in disagreement around the globe.

Care, Experience, and Moral Theory

One of the great strengths of the ethics of care is that it is based on experience, the experience of having been cared for and of engaging in care. That experience truly is universal. Every single person everywhere has been cared for when they were very young and most for much longer, and most persons also have some experience providing care. Every person has experienced care and can reflect on the values incorporated into its practices, and the values by which actual practices of care can be evaluated. They can recognize what was not good in the care they actually received, and recommend how care practices ought to be improved. Because it is based on experience, the ethics of care has no need to appeal to religious or cultural views that are divisive. And it does not rely on the individualistic outlook of the dominant theories, which only claim to be universal but in large part are not.

Another strength of the ethics of care is that it incorporates in many ways the best of the leading moral theories: Kantian ethics, utilitarianism, and virtue theory. While it should not be understood as a version of any of these, it can include many of their most persuasive aspects. Care ethics appreciates the motives and intentions emphasized by Kantians in the performance of right actions. Caring actions can be understood to have the intrinsic moral worth emphasized by deontological moral theories. The intentions with which persons engage in care are of moral importance, and caring actions should be evaluated on the basis of the motives they express as well as the effects they bring about. At the same time, as Utilitarians understand, effectiveness is of crucial importance in the ethics of care. It is not enough to intend to meet the needs of the person cared for. Good care must be evaluated in large part on whether it actually succeeds in contributing to health or growth or the other aims of care. Empirical findings about the actual effects of different components of caring practices, such as various styles of childcare, are highly relevant. Finally, the ethics of care can incorporate various of the insights of virtue ethics in coming to understand the traits of character that should be fostered in the providing and receiving of care in caring relations.

To the ethics of care, practices, actions, and persons should be evaluated on many grounds. Care ethics fosters care that effectively responds with empathy and sensitivity to actual needs, and that does so in ways conducive to trust, cooperation, and mutual concern.

The ethics of care understands care as a value at least as important as justice, and more fundamental. Much human life develops without justice; it cannot exist without care and the values it incorporates. Practices of justice such as the making and enforcement of law and the distribution of goods should reflect the values of justice. But society is both deeper and wider than these practices, and the values of care should be reflected in caring societies that determine the place within them of practices of justice. The ethics of care is potentially the comprehensive morality that should guide both the more personal and the more distant relations between persons and groups in given societies and around the world.

Conceptions of Persons and Groups

Attention to care and its activities leads us to understand persons as relational and interdependent, rather than as self-sufficient individuals seeking to further their own interests or recognizing the rational validity of universal norms. Good caring relations depend as much on how care is experienced by recipients as on how it is intended, and they depend on whether the relations between those involved are trusting and characterized by responsiveness and sensitivity, or not.

The relational views of the ethics of care are more compatible with Peter French's views on collective entities than with the thoroughgoing individualism of the prevailing theories.

To the ethics of care, it is caring relations between persons rather than individual utility or individual rights and obligations that are especially of value. When it was first developed, its attention was focused on the face-to-face interactions of those who give and receive care. The work and activities of mothering were of special interest. It has by now ventured far beyond the locations of its earliest explorations. Although we can perhaps most easily recognize the value of caring relations in the contexts of personal relations between members of families and among friends or persons in small groups, this understanding can be extended. We can recognize the value of caring relations even when relatively weak, between any number of persons in widely varying contexts. The emotions of empathy, caring, and concern for others that are so central to care may be felt most strongly in the case of those close to us, but forms of them can also be felt for those very distant. As Hume persuasively argued, and as fictional and reportorial accounts routinely demonstrate, we are not indifferent to the suffering of those we do not know personally (Hume 1957 [1752]; *Inquiry*, Section V, Part II).

Kantian ethics and utilitarianism employ conceptions of the person as equal, independent, autonomous, liberal individual. Such a person can recognize the universal principles to be accepted by all rational individuals, and he can enter into social contracts with his equals. Virtue theory is in many respects different, but it too sees persons as independent individual agents who can cultivate their virtuous dispositions. The ethics of care, in contrast, understands persons as inherently relational and interdependent. It does not assume, as do the dominant theories to an unhelpful degree, that social relations are entered into voluntarily. Care ethics takes account of the unchosen relations in which we find ourselves, and it can deal with the moral problems involved.

Social interactions are, probably most of the time, between persons and groups of very unequal power. While recognizing persons as of equal moral worth, the ethics of care can appreciate the vast inequalities of power that are part of the reality to which moral guidance should be addressed and from which it should be understood. Accordingly, it can recommend such practices as responding effectively and with sensitivity to the actual needs of unequal, embodied persons and groups. It can provide guidance on how to deal effectively, and nonviolently, with conflicts between persons and groups of very unequal power and influence.

Care ethics understands how trust is relational. It can only be developed *between* persons, since merely having a trusting disposition, or being trustworthy when others are not, may simply invite others to take advantage of the naïve, and free-load on the virtuous. Because the ethics of care should be built as much on the experience of recipients of care as of care providers, it offers guidance in avoiding paternalism or domination. As persons engaged in care reflect on their experience, they can learn how to deal appropriately with tendencies of the strong to impose their will on the weak, and to deceive themselves about their advantages (Khader 2011).

Care ethics does not assume, as do many moral and political theories, that the world to which they are to apply is one of individuals competing with all other individuals to further their own interests. It understands the contexts of family and much group life where the pursuit of individual interest is often not primary. But neither does the ethics of care assume that morality requires self-sacrifice. It challenges the terms of this dominant construal. Care ethics neither assumes nor recommends the egoistic pursuit of self-interest, but neither does it advocate an altruistic denial of self. It rejects the view that sees these as the only alternatives. It promotes, instead, the cooperative pursuit of the mutual good of persons, and the fostering of good caring relations. It understands how parents characteristically want what will be good for their children as well as themselves, and children characteristically want the same for their parents. Persons who care for one another can pursue what will be best for both or all together. And they can do this not only in families and small groups, but in wider and wider contexts.

Legal and Political Interactions

Political and moral theories resembling the traditional ones in which justice is primary may well be appropriate for many of the more limited legal and political interactions of persons within societies held together by weak relations of care. Care and its values, however, should still have overall priority, as caring relations form the wider and more fundamental context in which particular legal and political structures are developed, and can be expanded or reduced. In a caring society, for instance, in which persons would be enabled to obtain what they need, there could be far less of the coercion, often violent, inherent in law and its enforcement. Much of what goes on in society is not best thought of as a matter of law or of politics, and it is part of the distortions brought about by the dominant theories that these domains are often seen as all-encompassing. The ethics of care pays attention to such domains of society as education, healthcare, and social welfare, neglected by theories of justice. It can keep the various domains of society in perspective and is the better guide for both the more personal and the widest ties of persons and groups.

Care ethics is not always hostile to competition. Siblings compete within families, but in ways that are contained within broader relations of care. Sports teams and economic enterprises and artistic groups can compete within social groups but in ways that strengthen rather than undermine their communities. Such competition can contribute to replacing deadly or violent competition between groups with more acceptable forms of competitive interaction. However, if there is nothing else than antagonism and competition in the relations between persons and groups, families will fall apart, genuine friendship will not be possible, and social groups, at whatever level, will not cohere.

The familiar structures of liberal legal and political institutions are not possible without the social glue that enables persons and groups to form social communities. This has been recognized to some extent in recent years in the attention paid by social scientists to the importance of civil society (Keane 1998; Putnam 1994). What makes the solidarity of nation states and lesser social groups possible can best be thought of as a form of caring relation. Caring relations between strangers and those relatively distant from us can be thin and fragile, but without some concern for fellow-citizens or the other persons included in the group, assemblages of persons can easily disintegrate into harmful competition and deadly violence (Held 2006).

For the social groups that are nation-states and that have sufficient coherence to sustain legal and political institutions, liberal political and legal theories of justice and such traditional moral theories as Kantian ethics and utilitarianism may well be appropriate for a range of issues internal to these institutions (Held 2015), though they need to acknowledge, as Peter French would make clear, the realities and responsibilities of collectivities as well as of individual persons. Legal and political ways of interacting should not, however, be supposed to be the only ways people interact. They should be understood as embedded within wider and deeper networks of caring human relations. They should be seen as only a limited range of the ways that human beings in society are related and interact. For the wider context, the ethics of care is a more promising guide. We have been led to believe that the moral theories appropriate for legal and political interactions can be comprehensive moralities, but when we pay attention to care and all that it involves, we can recognize the deficiencies of these theories outside legal and political contexts.

Caring relations ought to be extended to everyone to the extent that we care what happens to them, care that their needs are met and their suffering alleviated. We ought to take responsibility for responding appropriately to their situations. We can also understand how people are divided into separate groups, societies, and states, and how their relations with one another within these are more restricted.

For the governing institutions within the various states, traditional liberal norms are usually to be recommended. These norms are not, however, universally accepted and they do not apply well on a global scale. Existing states should not be conceptualized as free and equal individual entities seeking to agree on a social contract. Caring concern for all persons, however, provides compelling reasons for all to accept the restraints of international law as valid (Held 2011). We should all, and together, strongly promote the avoidance of violence between states and groups, and promote the growth of human wellbeing.

The ethics of care can provide guidance for understanding the roles of legal and political institutions within societies, and for evaluating how their place in society ought often to be limited, or sometimes enlarged in situations of chaos. And the ethics of care shows great promise in providing recommendations on how groups and states ought to behave. It can show us how persons ought to act not only as citizens of given states, but as members of various groups and as belonging to a global community. We need to care for all persons everywhere for their rights to be respected, and their needs met.

Critics of Care Ethics

Some philosophers have dismissed the ethics of care as a moral or political theory, arguing that it is only relevant to personal relations, family contexts, and the like. An example is Susan Mendus's contribution to the volume *Philosophical Foundations of Human Rights* (Mendus 2015). Mendus doubts that we are psychologically capable of extending the care that arises in face-to-face relationships to unknown others or humanity as a whole. And she worries that for the recipient of care it is "humiliating and degrading" to be offered care rather than to have their claims of rights to justice recognized (Mendus 651). She sees the ethics of care as involving a "rejection of rights" (651).

These criticisms misinterpret the aims and positions of care ethics. In paying attention to practices of care, we can recognize various *values* neglected in other theories. Extending them to other contexts is not unlike extending such values as the rational pursuit of self-interest from the concept of a particular "economic man" to other persons and contexts, or extending the value of justice and the way an individual is obligated to obey the law from the legal context to all others. Values are inherently generalizable. The values of care – of responding to need, of sensitivity to the experiences of actual, rather than ideal and rational, others, and the promotion of trust – are eminently suitable for global and inter-group contexts.

As to the danger that receiving care may be degrading, the ethics of care includes understanding how care should enhance the growth of self-regard in recipients along with mutual wellbeing. In recognizing the perspective of recipients as fully as providers, it shows how providers of good care, in social services and development work, for instance, must learn to avoid domination (Barnes 2012; Khader 2011). Moreover, the categories of provider and recipient are not static: children become adults who become old and frail, groups of migrants in need become able to provide care for other groups, cities that are booming may fall into decline, and once wealthy countries may be superseded by others. As Peter French notes, corporations are born and live and die. What needs to be emphasized is the interdependence of human life. And the ethics of care does not *reject* rights, in their appropriate sphere; it understands the limits of that sphere.

The ethics of care is a feminist ethic calling for the transformation of the most fundamental domination, that of gender, and for the overthrow of gender domination not only in how our theories are applied, but in the very construction of the theories themselves. When we try to evaluate the potential of the ethics of care we should keep in mind that this new approach is only a few decades old, a very short time in comparison with the centuries in which most other moral and political theories have been developed. It is still at its beginnings, but there are already strong indications that it will be able to become a comprehensive morality providing guidance for the full range of human relations, from the closest in families and small groups to the most distant in political and social and global contexts.

Care Ethics and Ethnic Conflict

The ethics of care can well comprehend the social ties of groups and the special problems that can arise in dealing with them. Conflicts between ethnic groups are often between groups of very unequal strength, and they are often rooted in distant histories. Care ethics is better suited than traditional moral theories to deal with the problems of group conflict. It understands persons as interrelated, rather than imagining them as isolated, self-sufficient individuals. The values asserted by a care approach are especially promising for dealing with the hatred, anger, resentments, and disparagements that so often lead to conflicts between groups.

To build trust between conflicting groups is at the heart of replacing violence and antagonism with cooperation and mutual consideration. The ethics of care would guide and recommend the appropriate steps in such processes. To seek the wellbeing of both or various groups together rather than the gains of one's own group at the expense of others', is of fundamental importance. For a group to respond to the needs of another group, when in a position to do so, and to take responsibility for making such efforts, can help defuse group conflicts. If not in a position to meet the needs of another group, at least having sensitivity and empathy in understanding those needs can help considerably.

Care ethics would also reliably minimize violence. Violence destroys what care creates, and the ethics of care inherently seeks to reduce violence as much as possible. Unlike the preoccupations of justice that the violent enforcement of its rules by police and military forces be fair and justified, it seeks more fundamentally to minimize violence. It includes a deep awareness of the tendencies toward violence standard in human life, from children and caregivers to groups and states, but its practices and values include recommendations for heading off, limiting, and dealing with such violence (Held 2010; Ruddick 1989, 2009). Members of ethnic groups can learn from these practices of cultivating nonviolence.

Occasionally, the violence of those with morally indefensible aims must be met with violence, though such violence should always be minimized. In the long run, violence is defeated by undermining its appeal to potential recruits, and enabling them to see that there are more effective, as well as morally better, ways to make progress in achieving their legitimate goals (Held 2008). The responsibility to make nonviolent methods more effective lies with those with greater power. It is harder to appeal to some young adults by advocating tolerance and cooperation than by encouraging the excitement of rage and violence. But this only makes the task more challenging, and the demands greater for talents of imagination and persuasion devoted to aims of care.

References

Barnes, Marian. 2012. *Care in everyday life: An ethic of care in practice*. Bristol: The Policy Press.

Bowden, Peta. 1997. *Caring: Gender-sensitive ethics*. London: Routledge.

Bubeck, Diemut. 1995. *Care, gender, and justice*. Oxford: Oxford University Press.

Cruft, Rowan, S. Matthew Liao, and Massimo Renzo, eds. 2015. *Philosophical foundations of human rights*. Oxford: Oxford University Press.

Cushman, Thomas, and Stjepan G. Mestrovic, eds. 1996. *This time we knew: Western responses to genocide in Bosnia*. New York: New York University Press.

Engster, Daniel. 2007. *The heart of justice: Care ethics and political theory*. New York: Oxford University Press.

Engster, Daniel, and Maurice Hamington, eds. 2015. *Care ethics and political theory*. Oxford: Oxford University Press.

Ephron, Dan. 2015. *Killing a king: The assassination of Yitzhak Rabin and the remaking of Israel*. New York: W.W. Norton.

French, Peter A. 1972. The responsibility of monsters and their makers. In *Individual and collective responsibility: The massacre at My Lai*, ed. Peter A. French. Cambridge: Schenkman.

———. 1984. *Collective and corporate responsibility*. New York: Columbia University Press.

———. 1991. The corporation as a moral person. In *Collective responsibility: Five decades of debate in theoretical and applied ethics*, ed. Larry May and Stacey Hoffman. Lanham: Rowman and Littlefield.

———. 1992. *Responsibility matters*. Lawrence: University Press of Kansas.

Gilligan, Carol. 1982. *In a different voice: Psychological theory and women's development*. Cambridge: Harvard University Press.
Harrington, Mona. 1999. *Care and equality: Inventing a new family politics*. New York: Knopf.
Held, Virginia. 1993. *Feminist morality: Transforming culture, society, and politics*. Chicago: University of Chicago Press.
———. 2002. Group responsibility for ethnic conflict. *Journal of Ethics* 6: 159–181.
———. 2006. *The ethics of care: Personal, political, and global*. New York: University Press.
———. 2008. *How terrorism is wrong: Morality and political violence*. New York: Oxford University Press.
———. 2010. Can the ethics of care handle violence? *Ethics and Social Welfare* 4(6): 115–129.
———. 2011. Morality, care, and international law. *Ethics and Global Politics* 4(3): 173–194.
———. 2015. Care and justice, still. In *Care ethics and political theory*, ed. Daniel Engster and Maurice Hamington. Oxford: Oxford University Press.
Hume, David. 1957 [1752]. *An inquiry concerning the principles of morals*. New York: Liberal Arts.
Isaacs, Tracy. 2011. *Moral responsibility in collective contexts*. New York: Oxford University Press.
Keane, John. 1998. *Civil society: Old images, new visions*. Stanford: Stanford University Press.
Khader, Serene J. 2011. Beyond inadvertent ventriloquism: Caring virtues for anti-paternalist development practice. *Hypatia* 26(Fall): 742–761.
Kittay, Eva Feder. 1999. *Love's labor: Essays on women, equality, and dependency*. New York: Routledge.
Kovach, Karen. 2001. *Who we are and what we do: Ethnicity and moral agency*. PhD diss., City University of New York.
———. 2006. Genocide and the moral agency of ethnic groups. *Metaphilosophy* 37: 3/4 July: 1–22.
Lewis, H.D. 1991. Collective responsibility. In *Collective responsibility: Five decades of debate in theoretical and applied ethics*, ed. May Larry and Hoffman Stacey. Lanham: Rowman and Littlefield.
Mahon, Rianne, and Fiona Robinson, eds. 2011. *Feminist ethics and social politics: Towards a new global political economy of care*. Vancouver: University of British Columbia Press.
May, Larry. 1990. The responsibilities of inactive groups. *Noûs* 24: 269–278.
———. 1992. *Sharing responsibility*. Chicago: University of Chicago Press.
Mendus, Susan. 2015. Care and human rights: A reply to Virginia Held. In *Philosophical foundations of human rights*, ed. Rowan Cruft, S. Matthew Liao, and Massimo Renzo. Oxford: Oxford University Press.
Miller, Sarah Clark. 2012. *The ethics of need: Agency, dignity, and obligation*. New York: Routledge.
Moellendorf, Daniel, and Heather Widdows, eds. 2015. *The routledge handbook of global ethics*. New York: Routledge.
Noddings, Nel. 1984. *Caring: A feminine approach to ethics and moral education*. Berkeley: University of California Press.
———. 2002. *Starting at home: Caring and social policy*. Berkeley: University of California Press.
Olsaretti, Serena, eds. 2016. *Oxford handbook of distributive justice*. Oxford: Oxford University Press.
Pettit, Philip N. 2016. The conversable, responsible corporation. In *The moral responsibility of firms*, ed. Eric Orts and Craig Smith. Oxford: Oxford University Press.
Pogge, Thomas, eds. 2001. *Global justice*. Oxford: Blackwell.
———. 2011. Are we violating the human rights of the world's poor? *Yale Human Rights and Development L.J* 14(2): 1–33.
Poole, Ross. 1999. *Nation and identity*. New York: Routledge.
Putnam, Robert D. 1994. *Making democracy work*. Princeton: Princeton University Press.
Robinson, Fiona. 1999. *Globalizing care: Ethics, feminist theory, and international affairs*. Boulder: Westview Press.

———. 2011. *The ethics of care: A feminist approach to human security*. Philadelphia: Temple University Press.

Ruddick, Sara. 1980. Maternal thinking. *Feminist Studies* 6: 342–367.

———. 1989. *Maternal thinking: Toward a politics of peace*. Boston: Beacon Press.

———. 2009. On maternal thinking. *Women's Studies Quarterly* 37(3&4): 305–308.

Sevenhuijsen, Selma. 1998. *Citizenship and the ethics of care: Feminist consideration on justice, morality and politics*. London: Routledge.

Slote, Michael A. 2007. *The ethics of care and empathy*. London: Routledge.

———. 2013. *From enlightenment to receptivity: Rethinking our values*. New York: Oxford University Press.

Tronto, Joan C. 1993. *Moral boundaries: A political argument for an ethic of care*. New York: Routledge.

———. 2013. *Caring democracy: Markets, equality, and justice*. New York: New York University Press.

Young, Iris Marion. 2006. Responsibility and social justice: A social connection model. *Social Philosophy and Policy* 23(1): 102–130.

Theories of Moral Responsibility and the Responsibility Barter Game

Michael McKenna

In his influential book *Responsibility Matters* (1992), Peter French embraces a deflationary view of moral responsibility's nature: it amounts to nothing more than a collection of practices. We might be able to offer some general and illuminating insights about it, but we will not find out anything metaphysically distinctive about the world. Nor will we discover anything about moral responsibility required by our nature as practical reasoners. Hence, no substantive theory will be true to the metaphysical facts, or to the norms of living as practical agents. Moreover, when we tend to these practices, we will find some basic strategies for negotiating the Responsibility Barter Game, a game whose aim is for accountable agents to avoid bearing the burdens of being held to account for various outcomes (1992, 1–17). In this essay, I will assess French's view and resist him while advancing my own theory of moral responsibility. What I hope to show is that French's insights, such as those concerning the Responsibility Barter Game, are indeed amenable to a theory that pays adequate attention to the interpersonal relations between members of a moral community. What French's deflationary approach to theorizing about moral responsibility is really targeting—and properly so—is a way of theorizing about responsibility that is not sufficiently attentive to the practices that constitute our moral lives and ground our judgment of moral responsibility.

French's Challenge to the Theory-Builders

In the opening pages of *Responsibility Matters*, reflecting upon the collection of essays to follow, French offers the following observation about his overall position:

M. McKenna (✉)
University of Arizona, Tucson, AZ, USA
e-mail: msmckenna63@gmail.com

Z.J. Goldberg (ed.), *Reflections on Ethics and Responsibility*,
DOI 10.1007/978-3-319-50359-2_5

> . . . many philosophers who write about responsibility see it either as a truth of some sort about the world, or like Kant, they see it in terms of a necessary presupposition of practical life. I have defended, and continue to defend in this book, the position that responsibility is but a set of practices that we use to describe and understand individual and social behavior. Responsibility matters are matters that enter into our daily lives in myriad ways that cannot be reduced to simple formulas and principles. (1992, ix–x)

What is French's argument for this deflationary view? As I read him, it is revealed in his effort to show from the inside, so to speak, how our responsibility practices can be illuminated without first seeking some theory that unifies its nature and accounts for its norms. If we engage in a kind of ethnography, attending to various aspects of our practices and judgments, we will learn fresh and illuminating things about moral responsibility. If alternatively we try to force these insights into the confines of some compact list of necessary and sufficient conditions or set of principles, we will lose any of the details that are especially insightful. Suppose, for instance, we want to understand what moral innocence is and why in the course of our moral education we are forced to lose it. Then we need to look at its role in our thinking and consider the sorts of actual forces that put pressure on members of a moral community to bring the innocent to face the moral realities of the world we all must share (1992, 29–43).

So, on French's view, as regards moral responsibility, theorizing with general formulas or principles just won't do. Insight is found in the particular. In this respect, I have always found French's approach to philosophizing about moral responsibility refreshingly Wittgensteinian: Look to ways of life and social practices revealing various language games—like the Responsibility Barter Game—and show what there is to be understood. Leave matters there. Do not seek some overall theory to bring these insights together.

Consider in light of my interpretation of French's strategy what he calls the Responsibility Barter (RB) game. As he explains, the game is played in terms of trading to avoid maximal burdens when one is held to account for what she has done:

> The strategy is either not to be in the line of fire at all or to find a way to get as little dumped on one's plate as possible, trading off to others as much as one can (1992, 2).

Rather than find some general moral principle operative here that animates RB, French just calls attention to a plausible and familiar fact. People seek to avoid accountability for various untoward acts and outcomes by, in a sense, negotiating for a limited scope of what they might be properly accountable for. In doing so, they "barter" for distributions of burdens—and benefits—in a way that aims to diminish the risk of costs to them (1992, 2–3).

As French notes, philosophical theorizing about morality itself is in a certain respect orthogonal to the most interesting elements of the RB game. As French sees it, if we want a glimpse into how ordinary folk confront moral questions, it is usually by way of RB:

> . . . the Responsibility Barter Game (RB) is probably the most common experience ordinary people have with morality. Grand philosophical theories about THE GOOD, maximizing

> utility, gaining virtue, and doing one's duty enter the barter game only in oblique ways. They play a role in marking out what is good or right from what is bad or wrong at a theoretical level, and they are legitimate sources for appeals, though their authority is not always accepted. But when people get down to the business of moral assignments of responsibility, the question of goodness or badness, rightness or wrongness, have been at least tentatively answered, more often than not, by appeal to intuition, custom, or common convention. Then the game begins. (1992, 2)

As regards the goal of playing RB, French states his view plainly:

> We play RB to reduce liability, compensation costs, social discomfort, and so on. There are powerful economic, psychological, social, and legal reasons to do so. Hence, the basic reason to engage in RB is rational self-interest. (1992, 2–3)

French is not claiming any commitment to a specific theory of moral psychology, nor is he in this passage endorsing a Hobbesian account of the normative grounds of sociality. He is simply making a claim about what the basic reason is for most people to engage in RB.

French next turns to a specification of the scope of the game—the candidate behavior within the reach of the RB game. In this case, French seeks a principle, but the principle is simply extracted from attending to our actual practices and so is best thought of as a summary or description of them rather than as something carrying normative force that determines *why* the extension of responsible behavior is as it is. Here too, we have appeal to a kind of philosophical ethnography. How does French proceed?

French first considers a simple proposal defended by J.L. Mackie, "the straight rule of responsibility," according to which "an agent is morally responsible for all and only [its] intentional actions" (Mackie 1977, 208, as quoted in French 1992, 3). But as French explains, the straight rule just will not cover cases that need covering, since in RB we simply do hold people accountable for conduct even when it is not intended (1992, 4). Nevertheless, as French explains, the connection to intentionality remains. What one does unintentionally, perhaps by accident or through negligence, is still tethered to the intentional, since her so acting involves doing *something* that is intentional. I might, for instance, as in Davidson's (1963) famous example, flip a switch intending to turn on a light and in doing so unintentionally alert the burglar. Even if alerting the burglar is a doing of mine, it is so only in virtue of there being something I did that *was* intended. In this way, French explains, a constraint on RB is that it applies only to events understood as actions wherein there is *some* bit of intentional conduct and so something intended (1992, 10).[1]

[1]French weds his thesis to a further Davidsonian thesis about act-identity. For instance, in the case of Davidson's the act that is the turning on of the light is identical with the one that is the unintended alerting of the burglar. I am sympathetic, but it seems to me that it is not essential to French's thesis. Even if the alerting of the burglar is a different act than the flipping of the switch, it remains true that one counts as an act only insofar as there is some act or other (the same or different) that is intended and the two are suitably related in some way. I'll set this detail aside in the remainder of this paper.

French proceeds to identify yet further fine-grained distinctions between what is done intentionally and what is done deliberately and what is done willingly. One can do something deliberately in executing one's intention without doing so as part of one's plan to act as intended (1992, 11), such as drive over a toy when in a rush to get to the airport. Moreover, one can also do something willingly without deliberating about it (11). In all of these cases, the conduct in question can be cause for engaging in the RB game. This leads French to propose the Extended Principle of Accountability (EPA), wherein, so long as there is a relevant act that was intended under some description, the RB game can also apply broadly to what is unintended, due to accident or negligence, what one does deliberately, and what one does willingly. The net result, as French registers it, is an "extraordinarily rigid view" insofar as the scope of responsibility is pretty much as wide as the scope of any action linked to an agent's intendings. As a result:

> Only a limited range of behavior would be exempt. Such a latent tyranny of responsibility, however, is checked and balanced at the appellate level of excuse evaluation in RB. What EPA clearly indicates is that certain popular excuses such as "I did not mean that," "It was unintentional," "That was not what I wanted to do," are not necessarily exculpatory or even mitagatory in RB. That is especially true when RB is played over serious matters involving injury. (1992, 12)

French further qualifies his full examination of the scope of the RB game (1992, 12–15), but the preceding description is adequate for my purposes. Crucially, French simply sets out to identify how in fact the RB applies to the scope of action. In doing so, he tends to and also contributes to important work in the theory of action so as to accurately identify just what sorts of actions count as candidates for barter in the game. Nevertheless, he seeks no theory of moral responsibility beyond identifying the nature of our practices as they are actually played out.

At this juncture, a critical reader might protest that there is theory here after all, and so my contention that French makes do without appeal to a theory of moral responsibility is just mistaken. After all, French builds his treatment of RB and his extrapolation of EPA from the resources of a theory of action. He only achieves his results by way of distinguishing actions from other events, showing the relation between actions that are and are not intentional, and then explaining the link between deliberate behavior, willing behavior, and the like to intended action. Indeed, in doing so, he draws upon an important feature of intentional actions—their referential opacity (a detail I'll not set out here). And he then links this up with what is, basically, a theory about agency. Only certain sorts of entities can be intentional systems. Furthermore, as he rightly explains, these intentional systems have to be second-order intentional systems, capable of representing their own intentions and those of others as intentional systems, and in a way that allows for the formation of further intentions. Only in this way does French arrive at a view of moral persons. So, the critic might object, there is a lot of theory here, and it does the work in identifying French's EPA as playing a role in the RB game.

Of course, my imagined critic is right about this. There is a considerable amount of theory here. But all this means is that French is a philosopher. No surprise there. My contention is only that, as I read French, he is an anti-theorist *about the nature and norms of moral responsibility*. It just does not follow from this that he must make do without any appeal to theory at all. To the contrary, it seems rather that what French's view amounts to is that all the theory we need is just *theory of action*. While we can draw upon these resources to explain our moral responsibility practices, we can also do so to explain complex human agency *per se*—and so any set of human practices. It is this view of French's that I wish to resist, but it is also a view for which I have considerable admiration. It relies upon a laudable form of philosophical austerity that forces us instead to work cautiously in the Wittgensteinian fashion noted above. Better to pay attention to the details of our actual practices than to seek grand or general theories.

What a Theory of Moral Responsibility Shouldn't Be Like

Despite my plan to resist French and advocate for theory-building, I first wish to call attention to two ways of theorizing about moral responsibility that in my estimation are misguided. Each provide good reason for French and other likeminded philosophers to reject a proper theory of moral responsibility.

Theorizing by Way of Conceptual Analysis

One way to think of philosophical theory-construction is in terms of conceptual analysis. This strategy, familiar in twentieth century analytic philosophy, attempts to account for a concept like *moral responsibility* by way of identifying necessary and sufficient conditions. To theorize about moral responsibility, so understood, would be to seek a set of non-trivial necessary and sufficient conditions by which we could capture the proper extension of the concept's correct application and do so by means that would facilitate our understanding of it. Now there are quite general reasons that such an approach to theorizing has pretty much been abandoned in more recent times. There is, for instance, Quine's (1951) challenge to the analytic/synthetic distinction, and so to the tenability of any genuine analysis providing strict necessary and sufficient conditions for any philosophically interesting concept at all. Moreover, there are further worries about concepts understood in this classical manner (e.g., see Wittgenstein 1953). This gives rise to skepticism regarding the value of theorizing about them rather than the phenomena at which they are directed. Finally, there is also analytic philosophy's sad track record of successes achieving any remotely compelling classical analysis of any interesting concept. Indeed, French himself draws on Davidson's (1971) work on agency and intentions, and in Davidson's series of papers in the theory of action (1980), he offers one of the most instructive examples of a failed attempt to provide a proper analysis of intention (in terms of belief and desire).

Now perhaps reasons of the preceding sort were among those that motivated French to shun theory-building as applied to moral responsibility. These reasons, however, are all completely general. It seems to me that, even setting them aside, there are special considerations about this domain of inquiry that give good reason to be suspicious of theory-building and so to contend, as French does, that "responsibility is but a set of practices" (1992, x). Here are two.

First, the spectrum of responsibility practices is strikingly diverse. The phenomena does not present itself as the sort of thing that could be accounted for by way of any simple set of formulas or principles. Consider the vast array of conduct that a person might be accountable for, the differences between cultures as to what counts as blameworthy behavior—and so, in French's terms, what is worth bartering over. Consider how much variety there is in blaming practices, between cultures and among members of the same culture, or even members of the same family for that matter. Consider the emotions that animate our moral lives: sentiments like resentment and gratitude or guilt and pride. Think of how much variety there is here both in terms of the modes of expressing these emotions and the presuppositions regarding their propriety. Now consider pleas for excuses, and the practice of condemning or instead forgiving. Think here how much permissible variation there is.[2]

Second, as philosophers like Tamler Sommers (2012) have argued, it is unclear what the most general contours of moral responsibility are supposed to be. As Sommers argues, honor cultures have a very different set of practices associated with justice and responsibility as compared with ours. Admittedly, some tend to think of moral responsibility as limited to practices associated with deontic morality, and so limited to the domain of right and wrong, duty and obligation (e.g., Darwall 2006; Wallace 1994). Others, however, wish to be far more ecumenical about what counts as moral responsibility at all (e.g. McKenna 2012; Russell 2013; Shoemaker 2015). Williams (1993), for instance, writes of shame cultures rather than guilt cultures as enforcing an ethical viewpoint quite different from ours. Why not treat such cultures and practices as in the business of moral responsibility in some way (e.g., see Russell 2013)?

What both of the preceding reasons indicate is that moral responsibility is not well-suited for theorizing about in terms of classical conceptual analysis. It is not just that the diversity makes it likely that any theory postulated will be vulnerable to counterexample—though there is that. It is also that any analysis offered in terms of strict necessary and sufficient conditions will likely be too generic to tell us

[2]To avoid any misimpression, let me be clear. It is consistent with these considerations that there might be important theoretical work to do about some aspect of moral responsibility, like a freedom condition. Once such a condition is identified, it is open to important philosophical work. Likewise, suppose that the scope of responsibility includes obligations. A theory of obligation is not ruled out. But this would be to engage in philosophical theorizing about some element with which responsibility is concerned, just as French deploys work in the theory of action. What is at issue here has to do with a theory about moral responsibility's nature and norms *as such*. I am indebted to Ish Haji for raising a worry here.

anything interesting about the diversity of cases. This is even more so once we tend to Sommers's and Williams's considerations about how cultures can vary so widely as regards forms of ethical life. Instead, it seems far more appealing to think in Wittgensteinian fashion in terms of games and relations of similarity. Better to theorize by tending to the particular as French did in his *Responsibility Matters* (1992), looking to interesting details of particular aspects—or matters—of moral responsibility and doing philosophical work on them without seeking anything unifying to bring all of these insights together.

Treating Practice as If It Is Distinct

French contrasts his approach with views according to which moral responsibility involves some truth about the world or instead is a necessary presupposition of practical life. It is in contrast with these possibilities that French identifies moral responsibility as being nothing more than a set of practices (1992, ix–x). Here, I suspect French had in mind a familiar view of moral responsibility that I too wish to reject. On such a view, our moral responsibility practices are one thing. Moral responsibility itself is another. Our practices are in good standing depending upon whether they are true to or in accord with moral responsibility proper. On one model, moral responsibility facts about the world settle the matter. On another, normative standards of practical rationality settle the matter. Either way, a good theory determines what these things are, and our practices either do well in answering to or properly mirroring these things, or they do not. For a very simple example, built from a toy model, imagine that moral responsibility is a matter of whatever God judges is deserved as a response for one's moral conduct. Blameworthiness, for instance, just is culpable wrongdoing in God's eyes, and deserved blaming just is what God would think fitting as a response. Our moral responsibility practices could then be measured for veracity and compliance against these truths about reality as settled by God.

Clearly, French wishes to resist this way of theorizing about moral responsibility, as do I. In this regard, French and I are for the most part in agreement with P.F. Strawson. In his 1962 "Freedom and Resentment," when focusing on the web of attitudes "which form an essential part of the moral life as we know it," Strawson wrote:

> Only by attending to this range of attitudes can we recover from the facts as we know them a sense of what we mean, i.e., of all we mean, when, speaking the language of morals, we speak of desert, responsibility, guilt, condemnation, and justice. But we do recover them from the facts as we know them. We do not have to go beyond them. (1962, in Watson, ed. 2003, 91)

Now admittedly, Strawson here is talking about various attitudes, and French is more directly focused on practices. But this difference between them, at least on a view like my own (2012) is miniscule, since to understand the sorts of attitudes Strawson meant to feature—the morally reactive attitudes—we must do so in terms of how they are manifested in our practical lives.

Another philosopher who concurs is R. Jay Wallace. Wallace considers what he calls a "metaphysical interpretation" of the moral responsibility facts. According to it:

> . . . we would suppose that there is a fact of the matter about responsibility 'in itself,' a fact about what it is to be *genuinely* or *really* responsible, and that this fact is prior to and independent of our practices of treating people as morally responsible agents. That practice would be in good order to the extent that it succeeds in tracking or meshing with the prior and independent facts about moral responsibility. (1994, 87–88)

At one point, Wallace describes this interpretation as one in which the moral responsibility facts are construed as "conceptually independent from our practice of holding morally responsible" (1994, 87), and he reports that this metaphysical interpretation strikes him as "most unpromising" (1994, 88). Why? According to him:

> The trouble stems from the postulation of a prior and independent realm of "moral responsibility facts," to which our practices of holding people responsible should answer... I cannot see how to make sense of the idea of a prior and independent realm of moral responsibility facts. (1994, 88)

What Wallace found especially puzzling is that the way our moral emotions apparently animate our social lives would tend to suggest instead that somehow the conditions of being morally responsible must be alive to them. A metaphysical interpretation appears to be incompatible with this transparent fact. Here too, Wallace tends to various emotions, but the point is generalizable in a way friendly to French's approach. Our practices appear to have such a powerful role to play in structuring our expectations regarding moral responsibility that it would seem a peculiar picture, one not true to the on-the-ground facts, to think that the practices are meant to be tracking something independent from them.

Of course, we need to be cautious here. One worry about a strong deflationary view like French's, even if not on a view like Wallace's (1994) or my own (2012), is that we cannot make sense of an important feature of the norms we take to bear on these practices. In particular, as John Martin Fischer and Mark Ravizza (1993, 18) noted in assessing Strawson's view, it is possible that the practices could get things wrong. We could hold morally responsible people who are not and not hold morally responsible people who are (e.g., the severely mentally retarded and members of an oppressed race). It does appear that on a deflationary view like French's or Strawson's, there is a risk of eliding this important distinction—between actually being held morally responsible and it being appropriate to do so. But on this point, I think French and Strawson are not so badly off as it might seem. As I have argued elsewhere in reflecting on how best to interpret Strawson (2012, 154–5), it is a caricature of the sort of view Strawson or French develop to think that it would not have the resources to draw such a distinction. All that is needed is a way to show that norms used to assess our responsibility practices *themselves* bottom out in other presuppositions grounded in our practices.

A different approach for facing this problem, one to which I now turn, involves embracing the possibility that there could after all be moral responsibility facts and attendant norms. Hence, there could be a way of constructing a theory about them. The key is to conceptualize them as intertwined with our practices themselves. On such an approach, we could make sense of defective practices diverging from relevant facts and norms while still thinking that those facts and norms are in some way practice-dependent.

A Practice-Dependent Theory of Moral Responsibility

Consider again French's remark that "responsibility is but a set of practices that we use to describe and understand individual and social behavior" (2002, ix). I agree but for the word *but*. In my view, French is correct that moral responsibility is best understood in terms of a set of practices we use to describe and understand behavior. My only objection is with the deflationary suggestion brought out with that little three letter word. With it, French suggests that there is no reason to think in terms of there being any moral responsibility facts about the world—facts that could be the basis for developing a theory. I think there is room for theory-construction regarding moral responsibility facts, where those facts are themselves practice-dependent facts—facts of the very sort that help to account for the RB game as French understands it.

Before I turn to my own view, it is worth noting that recently two other prominent theories of moral responsibility have emerged, David Shoemaker's (2015), and Manuel Vargas's (2013). Along with my own (2012), these theories avoid the missteps I have identified above. Neither seek a classical analysis of the concept of moral responsibility, or for that matter any attendant concepts like morally responsible agency, blameworthiness, blame, and so on. Nor does either treat moral responsibility in a way that is entirely distinct from the practices and social contexts within which an agent presents as morally responsible and whereby others are liable to hold her to account. So it appears that the prospects for theorizing have evolved in the last quarter century or so. French's *Responsibility Matters* (1992) posed a challenge to theorizing about moral responsibility. But I suspect that it was a challenge targeting theories quite different from the sort now animating the debate. Moreover, one might see French's challenge as providing a desideratum for theorizing about moral responsibility. Any adequate theory must be one that can help to account for and minimally conform with the sorts of ethnographic insights animating French's own work. In this way, I think it is only fair to note that French has influenced the contemporary debate by forcing theorists like me to seek theories that fit more naturally with the compelling idea that moral responsibility is somehow deeply connected to our actual responsibility practices.

In *Conversation and Responsibility* (2012), I advanced a theory of moral responsibility that made the focal point for questions of a morally competent agent's responsibility the quality of will with which she acts. Following Strawson

(1962), I argued that when an agent is praiseworthy or blameworthy for some bit of behavior, she displays exemplary or objectionable regard for others or for salient moral considerations. At first blush, it might seem that this is in tension with the constraints laid down above for theory construction. Aren't our practices for holding responsible, say by responding with a reactive emotion of resentment or gratitude, to be guided by the independent facts about what sort of quality of will an agent actually had? No. On a Strawsonian view of the sort I advocate, reactive responses of holding responsible by way of our adult social practices do need to be alive to the facts about what an agent's quality of will really is like. But these facts themselves on a view like Strawson's and on my own cannot be conceptualized in a way that is *independent* of our practices of holding responsible. This is because our holding-responsible practices, and the emotions that are signaled and conveyed by way of them, are ways of expressing moral demands and expectations to members of a moral community.

Let me explain. Part of what is involved in, for example, a blameworthy agent showing lack of due regard for the wellbeing of another person is her failure to be sufficiently attentive to the pressures others are liable to place on her by holding her to account should she act poorly. Hence, her poor quality of will can itself be understood in terms of the practices whereby members of a moral community stand prepared to hold others to account. This is why when writing of our reactive emotions and the practices of holding responsible, Strawson described the making of the demand for goodwill from fellow members of the moral community in terms of the proneness of such attitudes: "The making of the demand *is* the proneness to such attitudes" (1962, in Watson, ed. 2003, 90). Stephen Darwall (2006) understands this in terms of second-personal reasons. One reason I might have not to step on your gouty toe is that it will harm you and so increase the amount of suffering in the world. But a distinct reason is that *you demand that I not do so*. That *itself* is reason-giving. Once we see this, we can widen the prospects for what counts as reason-giving for a morally competent agent. That others stand prepared to respond by holding a moral agent to account is *itself* an expression of moral demands. It is thus the sort of thing that, when disregarded, can be seen as showing insufficient regard for others. In this way, the facts about being morally responsible are, so to speak, infused with meaning by way of the practices of holding morally responsible. Hence, practice is essential to philosophizing about moral responsibility's nature. While this view is not French's, I take it to be amenable to his emphasis upon the relevance of our responsibility practices.

On the conversational theory I advance, morally responsible agency can be usefully elucidated on analogy with a competent speaker's ability to engage in a conversational exchange with an audience of competent speakers of a shared natural language. When a competent speaker initiates and then sustains a conversation with other shared speakers of the same language, she exploits all sorts of conventions in order to convey her meaning. Beyond the strict conventions for assigning meanings to types of sentences, innuendo and simple anticipation of shared background beliefs all enter into what resources she has available to communicate effectively and at the same time be prepared to receive replies that are in a certain respect cooperative.

Familiar Gricean considerations of implicature and the like all rely upon a shared set of expectations and loose conventions between speaker and audience. Consider an agent who speaker-means that her meal was terrible by uttering in a sarcastic tone "My meal was terrific! Way better than gruel." The sentence meanings of her utterance do not strictly imply that her meal was bad (quite the opposite!). But she uses these sentences among audience members who can pick up on what is conveyed by tone of voice and what is suggested by comparing a meal to Dickensian slop, and they are perfectly able to follow. Moreover, when others reply to our imagined speaker, we must expect that she too is alive to how they might exploit her understanding of various conventions to convey their intended meanings.

Here is how the analogy works. I argue that an agent's actions, the ones for which she can be morally responsible, can be bearers of a kind of meaning or significance. I call this *agent meaning* as distinct from action meaning—just like speaker meaning is distinct from sentence meaning. Agent meaning is a function of the quality of will with which an agent acts. When others respond to her by way of holding her morally responsible—say in manifesting a reactive attitude of resentment or indignation—this can be likened unto a conversational reply to a speaker who has initiated a conversation. Apologies, excuses, defiant displays of disregard can then be taken as further unfolding moves in an evolving conversation. Crucially, the meaning assigned to modes of holding responsible, or instead offering apologies and the like, will be structured by sets of social practices. For instance, to display blame and resentment by excluding a person from otherwise normal activities requires a background set of expectations about being included in such activities. Furthermore, a morally responsible agent, in acting in a way that might "initiate" a moral-responsibility exchange (as an analog to a conversational exchange) must be alive to the interpretive resources of her audience. That is, she must be able to modulate her behavior in ways that allow her to avoid the impression (or misimpression) that by so acting she has or lacks ill regard for others. This then requires that her competence as a moral agent depends on her appreciation of the practices and the interpretive standpoint of others prepared to hold her morally responsible.

Space will not permit further description of my overall theory, not to mention any argument for it. But what I have offered is enough to show how it might be that a theory could be constructed that shows considerable deference to the sorts of insight that animate French. As I have developed the conversational theory of moral responsibility, there is no pretense that the theory is meant to offer a set of necessary and sufficient conditions in the spirit of a conceptual analysis. Indeed, it is not even meant to capture without qualification the full extension of our moral responsibility practices and judgments. Clearly there are contexts in which an agent can be morally responsible absent anything like an analog to a conversational exchange. She can, for instance, be morally responsible when she seeks to avoid anyone even recognizing her objectionable conduct. Or instead, a person could act in a blameworthy way and be an apt target of blame, but immediately drop dead. There is no sort of conversing possible in a case like that. To handle all such cases, I mean only to offer a theory that I take to be able to explain adequately certain sorts of exemplar or prototype cases of moral responsibility. Other cases are then to be explained by relations of similarity to these cases. I take it that the central, salient cases that a theory of moral responsibility needs to be able to explain first and foremost are those cases that involve a morally responsible agent performing a blameworthy or praiseworthy act and then others being positioned to address that person directly by standards that bear on questions of desert and justice. It is in such contexts that an agent who is held accountable for a bit of conduct is then positioned to offer an apology, an excuse, admit wrongdoing and the like. If a theory of moral responsibility has the resources to explain these practices, the judgments implicit in them, and the norms regarding their proper application, as I see it, it is a success. It is gravy if such a theory can also then explain other cases that are in some way parasitic on or departures from these sorts of exemplar cases.

Now consider French's excellent observations about the RB game. Note three crucial features of his work in developing his treatment of the game. Each suggests a natural fit with the theory I defend. First, French did not pretend to be accounting for the full extension of the game—at least not without qualification. A person might be blameworthy for some terrible act but go unnoticed, and in such a case she would avoid the burdens of the game altogether. In this way, French's observations about the RB game are like mine about moral responsibility exchanges—they capture salient kinds of cases that need explaining but do not pretend to exhaust all cases. Second, the elements involved in being responsible for something or other involve a morally competent person's being sensitive to the likely responses of others with whom one is likely to barter for burdens or benefits. Third, French is not committed in anything he says to the idea that the RB game exhausts whatever there is of interest when attending to moral responsibility. All he claims is that this is one of the features of our moral responsibility practices, and he points out that the motivation for it, at least characteristically, is self-interest.

On this last point, I wish to dismiss a criticism of French that in my view would be uncharitable and based on a misreading of him. If French were claiming that the RB game and self-interested motives were at the heart of what is involved in an agent's being responsible and then others holding responsible, he would be a target for the sort of wrong-kind-of-reasons objection Strawson (1962) leveled against his compatibilist contemporaries. On their view, what accounts for moral responsibility is exhausted in the utility of a system of rewards and punishments. Strawson complained that these misguided compatibilists failed to see that when we hold responsible, we are not making calculations of this sort, or at least that is not what we are usually doing. Instead, we are responding with genuine concern or regard for how others have treated us. Questions of social utility are typically beside the point. Likewise, one might object to French that when we hold or are held responsible, we are not characteristically motivated by self-interest. Nor are we simply bartering so as to avoid moral burdens and the like. In short, our activity is not that calculating. We are instead animated by the moral significance of another's (or our own) good or ill will.

The reason that this criticism does not apply to French in his account of the RB game is that French in no way pretends to tell us that motives of self-interest are always in play when we are holding others responsible or when we are held responsible. Nor does he claim that in all cases when one is held responsible that one is even playing the game at all. All French is pointing out is something that is patently true. *This is a game we play*. We play it often, and it is the way most ordinary folks tend to come into contact with struggles about morality quite generally. Note that in this respect, French's insight is in accord with Strawson's when Strawson remarks in closing his paper that "it is far from wrong to emphasize the efficacy" of our responsibility practices (1962, in Watson, ed. 2003, 93). What is misguided is to think that those questions of social utility exhaust all there is to understanding responsibility. Likewise, we might say, for understanding motives of self-interest and the RB game. What would be misguided is to think that these considerations exhaust all there is to understanding responsibility. But French says nothing at all to lead us to think that they would exhaust them. He is simply describing an illuminating game that it turns out really does help us understand how various responsibility exchanges often unfold.

Conclusion

I close with a few very simple assertions followed by an invitation. The conversational theory of moral responsibility as I advance it offers support for French's treatment of the RB game. Indeed, it dovetails with his explanation of the scope of the game in terms of the candidate acts—intended, intentional, negligent, accidental, deliberate and willing—that are potential moves in the game. Any of these kinds of acts can take on meaning regarding the quality of an agent's will. And one way to engage in a moral responsibility exchange as the conversational theory understands it is by way of bartering for greater or lesser burdens in light of the moral salience of one's actions. Hence, I invite Peter French to come on board as an ally.

Acknowledgements I am honored to be included in this festschrift for Peter French. I was Peter's student in an NEH Summer Seminar for College Professors in 1995, held in the foothills of the Rocky Mountains in the outskirts of Boulder, CO. It was an experience I still recall fondly. Peter's work in the seminar and my experience with several of the other seminarians, especially Ish Haji and Marina Oshana, proved to be invaluable to me as my career unfolded. From that time with Peter and long afterwards, Peter was extremely kind to me, often offering me support and advice in facing some very hard professional challenges. He was, of course, also an excellent source of philosophical insight. I am very much indebted to him, and I would like to thank him sincerely for his kindness, wisdom, and generosity. I hope this essay honors him as he deserves.

For helpful comments on this paper, I would like to thank Ish Haji, Paul Russell, David Shoemaker, and Brandon Warmke. I would also like to thank Zachary Goldberg for editing this volume and inviting me to contribute to it.

References

Darwall, Stephen. 2006. *The second-person standpoint: Morality, respect, accountability*. Cambridge: Harvard University Press.

Davidson, Donald. 1963. Actions, reasons, and causes. *Journal of Philosophy* 60: 685–700.

———. 1971. Agency. In *Agent, action, and reason*, ed. Robert Binkley, Richard Bronaugh, and Ausonia Marras. Toronto: University of Toronto Press.

———. 1980. *Essays on actions and events*. Oxford: Clarendon Press.

Fischer, John Martin, and Mark Ravizza, eds. 1993. *Perspectives on moral responsibility*. Ithaca: Cornell University Press.

French, Peter. 1992. *Responsibility matters*. Lawrence: University of Kansas Press.

Mackie, J.L. 1977. *Ethics: Inventing right and wrong*. Harmondsworth: Penguin.

McKenna, Michael. 2012. *Conversation and responsibility*. New York: Oxford University Press.

Quine, W.V.O. 1951. Two dogmas of empiricism. *Philosophical Review* 60: 20–43.

Russell, Paul. 2013. Responsibility, naturalism, and the morality system. In *Oxford studies in agency and responsibility*, ed. David Shoemaker, vol. 1, 184–204. Oxford: Oxford University Press.

Shoemaker, David. 2015. *Responsibility from the margins*. Oxford: Oxford University Press.

Sommers, Tamler. 2012. *Relative justice: Cultural diversity, free will, and moral responsibility*. Princeton: Princeton University Press.

Strawson, P.F. 1962. Freedom and resentment. *Proceedings of the British Academy* 48: 187–211.

Vargas, Manuel. 2013. *Building better beings*. Oxford: Oxford University Press.

Wallace, R. Jay. 1994. *Responsibility and the moral sentiments*. Cambridge: Harvard University Press.

Watson, Gary, eds. 2003. *Free will*. New York: Oxford University Press.

Williams, Bernard. 1993. *Shame and necessity*. Berkeley: University of California Press.

Wittgenstein, Ludwig. 1953. *Philosophical investigations*. Oxford: Blackwell.

Reflections on Obligation and Blameworthiness

Ishtiyaque Haji

Appealing to Frankfurt examples (Frankfurt 1969), Peter French concurs that persons can be morally blameworthy for what they have done even if they could not have done otherwise (the "lesson"). However, if one accepts the principle that "ought not" is equivalent to "impermissible," and agrees that "ought not" implies "can refrain from" (as French presumably does[1]), then one is rationally committed to the view that impermissibility requires avoidability. If one further sides with the popular principle that a person is blameworthy for doing something only if it is impermissible for her to do it, then one will have to renounce the lesson. In this paper, I suggest that French has the resources to reject the popular principle and so can evade this conundrum altogether. I then give additional reasons against this principle partly by drawing on some of French's insightful thoughts about heroism and responsibility. Finally, exploiting cases in which one cannot do otherwise because of one's character, I broach some larger metaphysical issues. Does determinism preclude obligation in virtue of precluding freedom to do otherwise, and does indeterminism at apt junctures in the causal pathway to one's actions preclude obligation owing to such indeterministically caused actions being too much of a matter of luck?

[1] I say "presumably" because it seems that French (1992, 119) accepts the principle that "ought" implies "can."

I. Haji (✉)
University of Calgary, Calgary, AB, Canada
e-mail: ihaji@ucalgary.ca

Z.J. Goldberg (ed.), *Reflections on Ethics and Responsibility*,
DOI 10.1007/978-3-319-50359-2_6

A Conundrum Concerning Frankfurt Examples

In a discussion on fate and responsibility (1992, 44–54), French advances the following Frankfurt example:

> A person M [Mary] decides for reasons of her own to protest the treatment of the prisoners in the H-Blocks. She is then threatened by the IRA with horrible personal suffering if she does not protest. The threat is so horrible that any reasonable person would submit to it. M does protest....Is M morally responsible for protesting when she had no alternative to doing so? It will be suggested, of course, that M had the alternative of resisting the IRA threat, so the story can be modified to make M incapable of resisting the force that would make her protest. In other words, whatever that force is, M will protest, and she will do so either because she decided to do so or because she was forced to do so, but in no case will she fail to protest. The fact that she could not have avoided protesting is a sufficient condition of her having protested. However, that may play no role in the explanation of why she did protest....The point is that if our concern is the ascribing of moral responsibility, we should not place much weight on a fact that is irrelevant to explaining a person's behavior. Only the reasons a person did something in the circumstances should matter. Unavoidability does not explain Mary's behavior in the circumstances, so it is not relevant to the issues of her responsibility. (1992, 51–53)

The alleged lesson of Frankfurt examples, however, that responsibility—and here attention is limited to moral blameworthiness—does not entail that we have alternatives succumbs to pressure if one is partial to the ensuing popular principle and to what may be dubbed the "simple argument". The principle (*BRI*) says that blameworthiness requires impermissibility: One is morally blameworthy for performing (or failing to perform) an action only if it is morally impermissible for one to perform (or not to perform) that action. The simple argument seeks to show that moral impermissibility *does* require freedom to do otherwise: If it is impermissible for one to do something, one ought not to do it, assuming that one ought not to do something if and only if it is impermissible for one to do it (principle *Equivalence*). But if one ought not to do something, then one can refrain from doing it, since "ought" implies "can" and "ought not" implies "can refrain from" (principle *OIC*). Hence, if it is impermissible for one to do something, one ought not to do it.

To flesh out the concern, partition French's Frankfurt example into two stages and alter it to involve blameworthiness. In Stage 1, Mary decides on her own to attack a prison guard. She succeeds in severely injuring him. Assume that in this first stage, Mary could have refrained from attacking the guard, it is impermissible for her to attack him, and she is to blame for attacking him. In Stage 2, a counterfactual intervener, who fails to show his hand, would have forced Mary to assault the guard had Mary displayed an involuntary sign that she was about to decide not to assault him. But Mary acts no differently in this stage than she does in the former. It looks as though she is blameworthy for deciding to attack the guard, and for attacking him, in Stage 2 even though she could not have done otherwise, or so "Frankfurt defenders" would claim.

However, if the simple argument is sound, then in Stage 2, it is *not* impermissible for Mary to attack the guard (because she could not have refrained from attacking him). Furthermore, if blameworthiness requires impermissibility, then contrary to what Frankfurt defenders wish to conclude, in Stage 2 Mary is *not* blameworthy for assaulting the guard. So we have a conundrum, and something must give way to escape it. The relevant choices are: rescind the judgment that Frankfurt examples impugn the principle that blameworthiness requires alternatives; or, assuming *Equivalence* is beyond reproach, renounce *OIC*; or reject the view that blameworthiness requires impermissibility (*BRI*).

In addition to looking favorably upon Frankfurt examples, French accepts *OIC*. He says, "If you cannot swim, you have no duty to rescue a drowning person. But if you can, and attempt no rescue, you are guilty of moral failure" (1992, 119). Regarding the conundrum, French leaves himself no choice but to jettison *BRI*. Fortunately, jettisoning *BRI* is something French should approve of as I explain in the next section.

Morality's Complexity

In his engaging discussion on responsibility and heroism (1992, 111–121), French rejects a traditional threefold deontic classification of acts as obligatory, impermissible, or permissible (1992, 116). Commenting on what he takes to be the Kantian position that an act that is "neither commanded nor forbidden is merely permissible" and so "morally indifferent," he says that heroic "deeds are not morally indifferent. 'Hero' is surely a term of favorable moral evaluation" (116). In further support against the threefold classification, French writes:

> [A] heroic act must be undertaken with full knowledge that one's life is at risk....This self-sacrifice condition [of heroism] is noted by a number of philosophers, including John Rawls, who identifies heroic deeds as good acts that would be moral obligations except for the cost run by the hero. Heroic deeds, then, are not just benevolent acts of helping others or of acting in ways to achieve good ends. They must involve risk of life and limb. Insofar as many moralists, especially since the advent of the centrality of the individual in the social contract theories of Hobbes and Locke, believe that morality cannot require acts against self-preservation, heroic deeds should not be morally obligatory. They seem to be actions it is good to do but not bad not to do—deeds one cannot be held morally responsible for not doing. (1992, 114, note omitted)

Remarking on morality's complexity, French explains that removing

> the special moral status of heroism destroys important distinctions and shadings in the way we color our lives. Ethics should not be monochromatic when the moral world of the ordinary person is so colorful. More than numbers count and not all good acts are duties. In fact, if self-sacrifice to benefit others is always a moral responsibility [i.e., a moral obligation], there is no point in praising those who do it. (1992, 119).

These passages suggest that French may well be congenial to regarding heroic acts as supererogatory. This would dovetail nicely with his rejection of the threefold classification. Elaborating, among others, Paul McNamara has proposed that our ordinary moral conceptual scheme allows for the notions of permissibly doing the least one can do and permissibly doing more than one has to do (2008, 2011). He explains that a range of acceptable alternatives yields ranked permissible options with two extreme poles—the best of the permissible alternatives and the least of those—with the prospect of doing more than the least of those or permissibly less than the best of those. Here is an instructive example:

> [*Contact*:] Suppose that in virtue of promising to get in touch with you, I become obligated to do so. Suppose...I can fulfill this obligation in two ways: by writing you a letter or by stopping by....[M]y other obligations make me too busy permissibly to do both. Finally, suppose that, morally speaking, I put in a better performance if I pay you a visit rather than write you, even though either one is permissible. Then if I *do the minimum morality demands*, I will write rather than visit....The important thing to note is that what is necessitated by *meeting morality's demands in a minimally acceptable way* is not to be confused with doing what I am obligated to do....[S]ome such notion is vital to the concept of supererogation. For if it is possible for me to discharge my obligations in a supererogatory way (in a better than minimal way), then it ought to be possible for me merely to discharge them in a minimal way—and vice versa. (McNamara 1996, 424–26)

An act is beyond the call if and only if it is permissible and precluded by doing the minimum (McNamara 2011, 228). It is relatively uncontroversial that one can be praiseworthy for going beyond the call. For instance, one can be praiseworthy for doing what it is supererogatory for one to do. McNamara (e.g., 2011, 223) proposes this analysis of the supererogatory: An act is supererogatory for an agent, *S*, if and only if it is optional for *S* to do, praiseworthy for *S* to do, not blameworthy for *S* to omit, and precluded by doing the least *S* can do.[2] Since any supererogatory act is precluded by doing the (permissibly) minimum, and one is praiseworthy for such an act, one can be praiseworthy for going beyond the call. We may plausibly suppose that heroes, in doing the heroic, frequently go beyond the call, and are (or can be) praiseworthy for their heroic deeds.

Should one accept the category of the supererogatory, or at least the category of acts that go beyond the call, it seems that one should also accept the category of the *suberogatory*, or minimally, the category of permissibly suboptimal acts. It certainly appears that one can be blameworthy for doing what it is permissibly suboptimal for one to do. A variant of *Contact* confirms this.

Embellished Contact: Suppose I can fulfill the obligation to contact you in these ways: putting in a personal appearance at your store (*w1*); phoning you (*w2*); writing you (*w3*); or scribbling a message on your store window (*w4*). Suppose, again, that my other obligations make me too busy permissibly to do any two of these things; doing one of them precludes me permissibly from doing any of the others (but doing each is permissible). Finally, imagine that *w1* is the best of these four options, and in the progression from *w1* to *w4*, the "deontic value" of each decreases so that *w4* is relatively worst; morally, I put in a better performance if I visit than if I phone, write, or scribble a message. Lest one think these rankings arbitrary, these details should help. I'm a store owner, too, a few blocks away from you and you and I are friendly rivals. During early afternoons when business is slow, I can close the store for a bit to attend to other concerns, such as zipping over to the bank, post office,

[2]See also, Heyd (1982) and Mellema (1991, 17, 125–29).

and so on. To nurture our growing friendship, it would be better to put in a personal appearance than to phone you. Writing a note is acceptable but too impersonal; it is something neither one of us would do. Finally, scribbling a message on your store window would cause you some trouble; you would have to clean up the window, and so forth.

Suppose I'm aware of these relative rankings. Intuitively, at least, if I deliberately scribble, knowing it would hardly have taken much for me to do significantly better—I could have sauntered over in the afternoon—I'm blameworthy for scribbling. Similarly, if I deliberately write, aware that I could have done better by putting in a personal appearance, I am blameworthy even if only a tad for writing: I act in light of the nonculpable belief that I have done something it is, for lack of better expression, "morally amiss" for me to do.

Suberogatory acts are the roughly symmetric flip sides of supererogatory ones. McNamara (e.g., 2011, 231) proposes that an act is suberogatory for *S* if and only if it is optional for *S* to do, blameworthy for *S* to do, not praiseworthy for *S* to omit, and precluded by the maximum *S* can do.[3] Since any suberogatory act is precluded by doing the most one can do, and one is blameworthy for such an act, one can be blameworthy for doing what it is permissibly suboptimal for one to do. But then it is false that blameworthiness presupposes impermissibility (*BRI*).

Recall, the initial conundrum. If, as French proposes, Frankfurt examples may be invoked to question the principle that one is morally blameworthy for performing an action only if one could have done otherwise, then French has to face up to the following challenge. Blameworthiness requires impermissibility (*BRI*) and impermissibility, in turn, requires avoidability. But in Frankfurt examples, the agent (like Mary) who is supposedly blameworthy for doing something (such as killing the guard) seemingly *cannot* refrain from doing what she does. Hence, even if it is true that an agent, like Mary, could not have done otherwise in her "Frankfurt situation," it is false that she is blameworthy for doing what she did. I have proposed that French can evade this problem by exploiting his suggestion that ethics "should not be monochromatic." An important "shading" in our moral lives is that certain actions we may perform, suberogatory ones, are permissible actions with a special sort of disvalue, and we can on occasion well be to blame for performing them.

Changeability of Obligations Over Time and Blameworthiness

The "changeability" of obligations with the passage of time casts additional suspicion on *BRI*. To illustrate the phenomenon of changeability, imagine that on Monday, it is impermissible for you, the doctor, to give medicine B to a patient on Wednesday because medicine A, which is also available, will cure the patient with no unpleasant side effects. There are no other remedies for the cure. However,

[3]See, also, e.g., Mellema (1991) and Driver (1992).

suppose you deliberately plan on doing wrong by giving B, and you do give B on Wednesday. Next, initiate the following change: Unbeknownst to you, and owing to events entirely beyond your personal control, the supply of A is exhausted on Tuesday. Some unfortunate alcoholic, desperate to get her hands on some "good stuff," guzzles all the A in the belief that A is some exotic intoxicant. Now as of Tuesday, it is no longer impermissible for you to give B on Wednesday; indeed, you ought, as of the time A is unavailable, to give B on Wednesday as this is the only way in which your patient will survive.

On Wednesday morning, you give B in the nonculpable belief that you are doing something impermissible in giving B and that you could have done better for your patient by giving her some A instead. It seems you are just as blameworthy here for giving B as you would have been had some A indeed been available. But if in fact there is no A left, then you are blameworthy for giving B even if it's false that it is impermissible for you to give B; you are blameworthy for something that it is obligatory for you to do. Once again, French can call upon such examples involving changeability to deflect the challenge that Frankfurt examples do not undermine the principle that blameworthiness presupposes freedom to do otherwise because blameworthiness requires impermissibility, and impermissibility requires avoidability.

Character and Blameworthiness

In previous work (e.g., Haji 2002, 2012a, 2016) I have argued that if obligation requires basic control—it is obligatory for one to do something only if one can do it—then barring cogent reason to believe otherwise, impermissibility and permissibility also require this basic sort of control. Put briefly, "ought," "permissibility," and "impermissibility" each imply "can." We may now argue that obligation requires alternatives: If one ought not to do something, then it is impermissible for one to do it. If it is impermissible for one to do something, then one can do it. Therefore, if one ought not to do something, then one can do it. But it is also true that if one ought not to do something, then one can refrain from doing it. Hence, if one ought to do something, then both one can and one can refrain from doing it. Just as it is impermissible for you to do something only if you can refrain from doing it, so it is obligatory for you to do something only if you can refrain from doing it.

With this in mind, ponder these examples involving persons of strong moral character. With his typical wit and moral insight, in a passage (laced with irony) Mark Twain pronounces, "I am morally superior to George Washington. He couldn't tell a lie. I can and don't."[4] When Luther broke with the Church of Rome in the sixteenth century, he reportedly made the now famous declaration: "Here I stand. I can do no other." With no reservation and with pronounced emphasis,

[4]As quoted by Peter van Inwagen (1983, 63–64).

a mentally healthy and loving mother declares, "I couldn't but rescue my child from the monstrous waves." Whether someone can in fact be constitutionally or psychologically incapable of performing various actions is controversial. Far less contentious is that the sort of person one is, or broadly, one's character, influences the types of action one can or cannot perform. The *extent* of this influence is debatable. Suppose it was literally true of Washington that he could not bring himself to lie, given his disposition to be honest. Then since obligation requires avoidability, and he could not have prevented himself from telling the truth, it is false that on the relevant occasion it was obligatory for him to tell the truth on that occasion. Moreover, if it is conceded that there is a requirement of alternative possibilities for impermissibility and permissibility as well, then it was in addition to not being obligatory for him to tell the truth, not impermissible nor permissible either. We may say that in this case, it was "amoral" for Washington to tell the truth. It may, nevertheless, reasonably be judged that he was still praiseworthy for telling the truth.

At least some heroes may be like Washington in that they could not have refrained from engaging in their heroic deeds. French proposes that heroic acts must be performed to achieve morally desirable ends (1992, 113); they should be undertaken in the full knowledge that one's life is at risk (114); and they should not be morally obligatory (114). He also insists that heroes should be appropriately motivated—the hero must have the intention to help others, and this intention "must be proportional to his or her sacrifice" (115). None of these proposed conditions for heroism or heroic deeds precludes a hero from being unable to refrain from performing some heroic deed. At considerable risk to herself, Ann rushes into the inferno to save her neighbor's trapped baby. Badly burned, she succeeds. Maybe Ann simply could not have refrained from what she did. If she is praiseworthy for her heroic deed, then, again, she is praiseworthy for something that it was amoral for her to do.

Still, one might press the following concern. Aristotle and others have argued that we have the power to mold or influence our characters. Suppose Ann has taken deliberate steps to see to it that she would protect or come to the aid of her children (or the progeny of others) when called upon. Furthermore, suppose she has fashioned herself to become the kind of person who cannot do (or refrain from doing) various things, such as helping needy children in germane circumstances. It may be proposed that this sort of character formation should *not* undermine obligation or impermissibility. Even if Ann cannot refrain from saving the trapped baby, it is still obligatory for her to save him because she has freely made herself into the kind of person who cannot but rescue or attempt to rescue children from impending danger.

Whether agents freely mold themselves or to what extent they do to become the adults they are is controversial. I won't dwell on this concern. Rather, the objection can be parried if we attend carefully to certain features of the case. The key principle underling the objection is this: If you freely do some things at an earlier time to ensure that, later, you won't be able to refrain from doing something else, then this thing that you won't at some future time be able to refrain from doing may still be permissible, impermissible, or obligatory for you. However, an example involving changeability challenges this principle. You borrow a book from Fred on Monday. You promise you will return it not later than Friday. Assume that, because you promised, you morally ought to return the book by Friday. Now suppose that on Wednesday, you sell the valuable book because you're short on cash. Some may object that you still have an obligation to return it by Friday even though, as of the time you've sold it, you cannot return it. However, we are not compelled to this position. A credible alternative is that prior to selling the book, you ought to return it by Friday, partly, because you can, before selling it, keep your promise. After selling it, however, and so no longer being able to return it, it isn't true that you ought to return it by Friday. Of course, one can maintain that you ought, up to the time of selling the book, to return it later, and as this (remote) obligation is *not* satisfied, a wrong *is* done. But this is consistent with holding that as of the time you sell it, it is no longer obligatory for you to return the book, and, moreover, as of this time you acquire new obligations, such as the obligation to apologize, make reparation, or attempt to recover the book. Notice, in addition, that obligations do expire. If you ought to return the book not later than 9:00 a.m., and it is now 9:32 a.m., even if you haven't sold the book *this* obligation has now expired. At 9:32 a.m., you no longer have an obligation to return the book at 9:00, and you don't have this obligation because as of 9:32 you cannot return the book at 9:00. If obligations can expire after the proper time of discharge (9:00 a.m. in our example), why suppose they cannot expire before the slated time of discharge if the relevant inability has set in prior to this slated time? It is, then, perfectly in order to conclude that once you have sold the book, and the relevant inability has set in, your obligation to return it by Friday expires (see, e.g., Zimmerman 1996, 98–100; Haji 2002, 47–52; Vranas 2007, 175–179).

For whatever bizarre reason, suppose you have made yourself into the kind of person who will not return a borrowed book on time. The prior considerations lend support to the view that once the pertinent inability sets in, you do not have an obligation to return the book even if it is assumed that before this inability sets in you did have such an obligation.

Reverting to the mother's case, we may suppose that even if Ann has freely made herself into the kind of person who cannot but come to the aid of needy children, helping them is not something that is obligatory, permissible, or impermissible for her. For example, rescuing the baby does not have any of these moral statuses because she could not have done otherwise. Still, one may reasonably suppose that she is praiseworthy for saving the baby.

We can imagine a person who has so hardened his heart to morality that he simply cannot avoid doing things that, but for being unavoidable for him, would have been impermissible for him. Here, we may plausibly judge that such a morally depraved agent would be blameworthy for performing some heinous deed despite its being amoral for him to perform it.

Some existentialists (e.g., Camus 1946; Sartre 1953, 617–618) have proposed that, conceivably, one can do something even in the absence of any reason to do it—what is rationally inexplicable is not impossible. Suppose Annie does something—she *A*-s in the absence of any reason to *A*. Suppose that, had she not

A-ed at the time she did, she would have *B*-ed instead, and if she had *B*-ed she would have done so in the absence of any reason to do so. Can *A* be a moral obligation for Annie (at the relevant time)? One is indirectly obligated regarding something just in case one is obligated regarding it by way of being obligated regarding something else; one is directly obligated regarding something just in case one is obligated regarding it but not indirectly so. As Zimmerman (2006, 595, 602; 2008, 90–91, 149–150) cautions, direct obligations are restricted to intentional actions one can perform; not so with indirect obligations. Suppose Ted has a direct obligation to turn on the furnace. He cannot, however, turn it on without activating the relevant mechanisms within of which he knows nothing whatsoever; so he ought to activate these mechanisms. This indirect obligation is one that, in his circumstances, he can perform but not intentionally. We may now rephrase the central question concerning Annie: can *A* be a direct obligation for her? The answer seems clear at least if one favors a causal theory of action. An action one performs is an intentional action only if this action is suitably connected to one's reasons states. As Annie *A*-s for no reasons at all (if the example is to be believed), *A* is not an intentional action. For analogous reasons, neither can *A* be (directly) permissible nor impermissible for Annie. If Annie may still be blameworthy for *A*-ing, then once again we have reason to believe that blameworthiness does not presuppose impermissibility; so *BRI* is false. And yet again it may be proposed that French can help himself to this result to meet the challenge that Frankfurt examples do not show that blameworthiness does not require avoidability. However, as I argue below, I have my doubts about whether Annie can indeed be blameworthy for *A*-ing.

Wider Metaphysical Issues

The examples involving strong character—for instance, Ann's scenario in which Ann cannot but save the child—call to mind what many accept to be the case: if determinism is true, no one can do otherwise.[5] If impermissibility requires avoidability, and blameworthiness requires impermissibility, then with one qualification (to be introduced below), determinism is incompatible both with impermissibility (or, more generally, obligation) and blameworthiness.

Annie's case brings to mind the so-called "luck problem" that event-causal libertarians confront.[6] Libertarians affirm that determinism is incompatible with free action or moral responsibility, and at least some of us at times perform free actions for which we are responsible. Libertarians allow that an indirectly free action whose freedom derives from the freedom of other actions to which it is suitably related

[5]For our purposes, take determinism to be the thesis that at any instant there is exactly one physically possible universe (van Inwagen 1983, 3).

[6]I set aside agent-causal libertarian views although I have argued that such views also succumb to the problem of luck. See, e.g. Haji (2012a).

may be determined by its immediate causal precursors. A directly free action is free independently of inheriting its freedom from the freedom of other events. But libertarians insist that action *A* performed at time, *t*, is directly free only if there is another possible world with the same past and laws in which, at *t*, the agent does not do *A*. The sense of 'free' here is the personal one presupposed by true judgments of moral responsibility such as *she was morally blameworthy for lying*. The problem of luck to which libertarian theories seem susceptible highlights the relevant similarity between Annie's scenario in which she *A*-s at *t* for no reason, and a case in which some agent performs a putatively directly (libertarian) free action at *t*.

There are at least two ways to motivate this problem. In the *No Explanation Version* of the luck problem, imagine that in the actual world, *W*, Peg has reasons to decide to *A* (at some later time), and also reasons to decide to *B*. After some deliberation, she forms the all-things-considered judgment that it is best for her to decide to *A*, and she continently decides to *A*. Assume that this decision is nondeviantly and indeterministically caused by the reasons she has to so decide. To introduce a term of art, the causal trajectory, or a segment of such a trajectory, of an action or choice of an agent is *smooth* provided it is free of responsibility-undermining (or responsibility-diminishing) factors, such as, for instance, the impact of manipulation of the sort that vitiates responsibility or a breakdown in agency; the agent does not succumb to akratic or other irrational influences in making the decision she makes; and, barring unusual circumstances, such as the occurrence of events over which she lacks any control and which would prevent her from deciding consistently with her best judgment, and in the absence of new information, further deliberation, or reconsideration, she decides in accordance with such a judgment. Reverting to Peg's scenario, assume that the segment of the causal trajectory that "commences," roughly, with Peg's deliberations about whether to decide to *A* and extends to her making at *t* the decision to *A* in *W*, is smooth. We may suppose that Peg exercises self-control in deciding to *A*, and at *t* she indeterministically decides to *A*. Assume, furthermore, that there is an apt detailed reason-explanation of Peg's deciding at *t* to *A* in *W*: her reason-states nondeviantly cause her decision. It is vitally important that there be such a causal explanation because event-causal libertarians agree that the control necessary for responsibility just consists in one's actions being appropriately caused by one's reason-states. As at *t* Peg indeterministically decides to *A* in *W*, there is a world, *W**, that has the same natural laws as *W*, and is past-wise indiscernible from *W*, right up to *t* in which at *t* Peg decides to do something other than *A*—at *t* she decides to *B*. It appears that this decision is akratic; it is supposedly a free and intentional mental action that is contrary to Peg's consciously held best (or better) judgment. But then in virtue of what is it true that Peg indeterministically decides at *t* to *B* in *W** when this decision is akratic? With the stipulation that *W* and *W** have the same laws of nature and pre-*t* history, it appears that there are no appropriate causal connections between her deciding to *B* and her reason states to account for Peg's akratically deciding as she does in *W**. Without such connections, however, Peg does not exercise "responsibility-level" control in deciding to *B* in *W**. It would appear, then, that she is not responsible for deciding to *B* in *W** (Haji 2012a, section 6.3; 2016, chapter 7). Parallel reasoning, if it is cogent, sustains the view that Peg is not responsible for *A*-ing in the actual world.

The luck problem may be energized differently. The *Pure Luck* version takes it for granted that (or remains agnostic about whether) there is a reasons-explanation of whatever decision Peg makes in the relevant worlds. It focuses our attention on luck differently. With an indeterministic agent, such as Peg, it is false that the agent has some *further* power to influence causally which of her alternatives she realizes, a power over and above the mere chance of acting differently and to exercise "responsibility-level" control *in* making whatever decision she makes (e.g. Clarke 2003, 96; Pereboom 2014, 31–39). Alternatively, if one agent does one thing and another refrains from doing that thing, "and there is nothing about the agents' powers, capacities, states of mind, moral character and the like that explains this difference in outcome, then the difference really just is a matter of luck" (Mele 1999, 280).[7] An insightful underlying thought of proponents of the *Pure Luck* version, succinctly summarized by Mele, is that it is no more up to Peg at *t* whether she decides to *A* or instead decides to *B* than it is up to a genuinely random generator whether the number it outputs at *t* is 7 or 11 in a scenario in which it has only a few possible outputs at the time (Mele 2013, 244).

What fundamentally drives the *Pure Luck* version that Mele's thought concerning the randomizing machine captures is not what at rock bottom energizes the *No Explanation* version. As I have explained (e.g., Haji 2000, 2009, 2012b, 2016), what fuels the *No Explanation* version is the idea that the alleged outcome in *W**—Peg's deciding at *t* to *B*—is not appropriately connected to her reason-states or her deliberation, all of which favor her deciding to *A*. The issue meriting careful scrutiny concerns a detailed reason-explanation of why the agent—Peg in our example—seemingly akratically decides to *B* in *W**. We may concur that if Peg, for instance, were to fix her attention vividly on various salient factors during the time she deliberates about what it is best for her to do, this may raise significantly the probability that she decides at *t* to *A* (rather than *B*) in the actual world. To focus the enigma, imagine that in the actual world Peg successfully *does* do whatever she can do prior to *t* to raise the probability that she will decide at *t* to *A*, and *A*-s at *t*. Then in *W** in which at *t* Peg decides to *B*, it is also true that prior to *t*, Peg's relevant activities have raised significantly the probability that at *t* she will decide to *A*. Yet, at *t* she decides to *B* in *W**. Isn't this simply more fuel for the fire? What *is* the detailed reasons-explanation of her deciding at *t* to *B* when this decision is presumably akratic? All her pre-*t* reasoning supports her deciding to *A* in *W** but holding constant this reasoning she still decides at *t* to *B* in *W**. Needless to say, it will not do simply to claim that Peg's reasons that favor her deciding to *B* "prevail" in *W** (but not in the actual world). Why do they "prevail," given that *W**'s relevant pre-*t* history mirrors the relevant pre-*t* history of the actual world?

[7] See also, Mele (2006).

Reverting to our question, how is Annie's scenario in which Annie *A*-s at *t* for no reason relevantly similar to Peg's in which she indeterministically *A*-s at *t*? If the *No Explanation Version* is convincing, the similarity should be evident: Just as Annie's *A*-ing is not connected to her reason states, so Peg's *A*-ing is not appropriately connected to hers. But then the instances of their *A*-ing in the two cases are not intentional actions and, hence, cannot qualify as direct obligations. If one favors the *Pure Luck Version*, the germane lesson is that if an action is just a matter of luck (again, in the sense of 'luck' this version highlights), it seems that it cannot be permissible, impermissible, or obligatory for one. A comparison may be useful. Suppose you don't know the combination of a safe. But as a result of sheer luck you dial the correct combination on the very first attempt. It seems that you didn't have an obligation to open the safe on the first attempt. If impermissibility requires that one's actions not be fluky, in the relevant sense of 'fluky' that either version of the luck objection or the case of the safe bring out, and blameworthiness requires impermissibility, then the falsity of determinism is incompatible both with impermissibility (or, more generally, obligation) and blameworthiness.

I have argued that obligation (or impermissibility) requires that one could have done otherwise. Is the notion of "can" (or its cognates like "could") that obligation presupposes the strong (incompatibilist) notion (given exactly the same pre-*t* past and the laws of nature, although at *t* Ann did *A* she could at *t* have refrained from doing *A*)? Or is the notion some weak compatibilist notion (perhaps, as a rough first stab, although at *t* Ann did *A*, she would at *t* have refrained from *A*-ing if she had wanted, or attempted, or intended to refrain from *A*-ing)? In short, does obligation presuppose strong incompatibilist control or weak compatibilist control?

If *A* is a (direct) obligation for Annie, then Annie intentionally can do *A* and she intentionally can refrain from doing *A*. But if she *A*-s without reason, it seems that she does not intentionally *A*; again, if Annie intentionally *A*-s, Annie's *A*-ing must be suitably connected to her apt reason states. In addition, if *A* is a direct obligation for Annie, then it is not the case that *A* is fluky (in the sense of 'fluky') that either version of the luck objection highlights. Suppose one submits that, necessarily, one has a direct obligation to do *A* only if one can refrain from doing *A*, and the notion of "can" here is the strong incompatibilist one. In other words, assume that, necessarily, one has a direct obligation to do A only if A is a libertarian directly free action. Then no one in a suitably indeterministic world (and, needless to say, in a deterministic world) would have a direct obligation to do anything. (A world is suitably indeterministic only if the etiology of agents' actions in that world feature indeterminism at the right junctures; roughly, at the time of decision, the agent could have refrained from making that decision). For all putatively libertarian directly free actions are either not intentional actions (as the *No Explanation* version suggests) or are too fluky (as the *Pure Luck* version suggests). But why accept the view that obligation requires a sort of control the very exercise of which in performing actions would *undermine* obligation? With no good reason to support this view, it seems reasonable to conclude that the control that obligation requires is not strong incompatibilist control.

Ponder these claims:

R1: If impermissibility requires avoidability, and if blameworthiness requires impermissibility, then determinism is incompatible both with impermissibility (or, more generally, obligation) and blameworthiness unless obligation and blameworthiness require only weak compatibilist alternatives.

R2: If impermissibility requires that one's actions not be fluky, and blameworthiness requires impermissibility, then the falsity of determinism is incompatible both with impermissibility (or, more generally, obligation) and blameworthiness. The 'falsity of determinism' is shorthand for 'worlds in which determinism is false and the etiology of agents' actions in these worlds feature indeterminism at the time agents make decisions or perform overt actions.'

R1 is true if 'avoidability' denotes "strong" avoidability: consistent with the past and the laws remaining fixed, one could have done otherwise. For if impermissibility calls for one being able to do otherwise, and assuming determinism effaces alternatives, nothing is impermissible for any agent in a deterministic world. However, regarding impermissibility, if the "can" associated with one's being able to do otherwise when it is impermissible for one to do something is some weak compatibilist "can," then determinism does not preclude impermissibility (barring independent problems for the compatibility of obligation and determinism). As for R2, if obligation and impermissibility are incompatible with the sort of flukiness displayed in appropriate scenarios in which Peg indeterministically *A*-s, then R2 is true if the luck objection is sound; suitably indeterminsitic worlds will be devoid of moral impermissibility, and if blameworthiness presupposes impermissibility, devoid of blameworthiness too.

Consider another pair of claims.

R3: If impermissibility requires strong avoidability, then determinism is incompatible with impermissibility (or, more generally, obligation) unless obligation requires weak compatibilist alternatives.

R4: If impermissibility and blameworthiness require that one's actions not be fluky, then the falsity of determinism is incompatible both with impermissibility (or, more generally, obligation) and blameworthiness.

R3 like R1 is true if determinism expunges strong alternatives, and R4 like R2 is true if the luck objection is sound.

In conclusion, I first outlined why one might find oneself in a pickle if one accepts an alleged lesson of Frankfurt examples that blameworthiness does not require that one could have done otherwise (the "lesson"), but also looks favorably upon the "ought" implies "can principle (*OIC*), the principle that "ought not" amounts to "impermissible" (*Equivalence*), and the view that blameworthiness presupposes impermissibility (*BRI*). For, from *OIC* and *Equivalence*, we may infer that impermissibility requires avoidability. But this result, conjoined with the view that in Stage 2 of (suitably constructed) Frankfurt examples the agent could not have done otherwise, undercuts the lesson. I suggested, next, that French's promising way out of this puzzle is to reject *BRI* with his insight that ethics is not "monochromatic when the moral world of the ordinary person is so colorful." Whereas the moral hero goes (or may go) beyond the call, others do what it is permissibly suboptimal for them to do, and they may well be blameworthy for doing less than the morally permissible minimum. I then offered additional grounds to question *BRI*. One had to do with changing obligations over time. Another dwelt on cases relevantly analogous to ones in which persons of strong character (like the commendable mother) could not refrain from doing things that would have been morally obligatory for them if these things had not been unavoidable for them. These were cases in which persons performed actions that would have been morally impermissible for them had they not been unavoidable for them. Finally, pondering these sorts of cases generated discussion, first, of whether determinism precludes obligation and blameworthiness in virtue of precluding freedom to do otherwise; and, second, whether indeterminism precludes obligation and blameworthiness as a result of precluding non-fluky actions.

Acknowledgments Many thanks to Zachary Goldberg for the kind invitation to contribute to this volume, and for his useful comments. This paper was written during my tenure of a 2015–2016 Calgary Institute for the Humanities (at the University of Calgary) grant. I am most grateful to the Institute for its support.

References

Camus, Albert. 1946. The stranger. Translated by Stuart Gilbert. New York: Alfred A. Knopf, Inc.
Clarke, Randolph. 2003. *Libertarian accounts of free will*. New York: Oxford University Press.
Driver, Julia. 1992. The suberogatory. *Australasian Journal of Philosophy* 70: 286–295.
Frankfurt, Harry. 1969. Alternate possibilities and moral responsibility. *The Journal of Philosophy* 66: 829–839.
French, Peter. 1992. *Responsibility matters*. Lawrence: University Press of Kansas.
Haji, Ishtiyaque. 2000. Indeterminism, explanation, and luck. *The Journal of Ethics* 4: 211–235.
———. 2002. *Deontic morality and control*. Cambridge: Cambridge University Press.
———. 2009. *Incompatibilism's allure: Principal arguments for incompatibilism*. Peterbrough: Broadview Press.
———. 2012a. *Reason's debt to freedom: Normative appraisals, reasons, and free will*. New York: Oxford University Press.
———. 2012b. Reason, responsibility, and free will: Reply to my critics. *The Journal of Ethics* 16: 175–209.
———. 2016. *Luck's mischief: Obligation and blameworthiness on a thread*. New York: Oxford University Press.
Heyd, David. 1982. *Supererogation*. Cambridge: Cambridge University Press.
McNamara, Paul. 2011. Supererogation, inside and out: Toward an adequate scheme for common-sense morality. In *Oxford studies in normative ethics volume 1*, ed. Mark Timmons, 202–235. New York: Oxford University Press.
———. 2008. Praise, blame, obligation, and beyond: Toward a framework for the classical conception of supererogation and kin. In *Deontic logic in computer science*, ed. Ron van der Meyden and Leendert van der Torre, 233–147. Berlin: Springer Verlag.

———. 1996. Making room for going beyond the call. *Mind* 105: 415–450.
Mele, A. 2013. Moral responsibility and the continuation problem. *Philosophical Studies* 162: 237–255.
———. 2006. *Free will and luck*. New York: Oxford University Press.
———. 1999. Ultimate responsibility and dumb luck. *Social Philosophy and Policy* 16: 274–293.
Mellema, Gregory. 1991. *Beyond the call of duty: Supererogation, obligation, and offence*. Albany: State University of New York Press.
Pereboom, Derk. 2014. *Free will, agency, and meaning in life*. New York: Oxford University Press.
Sartre, Jean-Paul. 1953. *Being and Nothingness*. Trans. Hazel E. Barnes. New York: Washington Square Press.
van Inwagen, Peter. 1983. *An essay on free will*. Oxford: Clarendon Press.
Vranas, Peter B.M. 2007. I ought, therefore I can. *Philosophical Studies* 136: 167–216.
Zimmerman, Michael J. 2008. *Living with uncertainty*. Cambridge: Cambridge University Press.
———. 2006. Moral luck: A partial map. *Canadian Journal of Philosophy* 36: 585–608.
———. 1996. *The concept of moral obligation*. Cambridge: Cambridge University Press.

Responsibility, Obligation, and Climate Change

Tracy Isaacs

Introduction

Any philosopher who has ever worked on collective responsibility or collective agency (and indeed many who have not worked on these issues) has no doubt read Peter French's influential paper, "The Corporation as a Moral Person" (French 1979). The paper goes a long way to establishing that if any collective entities fulfill the conditions for moral responsibility or count as moral agents, corporations are the best candidates. They have clearly defined structures and decision-making procedures that, as French argues, make their reasons for action distinct from the reasons for action of their members. And they are themselves capable of intentional actions. But not all collective entities and groups have the tidy organizational structure of corporations.

In this chapter, I want to talk about a less frequently discussed contribution from French, found in his paper, "The Responsibility of Inactive Fictive Groups for Great Social Problems" (French 1998, 251–258). There he takes up the more slippery questions of agency and responsibility with respect to collections whose status as agents is less clear than the corporation. The issue of how to think about responsibility with respect to enormous global problems that clearly require collective solutions has taken on a pressing significance in recent decades because of the increasingly dire scenarios climate change threatens to bring. Individuals and

Many thanks to Zachary Goldberg for helpful comments on an earlier version and to an audience for lively and constructive Q and A at the Canadian Philosophical Association session on the first draft of this work, June 2015, Ottawa, Canada.

T. Isaacs (✉)
Western University, London, Canada
e-mail: tisaacs@uwo.ca

Z.J. Goldberg (ed.), *Reflections on Ethics and Responsibility*,
DOI 10.1007/978-3-319-50359-2_7

collectives (for example, nations) try to deflect responsibility for all sorts of reasons. Individuals worry that nothing they can do alone will make a difference. If I am the only one who changes my behavior, say by following Al Gore's advice to switch to "energy star" light bulbs, then my small contribution will make about as much difference as trying to douse a raging forest fire by spitting on it. For collectives, the objections often come down to economic considerations, an unwillingness to own up to the climate impact of past and current practice, the rejection of the "polluter pays" principle (Caney 2010), the rejection of the "ability to pay" principle (Caney 2010), and a refusal to make the sorts of changes to lifestyles, emissions, and consumption patterns that might make a difference.

Few will deny that an issue of this scale and kind requires a collective solution. If you look at the website for *An Inconvenient Truth*, Al Gore's 2005 film that attempted to wake up the world to the urgency of addressing climate change, you will see that the first three of the suggestions in the "Five Things You Can Do Now" section of the site invoke collective solutions, such as joining the Climate Reality Project, asking your employer to sign the Climate Declaration, and supporting companies that are doing good things on climate change. More recently, The United Nations Conference on Climate Change in November 2015 demonstrates a recognition that international agreements are essential if climate change is to be addressed at all.

In his paper on the responsibility of fictive groups, French grapples with the prospect of how groups that are in a sense not yet formed can be held responsible for the world's difficulties (such as widespread hunger, illness, poverty) in a constructive or meaningful way. The groups he wants to focus on are "fictive" in the sense that they have never "actually formed and so never performed any concerted action (or inaction)" (1998, 252). In the end, French claims that attempting to attribute responsibility to groups of people who might be, but are not at present, organized into effective collective agents "gets so incredibly complicated that we are likely to be wrapped up in an academic dispute over possible world scenarios so far into the future that any hope of actually making a positive contribution to solving the social problems will be utterly lost" (1998, 257).

My objective in this chapter is to engage with the ideas and issues French raises with respect to the idea of the responsibility of "inactive fictive groups" as it applies to responsibility for climate change. Of particular interest is his conclusion that "it would seem to make some practical sense to focus on already existing entities that have the resources and power to effect the changes we think morality recommends" (1998, 257). I challenge the focus on existing entities. Though we ought not ignore them, it is not enough to rely on existing groups. A coordinated effort that harnesses the potential of "fictive groups" and transforms them into real collective agents will have an impact collectively and individually because it will enable individual agents to insert themselves meaningfully into effective collective actions. This approach will allow individuals not just to feel good about themselves, but actually to make positive contributions that indeed will make a difference.

I use climate change as a focal point for this discussion because if anything is an issue of great global concern of the sort French talks about in his paper, climate change is. Despite that it arguably has a more serious impact on vulnerable groups such as the global poor, no one can completely escape its effects, which include rising sea levels and increased extreme weather events. As Simon Caney summarizes:

> The increased global warming will induce other malign effects, including higher deaths from drought and malnutrition. In addition to this the increased temperatures will increase the numbers of those exposed to infectious diseases, such as malaria, dengue and cholera. Higher temperatures will also result in death by heat stress. Climate change will, moreover, bring increased rainfall for some areas and this too will issue in harmful effects, causing destructive flooding. Finally, the majority of scientific experts hold that climate change heralds unpredictable weather events and such freak events will threaten human buildings and infrastructure. (2010, 203)

These are not simply natural occurrences attributable to expected and cyclical shifts in the conditions of our planet. Rather, the impact we are experiencing today and, based on climate models, we can expect to get more severe in the future, is the result of human activity. That is, climate change as we know it today is anthropogenic. It is not just that it has an impact on everyone, it is also that just about everyone makes some contribution to it. Given the scope of its impact, it cannot be ignored. Nor is it something that individual effort alone can influence.

As Caney points out, the facts about climate change give rise to two sorts of duties. In the first instance, there is a duty to mitigate its effects. This means reducing carbon emissions by doing such things as eating less meat to lower demand for livestock, the farming of which contributes enormously to the production of greenhouse gases, driving less frequently and driving more environmentally-friendly vehicles, and supporting initiatives of government and other organizations that promote changes with the goal of addressing climate change. But no amount of mitigating is going to protect us from experiencing some impact. Therefore, adaptation is also necessary—for example, when sea levels rise, communities will need assistance as people attempt to protect their homes and lands or seek safer ground. Thus the reality of climate change also yields what Caney has termed "duties of adaptation" (2010, 204). The reality and scale of climate change means that any plausible solutions will need to engage collective agents.

French opens his discussion by asking whether it is possible to hold such loosely structured groups responsible as "the cause of the problem" (whatever the great global problem may be) by virtue of their inattention to it. Think of climate change, which is the cumulative impact of generations of individuals and collectives living their lives in ways that are unsustainable when taken together. No one intended it. There was never and is not a joint effort, the goal of which was or is to destroy the planet by altering the climate. And individuals' actions cannot be isolated as "the cause" even though we might accurately say that just about everyone, on a daily basis, contributes. Though we should question whether it is actually the result of *wrongful* action, it is an incontestable fact that it is a harm to the planet and humanity. Many have pointed out further that affluent individuals and nations have contributed to the most. This makes French's fictive group of choice, "Upper- and Middle-Class People from the Western Industrial Democracies" (UMCPWIDs), appropriate for a discussion of climate change. What does French mean when he asks whether a group such as this might be considered responsible? We can break this question down into two different parts. First, we should think about how to understand responsibility. Second, we might ask what sort of group UMCPWIDs are and whether it makes sense to hold that kind of group responsible.

Taking up the first part of the question, the next section outlines the difference between responsibility and obligation at the individual and collective levels.

Responsibility and Obligation

Responsibility may be causal or moral, backward-looking or forward-looking. The discussion in this section serves two purposes. First, I distinguish between moral and causal senses of responsibility, making the claim that they are both typically "backward-looking" and attributable to individual human agents and to collective agents. Second, I distinguish between responsibility, on the one hand, and obligation or duty, on the other hand, making the claim that obligation and duty are forward-looking and that both individual human agents and collective agents may have duties or obligations.

For the purposes of this paper, *moral responsibility* is to be understood as the blameworthiness or praiseworthiness of agents for their actions. Agents are blameworthy when they perform actions that are morally impermissible (i.e. wrong) and praiseworthy when they do the right thing or go above and beyond. Of course, philosophers have written volumes about the conditions agents must fulfill in order to be considered morally responsible, both generally and in a particular case and about whether anyone actually fulfills those conditions. There is an ongoing dispute about whether moral responsibility is even possible. This paper does not venture into that territory. Rather, we will assume that moral responsibility is indeed possible, both at the individual and the collective levels.

Only moral agents are morally responsible in the blameworthy or praiseworthy sense. Earthquakes and tsunamis may cause lots of damage, but they are not "blameworthy" in any moral sense for the damage they cause because they lack the capacity for agency. In short, they are incapable of intentional actions and, therefore, lack a prerequisite for moral agency. Some philosophers of collective responsibility take issue with the claim that only agents may be responsible because they wish to make space for the possibility of collectives that are not agents but yet are responsible (Cripps 2011; Wringe 2014). I will return to this point later when considering the possible agency of what French calls "fictive groups." The pertinent point for now is that the difference between moral agents and natural disasters helps to highlight the difference between causal responsibility and moral responsibility. Earthquakes and tsunamis can be causally responsible because they can play a causal role in bringing about significant harm. Moral agents, by contrast, may be causally responsible and, in addition, morally responsible.

Both moral responsibility and causal responsibility are typically backward-looking attributions, applicable because of something in the past. I say "typically" because it is arguably the case that we might consider people causally or morally responsible in the present, as they are in the process of committing an act. The murderer may be blameworthy as she murders; the thief as he steals.[1] By contrast, we might sometimes understand responsibility in a more forward-looking way, as a responsibility to do something in the future. In everyday language, we often hear people talking about having *a responsibility*, when more technically they mean they have an obligation or duty. For example, when we say parents have a responsibility to look after their children, we mean they are obligated to do so.

It is also worth noting that responsibility and obligation can be individual or collective. Individual responsibility is a feature of individual human moral agents—such agents are morally responsible for their actions as individuals. Collective moral responsibility assumes that there are legitimate collective agents, that is, collective entities that are capable of collective action. Collective agents, such as organizations, corporations, governments, clubs, and the like, may be morally responsible—that is, praiseworthy or blameworthy—for their actions as collective agents. Similarly, individual and collective agents may both have moral duties or obligations.

The section "Collective Agents and Other Kinds of Collectives" takes a closer look at collective agency and types of collectives with the goal of gaining a clearer picture of what sort of things fictive groups are.

Collective Agents and Other Kinds of Collectives

What kind of collective agent, if agent at all, is a fictive group? There are two types of collectives that warrant agent status: organizations and goal-oriented collectives (Isaacs 2011, 24–28).

Organizations, such as corporations, governments, and non-profit groups, are highly structured, with formal decision procedures and clearly-articulated roles and responsibilities, often enshrined in governing documents such as constitutions or charters. Their structures generate and support agency by enabling intentional collective action. The organizational structure does this by providing mechanisms through which decisions may be made and actions may take place. This kind of collective agent is the least contested. Its structures make it easier to dissociate it, as an entity, from its members in so far as the same entity may persist through significant changes at the level of membership.

Goal-oriented collectives are less structured than organizations. As the name suggests, they exist when groups of people coalesce around a shared goal, the

[1] Zachary Goldberg raised this possibility in comments on an earlier version of this paper.

obtaining of which they pursue through collective action. They can be enormous, such as the goal-oriented collective that perpetrated the Rwandan genocide, or as small as two people going for a walk together or dancing the tango, or somewhere in between, such as a group of neighbors doing a community clean-up of their street in the early spring (Gilbert 1990; Isaacs 2011).

If there are only these two types of collective agents, then French's fictive groups, such as UMCPWIDs are not agents. They do not have the structures of an organization. Nor do they have a common goal around which they have coalesced and towards which they are acting together. Therefore, French is correct in his claim that UMCPWIDs is too unwieldy a group to think of as an agent. Not being agents calls into doubt their potential for being responsible, whether for actions or for omissions, because agency supports responsibility. Recall that earthquakes and tsunamis are not blameworthy in a moral sense because they lack the capacity for agency. They can not and do not perform intentional actions.

If UMCPWIDs are not collective agents, then what kind of group are they? Not all collectives are agents. Some, such as social groups, might constitute aggregates. In an aggregate, people are grouped together because they have some shared feature, such as belonging to the same religion, sharing a racial or ethnic identity, or being a member of the same gender-category. There are a range of reasons for carving out such groups, from the noble, since they may allow us to identify systemic patterns of privilege and disadvantage, to the not so noble, since identifying social groups can serve as the basis for racism, sexism, and other forms of discrimination. Social groups are aggregates. Apart from the shared characteristic, there is nothing else that holds these groups together. While we may not think of UMCPWIDs as a social group, per se, it makes sense to consider them a kind of aggregate in that having the shared feature (of being an upper- to middle-class person from a Western industrialized democracy) is what qualifies someone to be a member.

In considering groups whose agency is less clear than that of organizations and goal-oriented collectives, philosophers working on collective responsibility have variously referred to "random groups" (Held 1991),"loosely structured groups" (May 1998), "putative groups" (May 1998; Cripps 2011; Isaacs 2011), and, as we have seen in French's paper, "fictive groups" (1998). The members of these groups share some feature that may not necessarily be as socially and politically significant a feature as members of the same race or class or gender. It could be a passing shared feature, such as happening to be on a beach at the same time or being a member of the audience at a performance of *Hamlet.* These groups lack an organizational structure and, most notably, have no clear decision procedure that gives rise to collective action. The same question always arises in these discussions: can these types of groups be morally responsible? And if so, how?

In the next section, we take up the issue of responsibility in relation to groups that are not agents but may have agent potential.

Responsible Agency and Fictive Groups

What are we to make of these aggregates and their potential for moral responsibility? Before we consider how to answer this question, let us take a moment to reflect upon why we should care—generally and when thinking about climate change. Most thinkers seeking an answer to the question about what types of entities may be responsible are moved by a concern for accountability for wrongdoing. If we can think of such groups as collectively responsible, then we have someone or something to blame. But in addition to establishing blame, there is also a strong desire to establish accountability in a forward-looking sense. Attempts to establish responsible agency in these groups trade on a strongly felt intuition that those who cause something, particularly if they are morally responsible, ought to be held to account for its repair (Caney 2010; Isaacs 2014). Similar questions of agent-status or the possibility of responsibility have arisen for "the global collective," that is, all of humanity (Wringe 2014).

Note that the issue at hand is whether these types of collective entities should count as agents for the purposes of responsibility. This is not the same as the question of whether, in a particular case, such an entity is blameworthy or praiseworthy, that is, responsible, be it for actions or omissions. Rather, we are asking if it makes sense to think of them as agents at all.

On most criteria for agency, these types of groups do not count as collective agents. They lack the capacity for intentional collective action—no decision procedure, no sense of shared purpose and goals, no organizational structure for producing action. However, we cannot deny that they *could* become collective agents, especially goal-oriented collective agents, if the members came together around a shared goal and undertook collective action to achieve it. Consider, for example, a random collection of individuals on a beach. They might form themselves into a collective agent to save a group of children in peril, where the rescue requires a coordinated group effort. In this kind of case, the people on the beach may well have played no causal role in the children's peril. But let us assume that they are well-positioned to rescue the children if they band together and act quickly. When they do, they transform from a random group of individuals into an effective goal-oriented collective with a specific purpose. The key point here is that only in the transformation is effective collective agency possible.

The potential for these kinds of non-agent groups to become goal-oriented collectives suggests to some philosophers that these putative or would-be collective agents already have enough going for them to be considered not just obligated in a future-looking direction, but in some cases, such as climate change, in some sense responsible for the harms their members, cumulatively, have caused.

Elizabeth Cripps, for example, develops and defends a claim of weak responsibility, as follows:

> A number of individuals who do not yet constitute a collectivity (either formally, with an acknowledged decision structure or informally, with some vaguely defined common interest

> or goal) can be held *morally collectively* responsible for a harm which has been caused by the predictable aggregation of individual actions. (2011, 174)

She maintains that when these groups are collectively responsible in this weak sense, the individual members of these groups acquire individual duties to act in ways that do not contribute to the harm. "Predictable" is doing a lot of work in her analysis, since it sometimes takes some time before it is fair to assume that reasonable people should be aware of the harm their own actions, combined with the actions of others, might bring about.

In a similar vein, Bill Wringe argues that "the existence of collective obligations does not require that the collectives on whom the obligation falls be agents, but only that some agent or agents be answerable for the fulfillment or nonfulfillment of the obligation" (2014, 175). In other words, where there are groups of individual agents, collective obligation may exist in the absence of collective agency. Formal structure, he maintains, is not a requirement for collective obligation. He suggests that collective obligations help to ground individual obligations, and in the case of large global challenges such as climate change, these obligations take the form of obligations to support institutions, which constitute an effective collective level of agency. The conclusion, that individuals are in the end obligated to support existing institutions, bears close resemblance to French's conclusion that we ought to focus our attention on existing entities.

Elsewhere, I have argued that putative groups—groups that we can identify but have not in any way "formed" into agents—can have *putative* obligations, and that these obligations at the collective level can help to mediate and make sense of actions that individuals might take in the context of a collective action solution to a large global problem (Isaacs 2011, 130–155; Isaacs 2014). These putative obligations are would-be obligations that apply to the would-be agents. In this sense, they do not have the same binding force that actual obligations have. But they serve an important practical and conceptual function because they help to narrow the field of individual obligation, thus providing some direction for individuals to act in relation to the groups to which they belong, regardless of whether those groups are not as yet agents (Isaacs 2011, 130–155; Isaacs 2014). This narrowing function matters in scenarios such as climate change (or even would-be rescuers on a beach) because for a lot of people, the question is not, "should I do anything?" but rather, "what should I do?" People want to participate in improving the situation for themselves, more distant others, and future generations, but for challenges as enormous as climate change, they often feel as if their small contributions are hardly contributions at all. Finding ways to locate themselves within a group and, having done that, to determine constructive ways of taking part in the collective actions of that group makes "making a difference" a more achievable goal. Thus, we can think of putative groups and their putative collective obligations as helpful conceptual tools that enable the creation of effective goal-oriented collective agents and, at the same time, yield a clearer set of individual obligations to people who want to make a difference but do not know how.

When people can place themselves and their actions within a larger collective context, their understanding of what they are doing and, quite possibly, of what they have already done, can undergo a dramatic change. Drawing on Donald Davidson's action theory, consider that the actions of individuals bear different descriptions (Davidson 1980; Isaacs 2011, 101). Depending on which description we employ, we get more or less information about the action. To offer Davidson's well-worn example, with the same movement of my finger, I might flip the switch, turn on the light, and alert a burglar. We might think of these different descriptions as contracting and expanding to include more or less information about the consequences of simple bodily movements (Isaacs 2011, 101). For this reason, Joel Feinberg called it "the accordion effect" (1965).

This brief overview of action theory is relevant here because descriptions of individuals' actions might expand to include their contributions to collective outcomes and actions. For example, someone's self-understanding can change significantly if she starts to think of her consumption of animal products in terms of its cumulative impact—conjoined with other behaviors of her own and of others—as a contribution to climate change instead of simply as a dietary choice based on personal preference (a quite contracted, individualistic, and compartmentalized description). Similarly, looking to action potential, understanding our actions in terms of descriptions that capture the way they contribute to collective undertakings can open up new possibilities for effective agency. Moreover, some of the more expansive action descriptions may be normative in nature. Taking into account the obligations of putative groups, individuals can begin to understand what they might do as contributions to the fulfillment of collective obligations. In so doing, their actions take on a moral quality that they might otherwise not have.

In summary, though it does not make sense to think of these types of "fictive groups" as full-blown collective agents, conceptualizing them in terms of their potential to become goal-oriented collective agents through people coming together has positive normative outcomes. When individuals see these possibilities for themselves and think of their actions in a more collective light, opportunities arise for significant change through entities that do not yet exist as collective agents capable of intentional collective action. In what follows, we examine how thinking about groups that are not yet agents can help to give shape to individual and collective obligations concerning climate change. This possibility challenges French's claim that we ought to limit our focus to existing entities.

Climate Change, Collective Responsibility, and Collective Obligation

In a forward-looking sense, any solution to climate change will require a collective effort. Looking to existing entities, we already have a sense of some of the collective agents who might be able to contribute to a solution: governments, corporations, non-profit organizations with an environmental focus. But as we have seen, we may further think in terms of agents not yet formed, putative collective agents, who might be able to contribute to the solution. Those who are among the UMCPWIDs might form themselves into effective collective agents, mobilizing as goal-oriented collectives even if they are not yet there. Why? Very simply: because they can and, arguably, because they should.

This idea picks up on the "ability to pay" principle, in which those who are in a position to pay must, regardless of causal connection (Caney 2010, 204). Such an approach is wholly forward-looking, and captures the sort of scenario in which, like the people on the beach, taking a collective view of the situation yields a clear course of collective action and a clear view of the collective agent that ought to take it. But climate change differs from a drowning child situation because everyone, including those who would "rescue" or at least who would undertake a concerted effort to improve the situation, is also in peril. Climate change has a global impact.

Another respect in which this is different from the typical drowning child scenario is that the individuals who might become part of these coordinated efforts have also contributed to the current state of the climate. It is plausible to claim that it makes a moral difference that some groups of people have played a more significant causal role in the situation we find ourselves in today (Cripps 2011; Isaacs 2014). Agreements such as the Kyoto Protocol have taken this view, focusing on nations with industrialized economies. As the primary contributors because of their levels of production and consumption, they must now bear a heavier burden in a solution. Cripps singles out these "global elite" (2011, 184), similar to French's UMCPWIDs, as the cause of the harm, and identifies the world's poor and vulnerable populations as the recipients of it (2011, 184). She builds a case for collective responsibility for the global elite as a putative group, citing their actions as the primary cause of climate change and stating that they are the beneficiaries of it. Their responsibility, she argues, means that they may be coerced into fulfilling their environmental duties. This intuition lies behind the "polluter pays" principle: "those who caused the problem should pay" (Caney 2010, 204).

Some might object to implicating people on the basis of past contribution on the grounds that until quite recently people were ignorant of the impact our lifestyles were having on the planet. Cheshire Calhoun draws a distinction between two types of contexts in which moral ignorance may take place (Calhoun 1989). Moral ignorance occurs in a normal moral context or an abnormal moral context. In a normal moral context, someone may be morally ignorant of what everyone else knows to be morally true. For example, if someone pleads ignorance with respect to stealing a hat from a street vendor's display, that ignorance occurs in a normal moral context. Everyone knows or is expected to know that it is wrong to steal from street vendors. You have to pay for the items on street vendors' tables. But sometimes people are morally ignorant in a context where that ignorance is so widespread that it is difficult to grasp the mistake. For example, it used to be the case that it was not thought morally wrong to employ children, putting them to hard work for long hours with few or no breaks. In essence, in the early days of the industrial revolution, children, particularly poor children and orphans, were an exploited workforce. Were their employers wrong to employ them? Yes. Could they have been expected to know they were wrong? That is debatable when as a widespread social practice it was not thought wrong. If that is true, then according to this analysis the moral ignorance of the wrongness of child labor at that time in history took place in an abnormal moral context.

An abnormal moral context can serve as an excuse for ignorance. An excuse exonerates people from blame while at the same time affirming that they acted wrongly. The same can be said when we contribute to harms of which we are unaware. In those cases, we are ignorant of the harms to which we contribute. That ignorance takes place in something like an abnormal context—no one can be expected to know (Calhoun 1989; Isaacs 2011, 156–176).

Some might challenge the possibility that ignorance, no matter how widespread, might exculpate. Michelle Moody-Adams, for example, argues that in many cases, we should be suspicious of moral ignorance because it could be "affected," in the sense that people could know but do not want to know (Moody-Adams 1994). She maintains that we need to stay alert to the distinction between what is difficult and what is impossible. Or, someone might ask how widespread does it need to be to have this excusing effect? Throughout a particular society? Multiple societies? Over generations?[2] Moody-Adams might be right that some ignorance is affected, and we can concede that the borders between abnormal and normal contexts are fuzzy. Nevertheless, in at least some cases it would be unreasonable to expect people to know. And arguably, at least for a long span of human history, the epistemic position of the general population with respect to climate change was one of genuine ignorance.

Even if we assume for the sake of argument that not all ignorance is culpable and that ignorance in an abnormal moral context may serve as a legitimate excuse, knowledge, including moral knowledge, evolves and progresses. Abnormal moral contexts shift. They may become normal relative to particular issues. For example, ignorance of the wrongness of slavery no longer serves as an excuse because the moral context has normalized with respect to slavery: people are expected to know that it is wrong. It is no longer reasonable to believe it is morally permissible to own slaves. Hence, no one now can claim ignorance as an excuse. We live in a normal moral context concerning the wrongness of slavery.

We might think similarly about the way our lifestyles contribute to climate change. Though there was a time when we could claim ignorance concerning the harmful impact of our behavior on the planet, that time has now passed. It is simply not the case that reasonable people can claim ignorance as a justification for continuing to act in just the same way they always have. As Catriona McKinnon states in her paper about the current generation's unique position with respect to climate change mitigation, "Generations prior to us did not know the havoc they were wreaking, and it will be too late for those who come after us. The current generation is drinking in the last chance saloon of CC mitigation" (McKinnon 2011, 197).

[2]Zachary Goldberg raised these possibilities in his comments on an earlier draft.

"The current generation" is as unstructured and fictive a group as the global elite or UMCPWIDs. As we saw earlier, these groups are not collective agents. Attempting to hold them responsible is exactly the sort of view French rejects when he claims that it would just be too hard to figure out and, therefore, would be ineffective (1998, 257). The whole purpose, he claims, of holding such groups responsible is "to provoke otherwise inactive people to do the right thing in the first place" (1998, 257). Given his view that holding fictive groups responsible will fail to achieve the desired outcome, French concludes that we ought to focus on existing entities to get the job done.

French is right to think that it is complicated. Caney considers a similar objection, namely, that in order to use the Polluter Pays Principle "we need to be able to specify the harm done and trace it back to the causal actors and where either the nature of the harm is uncertain or unpredictable ... or the link between climate change and the harm is uncertain..., then this cannot be done" (2010, 207). Ultimately, Caney responds that the objection does not provide sufficient reasons to reject the principle. As he notes, practicalities do not, on their own, undermine the force of moral principles. This is not an issue of being able to use "ought implies can" to shirk a moral duty by claiming one cannot fulfill it. As the science on climate change improves, some scientists are "increasingly confident that it will be possible to attribute specific events to climate change" (2010, 257). Establishing at least some causal narrative concerning climate change is not completely out of the question.

But recall that though it makes sense to argue that those who played a causal role in bringing about a harm may be morally required to bear a heavier burden in the solution, those are not the only grounds for collective or individual obligation. The people on the beach did not have to have caused the children's peril to be obligated to rescue them. Nevertheless, this is not a strictly consequentialist view that makes demands only on the basis of what position people are in to act. While ability to act is relevant, prior contribution also matters. These two considerations combined help to identify putative collective agents because, as some have argued (Cripps 2011; MacKinnon 2011), "the global elite" or the "current generation" contribute more intensely in a causal if not blameworthy manner to the situation ("polluter pays" and furthermore collective agents made up of such people have the ability to enact change ("ability to act").

Besides the complexity of doing otherwise, there are other reasons for taking issue with French's claim that we should focus on already existing entities. We have reasons to believe that more initiative may be needed than what existing entities have to offer.

Existing entities such as governments and corporations have so far not proven themselves to be effective agents for change where climate change is concerned. International summits on climate change have seen some nations refuse to sign agreements at all, others willing only to sign watered down agreements that do not force real change. Or, when they do agree to more demanding revisions in current practices and seriously reduced emissions targets, they fail to follow through. Consider, for example, the Kyoto Protocol, drafted in 1997 to take effect in 2005, which was an international and supposedly legally binding agreement among industrialized nations to set targets for reduced greenhouse gas emissions (United Nations 1998). The most industrialized country in the world, the United States, refused to ratify the agreement (United Nations 2014a). Canada signed off originally, but signaled in December 2011 that it would withdraw its ratification effective December 2012 (United Nations 2014b). And while the Protocol has many signatories, the conduct of these two significant parties suggests that counting on the governments of "the global elite" to make appropriate commitments is not sufficient. While the late-2015 agreement in Paris (European Commission 2016) and the more recent push to move the year it comes into effect from 2020 to 2017 indicate a renewed international commitment (Goldenberg 2016), only time will tell how effective it will be.

A further worry about settling for the efforts of existing entities is that it could lead to complacence at the level of individuals. As we saw above, when individuals can be understood and can see themselves as members of groups, even putative groups, this enables a clearer picture of their obligations as individuals. But if the focus of attention is on governments and other already-formed collective entities, those individual obligations remain foggy and indeterminate in the face of an issue of such scale. The reason they remain indeterminate is that when seen only in the context of individual action, anything an individual might do seems ineffective (recall the futility of spitting on the forest fire). When individuals experience their actions as ineffective, making no difference one way or the other, there is no strong motivation to act. Hence, complacency is a predictable reaction. Thus, even though collective action is required, we want an approach that motivates individuals to see themselves as members of effective collectives. Relying heavily on existing entities is not a good way to achieve that outcome.

In the section "Responsible Agency and Fictive Groups", the idea of putative collective agents gained some traction. Among its merits, this idea enables individuals to see themselves as members of effective collectives and potential collective agents. The transformative potential of putative groups to become collective agents provides opportunities for individuals to participate in collective action. If only existing collective entities matter and get our attention, then we deny individuals opportunities for exercising their potential in coordinated efforts, joint ventures, and goal-oriented collectives. It is at the intersection of individual and collective responsibility, and individual and collective obligation, that individuals can imagine themselves acting, together with others, in ways that actually do make a difference. Without these imaginative possibilities, individuals have little reason to think of themselves as effective. Therefore, thinking of the agent-potential of new, not simply current, collective entities has an empowering effect on individuals who would be their members while at the same time helping to shape obligations at the individual and collective levels, making them clearer and more accessible, and therefore easier to fulfill.

Conclusion

People sometimes hesitate over the idea of collective agency, responsibility and obligation because instead of thinking about it in terms of opportunities for effective action, they worry that it will implicate or obligate innocent people who happen to be members of blameworthy collectives. But responsibility and obligation at the collective level does not have any necessary connection to responsibility and obligation at the individual level. That is, collective responsibility and obligation do not distribute in any direct way to individuals who are members of responsible collectives. It is not as if, having established that some collective is blameworthy, we have thereby established that every member of the collective is blameworthy for the collective's action. The reason for this is quite straightforward: collective agents, not individual human agents, perform collective actions. This is the case in collectives of small or large scale. Quite literally, it takes two, not just one, to tango. A corporate action is the action of a corporation, not of an individual person or even a group of individual persons. Decision procedures and corporate structures that empower individuals in relation to roles are essential for these actions to take place. Government decisions are made and enacted by governments. Since collective agents are the subjects of collective actions, they are also the subjects of attributions of collective responsibility and collective obligation. If a collective is responsible for its actions or obligated to perform some act in the future, it is not the case that individual members are responsible for that same act or obligated to do that same thing. Why not? As just noted, individuals cannot perform collective actions.[3]

This claim can be misunderstood to imply that individuals are never responsible or obligated in collective action scenarios. But that is not the case. Individuals are often implicated in collective action situations and, as we have seen, collective obligations, even putative collective obligations, can generate obligations at the individual level. What we need to avoid, however, is the conflation of collective responsibility with individual responsibility and collective obligation with individual obligation. Being a member of a blameworthy collective does not automatically render a person blameworthy, or if individual blame can be established, individuals will not be blameworthy for exactly the same thing as the collective. To the extent, however, that individuals' actions contribute to blameworthy collective actions, we gain a better understanding of the moral quality of their actions when we think of them in the context of the larger collective action of which they are a part. Recall the brief overview of action theory and the accordion effect discussed earlier. The same person's action might be described as "a contribution to genocide" or "a mass murder." Notwithstanding that both are morally deplorable actions, contributing to genocide has a different moral quality to it. Genocide is not the same as murder or mass murder, in so far as it targets people on account of their membership

[3]For a more fully developed account of this view, see Isaacs, *Moral Responsibility in Collective Contexts*, chapters 1 and 2.

in a group with the intent of destroying the group (United Nations 1948, Article II). It may include mass murder, but when we get more information about the same act, learning that it was a contribution to genocide, we learn new, morally relevant information that sets the act in a more collective context. Similarly, on the praiseworthy side of responsibility, doing my part with others to mitigate climate change has a laudable moral quality that simply deciding to ride your bicycle to work instead of driving, taken in isolation, does not. This does not mean that riding your bicycle to work cannot be a morally laudable action. It means only that *under that* description we have no idea that it is. Again, we might describe the same action in different ways and each may give us more or less information. Some of these bits of information may tip us off to moral qualities that our action have, others do not. Some might capture a more collective understanding of our actions in concert with the actions of others, others might not (Isaacs 2011, 97–102).

Why is this important in the case of climate change? Where climate change is concerned, taking a collective view can help to counter individuals' claims that they can do nothing to make a difference. While in some cases laments along the lines of "what difference will my small action make?" might come across as lazy ways of justifying the status quo, in other cases they may express legitimate worries about whether their actions might actually make a difference. These different ways of thinking about our actions can help people see their actions' impact as parts of the collective efforts of goal-oriented collectives.

This is not to say that we should ignore existing entities altogether. Instead, we want to encourage the formation of new groups as well. For this, we need to look to the potential of putative groups, such as UMCPWIDs and the global elite, to organize in ways that allow individuals to act effectively together. Does this mean that these groups are responsible, in the blameworthy sense, for the existence of climate change? No, it does not. They are not responsible because they do not constitute a collective agent that can be considered responsible. Similarly, individuals cannot be considered responsible for what they could not have been expected to know. Climate change, in the first instance, is more a harm than a wrong. However, the days of not being expected to know have come to an end. Continued inaction in this matter will take individuals and existing collectives into the territory of moral wrong. This is where putative collective agents can do noble work, offering real possibilities for individuals who wish to take part in the actions of goal-oriented collectives.

There is an undertone in moral philosophy that responsibility and obligation are burdens to be avoided at all costs. We want to be free moral agents, on the one hand, but if most moral philosophy is right, we spend a lot of time trying to duck out of morality's requirements. I want to suggest that in many cases this just is not the truth. We are not all like Gyges, looking for ways to shirk our moral duty and not get caught. Rather, there are a good many people who, given the opportunity, are interested in doing their part, particularly where climate change is concerned because people are acutely aware that it has an impact on all of us. Limiting action to existing collective entities denies these people valuable moral opportunities that they may, indeed, be seeking.

References

An inconvenient truth: Official website of the award-winning film. http://www.takepart.com/an-inconvenient-truth/film. Accessed 31 Mar 2016.

Calhoun, Cheshire. 1989. Responsibility and reproach. *Ethics* 99(2): 389–406.

Caney, Simon. 2010. Climate change and the duties of the advantaged. *Critical Review of International Social and Political Philosophy* 13(1): 203–228.

Cripps, Elizabeth. 2011. Climate change, collective harm and legitimate coercion. *Critical Review of International Social and Political Philosophy* 14(2): 171–193.

Davidson, Donald. 1980. *Essays on actions and events*. New York: Clarendon.

European Commission. 2016. Paris agreement. http://ec.europa.eu/clima/policies/international/negotiations/paris/index_en.htm. Accessed 19 Apr 2016.

Feinberg, Joel. 1965. Action and responsibility. In *Philosophy in America*, ed. Max Black, 134–160. Ithaca: Cornell University Press.

French, Peter. 1979. The corporation as a moral person. *American Philosophical Quarterly* 16(3): 207–215.

———. 1998. The responsibility of inactive fictive groups for great social problems. In *Individual and collective responsibility*, ed. Peter French, 251–258. Rochester: Schenkman Books.

Gilbert, Margaret. 1990. Walking together: A paradigmatic social phenomenon. *Midwest Studies in Philosophy* 15: 1–14.

Goldenberg, Suzanne. 2016. US and China lead push to bring Paris climate deal into effect early. The Guardian, April 18. http://www.theguardian.com/environment/2016/apr/18/us-and-china-lead-push-to-bring-paris-climate-deal-into-force-early. Accessed 19 Apr 2016.

Held, Virginia. 1991. Can a random collection of individuals be morally responsible? In *Collective responsibility: Five decades of debate in theoretical and applied ethics*, ed. Larry May and Stacey Hoffman, 89–100. Lanham: Rowman and Littlefield.

Isaacs, Tracy. 2011. *Moral responsibility in collective contexts*. New York: Oxford University Press.

———. 2014. Collective responsibility and collective obligation. *Midwest Studies in Philosophy* 38: 40–57.

May, Larry. 1998. Collective inaction and moral responsibility. In *Individual and collective responsibility*, ed. Peter French, 211–231. Rochester: Schenkman Books.

McKinnon, Catriona. 2011. Climate change justice: Getting motivated in the last chance saloon. *Critical Review of International Social and Political Philosophy* 14(2): 195–213.

Moody-Adams, Michelle. 1994. Culture, responsibility, and affected ignorance. *Ethics* 104(2): 291–301.

United Nations. 1948. Convention on the prevention and punishment of the crime of genocide.

———. 1998. Kyoto protocol to the United Nations framework convention on climate change.

———. 2014a. Status of ratification of the Kyoto protocol. United Nations Framework Convention on Climate Change. http://unfccc.int/kyoto_protocol/status_of_ratification/items/2613.php. Accessed 19 Apr 2016.

———. 2014b. Canada withdrawal. Status of ratification of the Kyoto protocol. United Nations Framework Convention on Climate Change. http://unfccc.int/kyoto_protocol/background/items/6603.php Accessed 19 Apr 2016.

Wringe, Bill. 2014. From global obligations to institutional obligations. *Midwest Studies in Philosophy* 38: 171–186.

The Ethical Morass of College Sports

William J. Morgan

> *There is plenty of reason for pessimism, but it would be better to do what one can to get people to follow an improbable scenario, than to simply throw up one's hands.*
>
> Richard Rorty (2006)
>
> *Everything I know about morality and the obligations of men, I owe it to football [soccer].*
>
> (Albert Camus 1960)

Elite college sports are an ethical minefield. Wherever you decide to set foot within their carefully demarcated precincts you will likely find your confidence in the moral ideals you hold dear severely tested. This is especially so of its two most lucrative sports, football and men's basketball. To be sure, neither the astonishing amount of money lavished on these two sports nor the huge public followings they typically command pose a serious problem for their professional counterparts, since professional football and men's basketball make no bones about their avaricious intentions. But college sports, we are told over and over again, are supposed to be importantly different from professional ones. Specifically, they are supposed to be about more laudable educational and moral values such as teaching moral character, fair play, respect for and appreciation of excellence, teamwork, perseverance, and the like. And it is because they stand for such values, we are further told, that they belong on college campuses since their main aims and values are fully consonant with the educational and ethical missions of institutions of higher education. The complication, of course, is that aside from the university names and logos that adorn the uniforms of student football and basketball players, one would be hard pressed to detect any substantive differences between the college and professional games.

That is why it will come as no surprise that both supporters and critics of big time intercollegiate football and men's basketball insist they need urgent and significant reform, that simply abiding the status quo is no longer an option. Two main camps have emerged as the leading forces behind the athletic reform movement, which the

W.J. Morgan (✉)
University of Southern California, Los Angeles, CA, USA
e-mail: wjmorgan@chan.usc.edu

Z.J. Goldberg (ed.), *Reflections on Ethics and Responsibility*,
DOI 10.1007/978-3-319-50359-2_8

New York Times Op-Ed columnist Joe Nocera colorfully dubbed "Team Reform" and "Team Market" (2012). Roughly put, proponents of Team Reform argue that it is the massive commercialization of college sports that have been their chief educational and moral undoing, and that the only way to make them right again and to justify their presence on college campuses is to contain if not quash these pernicious commercial forces. By contrast, proponents of Team Market argue that what plagues college sports today is not their undeniable commercialization, which is in any event, they confidently assert, too entrenched in the present intercollegiate athletic scene to be reined in let alone rooted out, but the clearly unjust way the distribution of these monies are meted out. After all, they point out, it is the athletic labor of student-athletes that drives the vast financial engine of college sports, and that, as a result, should be fairly compensated for their collective efforts.

As we shall see, French opts for the reform advocated by Team Market because he too thinks, in Tyler Branch's provocative words, that "The tragedy at the heart of college sports is not that some athletes are getting paid, but that more of them are not" (2011, 4). French not only wants to rectify this distributive injustice by paying college football and men's basketball players, but by paying them in terms proportional to the actual revenue they bring in. The specific justification he offers as to why college athletes should be paid as their professional peers are is that an important part of the mission of colleges and universities is to provide public service to the larger community, something which big-time sports do especially well by putting on athletic extravaganzas that draw impressively large numbers from the surrounding community. He also shares with other members of Team Market the view that coming clean as to the true commercial designs of elite intercollegiate sports is far more honest and ethical than to pretend they are something that they most assuredly are not: amateur affairs that teach moral virtues of fairness and respect for others.

I find French's case against Actually Existing Elite College Sports completely persuasive and devastating in its overall impact. No one who reads this part of his account with an open mind, I believe, will be able to put stock any longer in the ways they have traditionally been defended and justified. But when French turns his attention to their reform, to his claim that the best way to fix college sports is essentially to give market forces a free pass in running them so long as the athletes themselves are fairly remunerated for their efforts and not burdened by unnecessary academic obligations, I have serious doubts. Specifically, I have two principal misgivings. First, the resort to market norms both in and outside the university has become, of late, the go to remedy for just about everything that is thought to ail the social practices we presently cherish, and that far from making things better has made them much worse by undermining what it is that we most value about these practices, to include, of course, college sports. Second, despite French's insistence he has no beef against sports themselves, he does, I argue, end up shortchanging the positive non-moral and moral values sports at their best have to offer to student-athletes and their non-athletic peers, not to mention the faculty and the larger community. That is why I will argue that when suitably protected from the commercial forces that currently dictate when and how they are conducted and played, college sports can make a far more central educational and moral contribution to campus life than simply entertaining those who come to watch them.

French's Case Against Elite College Sports

I will focus principally on the moral part of French's critique of Actually Existing College Sports, since it is this part of his analysis that I find the most compelling and interesting. That is not to say that other parts of his critique that deal, for instance, with the financial justification of big time football and men's basketball – that they bring in significant sums of money to the university that is, or at least could be, used to finance its academic programs, are either unimportant or uninteresting. They are neither, since, for example, it will likely come as a big surprise to many to learn, as French reveals, that most of these college athletic powerhouses not only lose money but hemorrhage money (2004, 81).[1] What is surprising about this dirty big secret is that these elite powerhouses bring in so much money from ticket sales, broadcast rights, athletic merchandise, and the like, that it seems unimaginable they could possibly lose money let alone lose a lot of money. But most of them do for the simple reason that they spend far more than they bring in, and hide their extravagant spending by creative accounting tricks like, for instance, assigning coaches' salaries, a very large expense, to the general faculty salary pool. As eye-opening and troubling as the athletic department's financial profligacy and accounting sleights of hand are, not to mention the other non-moral parts of French's analysis, I find his moral critique of Actually Existing College Sports even more eye-opening and troubling. That is because, as we shall shortly see, he makes a strong case that college sports are essentially amoral, if not immoral, affairs, in which the vaunted moral ideals that they supposedly stand for and appeal to in order to justify their formal ties to institutions of higher education do not figure in the least in their actual practice. This is a stunning indictment of the college athletic scene to say the least.

French's critique of the moral failings of college sports takes aim at the two central moral ideals that are claimed to inform everything that they are about and do. The first is the well-worn claim that college sports are amateur enterprises that prize above all fairness and a love of sport for the sake of sport itself. By amateurism, however, French doesn't just have in mind fair conduct and participation in sport for the sheer love of the game, but as well several other features of the amateur ideal as originally envisioned by its nineteenth century creators. This more comprehensive

[1] The university of Michigan is a good example. As its former president, James Duderstadt, reported after its football team won the national championship in 1997, the athletic department ran a deficit of close to $ 3 million dollars that had to be covered by money taken from the general university fund (French, 82). This was, Duderstadt hastened to add, the rule rather than the exception throughout his reign as president.

notion of amateur sport claims that because sport is an avocation rather than a vocation, one should not only play fairly and for the love of the game, but additionally, refrain from trying too hard to win, avoid specialization in one sport, and eschew professional coaches. The traditional amateur ideal also included a well-noted social class animus against the engagement of the working class in gentlemanly athletic pursuits (11).

The second moral ideal of college sports often used to justify their affiliation with institutions of higher education is that they teach moral character. The aim of sport at this level, it is contended, is not just to play well, to aspire to athletic excellence, but to play virtuously, to exhibit loyalty, teamwork, dedication, and respect for authority in one's play (31). So understood, athletic accomplishment cannot be, and should not be, divorced from moral accomplishment, from playing the game in the "right" way. And here is where playing the game the right way leads us back to the amateur ideal. For if sport is to fulfill its moral educative role, if it is to teach character, it must curb the motive to win since if left unchecked playing in a morally upstanding way does not stand much of a chance. According to this view, therefore, the motive most conducive to virtuous athletic conduct is to play the game for its own sake, for the sheer joy of athletic competition itself (35).

French effectively argues that these two supposed moral ideals of college sports lack justificatory force because they have no basis whatsoever in fact. So while they undoubtedly look good on the pages of the mission statements disseminated by athletic departments and the official policy statements issued by their governing body the National Collegiate Athletic Association (NCCA), they are not worth the paper they are printed on, he argues, since they have no actual bearing on what takes place on college playing fields and courts (50). On the contrary, the ruling principle of Actually Existing College Sports can be summed up in one pithy and instantly recognizable mantra, "winning isn't everything, it's the only thing."

Hence, both the amateur ideal and the moral education ideal were sacrificed on the altar of, what else, the obsession with winning that gripped both the college and professional versions of these games. For when winning becomes the name of the game, the principal grounds upon which student athletes, coaches, and athletic administrators are evaluated, as French adroitly shows, cultivating an intrinsic regard for sports and educating players to morally respect their opponents become at best afterthoughts, and at worst obstacles to athletic success. Rather the order of the day, for coaches at least, is to ensure players toe the party line, which means above all doing whatever the coaches tell them to do without asking why. That explains why everything players do on and off the field is carefully scripted, constantly monitored, and painstakingly regulated by their athletic superiors. That this hardly makes for a moral education is obvious, since it not only deprives players of any opportunity to think for themselves as to how they should act in or outside of sport, but strongly admonishes against moral reflection of any kind (52). Not surprisingly, the empirical evidence confirms our worst suspicions in this regard, since it shows that moral respect for oneself and one's opponents is the exception rather than the rule in college sports, and, conversely, that egocentric, selfish behavior is the rule rather than the exception both on and off the playing field. French aptly sums up the gloomy findings, and conjectures, correctly to my mind, why proponents of college sports continue to give lip service to this wholly discredited idea that sports teach moral character, "the overarching conclusion of the empirical studies is that all this business about the inherent virtues of athletic participation is a myth concocted by the athletic enthusiasts to justify the inclusion of athletics in educational institutions" (55).

It may reasonably be asked at this point that if college sports can't be justified on moral grounds, not to mention on the other non-moral grounds typically offered in their defense, then on what grounds, if any, can they be justified? French's answer directs us back to the mission statements of colleges and universities, in which he asks us to take note of the increasingly wide-ranging ways these institutions have articulated the roles they think they should play in the lives of their students and the larger public. For what we will find if we canvas these various mission statements is that universities for some time now have rejected any notion that they are merely single-purpose institutions devoted exclusively to academic and moral education. Rather, they prefer to think of themselves as multi-purpose institutions that, in addition to their long-standing commitment to classical and scientific studies, are also committed to professional studies (the training of doctors, lawyers, teachers, entrepreneurs, etc.), and, most importantly for our purposes, to public service. And it is this commitment to professional service, French argues, that provides the best defense of college sports, since the entertainment they provide to the multitudes that flock to see them, in French's own words, "likely touch the lives of more members of the public in a positive and effective way than any other service the university may extend in this direction" (115). The biggest mistake the critics of these sports make, therefore, is clinging to their antiquated, tunnel-vision view that colleges and universities are exclusively in the education business. For if we (wrongly) think of universities as only being in the education business, then sports have no business being on college campuses, since, as the empirical news makes crystal clear, they are anything but educational endeavors. Indeed, when only viewed from this educational perspective, what goes on in athletic departments, to quote perhaps French's favorite observer of the contemporary intercollegiate athletic scene, Harold W. Stoke, is "inexplicable, corrupting, and uncontrollable" (quoted in French, 114). But if we (correctly) view them as the multi-purpose institutions they profess to be, which means we take into account their service obligations to the public and thus their obligation to entertain the public, then what goes on in these sports is perfectly coherent, justified, and utterly respectable.

The idea that colleges and universities are by virtue of their commitment to public service not only justified in having athletic departments on their campus, but in charging them with putting on athletic spectacles for the enjoyment and pleasure of the masses, is a hard one to swallow for many people, especially the faculty. To put it bluntly, it is a fairly radical idea, but one French seems to embrace. I say seems here because many of the arguments French advances to support it are cribbed, with due attribution, from an earlier essay written by the previously mentioned Harold Stoke, whom he credits with having "a far better grasp than many who have participated in the debate about intercollegiate athletics" (119). As a consequence, it is not always clear when French is simply channeling Stoke's view of college sports as public entertainments and when he is directly advocating for it. But he comes perhaps closest to endorsing it root and branch when he enthusiastically seconds the call by Michael Crow, the president of his own home institution, Arizona State University, that major public universities should stop thinking of themselves as state agencies, in effect, as public entities, and start thinking of themselves as self-supporting entrepreneurial entities who can financially benefit from serving the needs of the localities in which they are housed (120). While Crow had principally in mind technology transfers from theoretical and applied scientific and engineering research, French takes special note of how well it fits the athletic entertainment model. This, of course, is the model athletic departments have been following for some time. But what they failed to do, and what French exhorts them to do in the spirit of reform, is "to carry the entertainment model to its proper conclusions with respect to the rights and welfare of the athletes who make it all possible" (121). That means a number of things, to include making academic accommodation to the athletes' interests and needs when it comes to admission and taking courses, and even perhaps whether they want to be students at all, since, after all, universities recruit them not to excel in the classroom but on the playing field. But above all else, French underscores, it means compensating them proportionately to the revenue they generate. Short of just compensation for their arduous efforts, the amenities they presently receive, from separate dorms, training centers, to paid travel, "amount to little more than fancier plantations than those that existed in the antebellum American South" (121).

Critical Assessment of French's Reform Proposal

We are now in a position to ask what French's proposal to reform elite college sports has going for it critically speaking. As I see it, once again, the answer to this question turns on the normative, and more specifically, moral contribution it makes to this highly charged issue. I think its principal merit in this regard is its simple candor and honesty, its refusal to countenance the blatant hypocrisy of the present college athletic system and the baseless rhetoric that sustains it. It makes no pretense, therefore, that elite college sports are educational undertakings, pursued for the love of the athletic struggle itself, and arranged and conducted to teach student-athletes important moral lessons that will serve them well both on and off the playing field. Part of the normative strength of French's reform effort here derives, interestingly enough, from its descriptive fidelity both to the actual practice of college sports, in which, as duly noted, the untrammeled pursuit of winning has been the norm for decades, and to the actual wording of the mission statements of universities, in which, as also duly noted, the commitment to public service has been well documented. But a no less important part of the normative strength of French's proposed reform is that by de-mythologizing the fabled, reality-challenged conceptions of the aims of college sports perpetuated by the grandees of the intercollegiate sports' world, we will not only be able to see these sports for what they truly are (public entertainments), but what we must and ought to do to ensure the rights and the welfare of the athletes upon whose labor the entire entertainment franchise depends are honored. That entails, as we have seen, paying them what they are due, and eliminating academic constraints that get in the way of fulfilling their obligation to entertain the public.

However, if we further ask, as is now appropriate, what French's reform does not have going for it critically speaking, I am forced to say the same thing that I just said it has going for it: its candid and resolute market approach to the whole problem. For whatever the aforementioned virtues of French's spot-on diagnosis that intercollegiate football and men's basketball have become mainly commercial spectacles and his remedy of financially remunerating the grueling and risky labor of the athletes who make it all possible have in their favor, are called into question by his presumption that the commercial spectacles they have become is not itself to be faulted and, therefore, targeted for reform. Framing the moral issue in this way as one essentially of distributive justice, of rectifying the inequitable way in which those who control the market forces that fuel the commercialization of these elite college sports financially compensate the players' performances, strikes me as question-begging precisely because it glosses over the heavily commercially clad elephant in the room. For not only does it ignore the very real and extensive damage the commercialization of these sports has already visited upon them, but worse, it gives the market forces behind their commercialization a free pass to continue to impose their egoistic, profit-driven logic on them without regard either for their internal goods or the distinctive reasons people value athletic endeavors in the first place. If there is any doubt that French's reform is as market-friendly as I claim and worry, I need only point out that both French and his normative mentor in all things athletic, Harold Stoke, made their argument that intercollegiate football and men's basketball are best thought of and treated as public entertainments fully mindful of the fact that so far as their fans are concerned only winning teams are entertaining teams.[2] This suggests that not only do French and Stoke give a normative green light to athletic departments to continue to pour as much money as it takes to field winning (entertaining) teams, but do so without bothering to put in place any speed bumps that might at least slow the pace in which these elite sports are commercialized. But I think, and will argue, that giving market forces such wide berth in the affairs of these athletic endeavors works not only to the detriment of the universities that sponsor and house them but to the games themselves.

Let me begin with the harm the commercialization of college sports has done, and continues to do, to the colleges and universities that unapologetically sponsor and promote big-time athletic programs that place such a high premium on winning.

[2]I think I can safely say this with regard to elite intercollegiate football and men's basketball, since I am not aware of any example of outlier examples in professional sports like Chicago Cubs fans, who evidently, and I might add inexplicably, savor losing as much as winning if past history is any indication, in the ranks of these premier college sports.

That harm, I argue, has to do with their providing a financially costly service to the public virtually devoid of any educational aim, import, or value. I say virtually devoid of any educational dimension because while players of these sports certainly do learn how to perform and perfect their athletic skills (knowledge-how), and while learning and performing such skills at this advanced level does require some minimal level of propositional knowledge in academic disciplines such as physiology and psychology (knowledge-that), not to mention learning moral virtues such as perseverance and courage, those lessons count for little if anything in intercollegiate athletic contests in which coming out on top is the only thing that truly matters. So what is problematic about higher education institutions being in the athletic entertainment business is not anything intrinsic to these sports themselves, to epistemic and moral defects in their internal structural makeup, but to the win-at-all costs mentality that is the dominant ethos of sports at this level and a trademark feature of sports across the board wherever the market has successfully intruded itself. What especially rankles in this regard, then, is not just the enormous financial costs colleges and universities run up in putting on big-time sports, but the educationally and morally bankrupt way in which these big-time sports are produced and practiced, all in the effort to make them more entertaining to the student body, local community, and nationally televised audience.

French would likely reject my criticism of the educational failings of college sports on the grounds that it merely perpetuates the academic bias members of the professoriate like me have against them. Colleges and universities, he would likely once again point out, are multi-purpose institutions, which means their mission is not only to educate the student-body and surrounding community, but, among other things, to entertain them as well. So whatever educational deficiencies football and men's basketball might have at present, and both French and Stoke, as we have seen, openly acknowledge they don't measure up according to traditional academic standards, indeed, are not even intelligible practices by such standards (114), they more than make up for by virtue of the entertainment they provide to an adoring public.

But I don't find this reply persuasive. The reason why is that my above criticisms not only do not deny that institutions of higher education have an obligation to serve the larger community, but are premised on them having just such a public obligation. So I think French is entirely right in insisting colleges and universities recognize and honor their service commitments to the public.[3] Rather, my objection to French's reform of college sports is that the obligation colleges and universities have to serve the public is not an open-ended one but comes with an important, indeed crucial proviso, namely, that they do so with an overarching educational and moral aim in mind. After all, these institutions are first and foremost educational ones. And while that does not mean, as French convincingly argues, their educational

[3]In fact, he might have cited the oft-cited Morrill Act to bolster his case in this regard, which was passed by Congress in 1862 and provided grants of federal lands to states for the purpose of establishing new colleges that would extend their mission to include the teaching of agriculture and the "mechanic arts" (engineering). The addition of these new branches of learning was in response to a crying public need for experts in modern industry and agriculture (Delbanco 2012, 77).

purpose has to be understood and carried out in narrow academic terms, it does mean, as I see it, that whatever services they do offer to the student-body and local community should include an additional educative feature beyond that of simple entertainment. A quick glance at the range of entertainments typically made available by colleges and universities outside of elite sports suggests as much, whether it be theatrical productions, music concerts, dance performances, artistic exhibitions, TED talks, debates, public lectures, and the like. What these public oriented productions share in common is that they both entertain and educate the student-body and public, and that the entertainment they provide is parasitic, as it should be in the case of institutions of higher learning, on their educational contribution. What distinguishes elite intercollegiate athletic programs from these other university sponsored public "entertainments" is easy to see: they have gladly forsaken for some time now their educative role for their entertainment role in order to bolster their financial bottom line. That is why winning and moneymaking have become their central calling cards, and why, of course, their relation to the rest of the university has become increasingly strained if not unintelligible. And it could hardly be otherwise since the kind of public entertainment they put on offer comes without the requisite educational component that defines everything else higher education institutions pride themselves on doing whether in or outside the classroom. It is little wonder, therefore, why athletic departments have been allowed, greatly encouraged, even goaded, by their university superiors (typically university presidents and the board of regents they report to) to train all their attention, effort, and finances, on entertaining spectators as opposed to educating them on what college sports could be at their best, on the educational and moral lessons they are capable of imparting when winning is not their sole raison d'etre.

French would likely retort that my criticism of the present over-commercialized, winning obsessed intercollegiate athletic scene is still tainted by academic bias, since it never deigns to ask what French thinks is crucial to ask of any consideration, critical or otherwise, of the university's responsibility to the public: "who gets to define and determine what the public needs from universities?" (121) According to French, it is sheer "academic arrogance" if not a "moral defect" to presume that only academics like me, armed as I am with my insider, professorial take on what is wrong with commercialized college sports, are equipped to answer this question. For the public, as he sees it, has a right to weigh in on what it needs from universities, and this is as true of college sports as it is of most everything else that goes on in their hallowed confines. So even those members of the surrounding community who only venture on campus to watch a Saturday football game or a weekday basketball game are entitled to have their say as to what sports like these should be all about. There can be no doubt that what they want and expect from colleges and universities in this regard is to field winning teams that gratify them rather than losing teams that miff them. It is only by taking into consideration the wishes of the public to be entertained by these sports, French admonishes, that academic critics of intercollegiate football and men's basketball like me can see "the full spectrum of responsibilities that [educational] institutions may incur with respect to their different constituencies" (122).

Now, I would be the first to admit that we academics can be and frequently are arrogant to a fault, and, like everyone else, plagued by blind spots that occlude different ways we might profitably see the world and, of course, ourselves and our own institutions. But I think French greatly overstates his case in this instance. For it is one thing to say the public deserves a seat at the table when it comes to determining what the mission of universities should be, which it supports, private universities excepted, with its tax dollars (though, alas, at an alarmingly decreasing rate). However, it is quite another thing to say that what the public expects from universities they should simply deliver. I am sure French knows this full well, and would not hesitate to reject any public outcry, for instance, that a course on creationism be offered in the curriculum, or any demand by the student body that the university put on burlesque shows or gambling competitions for their enjoyment. This points up one of the most fundamental and important obligations universities have with regard to the public, which is to furnish their members with the latest and most thoroughly vetted knowledge of the natural and social world available to us, as well as the best critical commentary and arguments we can muster to address the great normative questions regarding how we should live our lives. Meeting this core public obligation, however, often pits the university against larger society, particularly when false beliefs and morally repugnant views have found their way into the public discourse and corrupted whatever discussion and inquiry takes place there. When this happens, as it does more often than we might care to admit, the university's obligation to speak truth to power and prejudice is not one to be taken lightly, and not one, therefore, it can either ignore or shirk without ceasing to be the special educational institution it fundamentally and at its best is.

As I said, I am fairly certain French sees the key adversarial role the university plays or should play in such instances in much the same way as I have just described it. The rub, however, is that his market remedy for college sports, which for all intents and purposes simply rubber stamps rather than critically challenges the public's dubious take on what it wants from college sports (entertaining winning teams), betrays nary a trace of what I think should be the university's contrarian response to this public demand. If ever a situation called for the university to flex its critical, adversarial muscle to oppose what essentially amounts to the public's consumerist demand that it put on elite athletic contests of brawn and skill that place the primary emphasis on winning in order to accommodate the viewing pleasure of the audience, it is surely this one. For it hardly needs saying that sports designed for the express purpose of entertaining the public and fixated on winning are poorly suited, if suited at all, to educate. While sports so designed and pitched ensure that the athletic public need not worry that their fun will be spoiled by unwelcome efforts to suffuse them with educational content, the university, as I see it, should worry very much that in coddling this particular public they have abandoned their most solemn obligation to educate rather than placate the community they serve. As I see it then, it is a far greater moral defect for the university to renege on its critical role in such instances than to risk coming off as an isolated, out of touch ivory tower peopled by arrogant iconoclasts who could care less about what the public thinks.

I turn now to my second and final criticism of French's Team Market approach to the reform of football and men's basketball, namely, that it simply ignores and thus lets stand the corrosive effects the commercialization of these sports has had specifically on them. The nub of my complaint here is that French's idea of paying athletes for the revenue they generate not only does nothing to redeem what these athletic endeavors could be educationally and morally speaking – if they were not held hostage by the do-whatever-it-takes-to-win mentality that is the inevitable, if not intended, result of their commercialization, but makes winning and money that more central to their practice. For now players and their athletic "superiors" alike both have a financial stake in what happens on the playing field. Why French did not see fit to critically take up this commodification of college sports is not immediately apparent. For he was both clear and firm that his unsparing critique of college sports was not intended to, and, in fact, did not, point the finger at these sports themselves, to some problem in their internal structural composition that explains their morally compromised status, but only to the way that the dominant parties fashioned them into mainly commercial affairs and then rigged the revenue they generate in their favor at the expense of the players (3). So I think I am on solid ground in saying that French is at least open to the idea that college sports could be much more than what they presently are, and, therefore, that he would not be opposed in principle to taking on the commercialization of these sports.

However, despite French's disclaimer that he has no bone to pick with sports themselves, he does in several crucial passages of his monograph insinuate that sports do, in fact, suffer from a crucial defect in their structural composition that is especially concerning in the case of college sports because it casts serious doubt on their ability to educate or morally uplift those who play and watch them. That fundamental, structural defect has to do with the wholly artificial character of athletic pursuits, with the fact that, in Peter Heinegg's words, approvingly quoted by French, sport is "a separate universe with a fully articulated structure which is a comic imitation of the real one, an ersatz creation [in] both design and purpose (wholly arbitrary, yet consistent)" (55). The artificial character of sport proves to be a defect because any resemblance between it and our real, everyday lives, is superficial at best. That means anything learned there would have no significant relation or relevance to what goes on in our real, ordinary lives. But it is French himself, following the lead of one of his sources, who drives a stake in the heart of the notion that sport has an important educative role to play, moral or otherwise, when he links Heinegg's metaphysical claims regarding the utter artificiality of sport to the empirical studies that show the behavior of college athletes in their chosen sports falls well below their non-athletic counterparts on all of the important moral measures. His argument for this important, damning link is that because athletes "grasp the artificiality of athletic contests" they are all too aware of the wide gulf that separates their actions in sport from their actions in the real world. It is owing to the "highly artificial rules" of sport, therefore, which govern the actions of players by providing them cover from the real world – by literally walling them within the artificial confines of the game, that players are given license to act in amoral, egocentric ways that defy the moral constraints of everyday life (56).

By laying the blame for the glaring problems with Actually Existing College Sports not only on the ill-considered and ill-begotten actions of the powers that be that currently control them but as well on the artificial structure of these sports themselves, it is easy to understand why he allied himself with Team Market rather than Team Reform. For if college sports are at bottom merely comic, amoral imitations of the real, morally freighted world, there would indeed be no point in trying to rein in the commercialization of their affairs in order to realize their educational and moral potential. That is because they do not have any apparent educational or moral potential to tap in the first place given their contrived, emulative status as pure diversions from the real world. Indeed, characterizing sport as a "comic imitation" of everyday life puts it in the same strange and benighted category as reality television, since everyone who has even a passing acquaintance with such fare knows, save perhaps the most naïve among us, that this genre of television does not, in fact, depict or otherwise represent the reality of our actual, ordinary lives, but rather offers a comic, and occasionally tragic, replication of those real lives. So it is no mystery why French claims that the only thing college sports have to offer is to entertain the public, to ply their legion of fans with pleasant diversions that take their minds off of the real world for a few precious hours. That we could say the same thing about reality television or any number of other manufactured diversions only confirms, for French and company, their view that sport is a part, perhaps even and integral part, of the vast entertainment industry

But I think that French has been badly misled by Heinegg and others of similar persuasion who insist sports are nothing more than inconsequential diversions from the real world. To see why we need only consider what precisely is contrived about sport that distinguishes it from everyday life, and that characterizes its special relation to everyday life. So while I agree with French and Heinegg that sport is an artificial, contrived endeavor, I disagree with them regarding the nature of that contrivance. And here I can turn, fortunately, to Bernard Suits's keen analysis of sport, and of the larger category of games to which it belongs, to show that the artificial character of sport does not consign it to the category of comic diversions designed mainly or only to entertain, but to the category of intrinsic goods, to social practices and the goods internal to them whose value does not depend on their connection to something else of greater value (2014).

Suits argues that athletic games of skill are defined by four main elements. The first two of those elements, that games of this kind have specifiable achievable goals (in golf to put a small ball in a hole, in basketball to put a larger ball through a circular rim) and allowable means to achieve these goals (in the former by standing at some distance from the hole using clubs to stroke the ball into the hole, in the latter to score by shooting the ball through a circular rim fixed at a certain defined height), are of little definitional significance because almost all human activities possess a similar means-end structure. The next two features of athletic games do, however, capture what is structurally distinctive about them.

Perhaps the more important of these two additional elements are the rules of games. The main rules of games, Suits points out, prohibit players from using the easiest, most efficient means to achieve the game goal (in golf simply stuffing the ball into the hole with one's hand) in favor of a more difficult, less efficient means to achieve it (as just noted, by standing at some distance from the hole and using specially designed clubs to propel the ball into the hole) (39–40). What is important about the means-limiting rules of games is that they are utterly unlike the rules that govern how we most typically go about choosing the means at our disposal to realize the goals we seek in ordinary life – which is, of course, to select the easiest and most efficient means to achieve our goals. Of course, athletic games like all other games would cease to be the challenging activities they fundamentally are unless they had such means-limiting rules, and it is safe to say no one would play them if players were permitted to use the easiest means available to achieve their game goals.

Lastly, athletic games, and games in general, require they be played with a certain attitude, what Suits calls a "lusory" attitude. He characterizes the lusory attitude as "the knowing acceptance of the rules just because it makes the game possible" (40). The lusory attitude is a necessary feature of sport and games because it explains the otherwise strange state of affairs in which one deliberately chooses to employ worse rather than better means for achieving an end (41). This attitude also markedly distinguishes sport and games from everyday life because in ordinary life the only plausible reason why we might on rare occasion do something less efficiently is if doing it more efficiently would be disastrous. So, for instance, if one has a headache surely the most efficient way to rid oneself of the pain is to simply blow one's head off with a gun. Of course, we do not do such things in real life because of the disastrous consequences, which is also, by the way, the same reason why in circumstances of war we usually, thankfully, employ conventional rather than nuclear weapons even though the latter are a more efficient way to eliminate one's enemies (41). Whereas in athletic games the reason why we accept their means-limiting rules is that otherwise we could not play them.

Suits's analysis helps us to see, then, that the structural makeup of sport is significantly different from the structural makeup of most other human activities, to include, of course, the typical activities of everyday life. His analysis also helps us to see, more importantly to the point at hand, that the structural makeup of sport is utterly unlike what Heinegg, and French after him, would have us believe that it is, a mere comic imitation of the real world. For there is nothing emulative of the real world to be found in the core features of sport, as Suits deftly showed, since it is these very features that are responsible for the reversal of the instrumental relation of means to end that typify our everyday dealings in the real world and that make sport the distinctive social practice that it is. What is contrived about sport is not, then, as Heinegg and French allege, that it artificially recreates the real world already known to us, but that it creates an alternative to that world replete with it own distinctive purpose and distinctive order of rationality that is mostly unknown to those of us who, like Nietzsche's "last man," prefer the predictability and familiarity of the mundane to the unpredictability and unfamiliarity of the extramundane.

This Suitsian distinction between the constitution of "real" life and that of sport and the like is not just of intellectual interest but crucial to understanding what place out-of-the-ordinary social practices like sport have or at least should have in our lives, to include our university lives. More importantly, it suggests that perhaps the worst way to understand and appreciate social practices like sport is to judge them from the instrumental standpoint of everyday life, that is, to value them primarily for the contribution they make to these "real" lives. For there is nothing even remotely instrumentally valuable about trying to achieve contrived trivial game goals like getting a small ball into a small hole save the pleasurable diversion and occasional respite they provide us from our unremitting and laborious struggle to achieve the serious goals that preoccupy us in our real lives, the successful achievement of which are vital to our very survival and well-being. However, since Heinegg and French seem to think there is no other normative way to evaluate sports and their kind, it is not surprising they treat them as mere pleasurable sideshows to the serious affairs that occupy us in the real world. But in doing so, they miss what Suits claims is so special about athletic endeavors, and, consequently, the special contribution they can make to our lives. For as he sees it, far from being "trifling fillers of the interstices in our lives, ... [sports and games] are clues to the future" once we are no longer burdened by problems of scarcity (194).

Suits's heady claim that sports are the "clue" to our possible future utopian lives, which as we shall shortly see depends on viewing them as intrinsic goods, might seem, well, too heady, were it not backed by other philosophers especially of the rank of a Hegel and a Marx. For when Hegel reflected on the ancient Greek Olympic Games he spotted and articulated the very same distinction between "real" life and sport that Suits spotted and articulated when he reflected on contemporary sports and games.

> If we look at the inner nature of these [Greek] sports, we observe first how sport itself is opposed to serious business, to dependence and need. ... Serious occupation is labor that has some reference to some need. ... In contrast with this kind of seriousness, sport presents the higher seriousness; for in it nature is wrought into spirit. In this exercise of physical powers, man shows his freedom, he shows that he has transformed his body into an organ of spirit. (1954, 55)

And as noted, Marx in *Das Kapital* penned his own remarkably similar distinction between paradigmatic real world occupations rooted in necessity like work and paradigmatic non-real world endeavors rooted in freedom like sport.

> The realm of freedom actually begins where labour which is determined by necessity and mundane considerations ceases; thus in the very nature of things it lies beyond the sphere of actual material production. ... Beyond [such material production] begins that development of human energy which is an end in itself, the true realm of freedom. (1977, 820)

What is so special about the artificial character of sport as Suits and company see it, then, is not, as French claims, that it relegates it to the margins of our real lives as a comic diversion from the serious business of life itself, but rather that it elevates sport to the status of an intrinsic good "whose only justification is that it justifies everything else" (182). Indeed, it is the very artificial makeup of sport that makes it just the sort of human endeavor one would expect to find in Hegel's sphere of Spirit, Marx's realm of freedom, and Suits's notion of Utopia, along with such things as art, music, poetry, literature, and the like. For what all these human contrivances share in common is that they were not primarily contrived to aid and abet those things we *have* to do if we are to survive, but rather contrived to enable us to do those things we *want* to do if we are to live full, meaningful, and flourishing lives. Minus the latter, they insist, there is not much point in the former.

The value of sport does not lie, therefore, as it does for work and all kindred activities rooted in necessity, in the value of the external goals they seek (putting a small ball in a small hole), which, as noted, possess little if any instrumental value, nor, it should also be said, any intrinsic value, but in the self-imposed limited manner in which we are required to achieve them. And the value we get when we factor in the rule-governed, arduous process in which such goals are to be achieved, the challenges created by deliberately placing unnecessary obstacles in our path to achieve them, is not whatever marginal utility to our everyday lives can be squeezed out of athletic endeavors, but the intrinsic value that comes from doing something supremely well, something excellent, when tested and pushed to the upper limits of our skill, dedication, and effort. What makes sport a valuable human undertaking, therefore, is the same thing that makes art, music, and all the other things that populate Hegel's category of Spirit valuable human undertakings: they are one and all significant human accomplishments that testify to the various ways we humans can pursue and sometimes achieve genuine excellence.

It is important to add here that there is no reason to exclude moral excellence from the above-mentioned excellences at least so far as sport is concerned. For whether or not one agrees with French and the sources he cites that sport is structured in such a way that it releases us from the moral constraints of everyday life, I think it is undeniable that sport introduces its very own moral constraints and entailments.[4] So even if it is conceded that by virtue of its artificial composition sport brackets out everyday moral concerns, it does not follow that it is a moral-free zone in which selfish, egocentric acts get a normative pass. That is because sport also has built-in moral features upon which its very intelligibility as a perfectionist practice, one dedicated to the pursuit of bodily excellence, depends. As LaVaque-Manty helpfully notes in this regard in his astute analysis of sport,"conceptions of excellence have always presupposed a baseline of equality and a set of constitutive norms" that are crucial to the normative judgments of excellence we observe on the playing field. In assessing athletic contests, he continues, "we want to know whether there was a meaningful contest in the first place" (2012, 190). That is why an unfair athletic competition is adjudged as a failed rather than an excellent one no matter the athletic prowess demonstrated.

So my complaint with this part of French's Team Market reform is that it does nothing to remedy the heavily commercialized athletic status quo that features an impoverished conception of sport that overemphasizes winning. His failure to challenge this one-dimensional conception of sport is owed in this instance not just to benign neglect, to the fact that he put, so to speak, all his eggs in the unjust financial remuneration of athletes basket, but further to his claim that the artificial

[4]For an excellent account that argues the moral principles fundamental to sport are expressions or reflections of the same moral principles found outside of sport, see Russell (2007).

character of sport is partly responsible for its present low moral standing. But as Suits and company have argued the opposite is actually true, that sport by virtue of its artificial makeup could be much more that what it presently is educationally and morally speaking, if it were not shackled by the win at all costs mentality that dominates elite sport at all levels today and that is seemingly hell bent in turning it into an entertainment spectacle for the masses. This is especially important in the case of college sports since, as Paul Weiss noted, one of the main attractions of sport is that "it offers a superb occasion for enabling young men to be perfected" (1969, 19).[5] That is to say, sport is the one human endeavor on Hegel's, Marx's, and Suits's lists of special human endeavors that gives young men, and we need to add, of course, young women, the opportunity to be excellent now when they are in their physical prime, and when they are capable of being the very best in the world at what they do. Why not, then, reform the sports they play in college so that athletic excellence becomes their trademark feature rather than moneymaking? College sports, I contend, would be the better for it, and, it goes without saying, I think, so would the universities that stand behind them.

Conclusion

I have argued for two main points. The first is that if one wants a clear headed, persuasive, and far reaching, not to mention entirely fair, critique of what presently ails college sports today, one need look no farther than French's impressive critical takedown of the present intercollegiate athletic scene. The second is that the same cannot be said for the remedy he proposes to justify sports on college campuses. By exclusively targeting the unjust financial compensation of athletes and by implicating the artificial character of sport in its own educational and moral downfall, French's reform effort leaves unchallenged the damage done to universities and to the games themselves by their present unprecedented commercialization. Any meaningful reform of college sports today must, as I see it, address and redress the ill effects of this intrusion of the market into their internal affairs. A Herculean task, to be sure, but an indispensable one if we hope to reconcile what goes on in elite sports at this level nowadays with the best educational and moral ideals of colleges and universities.[6]

---

[5]That sports are one of the few endeavors in which young people can achieve a level of athletic perfection beyond the reach of their older peers also accounts for why this particular positive value of sport cannot be achieved outside of elite, top-level sport. In this one particular respect then, I dispute French's claim that <u>all</u> of the positive values of sport can be achieved just as easily in pickup games or intramural sports as they can in elite athletic settings (3).

[6]I suspect French would retort that the task of such reform is too Herculean to stand a realistic chance of succeeding. This is, no doubt, a further reason why he opts instead for paying athletes their just desserts rather than taking on the powerful commercial forces that presently govern intercollegiate sports. A full response to this objection would require a paper in its own right. But I

References

Branch, T. 2011. The shame of college sports. *The Atlantic* (October 20th): 2–31.
Camus, Albert. 1960. The wager of our generation. In: *Resistance, rebellion, and death*, trans. J. O'Brien. New York: Vintage Books.
Delbanco, Andrew. 2012. *College: What it was, is, and should be*. Princeton: Princeton University Press.
French, Peter. 2004. *Ethics and college sports*. New York: Rowan & Littlefield.
Hegel, G.W.F. 1954. The philosophy of history. In *The philosophy of Hegel*, ed. C.J. Friedrich. New York: The Modern Library.
Lavaque-Manty, M. 2012. *The playing fields of Eton: Equality and excellence in modern meritocracy*. Ann Arbor: The University of Michigan Press.
Marx, Karl. 1977. *Das Kapital*. Vol. 3. New York: International Publishers.
Nocera, J. 2012. Let's start paying athletes. Nytimes.com 01/01/magazine: 1–10.
Rorty, Richard. 2006. Interview. In *Take care of freedom and truth will take care of itself*, ed. E. Mendieta, 100–101. Stanford: Stanford University Press.
Russell, John. 2007. Broad internalism and the moral foundations of sport. In *Ethics in sport*, ed. W.J. Morgan, 35–50. Champaign: Human Kinetics.
Suits, Bernard. 2014. *The grasshopper: Games, life, and utopia*. Ontario: Broadview Press.
Weiss, Paul. 1969. *Sport: A philosophic inquiry*. Carbondale: So. Illinois Press.

can make two brief replies that aim to show that driving the commercial forces out of college sports is not quite the quixotic venture it might at first appear to be. First, French's own suggested remedy of paying college athletes could similarly be dismissed as a utopian pipe dream. For the consensus among sports economists is that there is not enough money to go around to pay players, not, that is, without radically cutting back on the profligate ways athletic departments spend money especially on high profile football and basketball coaches. French himself, as already noted, observed that most big time athletic departments lose a lot of money. My second reply builds off the first. If it is true that most of the top intercollegiate programs are losing money in ever larger chunks, it is apparent that they cannot sustain their present spending levels without crashing and burning. That would mean my own proposal to attack the intrusion of the market into college sports is very much a distinct and realistic possibility, and an especially timely one.

References

Cassidy, Allen. 1966. The wages of consumerism. In *Sex, lies, and college sports*, ed. J. O'Brien. New York: Vintage Books.

Delbanco, Andrew. 2012. *College: What it was, is, and should be*. Princeton: Princeton University Press.

Rose, Peter. 1984. *Athletes and college sports*. New York: Praeger.

Hegel, G.W.F. 1954. The philosophy of history. In *The philosophy of Hegel*, ed. C.J. Friedrich. New York: The Modern Library.

French on Innocence Lost

Deborah Tollefsen

In "Losing Innocence for the Sake of Responsibility" (1992) Peter French argues that the loss of innocence is required for moral responsibility and that adults have a responsibility to facilitate the child's loss of innocence. Drawing on the work of Herbert Morris, French provides a compelling account of the knowledge that is acquired in the process of losing one's innocence and the sorts of experiences required for its loss. Although I agree with French that moral maturity requires the sorts of conceptual knowledge he identifies, I do not think that the loss of innocence is where we gain such knowledge. I shall argue that the experience of losing one's innocence provides a more fundamental knowledge on which this conceptual capacity is based.

As French notes philosophers have stayed clear of the topic of lost innocence:

> Lost innocence seems to create problems that moral philosophers have almost utterly ignored despite its apparent significance in each of our lives. Theologians, novelists, and poets have made loss of innocence perhaps the central theme of Western culture. Where would psychiatrists be without it? And the moral philosophers? Concentrating on guilt and punishment, no doubt. Innocence is a very elusive moral notion, one better looked over than looked at, loaded with the sort of emotional complications that resist the clear and clean principles of philosophers. Theologians and novelists rush in where wise folks fear to tread. (1992, 29)

It is not without a great deal of trepidation that I offer my own reflections on the loss of innocence. But, as always, French's thoughtful and provocative work, has inspired me.

D. Tollefsen (✉)
University of Memphis, Memphis, TN, USA
e-mail: dtollfsn@memphis.edu

Z.J. Goldberg (ed.), *Reflections on Ethics and Responsibility*,
DOI 10.1007/978-3-319-50359-2_9

The Loss of Innocence

Following Herbert Morris, French (1992) begins his discussion with the story of Adam and Eve's fall from grace. Having eaten from the tree, Adam and Eve's "eyes were opened" and "they realized that the were naked; so they sewed fig leaves together and made loincloths for themselves." What could it mean that they come to realize that they are naked? Surely, before eating the fruit they recognized that their bodies were not covered. This is not the first time they have seen each other's bodies. Their eyes were not literally opened. After eating the fruit, they do not come to see something new. Rather, they come to *know* something about what they have seen all along. They come to recognize their bodies *as* naked. They have what Morris (1976) describes as "insight." To see the body as naked is to undergo a conceptual shift. As French puts it:

> Coming to see *that* or to know, unlike mere seeing, depends on the acquisition of concepts and even theoretical information... Acquisition of a conceptual structure, such as the one that includes or focuses on nakedness, causes one to see *that* something one had long seen one way takes a description one had not previously used with respect to it. Eve's seeing *that* (or knowing) Adam is naked is quite a different thing from her seeing him naked. In the latter case, she merely "lays eyes on him." (1992, 32)

The knowledge that Adam and Eve gain, and, by extension, what we gain when innocence is lost is not propositional in nature. Rather French describes it as a sort of know-how. We acquire a conceptual structure that allows for the proper *use* of concepts. One does not really have knowledge of a concept if one cannot use that concept appropriately. When we lose our innocence, according to French, we come to see that our actions and the actions of others are capable of being brought under certain descriptions, descriptions that were not available to us prior to our loss of innocence. What Adam and Eve acquire and that which we all need to acquire in order to mature morally is the ability to use moral concepts appropriately and to invoke the conceptual scheme of responsibility. Within this scheme killing can be described as murder, issuing a false statement can be described as lying, failure to meet expectations as a betrayal.

If we gain a facility with moral description, what is lost when innocence is lost? What we lose is the ability to appeal to the simple narratives of the "good" and the "evil" we may have acquired through myth and literature. As French describes it: "...once the re-description has been learned, one loses the option of seriously using the illusions of innocent description" (36). As Michael McKenna (2008) points out in his helpful commentary on French's article, the child is not without some understanding of good and evil. But the categories are simple and the lines between them black and white. When we lose our innocence we lose the illusion of a simple moral order. Zachary Goldberg (2015) also identifies moral illusion as the defining feature of moral innocence. According to Goldberg moral innocence should be defined as a trust in moral illusions.

In losing our moral illusions we come to gain a new insight into the moral order. According to French, the knowledge that is acquired when one loses innocence must be acquired in a certain way. He appeals to Russell's (1910) distinction between knowledge by description and knowledge by acquaintance. The concepts acquired in the process of losing one's innocence must be known through direct acquaintance. "...(T)hose who lose innocence learn in a very personal way how to re-describe their situations, their experiences, and their actions. In effect, they learn first hand or in the first person how to appropriately use the language of responsibility with respect to themselves" (35).

One cannot come to lose one's innocence through a description—through a narrative, for instance. The first person experience is crucial.

Adam and Eve lost their innocence by eating fruit. How do we come to lose our innocence? French suggests that confronting evil precipitates the loss of innocence,

> ...it is a certain type of possibility that one must come to know. Experiencing evil in the loss of innocence is grasping for the first time the possibility that things might have gone differently, and so seeing what would have been good in the situation, and so seeing yourself as capable of evil. (39)

And the confrontation with evil must expose the child to knowledge of the universal. If one comes to hold beliefs about a particular person, perhaps that Bob is a liar, but fails to recognize that Bob's actions and motives are generalizable, then innocence is not lost.

> ...one needs to know evil in the universal sense to which Aristotle alludes. Ignorance of that sense of evil (and therefore good) is just what characterizes innocents. They may in fact be quite knowledgeable of particulars (knowing that it is Bob and not Bill they are hitting, and that the end of hitting will be a bruised and battered Bob), but their ignorance of the universal shields them from responsibility. (39)

What does French mean by evil? Is confronting human suffering sufficient? Given that the child must come to understand actions as falling under different *moral* descriptions, evil needs to be understood in a rich normative sense. A child who is present at her grandmother's deathbed and witnesses the passing of a life has not experienced evil though they may have experienced human suffering. French seems to mean by evil, undeserved human suffering.[1] Death from natural causes is not clearly undeserved. Human suffering at the hand of another would, however, count as a case of evil because it is generally undeserved and admits of moral description. It is intentional descriptions that the child comes to understand and become proficient in. The re-description isn't just a re-description of events, but of human actions (a particular type of event with a particular causal history—i.e. those that are caused by reasons). Morris is particularly clear on this point: "...the knowledge is not merely about matters in relation to human beings but knowledge

[1]Thanks to Zachary Goldberg for identifying this definition in French's work. In later work French defines evil as the willful infliction of undeserved harm on an individual that jeopardizes that individual's aspirations to live a worthwhile life. See Goldberg's contribution to this volume for a discussion of this definition. The focus on an individual's aspirations to live a worthwhile life might be problematic for those who have no aspirations—infants, severely disabled, persons on life-support? If they lack aspirations are they not subject to evil?

gained about the nature of human beings as persons of a certain kind with relations of a certain kind through their mental states and conduct to what is of value…" (1976, 148).

Having identified what is lost in the loss of innocence and how it is lost, French goes on to argue that adults have an obligation to facilitate the loss of innocence. The inclination to protect and shelter children from evil is, according to French, inconsistent with obligations we have to help them grow into morally responsible adults. How does one facilitate acquaintance with evil without doing harm? What sorts of innocence-losing experiences would facilitate the loss of innocence? French doesn't say. He alludes to certain rituals that in times past served the purpose of ushering the child "down the aisle of experience," but we don't get any concrete suggestions. French is clear that adults' duty to help the child lose innocence is not a license for child abuse. Nor is it to be construed as a duty to destroy all of the child's illusions. "The moral imperative to end innocence must be tempered with the restriction that only those illusions that prevent full responsible moral citizenship need be destroyed" (1992, 43).

French's discussion is rich and provocative. In what follows I offer some criticisms and refinements. I do not dispute the claim that the conceptual knowledge French describes is necessary for moral maturity. Rather, I think the innocence losing experiences that French and Morris highlight provide us with something more fundamental.

Innocence-Losing Experiences

I begin with a passage from an autobiography of Madeleine L'Engle, an award winning author known best for her series of children's books—*A Wrinkle in Time* (1963), *A Wind in the Door* (1973), and *A Swiftly Tilting Planet* (1978). In this passage L'Engle is describing an unfortunate event from her childhood.

> I was about eight, certainly old enough to have forgotten what it was like to wet one's pants. One day in French class, I asked to be excused. The French teacher must have been having problems with children wanting to leave the room for other reasons, and using the bathroom as an excuse, because she forbade me to go. I asked her three times, and three times was told, No. When the bell for the end of class rang I bolted from my desk and ran, but I couldn't quite make it, and spent the rest of the afternoon sodden and shamed. When my mother heard what happened, she demanded to see the Principal. I remember with awful clarity the scene in the Principal's office, after the French teacher had been summoned. She said, "But Madeleine never asked to go to the bathroom. If she had only raised her hand, of course I would have excused her." She was believed. To have an adult lie and to have another adult not know that it was a lie; to tell the truth myself and not be believed: the earth shook on its foundations. (1971, 143)

The passage is illustrative for a variety of reasons. First, I think it serves as an example of an innocence-losing experience. Whether L'Engle lost her innocence at this time is irrelevant. Her moral development is not the subject of this paper. It is, however, the sort of experience in which a child's eyes, like the eyes of Adam and Eve, are opened. They were opened to the complexities of the moral order. This is the sort of experience that is under philosophical reflection by French and Morris. There is an instantaneous insight into moral reality. I want to understand what is happening in these cases. What is the nature of the insight gained? Second, it involves a confrontation with evil that is, by many standards, mild. The child need not confront murder or rape in order to experience the loss of innocence. It is the sort of evil a child might well encounter in the course of their upbringing and it comes with no real effort on the part of adults to bring it about or facilitate it.

If we take L'Engle's story as an example of an innocence losing experience, we can ask what is lost and what is gained. She loses, it seems to me, the innocent view of the world that includes the idea that adults are morally superior and that all adults are morally mature. What does she gain? L'Engle clearly comes to see that the teacher's false statement is a lie. She comes to see it as a *lie*, as an intentional deception meant to hide the truth. It is, however, implausible to think that in this one experience she gains the facility to use moral descriptions in appropriate ways. Perhaps Adam and Eve acquired the conceptual knowledge French identifies as necessary for moral maturity instantaneously, but it is psychologically implausible that we do so. If losing innocence means acquiring a rich conceptual schema that makes possible the appropriate application of certain concepts, then it is difficult to see how such knowledge could result from a single experience of evil. In *War and Moral Innocence* (2011) French attempts to address some criticisms of his view by admitting that some loses of innocence, for example being molested, may not bring about the conceptual gains needed for entry into the moral community. My point here is not just *that certain moral evils* are insufficient for bringing about the conceptual knowledge required for moral maturity but that *no single* experience is capable of bringing about the conceptual knowledge required.

If we understand the loss of innocence as French does, then it is not an event but rather a process. Morris seems to acknowledge this when he writes:

> First, the tale (of Adam and Eve) can mislead if it suggests that the acquisition of the knowledge of good and evil, the acquisition of the capacity to apply these concepts appropriately, something that is an essential component of any loss of innocence is an instantaneous achievement. Loss of innocence is sometimes, perhaps most often, a gradual affair, for it is associated less with a sudden insight than it is with gradually realizing some truth. (1976, 152)

Though it is important to note here that this passage does not rule out gaining the requisite knowledge instantaneously. French, too, says that innocence is a scalar concept and that the loss of it is a process. He writes: "I have said that the *process* of losing innocence is one of learning how to re-describe things" (1992, 36). It is a *learning-how*, not a *learning-that*. French explicitly says that what is acquired in innocence losing experiences is not the full conceptual capacity but merely the knowledge that one could be the subject or object of evil.

> Whatever Eve tasted in that first bite of the forbidden fruit, it did not have to be complete knowledge of good and evil or the destruction of all of her illusions for her to lose her innocence. All that was needed was an immediate acquaintance with her capacity to do and be done evil, that is, knowledge by acquaintance of the rudiments of Aristotle's knowledge of the universal. (41)

But at other times he seems to identify a point in the process of losing one's innocence when the concepts are acquired all at once.

> Making the acquaintance of evil need not be sudden or dramatic. It need not occur in startling event in the skies over Belgium or in a sleazy motel room. Knowledge of good and evil, without the forbidden fruit, is usually incremental, and once the requisite acquaintance occurs, much of it is by description. Innocence is a scalar notion—there are degrees of it. Still, *for each of us there is a threshold somewhere along the scale, and when one crosses it, when one acquires that array of concepts or that extension of a concept, one becomes morally responsible.* (41)

And again,

> People *can lose innocence in a moment in an experience that triggers a different way of seeing the world and the humans, especially themselves, in it.* Such dramatic moments do not happen for all of us, yet we lose innocence. (35)

But now I am confused. Is the loss of innocence a process or an event? Both French and Morris seem to acknowledge that it could be either. French argues that to lose one's innocence is to gain a rich conceptual capacity; but if that is so, then we do not really lose our innocence when we undergo an innocence losing experience because such a capacity cannot be gained instantaneously.

Perhaps we need to confront evil multiple times in order to fully lose our innocence? Innocence losing experiences loosen our grip, so to speak, and eventually, after multiple exposures, we fall from the ledge? This seems to be what French has in mind. Losing one's innocence is a process, but at some point in the process a threshold is crossed such that the individual is the appropriate target of moral evaluation.[2]

But it is not clear how the mere experience of evil, however many times, is sufficient to acquire the conceptual knowledge French describes. After all, what French is describing is a skill. Being hit multiple times by a bike will not impart the knowledge needed to ride it. You need to get on it and practice. If knowledge of good and evil is more like procedural knowledge—know-how—then it requires practice and habituation. It must be acquired by participating in a practice that makes use of moral descriptions. Learning how to do this will take time and must be done in a context in which their uses are corrected and adjusted. They must go through a process of training and refinement. It requires not a confrontation with evil but an immersion into the practice of praising and blaming.[3] Confrontation with evil, then, seems insufficient to provide us with the conceptual knowledge French identifies as definitive of the loss of innocence.

And what of innocence losing experiences? The focus of French and Morris is on definitive moments in one's moral life when the "eyes are opened." Literature and our own personal biographies provide ample examples of such experiences. What do they give us if not the rich conceptual capacities French identifies? Perhaps

---

[2]Thanks to Zachary Goldberg for clarifying this point.

[3]See McKenna (2012) and his contribution to this volume for a discussion of the relationship between the capacity to engage in moral address and responsibility.

what we gain during innocence losing experiences is simply the realization that we can do or be done evil (rather than full knowledge of good and evil). We lose our innocence when we come face to face with this. But if so, then, losing innocence is not a process after all and it is not about gaining conceptual abilities. And how do we move from the recognition that we are a potential subject of evil to the rich conceptual abilities French argues are definitive of losing one's innocence?

What I want to suggest here is that innocence losing experiences provide us with a much more foundational knowledge. Let's return to the myth of Adam and Eve. French's understanding of the myth doesn't really account for the role nakedness plays. He focuses on the fact that Adam and Eve see *that* they are naked and this ability to see something in a new way is associated with the acquisition of a conceptual knowledge. But why do they cover themselves? And why is it that they come to see that they are naked rather than some other aspect of themselves? On some interpretations the recognition that they are naked is taken to mean that they recognize their sexual nature. It seems to me, however, that what Adam and Eve acquire when they eat the forbidden fruit is something more basic. They recognize that they are vulnerable. Nakedness is a symbol for vulnerability. Such a feeling of vulnerability arises from a basic understanding of our capacity to affect and be affected. Adam and Eve's recognition of their own vulnerability leads them to cover themselves. With the recognition of vulnerability comes the knowledge of all the various possibilities for human interaction, for our vulnerability makes possible murder and betrayal but it also makes possible love and friendship. Through the recognition of vulnerability Adam and Eve acquire knowledge of good and evil (perhaps instantaneously). Vulnerability refers to our capacity to be affected (good or bad) by others. Often associated with weakness, vulnerability is, on the contrary, the condition upon which all human relationships are built. It is a basic human condition. The idea that vulnerability is the foundation of ethics is found in the work of Judith Butler (2010) and more recently Erinn Gilson (2014) and is a core insight of feminist ethics. Gilson's analysis of vulnerability begins with a compelling argument that the principal error of most discussions of vulnerability is their wholly negative definition of the concept. She challenges the standard accounts of vulnerability by exposing the ideal of invulnerability. Exposing the masculine ideal of invulnerability has a long history in feminist theory. If vulnerability is not defined negatively in terms of the ideal of invulnerability then we can see that being vulnerable is the basic state in which we enter the world and remain in the world due to the various ways in which our lives, even as adults, are interdependent.

If the myth of Adam and Eve is illustrative of our own journey to moral maturity then innocence-losing experiences involve acquiring an understanding of vulnerability, either one's own vulnerability or the vulnerability of others. With the insight into human vulnerability comes, perhaps more slowly than for Adam and Eve, the knowledge of good and evil. One comes to appreciate the variety of human interactions that depend upon human vulnerability. The ability to describe these interactions in various moral terms, French's loss of innocence, it seems to me, must come later and is developed over time through a process of habituation.

Consider again the young L'Engle, she confronts evil and recognizes her own vulnerability as an epistemic and moral subject. She recognizes her dependence on others and the ways in which others depend upon each other for the transmission of truths. She recognizes that this dependency can be taken advantage of, that certain judgments of credibility can be manipulated in one's favor, that telling the truth isn't enough to be believed. She sees adults don't always tell the truth even if they claim that such truth telling is what one should do. And as a result L'Engle becomes, no doubt, guarded. She "covers" herself. She changes the way she interacts with others and becomes less gullible. Morris describes this new self-consciousness that comes about from a loss of innocence in the following way:

> ...lost innocence is characterized by self-consciousness in a different sense, a sense captured by the imagery of Adam and Eve covering their nakedness. For reasons yet to be stated, but essentially related to the first kind of self-consciousness, one becomes less natural, less spontaneous; hesitancy enters one's life. One thinks before one acts, and, as it were, adjusts a mask before making an appearance. One acts as if the self of which one is now conscious were vulnerable. (1976, 156)

Morris gets it partly right and partly wrong here. We act vulnerably because we are vulnerable and it is consciousness of our vulnerability that leads to us to "mask" ourselves. He describes things more accurately here:

> With the loss of innocence... we are conscious of our vulnerability, both as we may be pained by what others do and we ourselves do and may do. Our guard goes up to protect us from the evil that we now believe may be done to us; and we cover up to hide from other and ourselves the evil we sense within us, that we may do and have done. (157)

Innocence losing experiences, then, do result in the loss of innocence, though we might lose our innocence in various other less dramatic ways. Prior to such experiences we are ignorant of our own vulnerability or the vulnerability of others. When we lose our innocence we gain an understanding of that vulnerability and with it the possibilities for human action, good and bad. On the basis of this we are able to begin the process of moral development that involves the acquisition of the sorts of conceptual capacities French identifies.

Understanding the experience of the loss of innocence in terms of a recognition of vulnerability may also help to understand why it is that the morally innocent are unaware of their innocence. When one is morally innocent they do not know that they are. The morally innocent cannot reflect on their status as an existing condition. Rather, it is only possible to recognize one's innocence after it has been lost. The recognition of one's vulnerability is a form of metacognition that opens the door, so to speak, for further reflection on one's own moral status.[4]

Let's turn now to the issue of the moral obligations adults have to bring about the loss of innocence. It is not clear to me what the content of the adult's obligation is to the child. Is the adult really obligated to expose the child to evil? Or simply to allow the child to explore the world in a way that makes such exposure possible?

---

[4]Thanks again to Zachary Goldberg for suggesting the link between a recognition of vulnerability and self-reflection.

The latter seems more plausible. In "The Loss of Innocence and the Things that Remain" Michael McKenna fleshes this out a bit more in attempt to answer the question of just what adults/parents are obligated to do.

> Given the above reflections, what does seem clear is that the moral obligation of adults is to foster innocence-ending experiences that are naturally suited for the moral life young adults are liable to face. Perhaps, then, the obligation is to create the possibility for multifarious moral experiences, ones in which the young are exposed to the travails of life on the economic edge, life in the interstices of racial conflict, life at the front of environmental destruction, life as an outsider or foreigner on the global scene, as well as, of course, the typical experiences any person must face while emerging into adulthood, such as learning to cope with one's sexual urges, or resist the temptation to act from anger or hatred. (2008, 8)

The idea here is that the adult provides the possibility of innocence-ending experiences, suited to their age and emotional maturity, rather than, say, dropping them off in the middle of the city one day and telling them to find their way home. Still one might wonder whether such efforts are ever really necessary. Don't we all, in the course of normal human interaction, confront evil of some degree? The child bullied in the playground, lied to by a parent, manipulated by a sibling, surely comes "face to face" with some degree of evil. Unless we are Rousseau's Emile, sheltered from society for most of our childhood, we inevitably confront the capacity to do and be done evil regardless of whether our parents provide us with exposure to the dark side. Are we really obligated to send our children into the Peace Corps in order to ensure their loss of innocence?

What we are obligated to do depends on the nature of the obligation under question. It seems to me that our obligation as caretakers is a *negative* duty rather than a *positive* one. We are obligation *not* to prolong innocence or prevent its loss. But we do not have a positive duty to end innocence.[5] Understanding our obligations in this way would help French avoid the criticism that his view recommends child abuse.

Further, if we understand innocence-losing experiences in the way that I have described, it calls into question French's claim that a confrontation with evil is required for the loss of innocence. Although confronting evil may provide the most compelling examples of human vulnerability, confronting good (perhaps heroic acts of self-sacrifice) might equally well open our eyes to human vulnerability and confronting human suffering (of a non-moral sort) might well produce an understanding of vulnerability as well.

[5] What about cases of "affluenza"? The term was coined in the early 2000s in response to a highly publicized court case. A teenager from an affluent family killed someone in a drunk driving accident and his lawyer successfully argued for reduced charges because the child's upbringing had been so sheltered that he couldn't fully appreciate the consequences of his actions. Don't we have an obligation to prevent our children from suffering from affluenza? We do. But I am doubtful that exposing them to evil is the way to prevent it. The development of empathy seems crucial in developing caring human beings. Thanks to Tailer Ransom for raising this objection.

Conclusion

I have argued that what is gained during innocence-losing experiences is not a rich conceptual capacity but the knowledge of human vulnerability. We lose our innocence when we gain this understanding. This understanding of the human condition provides the foundation for knowledge of good and evil and for the sorts of conceptual knowledge French identifies as necessary for moral maturity. Perhaps an understanding of human vulnerability is just an understanding of one's capacity to do evil and have evil done to one. If so, my proposal is not a radical departure from at least one reading of French (though I would argue that an understanding of human vulnerability goes beyond a mere understanding of the capacity for evil). But French seems, at times, to suggest that the loss of innocence involves gaining a rich conceptual capacity. If this is so, then one does not lose innocence during innocence-losing experiences. This is an unhappy result. French and Morris begin with the myth of Adam and Eve and the event of losing innocence in the garden and they appeal to various examples of innocence-losing experiences from literature. It is these life altering events, and not simply the process of moral maturity, that seems to be under analysis. I have tried to offer an account of what is lost and gained during these experiences that fits within a broader story of moral development.

References

Butler, Judith. 2010. *Frames of war: When is life grievable?* New York: Versos.

French, Peter A. 1992. Losing innocence for the sake of moral responsibility. In *Responsibility matters*, 29–43. Lawrence: University Press of Kansas.

———. 2011. *War and moral dissonance*. New York: Cambridge University Press.

Gilson, Erinn. 2014. *The ethics of vulnerability: A feminist analysis of social life and practice*. London: Routledge.

Goldberg, Zachary J. 2015. Moral innocence as illusion and inability. *Philosophia* 43(2): 355–366.

L'Engle, Madeleine. 1963. *A wrinkle in time*. New York: Square Fish.

———. 1971. *A circle of quiet*. San Francisco: Harper Collins.

———. 1973. *A wind in the door*. New York: Square Fish.

———. 1978. *A swiftly tilting planet*. New York: Square Fish.

McKenna, Michael. 2008. The loss of innocence and the things that remain. *American Philological Association Newsletter* 7(2): 5–9.

———. 2012. *Conversation & responsibility*. New York: Oxford University Press.

Morris, Herbert. 1976. *On guilt and innocence: Essays in legal philosophy and moral psychology*. Berkeley: University of California Press.

Russell, Bertrand. 1910. Knowledge by acquaintance and knowledge by description. *Proceedings of the Aristotelian Society* 11(5): 108–128.

Evil and a Worthwhile Life

Zachary J. Goldberg

The concept of evil plays a central role in many of Peter French's publications.[1] He defines evil as "a human action that jeopardizes another person's (or group's) aspirations to live a worthwhile life (or lives) by the willful infliction of undeserved harm on that person(s)" (French 2011, 61, 95). Inspired by Harry Frankfurt's work on the importance of what we care about, French argues that "the life a person leads is worthwhile if what he or she really gives a damn about satisfies some condition(s) of value" (French 2011, 189). Through an analysis of the concept of "worthwhile", I endeavor to show that French's account of evil is correct although his definition of a worthwhile life is too demanding.

Defining an evil act as one that willfully imperils another's aspirations to live a worthwhile life is a welcome addition to the philosophical literature dedicated to the analysis of evil. Much of this literature identifies evil as severe, intolerable, or excessive harm, but these descriptions remain vague. At what precise point does harm cross over from mundane to severe, intolerable, or excessive? French provides an original and plausible interpretation of these kinds of evil harm by explaining them in terms of an impediment to aspirations to live a worthwhile life.

However, French's definition of a worthwhile life is too strong and hence excludes unmistakable instances of evil. It is quite possible that someone who cares about nonvaluable things, or someone lacking cares altogether, or non-human animals (who might fall into either one of these two categories), could be victims of evil. Therefore, if evil is an act that jeopardizes another's aspirations to live a

[1] See French (1992, 2011).

Z.J. Goldberg (✉)
Ludwig-Maximilians-Universität, Munich, Germany
e-mail: zachary.goldberg@lrz.uni-muenchen.de

Z.J. Goldberg (ed.), *Reflections on Ethics and Responsibility*,
DOI 10.1007/978-3-319-50359-2_10

worthwhile life, then the necessary condition of a worthwhile life cannot be that one gives a damn about something of value; it must be something far less demanding.[2]

In order to retain the central insight in French's account of evil, I offer an alternative suggestion concerning what makes a life worthwhile. To this end, I distinguish a worthwhile life from a meaningful, valuable, significant, or good life. Focusing on the definition and use of the word "worthwhile", I find that a worthwhile life is one that is worth the time and effort of the individual whose life it is. Jeopardizing another's ability to make such a determination about her life lies at the hardened heart of evil.

Some scholars think that "evil" does not belong to philosophical discussion. For many this term has connotations associated with the religious or the supernatural. It may conjure up images of the devil, or monstrous beings that haunt children's nightmares. It belongs perhaps only to fictional settings such as horror movies that titillate through their portrayal of psychotic killers terrorizing teenagers with murderous tenacity. More insidiously, the term "evil" has been used by political regimes to demonize their enemies sometimes with the aim of justifying military attacks as the most recent Bush regime did with its identification of the "axis of evil" following the attacks on September 11th. Indeed, Phillip Cole argues that:

> [Evil] only works as an explanation at a mythological level, and it only works if we suppose there is some other force at work other than the [agent] in question, either some kind of force that chooses to work through her, or some kind of narrative force, a story unfolding in which she is simply a character playing a specific and prescribed role. If we do not believe in the existence of these forces, then there is no explanation here at all, and the concept of evil has no role to play in a secular understanding of human behavior. (Cole 2006, 5–6)

In addition, in *Reading the Holocaust*, Inga Clendinnen argues that labeling Nazis and their actions as "evil" serves to categorize them as devilish or monstrous individuals whose behavior is exceptional to the realm of ordinary human conduct. The historian, Christopher Browning, likewise describes the actors in the Holocaust as recognizably ordinary individuals executing horrible orders (Browning 1992). In Scott Straus's analysis of the motives of the perpetrators of the Rwandan Genocide, he discovers that neither ethnic hatred nor a malicious bloodthirstiness was widespread among the ordinary men that participated in the mass violence (2006, 122).[3] To refer to any of these individuals as "evil" might foster the belief that perpetrators of horrible and brutal acts are so malevolent they no longer share

---

[2]One might suppose that even though such creatures cannot actually achieve a worthwhile life because they lack the capacity for care or for caring about things of value, they could nevertheless *aspire* to live a worthwhile life and hence be considered victims of evil on French's account. However, French's and Frankfurt's analysis of caring shows that the capacity to aspire is dependent on the capacity to care. An individual can *want* or *like* something in a temporally discrete moment without consideration of the future, but *caring* about something is inherently prospective. Insofar as an individual's cares structure her identity and bind together the moments of her life, aspirations for that life are rooted in what she cares about. See Frankfurt (1998, 83). I am grateful to Andrew Khoury for raising this point.

[3]See also Fuji (2009).

many of the features that are characteristic of humanity. Pushing such individuals or their acts outside of the boundaries of humanity leads to a halt to inquiry concerning the reasons for their actions. If perpetrators of grievous wrongdoing are inhuman monsters, then we can categorize them as irrational creatures who cannot be understood, setting them aside as tragic exceptions to a humankind that is fundamentally good. Clendinnen's argument, supported by the views of Browning and Straus, can be summed up in the following way: perpetrators of heinous atrocities like the Holocaust and other genocides are either diabolical monsters, or they are ordinary people. If they are diabolical monsters, then they are evil and if they are ordinary people, they are not evil. The facts show that they are ordinary people. Therefore, they are not evil. "We are a long way from monsters here" (Clendinnen 2002, 111). To make the contrary claim would be to misunderstand that ordinary human beings are the sole harbingers of atrocity.

Conversely, one might worry that calling such individuals ordinary or locating their acts and motives within the boundaries of humanity might diminish our abhorrence at the atrocities they committed. Responding to this worry, Clendinnen observes that if perpetrators were ordinary after all, this recognition does nothing to decrease the horror of their actions. In fact, it increases it. As one survivor of the Holocaust said of the Nazi doctors: "It is *demonic* that they were not *demonic*" (Lifton 2000, 5).

I disagree with Cole and Clendinnen regarding the appropriate use of the term "evil". The fact that perpetrators of atrocious violence are ordinary does not entail the further claim that "evil" cannot be applied to their acts. In fact, I am in agreement with the survivor's assessment; the term "evil" is appropriate precisely because ordinary humans are the agents of appalling acts of horror.

Hannah Arendt's well-known analysis of Adolf Eichmann helpfully illustrates this point. Her coverage of Eichmann's trial became notable because she suggested that evil has banal rather than diabolical or malicious motivations. She argues that Eichmann's actions during his trial in Jerusalem indicated that his thoughtlessness and ambition rather than murderous anti-Semitism motivated his despicable acts during the Holocaust. She points to the fact that he spoke in clichés and hackneyed idioms while continually referring to himself in the third person. Arendt draws a connection between Eichmann's inability to speak and an inability to think. She concludes that he is not a monster, and wonders if he is instead a clown (Arendt 1964, section 3). Although one might misunderstand her analysis as belittling the gravity of Eichmann's actions, her conclusions actually increase our alarm at the ease with which he performed acts of evil.[4]

[4]One wonders whether Eichmann's performance at his trial was sincere. New evidence has been uncovered to indicate that it was not. Bettina Stangneth challenges Arendt's portrayal of Eichmann as a thoughtless, yet ambitious, bureaucrat. In a compelling retelling of his story she proposes that his actions were the intentional acts of a "fanatical Nazi" ardently committed to the annihilation of the Jews (Stangneth 2015, 7). Despite this revelation about Eichmann's true motivation, we need not abandon the contention that evil may be caused by banal motives. A significant number of empirical studies support the position that acts of grave wrongdoing begin with ordinary and

The term "evil" refers to the very worst kind of human action. It need not entail connotations of supernatural inhumanity. Rather, it is a familiar feature of human interaction and its effects on its victims are severe, tragic, and oftentimes unbearable. The term "evil", when used precisely and in a secular context, is meant to be the worst term of moral opprobrium possible.[5] It has an explanatory purpose insofar as it allows us to categorize certain acts when adjectives like "bad" or "wrong" are insufficient to do so regardless of how many times we intensify them with the word "very". If the concept of evil allows us to make appropriate normative assessments regarding an extant category of human action, then it is constructive to attempt to clarify it further.[6]

French concurs that evil plays a central role in ethics, and that it therefore deserves our attention. He states that although ethics can aim at making people good, its most important function is to minimize actions that cause undeserved harm (French 2011, 65–66). Despite the great number of treatises dedicated to making people good and focusing on doing the right thing, evil is still a pervasive feature of human interaction. For this reason, the concept of moral evil is pivotal to many of French's chapters and articles.

French begins his discussion of evil with a number of important insights crucial for understanding his subsequent definition of the concept. First, he notes that "victimization is the identifying characteristic of evil" (French 2011, 62–63). This observation identifies an act as evil when it results in a certain kind or degree of suffering. When we reflect on examples of evil acts such as genocide, aggravated torture, and forced mass starvation, we are immediately confronted with the immense amount or perverse kind of suffering that the victims of those acts must endure. John Kekes and Claudia Card also offer harm-based account of evil,

---

comprehensible motives and beliefs. The well-known Milgram experiments and the Stanford Prison Experiment support this observation. Each set of experiments showed how easily ordinary individuals subject their peers to severe harm. Furthermore, psychologists Melvin Lerner and Carolyn Simmons reveal that when confronted with seemingly inexplicable suffering, people tend to believe that the suffering victim deserves her fate (1966). Similarly, Vicky Wilkins and Jeffery Wenger discovered that individuals who think the world is a just place, that is, those who believe that both suffering and prosperity are deserved rather than in large part a matter of luck, are more likely to oppose social policies aimed at rectifying injustices (2014). Still in another experiment, Zick Rubin and Letitia Anne Peplau discovered that people who believe that evil and injustice has a purpose or justification are more likely to support authoritarian political leaders (1975). These studies indicate that one need not have cruel or malicious beliefs or motivations in order to cause injustice or even evil. See also Imhoff and Banse (2009).

[5]See also Singer (2004); Kekes (2005).

[6]One way to examine evil is to say that it exists, that it plays a prominent role in human history, and even in philosophy, but that it cannot be defined. See Susan Neiman (2002). Neiman defends this approach by arguing that the problem of evil understood in both religious and secular contexts was *the* pressing problem from modern philosophy to the present. However she also insists that a precise definition of evil is neither possible nor helpful.

defining it as "excessive harm" (Kekes 2005, 2) and as "foreseeable intolerable harms produced by culpable wrongdoing" (Card 2002, 4) respectively.[7]

By emphasizing that evil acts are characterized by the kind and degree of suffering they cause, French's account can accommodate the plausible suggestion that evil is brought about by a plurality of different motives and intentions. The identification of the locus of evil in the suffering of victims, allows his theory to remain conceptually open to the possibility that evil is plural in its psychological causes.[8] Kekes explains:

> Most of the explanations given in the framework of the religious or the Enlightenment world view assume that evil has a single cause. Evil, however, has many causes: various human propensities; outside influence on their development; and a multiplicity of circumstances in which we live and to which we must respond. Because these causes vary with person, time, and place, an attempt to find the cause of evil is doomed. (Kekes 2005, 4)

The continuum of cruelties staining human history are too numerous and varied to attribute to a single psychological cause. French concurs: "The mental states, the conscience or lack thereof, the quality of will attributed to the evildoer might play a central role in justifications of responsibility ascriptions, blameworthiness, and the appropriateness of punishment, but not in the determination of whether or not an act or a person is evil" (French 2011, 64). If the motives and intentions behind evil acts vary, then it is reasonable to locate evil in the kind and degree of suffering that victims experience. One of the evident strengths of French's account of evil is that it identifies this salient feature of an evil act, while accommodating both the plurality and banality of the motives that cause evil.[9]

French's complete definition of evil is that it is "a human action that jeopardizes another person's (or group's) aspirations to live a worthwhile life (or lives) by the willful infliction of undeserved harm on that person(s)" (French 2011, 61, 95). The inclusion of "human action" in this definition functions to exclude natural disasters, which although they may have calamitous effects and cause a great deal of suffering, are clearly not evil in a secular moral sense. Only human agents can bring about moral evil. "Willful" serves to rule out accidents, inadvertent negligence, and

---

[7]See also Kekes (1990); Vetlesen (2005); Card (2010); Russell (2012, 2014) for additional harm-based accounts of evil.

[8]There are also numerous accounts of evil that attempt to define the concept by reference to features of the perpetrator—specific intentions, motives, desires, or a lack thereof. For example, see Garrard (1998, 2002); or Singer (2004). For a clarifying overview of different kinds of approaches to theories of evil, see Russell 2014. Although perpetrator-based theories are compelling, they also risk limiting evil acts to a single psychological cause. Since my current goal is an analysis of French's theory of evil, I shall not further evaluate the advantages and disadvantages of these different approaches to defining evil in this chapter.

[9]French's emphasis on the suffering of victims is not limited to physical pain. He acknowledges that "in some of its more dastardlier instantiations, [evil] may be entirely psychological" (2011, 62).

unforeseeable consequences from the category of evil. Finally, harm is undeserved when it is "not a morally justifiable hostile response to wrongdoing" (French 2011, 95).[10]

The unique feature of French's definition is its necessary connection to an individual's aspirations to live a worthwhile life. Acts of evil clearly inflict an immense amount and/or perverse kind of undeserved suffering on victims, but what makes the suffering perverse or excessive is that in each case the victims' aspirations for living a worthwhile life have been jeopardized or even destroyed. French affirms: "Victimization lies at the hardened heart of evil" (French 2011, 63). Specifically, the victim's hope to live a worthwhile life has been imperiled or shattered.

The immediate question demanding our attention is what makes a life worthwhile. French provides the following definition: "The life a person leads is worthwhile if what he or she really gives a damn about satisfies some condition(s) of value" (French 2011, 189). As previously mentioned, French's definition is inspired by Harry Frankfurt's work on the importance of what we care about.

In his influential study of care and volition, Frankfurt calls attention to the simple, but crucial fact that humans are principally creatures to whom things matter. Frankfurt writes, "A person who cares about something is, as it were, invested in it. He identifies with what he cares about in a sense that he makes himself vulnerable to losses and susceptible to benefits depending on whether what he cares about is diminished or enhanced" (Frankfurt 1998, 83). Further, the moments in the life of someone who cares about something are bound together by a "continuing concern with what he does with himself and with what goes on his life" (Frankfurt 1998, 84). In essence, caring about something involves structuring one's life in a certain way and constructing a roughly consistent self-identity over time.

We can further identify in persons a unique capacity for second-order caring. A defining feature of personhood is that each person cares about the fact that she cares about something. Frankfurt writes: "Not only does he care about following the particular course of action which he is constrained to follow. He also cares about caring about it" (Frankfurt 1998, 87). The individual identifies with her cares and guides herself away from being affected by anything that might dissuade her from caring as much as she does (Frankfurt 1998, 93–94).

The so-called wanton stands in contrast to the person who cares about her own carings. According to Frankfurt, a wanton does not care about her will. Her desires move her to act without it being true that she wants to be moved by those desires or prefers to be moved by them. Although a wanton may have developed rational faculties and be able to reason well, she is not concerned with the desirability of her desires themselves. She ignores the question of what her will is to be. She pursues whatever action she is most strongly inclined to pursue, but she does not care which inclination is the strongest (Frankfurt 1998, 16). I shall revisit the case of the wanton later in the chapter.

---

[10]See also French (2001).

French builds on Frankfurt's account by adding a normative element. Not only is caring important to persons, but caring about something of value is also critical. Particularly, it is caring about something of value that constitutes a worthwhile life.

This definition requires closer scrutiny. Even if it is true that cares play a crucial role in the lives of persons, it is not immediately clear that a *worthwhile* life requires having cares, nor the stronger claim that it requires caring about something of value. By distinguishing a life that is worthwhile from lives that are meaningful, significant, valuable, or good, I will argue that French's definition of a worthwhile life is too demanding. At the same time I will defend his definition of evil as correct—evil is that which jeopardizes aspirations to live a worthwhile life. In order to salvage this definition of evil, I offer an alternate definition of a worthwhile life: a life is worthwhile when it is worth the time and effort of the person whose life it is. Subsequently, I discuss what makes a life *not* worthwhile and how this understanding helps us clarify the nature of evil.

I begin with an analysis of the notion of a meaningful life in order to reveal how it is conceptually and substantively distinct from a worthwhile one. First, we must be careful to distinguish two separate ways that (a) human life can have (a) meaning. First, we can ask: what is the meaning of human existence? What is the meaning *of* life? This question seeks to provide an answer that purports to be valid for humankind as a species. A second and distinct question asks: what is the meaning of the life of a particular person? What is meaning *in* life? This question seeks to provide an answer that is valid for a specific individual. Kurt Baier observes that we can see the conceptual distinction between these two questions by noting that a positive or negative answer to one of the questions does not entail a correspondingly positive or negative answer to the other (Baier 1997, 46). Human life as such may have meaning if there is some purpose for its existence, for example, "to fill the earth and subdue it" (Genesis 1:28), or to evolve towards a state of perfection. However, it would not follow that each individual life exhibits this meaning or that each life is necessary to achieve the stated end. Conversely, individual lives may have meaning without their being any cosmic or metaphysical meaning to human existence as such.[11] That some individuals give their lives meaning does not result in meaning for humankind as a species. From my perspective, the issue concerning the meaning of particular lives is more important than speculations concerning meaning at the cosmological level.

What is meaning in life? To answer this question many philosophers focus on the manner in which a person interacts with objects of objective value.[12] Susan Wolf argues that "meaning arises from loving objects worthy of love and engaging with them in a positive way" (Wolf 2010, 8). Like Frankfurt and French she contends that an individual's life has meaning when it is committed to and engaged with objects of

[11]See also Nagel (1986); Sartre (2007). Of course, understanding the issue of creating individual meaning in a meaningless world is central to the Existentialist project.

[12]For a psychological analysis suggesting that meaningfulness is subjective, see Hicks and King (2009).

value. "One must be able to be in some sort of relationship with the valuable object of one's attention—to create it, protect it, promote it, honor it, or more generally, to actively affirm it in some way or other" (Wolf 2010, 9–10). Thaddeus Metz offers a "fundamentality theory" which states that "meaning in life is a matter of positively orienting one's and others' rational nature towards fundamental objects, conditions of human existence that are largely responsible for many of its other conditions (Metz 2013, 239). Metz's theory finds meaning in an individual's ability to engage in a certain way with objects, persons, ideas, and projects that possess a particular status in the world. Both his and Wolf's theories represent an objectivist approach to defining meaningfulness. A person's life is meaningful when she cares about objects of objective value.

Although such theories are plausible accounts of what gives a life meaning, it is precisely in demonstrating this plausibility that they reveal a sharp distinction with the notion of a worthwhile life. This divergence is most noticeable in Wolf's description of a life devoid of meaning. She writes: "A person who loves smoking pot all day long, or doing endless crossword puzzles, and has the luxury of being able to indulge in this without restraint does not thereby make her life meaningful" (Wolf 2010, 9). According to Wolf, the reason that such individuals do not have meaningful lives despite being actively engaged with objects they value, is that the objects themselves are not worthy of the attention they receive. The pot smoker and the crossword enthusiast lead meaningless lives because smoking pot all day and doing crosswords endlessly do not have objective value. Or as Metz might put it, such activities are meaningless because they are not connected in any way to fundamental objects or conditions of existence. Although I cannot so readily agree that such activities are unworthy of the attention they receive, I agree that they are not candidates for a meaningful life. Nevertheless, there is no reason to conclude in addition that such lives are not *worthwhile*.

It becomes especially clear that a meaningful life and a worthwhile life are conceptually and substantively distinct after looking more closely at the definition of the word "worthwhile". One might think that a worthwhile life is synonymous with a worthy life or a life of worth. But these latter formulations express meanings that differ from worthwhile. The worth of something is its value (*Oxford English Dictionary* 2nd ed. Revised, 583), and something is worthy when it is "possessed of value, deserves to be valued, is excellent or good" (*OED*, 587), or if it is "deserving effort, attention, or respect; having or showing the qualities or abilities that merit recognition in a specified way" (*The New Oxford American Dictionary* 2nd ed., 1939). These definitions correspond nicely with the notion of meaningfulness as defined by Wolf and Metz. However, being worthy is not identical with being worthwhile. One's "while" is "the time spent in doing something" (*OED*, 231). Something is worthwhile when it is "worth the time, money, or effort spent" (*OED*

232; *The New Oxford American Dictionary*, 1939). Consequently, a worthwhile life is likewise one that is worth the time or effort spent.[13]

Furthermore, the definition and ordinary use of the word "worthwhile" also reveal it to be a term used to evaluate a particular individual's time or effort rather than time or effort in any objective sense. The time or effort spent in (or on) a particular life, and the evaluation thereof, belong to the individual whose life it is. This subjectivism is demonstrated by the phrases that something is "worth your while" or "worth her/his/my while". Even the common expression "I'll make it worth your while" affirms that the term or phrase references some time or effort that must be invested for some return or advantage for the individual who invests her time and effort. There is no necessary connection between something being subjectively worthwhile and it being objectively of worth.

One might counter that anything that is objectively of worth is worthwhile—that is, certain objects, activities, cares, and projects are worth everyone's while. But this is not correct. Only particular individuals can decide whether a specific pursuit is worth their time and effort. Indeed, a particular individual can even decide that an objectively meaningful pursuit is not worth her while. An activity's meaningfulness in no way entails it being worthwhile for the individual in question, and its meaninglessness does not entail it not being worthwhile. Whether something, including a life, is worthwhile, is simply a subjective determination.[14]

To illustrate, consider the story of Sisyphus whose fate for contemporary philosophers is meant to exemplify a meaningless existence.[15] By altering a small detail in the story we can further demonstrate the distinction between meaningfulness and worthwhileness in life, while observing the objective character of the former and the subjective character of the latter. Imagine that the gods took mercy on Sisyphus and implanted in his brain the desire to roll the boulder repeatedly up the hill.[16] Nothing in this scenario has changed but for his internal outlook. Despite this significant change in his perspective, there is no reason to suppose that his life has gained meaning. Even if he psychologically endorses the act of endlessly rolling the boulder up the hill, it is still meaningless. The object of his care remains unworthy of his attention regardless of his favorable attitudes towards it. However, this alteration to the story does have a significant effect. Sisyphus's life is now worthwhile. As a result of his changed perspective, he now judges his life to be worth his time and

---

[13]I exclude money since only on very rare occasions will an individual evaluate the worthwhileness of continuing her life based upon money. It is not unheard of to do so, but it is not the norm for determining whether continuing one's life is worth one's while.

[14]"Subjective determination" means that there are no standards independent of the individual's desires, beliefs, or mental states to determine whether her life is worth her time and effort to continue. Of course a person may determine her life to be worthwhile because it is meaningful, valuable, significant, or good, but she need not do so on these grounds. For a discussion of subjective and objective theories of meaningfulness, see Metz (2013).

[15]See also Camus (1991).

[16]I am indebted to Richard Taylor for this example, although Taylor employs this example to arrive at a different conclusion. See Taylor (1970).

effort. It is worthwhile regardless of its meaninglessness and due to factors internal to his life.

Further, recall Wolf's examples of the pot smoker and the crossword enthusiast. Each of these individuals has decided that smoking pot and doing crosswords endlessly is worth their respective whiles. Nevertheless, these pursuits lack meaning because they are not deserving of the attention they receive. It is implausible that these individuals are unaware of the existence of more meaningful projects and activities, and yet they still make the subjective determination to spend their lives as they do. Insofar as smoking pot and doing crosswords are worth the time and effort spent for the return or advantage each receives, the two individuals in question lead worthwhile lives even if they lead meaningless ones. In fact, the life of any ardent hedonist may be one that lacks meaning but is still worthwhile. In any event, worthwhile lives need not be meaningful ones.

We can further distinguish between worthwhile and meaningful lives by arguing that the converse holds as well: a meaningful life may not be worthwhile. Imagine a martyr whose "life would be more meaningful if she underwent a life not worth living so that other individuals would not have to undergo that" (Metz 2012, 443). The martyr-individual gives meaning to her life by rendering it not worth living for the sake of others. Examples such as the life and death of Jan Palach come to mind. In 1969 Palach committed self-immolation to protest the end of the Prague Spring and the invasion of Czechoslovakia by Soviet occupying forces. He became a national folk hero to many Czechs, leading to songs and documentaries made in his honor, streets named after him, as well as inspiring protests against the totalitarian rule of the country. His act is commemorated with a plaque outside of the National Museum on Wencelas Square in Prague. His life is meaningful precisely due to the fact that he decided that it was not worthwhile. Whereas the pot smoker and the crossword enthusiast illustrate that a worthwhile life is not necessarily meaningful, the martyr shows that a meaningful life is not necessarily worthwhile.[17]

Now, the term "worthwhile life" is ambiguous and could refer either to the worthwhileness of starting a new life or of continuing a life already in existence. There has been a significant amount of philosophical attention paid to the first topic, and some attention but markedly less paid to the second. When thinking about the worthwhileness of starting a new life, one takes into consideration the entire potential life. Much of the literature concerning this matter focuses on an evaluation made by external observers. These external observers usually arrive at

[17] Although the martyr-case shows this conceptual division most clearly, we do not need to appeal to such dramatic cases to support the thesis that a meaningful life is not necessarily worthwhile. There are individual examples that also support this claim. For example, George Eastman, the founder of Eastman-Kodak, was a major philanthropist and helped popularize amateur photography. He also committed suicide. He shot himself twice in the chest and left a note that read: "To my friends: My work is done, Why wait? G.E." (Etkind, 12). The actor George Sanders, who has two stars on the Hollywood Walk of Fame, swallowed five bottles of barbiturates and left a suicide note that read: "Dear World, I am leaving because I am bored. I feel I have lived long enough. I am leaving you with your worries in this sweet cesspool. Good luck." (Etkind, 67).

their conclusions by assessing the foreseeable wellbeing or lack thereof of the potential individual in question. It is often thought that if a potential life will foreseeably cause itself or others more disutility or harm than not, then it is not a worthwhile life (e.g. Singer 1993; Benetar 2006). This debate appears frequently in population ethics and medical ethics.[18]

When French defines evil as that which jeopardizes aspirations to live a worthwhile life, he focuses on what constitutes a life worth continuing. When we think of evil acts such as genocide, aggravated torture, and forced mass starvation, the ruinous effects of these acts go beyond the severe suffering they inflict immediately, and often continue throughout the victims' lives. Assuming the victims survive the initial violence, many targets of evil acts may be unable to live worthwhile lives.[19]

We have established that a worthwhile life is not necessarily a meaningful one, and that a meaningful life is not necessarily a worthwhile one. To further specify the concept, we must distinguish a worthwhile life from a valuable one and also from a significant one. A valuable life is characterized by the value it produces or elicits, whereas a life is significant if it has some sufficient amount of impact on others.[20] This impact need not necessarily be positive. One may live a life of significance, but one that lacks value. For example, Pol Pot led a significant life insofar as his life impacted millions. Nevertheless, he certainly did not lead a valuable life since the impact his life had on others was evil. As Baier writes:

> We judge a life more valuable or more significant than another, e.g. that of Mother Teresa or Arthur Ashe more valuable, that of Churchill and the Ayatollah more significant, than mine or yours: the former more valuable on account of the good they have done to others, the latter more significant on account of the impact, whether for good or evil, which they have and are generally known to have made on others. (Baier 1997, 58)

To be even more precise, we can argue that a valuable life and a significant life have objective criteria that are established external to the life in question. As with its meaningfulness, we can judge a life's value or significance without needing to understand what the individual thought of her own life. In contrast, a worthwhile life is determined subjectively insofar as the life must be worth the while of the individual whose life it is.

Given that only an individual can determine the worthwhileness of her life, a seemingly counterintuitive conclusion follows. If neither objective value nor meaning are necessarily parts of a worthwhile life, then perpetrators of evil can be said to lead worthwhile lives as long as their subjective criteria for what constitutes such a life are fulfilled. But how can it be true that people like Pol Pot live

[18] See also: Parfit (1984); Smuts (2013, 2014).

[19] To name two prominent examples: The authors Jean Amery and Tadeusz Borowski committed suicide years after surviving the Holocaust.

[20] The definitions of a valuable or significant life are important in their own right and deserve further scrutiny. However, given the scope of this chapter, my current goal is to show that these kinds of life are conceptually and substantively distinct from a worthwhile life, not to provide a robust analysis of their defining characteristics.

worthwhile lives? Aaron Smuts identifies this apparent contradiction by stating, "it seems that a life that significantly advances horrendous evil is not worth living" (Smuts 2014, 440). Although this claim may be seem correct at first appraisal, it fails to recognize the distinction between a life's worth and it being worthwhile. We argued above that "worthwhile" does not entail worth or being worthy in any objective sense; worth in the objective sense reflects its value. We added that a life is valuable when it produces value or elicits good for others. In addition, a life is significant when it impacts others. And a life is meaningful when the individual cares about things worthy of her care. In contrast to these three kinds of life, a worthwhile life is one that is worth the time or effort of the individual whose life it is. Therefore, although it is certainly true that perpetrators of evil do not live valuable or meaningful lives, they do live significant ones insofar as they impact others, and worthwhile ones insofar as their lives satisfy their own subjective criteria concerning what is worth their time and effort.

This analysis prompts a slight alteration to French's definition of evil. Once again, French defines evil as an act that jeopardizes another's aspirations to live a worthwhile life. We must ask, however, whether the life of a perpetrator of evil, such as Pol Pot or Adolf Hitler, does not create the moral obligation to stop that individual's aspirations, thereby serving as a counterexample to French's account. For putting a stop to an individual's aspirations to do evil would not itself be evil; the prevention of their evil would be the opposite of evil-a moral good and obligation. As a consequence of the moral obligation to prevent evil, we must alter French's definition: An evil act is any act that jeopardizes another's aspirations to live a worthwhile life, unless those aspirations are held by someone who intends to jeopardize another's aspirations to live a worthwhile life. This qualification does not make any substantive changes to the definition, though it does preclude the objection that French's account, or my version of it, protects the aspirations of evildoers.

Clarifying these concepts provides us with distinct kinds of life. A meaningful life is one that arises out of loving or caring about objects worthy of love or care. A valuable life is one that engenders or elicits good for others. A significant life is one that has impact on others.[21] A worthwhile life need not fulfill any of these criteria. Its criterion is much less demanding. It is simply a life that is worth the time and effort of the individual whose life it is.

I have not yet discussed the kind of life that has received the most philosophical attention throughout the history of philosophy: the good life. I find it plausible that a good life is one that is meaningful, valuable, and worthwhile, while sometimes but not necessarily significant. That is, the good life is one in which one cares about things worthy of care, engenders or elicits good for others, and is worth the time and effort of the individual whose life it is. Nevertheless, I will not defend this position

---

[21] Almost all lives impact others. Therefore, most lives are significant for at least one other person. For a life to be significant for human history or for all of us it must surpass some threshold of impact. Further, if a life is valuable it may be necessarily significant since by engendering good for others one impacts them. I leave this discussion for another time.

here because a robust definition of the good life falls outside the particular goals of this chapter, and defining the good life is not necessary for defining a worthwhile life.

However, the concept of the good life can still be indirectly useful for our present purposes by serving as an obverse to the concept of a worthwhile life. Imagine that the concepts of a worthwhile life and a good life occupy opposite ends of a scale. A worthwhile life is at the bottom of the scale as long as it is also not meaningful, valuable, significant, or good. Fulfilling the subjective criteria that define a life worth continuing is not demanding. A particular individual must simply think that her life is worth her time and effort to continue. Conversely, a good life (however it is defined) would be at the top of the scale. Fulfilling the standard of a good life is demanding and is consequently difficult to attain.

Why is a good life so demanding? Michael A. Bishop observes that treatises regarding what constitutes a good life are dominated by three general categories all of which attempt to define the good life in terms of wellbeing: hedonism, Aristotelianism, and informed desire theory (Bishop 2015, 2–3). Hedonism defines wellbeing through measuring a life's balance of pleasure over pain. Aristotelian theories promote the cultivation of virtue that leads to, or is identical with, a flourishing life. Informed desire theories argue that a good life consists of getting what one wants. In each case the concept focuses on providing a definition of *maximum* wellbeing. In contrast, the notion of a worthwhile life is concerned with the *minimal* conditions of what makes a life worth the time and effort of the individual whose life it is. Consequently, theories of maximum wellbeing and the good life exist on the opposite end of the spectrum from the notion of a worthwhile life.

Imagining a scale of this sort may help us explain why we are able to speak of lives that are better or worse than others relative to a specified standard that defines the good life (Baier 1997, 59). Nevertheless, our scale is too stark and incomplete. Between a worthwhile life on one end and a good life on the other end of the scale, we might locate valuable, significant, and meaningful lives. Again, we might speak of lives as more or less valuable, significant, or meaningful relative to these standards. In any event, we see that these kinds of life are conceptually and substantively distinct.

Despite these conceptual distinctions, we often find discussions that confuse or conflate a worthwhile life with meaningful, significant, valuable, or good lives. It is well known that many of the ancient philosophers defined the good life as the exercise of rationality, the cultivation of virtue through philosophical contemplation or reflection, and the pursuit and achievement of the good, the true, and the beautiful.[22] Based on such arguments, Socrates claims famously "the unexamined life is not worth living" (Plato *Apology*, 38a). However this utterance is either about one of the other kinds of life, or it is false. Socrates may be correct that a meaningful, valuable, significant, or good life requires examination, but a life can be

[22]For example: Plato *The Republic* 508e2, Aristotle *Nicomachean Ethics*, 1098a7-1099a12, Epicurus *Letter to Monoeceus*, Epictetus *Enchiridion*.

worth continuing even in the absence of philosophical reflection. To insist otherwise would be to claim that only contemplative individuals have lives that are worth their time and effort. This conclusion is plainly absurd. Non-contemplative individuals may live worthwhile lives even if the argument can be posited that they do not live meaningful or good lives. Although this latter claim also strikes me as suspect, its defense has produced a common thread throughout the history of philosophy.[23]

Contemporary philosophers also tend to focus on the good or meaningful life even when they purport to say something about a worthwhile life. For example, despite the title of her book, *Well-Being: Happiness in a Worthwhile Life*, Neera K. Badhwar outlines a theory of wellbeing and defines it as the highest prudential good consisting of happiness and the cultivation of the virtues (Badhwar 2014, 23). Her definition betrays her purpose. The author gives us a compelling theory of what the highest good is, rather than the minimal conditions of a worthwhile life. Similarly, given its title we might think that Owen Flanagan's "What Makes Life Worth Living?" purports to identify defining characteristics of a worthwhile life. Instead, he focuses on possible characteristics that make life meaningful such as expressing oneself and finding projects that matter to the individual.[24] Although discussions of what makes life meaningful, significant, valuable, or good are important to philosophy, they do not address the question of what makes life simply worthwhile.[25]

These comparisons with treatises outlining the good life or a meaningful life support our earlier analysis showing that a worthwhile life cannot be equated with that which is meaningful, significant, valuable, or good. Even if an individual did not cultivate the virtues, or become excellent in the exercise of her rationality, or love objects worthy of love and become engaged with them in an active way, it does not follow that the individual's life is not worth her time and effort to continue. Consequently, whatever the criteria of a meaningful, valuable, significant, or good life, the conditions that make a life worthwhile are much easier to fulfill.

As a result of this analysis we see that French's claim that "the life a person leads is worthwhile if what he or she really gives a damn about satisfies some condition(s) of value" is simply too demanding (French 2011, 189). This criterion is plausible as a defining characteristic of a meaningful life, and perhaps gives us insight regarding what is essential for a valuable or a good life. However, as the examples of the

[23]It is not that I do not think that philosophical reflection is an important ingredient to a good life. Rather, I think that good lives can be reached in many ways. Further, being excellent in rationality or virtue is no guarantee of attaining a good life. See also, Kekes (1990).

[24]See also Flanagan (1996). Here he discusses meaningfulness while referring without distinction to worth, value, meaning, and wellbeing.

[25]See also: McDermott (1991), Cottingham (2003); Bortolotti (2009); Smuts (2013); and May (2015). Although Smutz argues that worthwhileness and meaningfulness are distinct, he conflates worth/worthiness and worthwhileness. Notable exceptions are: Metz (2012), where he explicitly distinguishes the meaningful and the worthwhile; Trisel (2007), where he distinguishes among different ways of testing whether a life is worthwhile before concluding the best test is whether an individual would choose to be born into this world *and* continue her life.

pot smoker and the crossword enthusiast show, a particular individual can lead a worthwhile life even if what she cares about does not satisfy some conditions of value.[26]

Moreover, by bundling his definition of a worthwhile life into his definition of evil, French excludes wantons and non-human animals from being potential victims of evil. Under French's definition only persons can be victims of evil because only persons have the capacity to give a damn about something of value. Consequently, only persons can live worthwhile lives and *ipso facto* can have their aspirations to live worthwhile lives jeopardized. Yet it is clear that animals and wantons can be victims of evil regardless of their incapacity to care about something of value.[27] They too can have lives that are worth their time and effort even if they do not or cannot reflect upon whether their lives are in fact worthwhile. An animal or wanton's ability to lead a worthwhile life can also be jeopardized even if it does not have occurent aspirations concerning how this life should be. With our revised definition of a worthwhile life, we confirm French's account of evil while expanding its range to include wantons and animals in addition to persons.

Although French's claim about a worthwhile life is too strong, I have stated but not yet defended my position, that his definition that "evil is a human action that jeopardizes another person's (or group's) aspirations to live a worthwhile life (or lives)" is correct (French 2011, 61, 95). The defense of this definition begins with its most apparent objection. Subjective human aspirations taken as a whole are too varied to make this definition of evil nontrivial, thereby reducing evil to simply that which impedes people from getting what they want. However, if the concept of evil is to do any normative work, then it must be a nontrivial concept that allows us to make appropriate assessments of human action.

To respond to this objection, I want to briefly identify those conditions that undermine the possibility of living a worthwhile life for all. Although specific aspirations for a worthwhile life are subjective, there may be conditions of existence that jeopardize the aspirations of any individual regardless of their particular aspirations or their subjective evaluation. Debates surrounding a meaningful, valuable, significant, or good life involve the identification of positive characteristics or conditions that must obtain for each one of these lives to develop. Whether it is the promotion of wellbeing, excellence in the exercise of rationality, cultivation of the virtues, or the just distribution of certain primary goods or basic liberties, the rich and suggestive philosophical literature on these themes corroborates this hypothesis. However, insofar as the evaluation of whether a life is worthwhile or not

[26]French may be open to the suggestion that one can live a worthwhile life even if one gives a damn about something that does not satisfy external conditions of value. See French (2011, 192). However, I make the further claim that one can live a worthwhile life even if one does not give a damn about anything at all.

[27]By definition wantons do not care about their cares and therefore would only care about things of value by mere luck. Also, I am assuming for argument's sake that animals do not care about things of value, but I readily acknowledge that this may not be the case. If it is not, then they already belong to the class of moral persons that French has argued can be victims of evil.

is a subjective determination, we only need to identify those conditions that must *not* obtain in order for an individual to believe that her time and effort are worth her while.

In other words, rather than debating what criteria are necessary for a worthwhile life, I propose that we need to ask what conditions must be avoided that would otherwise impede such a life. Here I propose that a worthwhile life is ordinarily one that is not spent under enduring conditions of fear or humiliation. We can think of such conditions as "what anyone can be presumed to want to avoid and what no one should have to suffer" (Card 2002, 114), as offering "a *summum malum*, which all of us know and would avoid if only we could" (Shklar 1989, 29), the absence of which is basic to most lives worth continuing.[28] Focusing on the political conditions that make any life indecent, Judith Shklar adds that the belief that every person ought to puruse their lives without fear is the only defensible meaning of liberalism (Shklar 1989, 21). Avishai Margalit argues compellingly that "a decent society is one whose institutions do not humiliate people" (Margalit 1996, 1). The decency of a society is a precondition for it being just. Similarly, a worthwhile life is one not subject to enduring conditions of fear or humiliation. It is ordinarily in the absence of such conditions that one can positively evaluate the time and effort spent continuing one's life. Experiencing continuous fear and undergoing persistent humiliation jeopardize the worthwhileness of almost any life.[29]

Fear is intertwined with autonomy just as humiliation is with dignity. Unrelenting fear, especially of cruelty, terror, or injustice, has the potential of permeating a life leaving insufficient space for pursuing the satisfaction of personal desires or subjective projects and interests. Acts of humiliation transgress a person's dignity, assaulting the individual's status as a moral person. One might think that fear and humiliation are of secondary importance to autonomy and dignity such that fear and humiliation appear sinister only as repudiations of their positive counterparts. Certainly, discussions surrounding the latter take pride of place in the history of moral philosophy. However, autonomy and dignity may be of crucial importance precisely because fear and humiliation are so pernicious. In whatever way we answer the question of conceptual primacy, one thing is clear: when present, enduring fear and humiliation dominate an individual's life overshadowing all other worthwhile-making characteristics in a life. The absence of such conditions allows an individual to consider continuing her life to be worth her while.

Before concluding, this characterization calls for two qualifications. First, it is worth noting that political regimes and institutions need not be the sole cause of enduring conditions of fear and humiliation. They can be, and perhaps often will be, given their power and impact. However, other individuals or group agents often

[28]Hobbes famously describes the *summum malum* as fear of a violent death. I would extend this notion to include not only that which makes death unbearable, but that which makes life unbearable as well.

[29]Paul Formosa characterizes evil in terms of "life-wrecking harm". He defines this harm as that which interferes "with a person's ability to live a full and complete life" (2008, 229). This definition is similar to French's and is likewise too strong.

bring about such conditions. Further, this claim is not meant to be a necessary or sufficient condition of a worthwhile life. There may be people who can lead worthwhile lives under such conditions, and there may be people who do not lead worthwhile lives in the absence of them. The presence of such conditions, however, makes living a worthwhile life extremely challenging.

Conclusion

Peter French defines evil as a human action that jeopardizes another person's (or group's) aspirations to live a worthwhile life (or lives) by the willful infliction of undeserved harm on that person(s). He adds that the life a person leads is worthwhile if what he or she really gives a damn about satisfies some condition(s) of value. I have argued that his definition of evil is correct while his description of a worthwhile life is too demanding and in fact identifies a plausible characteristic of a meaningful life.

I arrived at these conclusions by analyzing the meaning and use of the term "worthwhile" while distinguishing it from meaningful, valuable, significant, and good lives. For a life to be worthwhile it must be worth the time and effort of the individual whose life it is. Fulfilling this subjective criterion is not highly demanding. It is up to the particular individual to decide whether her life is worth her time and effort, and she need not engage in any meaningful, valuable, significant, or good-making endeavors. In contrast, living a meaningful, valuable, significant, or good life is demanding and requires the fulfillment of the objective criteria corresponding to each kind of life. My goal was not to scrutinize the essential components of each of these kinds of life, but to show that they are conceptually and substantively distinct from a worthwhile life.

Despite the worthwhileness of a life being a matter of subjective determination, we can identify certain conditions that ordinarily jeopardize aspirations to live a worthwhile life. Enduring conditions of fear and humiliation are ones that any individual wants to avoid and the absence of which is a precondition for the worthwhileness of most lives—person, wanton, or animal.

Peter French's insightful theory of evil has illuminated the nature of moral evil. By connecting the desire to live a worthwhile life to the endangerment of another's aspirations in this area, French has provided an important addition to philosophical discourse and has identified what makes certain evil acts so devastating. Evil acts certainly inflict immense and perverse suffering on victims, but they also jeopardize one's ability to look upon one's life as worth one's while. This harm truly lies at the hardened heart of evil.

References

Arendt, Hannah. 1964. *Eichmann in Jerusalem: A report on the banality of evil*. New York: Viking Press.

Aristotle. 1984. Nicomachean ethics. In *The complete works of Aristotle*, ed. Jonathan Barnes, vol. Two. Princeton: Princeton University Press.

Badhwar, Neera K. 2014. *Well-being: Happiness in a worthwhile life*. Oxford: Oxford University Press.

Baier, Kurt. 1997. *Problems of life and death*. Amherst: Prometheus Books.

Benetar, David. 2006. *Better never to have been: The harm of coming into existence*. Oxford: Oxford University Press.

Bishop, Michael. 2015. *The good life: Unifying the philosophy and psychology of well-being*. Oxford: Oxford University Press.

Bortolotti, Lisa, eds. 2009. *Philosophy and happiness*. New York: Palgrave Macmillan.

Browning, Christopher. 1992. *Ordinary men: Reserve police battalion 101 and the final solution in Poland*. New York: Harper Collins.

Camus, Albert. 1991. *The Myth of Sisyphus and Other Essays*. Trans. Justin O'Brian. New York: Penguin.

Card, Claudia. 2002. *The atrocity paradigm: A theory of evil*. Oxford: Oxford University Press.

———. 2010. *Confronting evils: Terrorism, torture, genocide*. Cambridge: Cambridge University Press.

Clendinnen, Inga. 2002. *Reading the holocaust*. Cambridge: Cambridge University Press.

Cole, Phillip. 2006. *The myth of evil*. Edinburgh: Edinburgh University Press.

Cottingham, John. 2003. *On the meaning of life*. London: Routledge.

Epictetus. 2004. *Enchiridion*. Trans. George Long. New York: Dover Publications.

Epicurus. 2010. Letter to menoeceus. In *The ethical life: Fundamental readings in ethics and moral problems*, ed. Russ Shafer-Landau. Oxford: Oxford University Press.

Etkind, Marc. 1997. *Or not to be: A collection of suicide notes*. New York: Riverhead Books.

Flanagan, Owen. 1996. *Self expressions: Mind, morals, and the meaning of life*. Oxford: Oxford University Press.

Formosa, Paul. 2008. A conception of evil. *The Journal of Value Inquiry* 42: 217–239.

Frankfurt, Harry. 1998. *The importance of what we care about*. Cambridge: Cambridge University Press.

French, Peter A. 1992. *Responsibility matters*. Lawrence: University Press of Kansas.

———. 2001. *The virtues of vengeance*. Lawrence: The University of Kansas Press.

———. 2011. *War and moral dissonance*. Cambridge: Cambridge University Press.

Fuji, Lee Ann. 2009. *Killing neighbors: Webs of violence in Rwanda*. Ithaca: Cornell University Press.

Garrard, Eve. 1998. The nature of evil. Philosophical Explorations: An International Journal for the Philosophy of Mind and Action January, No. 1: 43–60.

———. 2002. Evil as an explanatory concept. *The Monist* 85(2): 320–336.

Hicks, Joshua A., and Laura A. King. 2009. Meaning in life as subjective experience and a lived experience. *Social and Personality Psychology Compass* 3(4): 638–653.

Imhoff, Roland, and Rainer Banse. 2009. Ongoing victim suffering increases prejudice: The case of secondary anti-semitism. *Psychological Science* 20: 1443–1447.

Kekes, John. 1990. *Facing evil*. Princeton: Princeton University Press.

———. 2005. *The roots of evil*. Ithaca: Cornell University Press.

Lerner, Melvin J., and Carolyn H. Simmons. 1966. Observer's reaction to the 'innocent victim': Compassion or rejection? *Journal of Personality and Social Psychology* 4(2): 203–210.

Lifton, Robert Jay. 2000. *The nazi doctors: Medical killing and the psychology of genocide*. New York: Basic Books.

Margalit, Avishai. 1996. *The decent society*. Cambridge: Harvard University Press.

May, Todd. 2015. *A significant life*. Chicago: University of Chicago Press.

McDermott, John J. 1991. Why bother: Is life worth living? *The Journal of Philosophy* 88(11): 677–683.
Metz, Thaddeus. 2012. The meaningful and the worthwhile: Clarifying the relationships. *The Philosophical Forum* 43(4): 435–448.
———. 2013. *Meaning in life: An analytic study*. Oxford: Oxford University Press.
Nagel, Thomas. 1986. *The view from nowhere*. Oxford: Oxford University Press.
Neiman, Susan. 2002. *Evil in modern thought: An alternative history of philosophy*. Princeton: Princeton University Press.
Parfit, Derek. 1984. *Reasons and persons*. Oxford: Oxford University Press.
Plato. 1997. Apology. In Plato: Complete works, ed. John M. Cooper and trans. G.M.A. Grube, 17b-42. Indianapolis.
Rubin, Zick, and Letitia Anne Peplau. 1975. Who believes in a just world? *Journal of Social Issues* 31(3): 65–89.
Russell, Luke. 2012. Evil and incomprehensibility. *Midwest Studies in Philosophy* XVI: 62–73.
———. 2014. *Evil: A philosophical investigation*. Oxford: Oxford University Press.
Sartre, Jean-Paul. 2007. *Existentialism is a Humanism*. Trans. Carol Macomber. New Haven: Yale University Press.
Shklar, Judith. 1989. The liberalism of fear. In *Liberalism and the moral life*, ed. Nancy L. Rosenblum. Cambridge: Harvard University Press.
Singer, Marcus. 2004. The concept of evil. *Philosophy* 79(308): 185–214.
Singer, Peter. 1993. *Practical ethics*. Cambridge: Cambridge University Press.
Smuts, Aaron. 2013. Five tests for what makes a life worth living. *Journal of Value Inquiry* 47: 439–459.
———. 2014. To be or never have been: Anti-natalism and a life worth living. *Ethical Theory and Moral Practice* 17: 711–729.
Stangneth, Bettina. 2015. *Eichmann before Jerusalem: The unexamined life of a mass murderer*. New York: Vintage Books.
Straus, Scott. 2006. *The order of genocide: Race, power, and war in Rwanda*. Ithaca: Cornell University Press.
Taylor, Richard. 1970. *Good and evil: A new direction*. New York: Prometheus Books.
Trisel, Brooke Alan. 2007. Judging life and its value. *Sorites* 18: 60–75.
Vetlesen, Arne Johan. 2005. *Evil and human agency: Understanding collective evildoing*. Cambridge: Cambridge University Press.
Waller, James. 2002. *Becoming evil*. Oxford: Oxford University Press.
Wilkins, Vicky, and Jeffery Wenger. 2014. Belief in a just world and attitudes toward affirmative action. *Policy Studies Journal* 42(3): 325–343.
Wolf, Susan. 2010. *Meaning in life and why it matters*. Princeton: Princeton University Press.

Responsibility to Remember Injustice

Margaret Urban Walker

When Prime Minister Benjamin Netanyahu of Israel claimed bizarrely in a recent speech that a Palestinian leader was responsible for giving Adolph Hitler the idea of exterminating European Jews in World War II, reaction was swift and decisively negative both within and outside of Israel. German Chancellor Angela Merkel, at a joint press conference with the Prime Minister, remarked simply: "We don't see any reason to change our view of history." "We abide by our responsibility, as Germany, for the Holocaust" (Huffington Post 2015). Merkel's spokesperson, Steffen Seibert, added, "This is taught in German schools for good reason; it must never be forgotten . . . We know that responsibility for this crime against humanity is German and very much our own" (Times of Israel 2015).

If it is unsurprising that Germany, with its multigenerational history of public atonement for the Holocaust, would refuse any interpretation that relocated this responsibility, we should still find it remarkable. The German historian Ulrich Herbert refers to taking responsibility for the Nazi past revealingly as "the German peculiarity" (Smale, *New York Times*, 2015). Far from immediate or automatic, German recognition of the crime of the Holocaust took decades to become central to its public remembrance.[1] Nations do not easily accept, much less tenaciously defend, their unqualified responsibility for human rights outrages, massive crimes, systemic and grave abuses, or lengthy histories of massacre, cultural destruction and dispossession of subjugated peoples. Assertions of state responsibility for genocide, in particular, typically prompt angry denial by states and by many of their citizens, whether it is the long-running denial by Turkey of its genocide of

[1] On this uneven progression toward acknowledgment, see Weinke (2014) and Wouters (2014).

M.U. Walker (✉)
Marquette University, Milwaukee, WI, USA
e-mail: margaret.walker@marquette.edu

Z.J. Goldberg (ed.), *Reflections on Ethics and Responsibility*,
DOI 10.1007/978-3-319-50359-2_11

the Armenians; denigration of "black armband history" in describing Australia's treatment of indigenous people present for tens of thousands of years prior to British settlement; resistance to Canada's Indian Residential Schools Truth and Reconciliation Commission finding that Canada engaged in genocide against its First Nations; or resistance to similar claims about the dispossession and decimation of American Indian peoples, and deliberate attempts to destroy their languages and cultures, in the United States.

There is also the phenomenon of a formal gesture of responsibility-taking for grave wrong that is sealed off from practical effects or from consistency with other publicly stated or institutionally embedded positions. Stephen Harper, Prime Minister of Canada in 2008, made a ceremonial apology to Native Canadians for the "sad chapter in our history" in which children were removed from families and homes to residential schools at which many suffered physical and sexual abuse, deprivation, humiliation and cruelty while all were subjected to coercive attempts to strip them of tribal identity, language, and belonging. Yet in 2009, Harper stated in a G20 address that Canada, enviably, had "no history of colonialism" (Ljunggren 2009). The United States, unlike Australia and Canada, has so far made no attempt to publicly investigate its own use of Indian schools as merely one device in a long history of trying to solve its "Indian problem." But the United States Congress, in 1993, passed into law an "Apology Resolution" signed by President Bill Clinton that officially apologizes to Native Hawaiian people on behalf of the people of the United States for the "overthrow of the Kingdom of Hawaii on January 17, 1893" and "deprivation of the rights of Native Hawaiians to self-determination" (US Public Law 1993). While the same resolution includes a "commitment to acknowledge the ramifications of the overthrow," in 2009 the U. S. Supreme Court unanimously ruled, against the finding of the Supreme Court of Hawaii, that the resolution did not have the "weight" to block a transfer of state land pending claims of Native Hawaiians.

Sometimes, at an official level, societies cannot decide what or how much truth they are prepared to tell. In Tunisia today, the Truth and Dignity Commission – an official truth commission with a 5-year mandate charged to investigate crimes and corruption of past regimes – is under siege from the state that created it. As the President of Tunisia pushes new legislation to create a general amnesty for public officials and businesspeople accused of corruption, the Commission's head, human rights activist Sihem Bensedrine, finds it remarkable that a state-authorized truth commission is being overtly attacked by the state that authorized it. While the administration pleads pragmatic economic concerns, Bensedrine holds that corruption lies at the root of the human rights abuses of the previous dictatorships and at the heart of the "national memory" that the Commission is charged to preserve (Gall 2015). In yet another variation, attempts at official acknowledgments of the truth may be met with vocal resistance by the societies or communities they purport to represent. In a famous incident in 2001, then Polish President Aleksander Kwasniewski begged forgiveness "in the name of the Polish people" for the murders of 1,600 Jews by their Polish neighbors in the town of Jedwabne in 1941. The gesture was met with significant public resistance and anger in Poland and in

Jedwabne itself by many Poles who blame the Nazi Germans for the killings and see the Poles of that time as victims of German aggression (Fisher 2001).[2] Dissensus surrounding public apologies for grave injustices in history is not uncommon, even as such apologies seem to proliferate.

The instances just discussed are illustrative, but not exemplary in any special way. The phenomenon of resistance to or direct denial or evasion of dark aspects of societal histories seems to be the rule.[3] Is it perhaps futile to say that there is a "responsibility to remember" specifically in the case of histories of violence, oppression, or genocide? If there is such a responsibility, what forms does it take and upon whom does it fall? Few philosophers have addressed this issue, but in international law and a multidisciplinary transitional justice literature, a "right to the truth" and a "duty to remember" have emerged as guiding principles, to the point that international judicial bodies have in some cases ordered states to undertake particular public memorial measures in connection with specific atrocities (Campisi 2014).

I will argue that a responsibility to remember societal histories of wrongdoing is, for individuals, not feasible if it is coherent at all. Instead, I hold that a distinctive duty to remember can only reasonably fall upon societies as continuing historical entities who exercise agency through their governing institutions. While it is true that individual members of society have general civic obligations to accept and to contribute to the means of support of their society's actions in fulfillment of its obligations, this obligation applies to all legitimate actions and only incidentally to societal remembrance. In the first section, I consider Peter French's suggestion that the flattering collective memories that bind citizens to each other and to national (or group) identities are resistant enough to disruption or revision that they can render group members "morally challenged," that is, impaired with respect to recognizing or being able to act upon moral reasons. While French's claim oversimplifies the complexity and dynamic operations of collective memory, the idea of a "moral challenge" to individuals captures something important about our attachment to certain kinds of collective memories and I return to it in conclusion. In the section "For which memories are "we" responsible?", I explore some lines of support for consequentialist or deontological arguments for a "duty to remember" in cases of histories of grave injustice, looking at Jeffrey Blustein's sustained work on this issue. In the section "Who is responsible for memories some might prefer to forget?", I advance the claim that it is states through the agency of their governing structures that have duties to keep public memory responsible to accurate history. In conclusion, I suggest that nonstate institutions might also have obligations of memory and that it is a civic virtue of individual citizens to be actively supportive of their society's responsibility to remember injustice.

---

[2]On the careful reinvestigation of Jedwabne by Poland's Institute of National Remembrance, see Karn (2015).

[3]An extensive direct study of denial of atrocities, its many ways and means, is Cohen (2001).

Collective Memories as Memory Narratives

In "The Moral Challenge of Collective Memories," Peter French suggests that collective memories prevalent in societies – acquired through acculturation, education, and exposure to commonly held beliefs – can render us "morally challenged" (French 2011, 248). Collective memories, for French, are narrative representations of events that form part of the story an encompassing and enduring group tells about itself, contributing to its self-definition as a collective and to its members' sense of belonging and identity. Where belonging and identity are deeply valued, group members will react angrily, even violently, if the truth of these stories is denied or contested (French 2011, 250). Yet these "memories" are often – perhaps typically – mixed with fabrications, myths, and noble lies (French 2011, 252).[4] Shared narratives of dubious veracity about "our" group may promote hatred or suspicion of "other" groups, within or without. Mythic national memories often erase, if they do not distort, the stories of some groups within the same society whose actual histories of mistreatment or exclusion would question, discredit, or shame the nation as a whole; memories of oppression within mistreated or excluded groups may also function as unquestionable stories that anchor the righteousness of the group's claims of injustice. French argues that group members' investment in these "collective memories" (through early, deep, and persistent acculturation) produce attachments or commitments ("cares") that can render individuals unresponsive to relevant moral reasons or unable to act on recognizable moral reasons, if those reasons would require the individual to desert or reject some cherished identity-mooring beliefs. Individuals no doubt could believe and act otherwise and sometimes do. So while we remain morally responsible for what we do (or fail to do) in the grip of these seductive narratives, we are "morally challenged" in being able to see and do what is right.

The "moral challenge" of responsible historical memory, for societies and their members, is quite real, even as French's depiction of "collective memory" doesn't capture the complexities of historical memory, and hence, of that challenge. French uses the term "collective memory" to refer to learned representations and stories of events of which current members of the group could not have a "personal perceptual or a shared memory" (French 2011, 250). Collective memory in this sense refers to what might be more helpfully called shared "memory narratives" (i.e. narratives about the past learned and remembered). Memory narratives are not only specific narrations that and how certain things happened but also schemas or templates for the right sort of memories about those events. In settler colonial societies that dispossessed and decimated indigenous peoples, for example, certain

[4]French also entertains (without endorsing) the more radical view of the historian David Lowenthal that the collective memories that define the group-based identities and sense of belonging of group members – what Lowenthal calls "heritage" – are "typically fabricated," since only self-flattering stories of origin, character, or achievement will supply a source of positive self-reflection (French 2011, 253).

themes (in Australia, *terra nullius*; in the United States, "manifest destiny") require foregrounding adventures of exploration, claiming and taming the "wilderness," and building society where there was "emptiness," while rendering histories and actions of Native peoples secondary, invisible, or subsumed as material for tales of European daring, conquest, and achievement. Contrary to French's description, it need not be the case that group members *could not* have direct experiential memories of events involved in shared memory narratives, but rather that they need not. Where they in fact do have such individual memories of a period or series of events, a predominant memory narrative may allow them to remember the matter with others as the narrative represents it whether or not their individual experiences concur. A famous example of this is the post-World War 2 "myth of heroic resistance" that dominated French remembrance of its German occupation for several post-war decades: "Vichy was not France."[5] Emphasis on the Nazi occupation and effacement of complicity and active collaboration in the Holocaust by French elites and many French citizens was the prevalent memory narrative for a society whose population had just experienced and survived the period in question, in which many were complicit or collaborated or took active initiative in implementing murderous policies. This kind of case helps to illustrate some features of memory narratives that matter for considering our responsibilities for whether and what we collectively "remember."

Memory narratives are not necessarily fully articulate stories but are also story-templates that foreground certain protagonists and certain actions and achievements; others are cast into shade, ignored, or rendered in ways controlled by the required themes.[6] The memory narratives abroad in societies (or for that matter, within groups) are typically multiple. As Elizabeth Jelin says: "There may be moments or historical periods when a consensus is more pervasive, when a single script of the past is widely accepted, or even hegemonic . . . Yet there will always be other stories, other memories, and alternative interpretations. These endure in spaces of resistance, in the private sphere, in the 'catacombs' of history" (Jelin 2003, xviii). It follows that different individuals within a community permeated by certain memory narratives will have different relations to those pervasive stories in virtue of their own experiences and histories. They might reproduce or otherwise participate in the very "collective memories" that efface their own remembered experiences. They might struggle individually with that dissonance and with the erosion likely to afflict the memories they preserve in isolation. Or they might inhabit, seek out, or catalyze communities of memory with others whose remembered experiences are effectively exiled by a dominant memory narrative; they might together struggle for recognition of their version of the story. Memory narratives, dominant or socially submerged, are, like memory generally, dynamic. How we remember is a function

[5]Karn (2015, 33–40). See also, Baruch (2014) and Rousso (2003, 283), on "the spectacular evolution in France's collective memory in the last thirty years."

[6]Francesca Lessa attributes to John Gillis the claim that memory narratives are "things we think *with*" rather than "things we think *about*" (Lessa 2014, 78).

not only of what we have experienced or learned about events but also of the conditions under which we acquire and retrieve memories; these conditions include available information, concepts, and related experiences, the demands of the context of remembrance and other people with whom or for whom we are remembering (Campbell 2014, 13–18). When collective memories concern political conflict, violence, or injustice, "[m]emory narratives emerge through the conscious and sustained efforts of their creators – particular individuals, institutions and organizations such as victims' associations, politicians, armed opposition groups or security forces . . . ," who seek recognition and legitimacy for their version of the contested past (Lessa 2014, 78).

Within a society or group, some memory narratives achieve public or official status, with the sponsorship (if not enforcement) of elites or leaders. Yet powerful as such memories (and the resources available to promote them) may be, "[p]olitics of memory cannot always produce 'effective mental shackles,'" because "popular and local memories are hard to control" (Wouters 2014, 379).[7] Collective memory is an ongoing contest, especially where power, accountability, justice, and identity are at issue. Memory narratives are produced and advanced by human agents who often (at least in certain kinds of societies) "try to 'materialize' the meanings of the past in different cultural products . . . such as books, museums, monuments, films, and history books" (Jelin 2003, 25). Shifts in memory narratives or memorial regimes, however, cannot be explained entirely in terms of actions intended precisely to shift memories. While political memory activism can play a significant role, so can policy choices with respect to the past – such as criminal trials, truth or investigative commissions, creation or opening of archives or records, or public memorialization – as well as historical research, popular entertainment, international pressures, and generational change (Wouters 2014, 387). There is no question that the state and its institutions typically enjoy a huge advantage in advancing a view of the past, but even this does not guarantee that contrary memory narratives will not abide.[8] As noted earlier, states and their leaders may not adopt consistent stances concerning their histories; segments of the public may overtly or covertly resist the stances taken.

For Which Memories Are "We" Responsible?

The duties or responsibilities of memory I am concerned with here are ones related to societal histories of conflict, violence, oppression, repression and injustice that societies are tempted to evade or bury. In the case of a responsibility to remember episodes and eras of grave wrong and those who suffered in them, the most prevalent

[7] For a series of studies of popular and local resistance to official stories, see Bilbija et al. (2005).

[8] Three accounts of memory conflict triggered or exacerbated by state-authored memorial measures are found in Lessa (2014), Stockwell (2014), and Campisi (2014). On limitations of truth commissions as state-sponsored truth-telling projects, see Walker (2015).

view is that remembering the past can or might serve to prevent a repetition of similar grave wrongs. It is found invariably, for example, in the mandates of truth commission reports and embodied in the slogan "never again," employed widely in the connection with the Holocaust and with military repression in Latin America. It figures centrally in the emergence of a societal "right to the truth" affirmed in international documents, discussed below. It is unclear whether truthful accountings do in fact contribute to prevention of future violence; as widely as this is claimed, the mediating causal links between truth telling and prevention are virtually never supplied in any detail.[9] As a moral rationale for remembering the violence of the past, it can be given a consequentialist interpretation: recovery and dissemination of the truth about injustice is obligatory only if truth recovery would produce better outcomes in a given case than the alternatives (silence; edited versions; useful myths; or face-saving lies). On a nonconsequentialist construal of it, a truthful accounting would only be morally obligatory to the extent that it uniquely or effectively fulfilled some other obligation of independent weight, such as, perhaps, securing peace or stability. Neither of these construals is promising in supplying a *consistent* moral basis for accurate historical remembrance.

Jeffrey Blustein has produced the fullest account of nonconsequentialist duties to remember the past and the dead. His most novel "ethical expressivist" argument holds that, if persons, living or dead, deserve to be treated with a certain attitude – love, honor, respect, fidelity, gratitude – we have a nonconsequentialist moral reason to behave toward them in ways that adequately express the appropriate attitudes, including rituals and ways of remembering them.[10] This view captures something that explains what people do and may feel compelled to do when they remember, celebrate, and commemorate the dead. They are, in effect, continuing the relationship by exhibiting the attitudes that would have mattered to those who have died when they were living. Keeping faith with the dead is known to be important to human beings (including many cultural variations that involve honoring, assisting, appeasing, and sometimes warding off the dead). Keeping faith with the dead and not "closing the books" also play significant roles in struggles for justice and reparation by those who have lost loved ones to terror and oppression (Hamber 2009, 85–93). Direct obligations to the dead might be found incoherent by some who think the dead themselves cannot be harmed or wronged. An expressive rationale, however, might explain obligations to remember and memorialize in other ways that involve "character and conviction," as Blustein says of the act of bearing witness (Blustein 2008, 329). The guiding thought of individuals who hold themselves responsible to love, respect, honor, and commemorate their dead need not be that they are wronging or harming the dead if they do not. It might be: what kind of

[9]See Walker (2013) on linking truth telling to prevention through progressive strengthening of a human rights culture.

[10]See Blustein (2008), Blustein (2014) on several non-consequentialist lines of argument for remembrance of the dead. The few other philosophers who have seriously engaged the ethics of memory include Margalit (2002), McCarthy (2002), and Campbell (2014).

person am I if I act as though they, our shared lives, all the meaning they had for me, and all the feeling I had for them is simply cancelled by their death? Expressive acts might serve as a testament to what and whom a person values.

These rationales, however, do not meet the question I have put about accurate societal remembrance of violent, repressive, and unjust histories. Certainly surviving families and friends are likely to consider themselves obliged to remember those who perished in such circumstances with attitudes appropriate to their prior relationship. Memories of those who lost their lives in service to their country or those who conferred great benefit to their society might fit this model as well, for they are to be remembered with gratitude (and perhaps pride or sadness). But the question I have put is whether there are duties to remember that pertain to societies or their members generally in the case of gross injustice. I have asked whether there is a duty of *accurate* historical remembrance in such cases, that is, not only an obligation to remember the victims of injustice (living and dead) with fitting attitudes, but to preserve for public memory the truth about what happened to them, at whose hands, with whose support, for what reasons.

The sort of obligation of memory I am seeking is one that follows the contours of recent developments in human rights and humanitarian norms for societies dealing with gross violations of human rights and grave breaches of humanitarian law, such as disappearance, execution, illegal detention, torture, slavery, and genocide or other crimes against humanity. In a remarkable development, norms against impunity and in support of reparations for such acts increasingly entrench a "right to the truth." The Set of Principles to combat impunity (UN Commission on Human Rights 2005) asserts an "inalienable" right to the truth for victims and their families (Principle 4) but also for "every people" to know the truth about such violations as a "safeguard against the recurrence of violations" (Principle 2). Principle 3, here quoted in full, specifically enunciates "The Duty to Preserve Memory":

> A people's knowledge of the history of its oppression is part of its heritage and, as such, must be ensured by appropriate measures in fulfillment of the State's duty to preserve archives and other evidence concerning violations of human rights and humanitarian law and to facilitate knowledge of those violations. Such measures shall be aimed at preserving the collective memory from extinction and, in particular, at guarding against the development of revisionist and negationist arguments. (UN Commission on Human Rights 2005, Principle 3)

The following year, a UN Study on the Right to the Truth reiterated the entitlement of victims, their relatives and representatives, and "society as a whole" to the truth (UN Commission on Human Rights 2006, para. 36). The right to the truth covers the causes of victimization; causes and conditions of the violation; progress and results of investigation; circumstances and reasons for the perpetration of the crime; circumstances in which violations took place; the fate and whereabouts of victims; and the identity of perpetrators (UN Commission on Human Rights 2006, para. 38). The right to the truth corresponds to "the State's duty to protect and guarantee human rights," the Study concludes, and it is "closely linked to the rule of law and the principles of transparency, accountability and good governance in a democratic society" (UN Commission on Human Rights 2006, para. 56). More recently, the UN

Special Rapporteur for transitional justice Pablo de Greiff adds that "the right to the truth should be understood to require States to establish institutions, mechanisms, and procedures that are enabled to lead to the revelation of the truth ..." (UN Human Rights Council 2013). Finally, while these norms refer explicitly to the aim (and State obligation) of preventing future violations, and while the truth is seen as a mode of reparation for victims, the right to truth is nonetheless asserted to be an "inalienable and autonomous right," and a "stand-alone right" not subject to limitations (UN Commission on Human Rights 2006, paras. 55 and 60). That is, it is not a mere instrumentality, whatever positive effects individual processes of truth recovery or a general practice of truth recovery might be hoped to produce.[11]

The emergent international norm just described characterizes a duty to remember heinous acts of atrocity, not only for victims and survivors, but for society as a whole. It barely touches on historical truth, but this can be seen as an extension of the emphasis on the right of "any people" or "society as a whole" to an account of such acts in its history, especially acts that by contemporary standards constitute genocide, war crimes, and crimes against humanity.[12] Political documents articulating the advancing consensus on international norms justify these norms by reference to other established international norms, with broad references to the dignity of victims and the importance of preventing future violence. What kind of moral justification might be given that these grave violations, recent or distant, are ones that societies are both entitled to know and obliged to remember?

Avishai Margalit believes that humanity as a "moral community" ought to remember "striking examples of radical evil and crimes against humanity," because these acts "undermine the very foundation of morality itself" (Margalit 2002, 78–79). Of the "source of the obligation to remember" he says only that "it comes from the effort of radical evil forces to undermine morality itself by, among other means, rewriting the past and controlling collective memory" (Margalit 2002, 83). This might be read as a variation on the idea of prevention, in this case perhaps prevention of the erosion of moral standards, but Margalit does not elaborate on this remark. Blustein, however, does address the obligation of societal memory with what he calls an "argument from recognition of a distinct history and identity" (Blustein 2008, 169). The argument is that getting others to remember a history of injustice is "crucial to the self-respect of those who inherit the legacy of past injustice" (162). Public recognition of a history of injustice, including memorializing activities, must provide "not merely recognition of a group's understanding of its past," but recognition that can support for the current group "an understanding of its history that supports a sense of its own worth and a dignified sense of its collective identity"

---

[11]Information about violations as a remedy and a form of reparations is enunciated in UN General Assembly (2006). On truth as reparations, see Walker (2010).

[12]An interesting reflection on the implication of the human rights regime for history and historians, including the UN Universal Declaration of Human Rights and the emergent "right to truth," is found in de Baets (2009). See also, Karn (2015, 20–26), on historical commissions of clarification in a human rights framework.

(Blustein 2008, 164). Failure to publicly acknowledge their history of injustice, on the other hand, is frequently "but one aspect of the continued marginalization, oppression, and domination" of their group (Blustein 2008, 165).

This argument reminds us of deeply harmful effects on afflicted groups when their histories of unjust treatment are ignored or effaced. It is true that members of groups targeted for exclusionary, demeaning, and violent treatment may struggle with feelings of humiliation and shame even if they are aware that the mistreatment and insult they experience are utterly unwarranted. Some group members may internalize elements of a view of themselves and their group's language, practices, and cultural expressions as inferior or contemptible. Societies that claim to respect the dignity of individuals should aim to prevent these humiliating experiences and serious harms to individuals based on their membership in communities of origin, heritage, or affiliation that should not be denigrated.[13] But I do not believe that Blustein's argument is an argument for an obligation to sustain accurate histories of group oppression and violent mistreatment. I leave aside his idea that a group is entitled to an understanding of its history in which it can take pride; this might be a requirement for something other than an accurate history of its historical mistreatment. I pass over also the apparent implication that a group once maligned and persecuted will want the history of victimization to be defining of their identity; this history might rather be seen as an impediment to the expression of their identity as they see it. Instead, I think the emphasis in this argument is in the wrong place. The argument suggests that societies are obligated to remember unjust episodes and histories with the aim of allowing *the afflicted group* to enjoy a more dignified self-understanding and sense of its history. For members of the afflicted group, I would say, the point of acknowledging histories of injustice is not that they might enjoy a more dignified self-understanding but that they might enjoy greater relief from the injustices they have suffered and from their continuing negative social and political legacies, including additional injustices that their diminished status may carry.

My argument assumes that duties to remember gross injustice apply to political societies in virtue of their commitment to the basic moral and political equality of their members.[14] If societies are obligated to remember their episodes of mistreatment or their systemic injustice toward certain groups, it is because only in this way will more members of the society understand (to borrow a phrase Blustein uses in the context of his argument) "the meaning that a particular history possesses for those whose history it is" (Blustein 2008, 162). The history in question is the *society's* history of oppression. The meaning of that particular history (or no doubt particular histories, in the plural) is that without attention to an accurate account of the past situation and societal mistreatment of particular groups, the present

[13]The presumption here is that a history of unjust treatment is based on stigmatization, discrimination against, or persecution of groups that is itself unjust. The groups at issue in cases of persecution or systemic injustice would typically be national, ethnic, racial, religious, cultural or political groups.

[14]I don't hold that a hierarchical society does not have duties of memory of the type here discussed, but these duties could not be made sense of in the way I suggest here.

actual terms of relationship among members of the society is almost certainly misunderstood. As members of society are parties to an ostensibly cooperative venture, their "actual" terms of relationship within that venture are likely to depart in some respects if not radically from the "ideal" terms of relationship by which the society likes to characterize itself. The ideal terms are typically set both by formal legal status (as in founding precedents or constitutional arrangements) and by broader political traditions and social ideals which the formal structure overlays and within which it is interpreted. In contemporary democracies, these traditions tend to revolve around some basic forms of individual equality and liberty, often guaranteed by rights, and the ideal of sharing fairly in the common goods produced and the burdens required by the social cooperation that sustains society. When Americans claim that they enjoy equal opportunity, Australians a "fair go," or French citizens *liberté*, *egalité*, and *fraternité*, they invoke precisely the ideal terms of co-existence and cooperation enshrined in their founding formulations.

Episodes or extended histories of unjust treatment of groups, however, reveal precisely that certain groups either were never eligible for the position ideally envisaged or faced extraordinary and entrenched obstacles to realizing something approaching the idealized status with which other members of society did not contend. Having available accurate histories in precisely these cases makes the difference between a society that is prepared to acknowledge not only the past but the present predicaments of some individuals and groups, and to understand how the present – not just of certain groups but of society as a whole, including the relative status of social groups – is shaped by that past. As Thomas McCarthy puts it, in discussing policies to transform racial inequalities in the U.S., there needs to be "a serious upgrading of public memory to provide the necessary background for public justifications of a historical sort" (McCarthy 2002, 641). Accumulated disadvantages (both dignitary and material) due to histories of injustice can, without some historical understanding, appear as failures or evidence of the inferior ability or effort of disadvantaged groups. When groups in this situation argue for relief and redress of continuing disadvantage, they face skepticism (or ridicule) that shifts an unfair burden of proof on to them. It is they who must struggle to overcome ignorance or denial of the current reality and the historical roots of their situation. Others feel free to challenge their claims, not only morally but factually, and to impugn their credibility or their motives. It is with good reason that the Set of Principles to combat impunity speaks of the role of the right to truth in rebutting or preempting revisionist and negationist arguments (UN Commission on Human Rights 2005, Principle 3). For if victims and heirs of injustice have an interest in an accurate history, others have interests in denying or challenging that same history.

A society that is historically accountable at least sets conditions that make it *reasonable* for its members to believe what is in fact true about the history of its actual distributions of opportunity, recognition, and security (Walker 2014). To the extent that accurate histories are available, they make it unreasonable (although not, of course, impossible) simply to deny the reality of the past; they create the opportunity for public examination of the nature and impact of historical conditions. This is most consequential in cases of what Jeff Spinner-Halev calls "enduring injustice," those radical injustices that persist for at least two generations and that seem as if "they will continue on without some clear change in policy or attitudes" (Spinner-Halev 2012, 10). But it applies to all cases of severely degrading and violent mistreatment; mistreatment, ironically, creates its own self-reinforcing stigma, as onlookers attempt to reassure themselves and make sense that what is happening to others (especially at the hands of authorities they want to have reason to trust) is acceptable. It is reported that many people implicitly justified repressive acts (including tens of thousands of disappearances and illegal detentions) under Argentina's military junta (1975–1983) with the idea "*por algo será*" (i.e., there must be a reason) (Jelin 2003). It is much easier to believe that what is happening – or what has happened – is justified; to believe it is gravely wrong is to be taxed with considering what we or others should have done or might yet be obliged to do. The responsibility to remember, I suggest, requires a society to begin to reckon with the actual unequal terms of inclusion and participation among its members that constitute its most pressing questions of justice. Accurate historical understandings are hardly sufficient, but they are necessary to this task.

Who Is Responsible for Memories Some Might Prefer to Forget?

I have argued for a moral basis for a responsibility to remember within democratic communities that purport to recognize, secure, and protect the actual basic equality of their members. For accurate histories – in particular accurate histories of mistreatment and severe injustice – need to be uncovered, preserved, and revised (as needed for relevance and accuracy) in order to fairly examine the actual terms of inclusion and relationship and among their members and between their members and governing institutions. Exactly where, however, is this responsibility to be lodged? Is it an obligation of individual members, of the collectivity constituted by all members, or of institutions that represent the social body to remember all such relevant histories?

Both Margalit and Blustein seem drawn to versions of the idea that collective memory, including memory of profound injustice to some groups, is in some sense performed by the members of a collectivity as a group. Margalit writes that "the responsibility over a shared memory is on each and every one in a community of memory to see to it that the memory will be kept," but a "division of mnemonic labor" requires from each member only a "minimal measure of memory" (Margalit 2002, 58).[15] Blustein (drawing on Margaret Gilbert's plural subject theory) adopts

[15] In part because he distributes collective memories over the individual members of a community, Margalit struggles over whether humankind could be "a moral community of memory" of atrocities, and instead sees "natural communities of memory" bound by ties of caring, such as families, clans, tribes, religious communities, and nations, as the likely bearers of collective

the idea that a "joint commitment on the part of individuals to do or experience certain things as a body" can constitute a "plural subject of remembrance" to fulfill memory obligations (Blustein 2015, 88–89). I believe these views are mistaken (or perhaps misplaced) in holding that collective memory, in the sense relevant here, must be accomplished either by bits of remembering on the part of all members of a collectivity or by acts intentionally authored or affirmed jointly by all the members of a collectivity. While I doubt this is true even for those families, clans, tribes, or religious communities that Margalit calls "natural communities of memory," it is certainly false for political societies, such as nations (Margalit 2002, 69).

Collective memory as considered here consists in narratives or narrative templates that achieve currency or dominance within a collectivity concerning its past. Memory narratives emanate from various places and get traction under varying conditions. If collective "memory" results from the production, dissemination, and (more or less) effective reinforcement of memory narratives within a group or community, it will involve varied intentional actions of individual agents (e.g., transmitting memory narratives to children by teaching them) and might involve intentional memory-directed interventions by individuals (e.g. publishing a history that contests or supports particular views) or coordinated actions or campaigns of memory politics by groups (e.g. the Madres of the Plaza de Mayo in their weekly public demonstrations for their disappeared relatives). Individuals might individually or in concert have obligations of memory by virtue of special relationships or group affiliations (where Blustein's expressive theory is most relevant) or they might have adopted or accepted roles or offices in particular organized memory projects or institutions committed to memory preservation (where a "division of mnemonic labor" makes sense). But not all members of the social group or society need to accept or be committed to the task of preserving memory or particular societal memories, nor is it clear how they could all be so involved. Many (in some cases most) members will acquiesce passively in the circulation of memory narratives and others will ignore them or privately reject them, while some (likely a minority) take up the cause of defending or defeating them. It seems to me a mistake about what collective memory is to think that members of society *indifferently* bear *individual* obligations for the production and preservation of accurate societal narratives involving injustice, or indeed bear an obligation to make an individual contribution specifically to the maintenance of societally needed memory narratives in general.

An obligation to remember atrocities and histories of injustice should be lodged at the level of agency with both the general scope of responsibility that fits the task (to make available accurate histories to society in the interests of justice to all their members) and the powers and resources that give substantial promise that

memories (Margalit 2002, 69). The idea of a nation as one such "natural" community, however, seems to be a wishful communitarian view given the inevitable plurality, contesting, and dynamism involved in generating and sustaining memory narratives.

the task can be accomplished in a concerted way.[16] I suggest that the primary bearers of responsibilities to remember are, as current international standards have it, states. In cases of mass violence or systemic injustice, States are invariably either directly involved in committing or perpetuating wrongs or have failed in their responsibilities to protect their citizens from massive wrongdoing by nonstate actors. They are thus agents with causal connection, by commission or omission, to the wrongs in question. The scope of their responsibility extends (at least) to all their citizens. They are uniquely able to pursue and make available an accurate historical accounting by means unequalled command of the power and resources of public education, public media, and public institutions that produce and conserve historical knowledge (including public museums, public universities, and publicly funded research institutions). The state through its institutional and governmental apparatus also has access to a vast discursive field in which it can intervene with the intention of contributing to an accurate historical record. Interventions include public proclamations, apologies, or commemorative activities. Adapting a position Robert Fullinwider takes concerning reparations for historical injustice, there is "corporate" responsibility of the nation as a whole (a historically continuous institutional actor) for profound injustices that it imposed or tolerated; this in turn entails a "civic" responsibility of each citizen to do her or his part in honoring the nation's obligations (Fullinwider 2000, 2).[17]

To say that states, through the formal apparatus by which they govern and purport to represent a nation, bear a duty to remember grave injustices is not to say that states have either a duty or a right to demand specific forms of remembrance from individuals. The idea is rather that states possess the means to make available accurate understandings of these consequential histories and have a responsibility (both in virtue of prior wrongdoing or wrongful failure and in virtue of unique capacities and resources) to make historically accurate accounts generally available and to lend authority to those accounts. I have claimed that the rationale for duties of memory is based in the nature of democratic societies committed constitutively to honor and protect the political equality and freedom of their members. This means, first, that the state cannot responsibly be merely an impartial referee of, or host for, contending views, no matter how epistemically and morally disreputable the views may be, for the democratic state has a commitment precisely to protecting the equal

[16]Here I simplify by focusing on the national level and the responsibility of nation-states. But the same argument can be made as various levels of governance, including cities, provinces, or states. The first government authorized truth commission in the United States, the Maine Wabanaki-State Child Welfare Truth & Reconciliation Commission, investigating the effects of the Maine child welfare system on the Wabanaki peoples of Maine, presented its final report in June, 2015.

[17]Fullinwider's discussion involves reparations from the U.S. government for its failure to secure the rights and protections of citizenship for freed slaves. While accurate historical remembrance is increasingly recognized as a form of reparations, I here adapt the argument to locate accurate historical remembrance as a state obligation independently of its link to reparations. On corporate institutional responsibility of states, see, Erskine (2000); for the famous prototype account of corporate collective responsibility applied to corporations, see, French (1979).

standing of its members. This means the state should not itself authorize or subsidize the promotion of historically unsupportable narratives; it does not mean that part of the protection of citizens does not include a wide zone of freedom for citizens to develop and profess their own views. In other words, the responsibility of the state for accurate remembrance is to seek it, affirm it, and make it widely accessible.

There are inevitably, however, unclear boundaries or disputed questions about this responsibility that require political judgments to balance or reconcile conflicting values and responsibilities. One of these arises from the reality that facts are susceptible of varying emphasis and interpretation. A 1995 attempt of the Smithsonian Institution's National Air and Space Museum to commemorate the use of atomic bombs by the U.S. to end World War 2 in the Pacific ended up imploding over the inclusion of a display of effects on Japanese victims, including graphic images and disturbing mementos, such as a schoolgirl's lunchbox. The attempt to combine a profoundly emotional commemoration of an event within living memory with a critical scholarly treatment, some have argued, was a mistake (Kohn 1995 and Linenthal and Engelhardt 1996). This is a cautionary tale about finding effective and respectful ways, and appropriate occasions and spaces, in which to provide accurate accounts, not a repudiation of the importance of producing them. Another challenging area for democratic societies is that of balancing freedoms of expression and association with the objective of promoting and preserving truthful remembrance. Here, a stark example of dispute are the "memory laws" adopted by some nations that explicitly criminalize Holocaust denial or can be used to prosecute individuals who deny the Holocaust or other historically documented atrocities (Lechtholz-Zey 2012). Democratic societies with distinct traditions concerning the extent and valid exercise of basic freedoms of opinion and association have made different choices regarding this particular exercise in state promotion of truthful historical accounts. To say that states have a duty to remember grave and systemic injustices is not to say it is simple to decide which acts in fulfillment of this responsibility are politically defensible or practically viable.

Conclusion: State Obligation and Civic Virtue

Pablo de Greiff has said "we have an obligation to remember what our fellow citizens cannot be expected to forget" (quoted in McCarthy 2002, 629). I have given one interpretation of this thought-provoking maxim: that the obligation "we" have to remember falls upon the state, the representative agent of its people, to remember on their behalf and in their interest profound injustices that shape the history and often the present of their society. For what, then, are the people themselves responsible?

First, it is worth considering if a responsibility to remember might also fall upon private non-state institutions. Influential institutions may have been directly involved in grave injustices; they have some kind of representative standing, powers to reach widely into or beyond their communities, and resources to affect understandings of shared histories. Candidates for such responsibility might include churches, universities, or corporations. Brown University's President Ruth Simmons appointed a committee in 2003 to investigate the University's historical relationship to slavery and the slave trade. In 2007, the Committee' Report, describing universities as "conservators of humanity's past," surveyed both the deep historical roots in the slave trading of the Brown family, the general situation of slave trading and slavery in New England, as well as contemporary questions of justice and reparations (Brown University Steering Committee on Slavery and Justice 2007, 6). In July 2000, The Hartford Courant newspaper made a front-page apology for its publication of ads to sell slaves in the eighteenth and nineteenth centuries, having earlier published an investigation of the Aetna Inc. insurance giant for insuring slaves as their masters' property (Zielbauer 2000). Some Christian churches have issued public apologies for their complicity with slavery or their active participation in the removal of indigenous children to residential schools. Are these admirable optional actions or did these entities have a responsibility to disclose these parts of their institutional past?

Second, individuals as citizens have civic duties that are not only legal but moral obligations *as citizens* to comply with and contribute their fair share to support the (legitimate) state's fulfillment of its responsibilities, independently of any (other) individual implication in those responsibilities. This civic duty is entirely general, however, with no special connection to collective memory. In the case of civic duties to support the state's responsibilities to remember injustice, however, individual members of political communities often find it challenging to accept, seek out, or actively endorse and support their state's pursuit of accurate accounts of the shaming aspects of its history. Some individuals might be gripped with the force of Frankfurtian volition necessity, as Peter French suggests, by pleasant or elevating stories that affirm their group's goodness and glory; they will *feel* they cannot think or do otherwise (French 2011, 246–49). For the most part, though, individuals are commonly "morally challenged" by their society's historical accountability in much more pedestrian ways. On the one hand, many individuals are indifferent to many aspects of their society's history which they do not feel particularly concern them; they can be impatient or annoyed at the thought that they are supposed to pay attention to things they do not – and should not have to – care about. On the other hand, individuals are deflated, upset, or angrily (and occasionally violently) defensive when their preferred mythic or edited stories are challenged or impugned. Whether or not people care about the preferred story itself, they often care very much about how it makes them feel about themselves and others with whom they share it, and about individuals from whom, or events and places where, that story was learned. So, powerful feelings and desires to have things as we want them to be make us here, as elsewhere, tempted to avoid what is right, good, or true for what is pleasant, reassuring, or safe.

Virtue, not duty, might be the right ethical category here to capture what can be morally admirable here. Some people cultivate a firm disposition to want to live with their fellows and debate their reciprocal demands in the light of a truthful history; to be open to efforts to find it whether or not the results are comfortable or pleasing; and to expect and demand that the social institutions with the most power to make accurate understandings available will see to their responsibilities. Elsewhere, I have called this "civic integrity," a civic virtue (a virtue appropriate to individuals as citizens of a democratic society) that allows individuals to reliably support and insist on their society's fulfillment of basic standards of honesty and truthfulness and to disapprove actively of dishonest or corrupt activities of their society (Walker 2014, 48–52). Those with civic integrity support (among other things) a societal commitment to historical accountability and the avoidance of myth, fable, or lies about their society's history. When it comes to dark and discrediting histories, individuals with civic integrity are not necessarily less saddened, angry, disappointed, or uncomfortable to learn the awful truth. But they have learned to be moved in these cases by "the idea that justice must be the principal vector of memory" (Rousso 2003, 286). This is a virtue that democratic societies committed to the equal standing of their citizens have reason to encourage by instruction and example.

References

Baruch, Marc Olivier. 2014. Changing things so everything stays the same: The impossible '*Épuration*' of French society, 1945–2000. In *Transitional justice and memory in Europe (1945–2013)*, ed. Nico Wouters, 63–93. Cambridge: Intersentia.

Bilbija, Ksenija, Jo Ellen Fair, Cynthia E. Milton, and Leigh A. Payne, eds. 2005. *The art of truth-telling about authoritarian rule*. Madison: University of Wisconsin Press.

Blustein, Jeffrey. 2008. *The moral demands of memory*. New York: Cambridge University Press.

———. 2014. *Forgiveness and remembrance: Remembering wrongdoing in personal and public life*. New York: Oxford University Press.

———. 2015. How the past matters: On the foundations of an ethics of remembrance. In *Historical justice and memory*, ed. Klaus Neumann and Janna Thompson, 74–92. Madison: University of Wisconsin Press.

Brown University Steering Committee on Slavery and Justice. 2007. *Slavery and justice: Report of the brown university steering committee on slavery and justice* http://brown.edu/Research/Slavery_Justice/report/. Accessed 29 Nov 2015.

Campbell, Sue. 2014. *Our faithfulness to the past: The ethics and politics of memory*. Ed. Christine M. Koggel and Rockney Jacobsen. New York: Oxford University Press.

Campisi, Maria Chiara. 2014. From a duty to remember to an obligation to memory? Memory as reparation in the jurisprudence of the Inter-American Court of Human Rights. *International Journal of Conflict and Violence* 8: 61–74.

Cohen, Stanley. 2001. *States of denial: Knowing about atrocities and suffering*. Cambridge: Polity Press.

De Baets, Antoon. 2009. The impact of the Universal Declaration of Human Rights on the study of history. *History and Theory* 48: 20–43.

Erskine, Toni. 2000. Assigning responsibilities to institutional moral agents: The case of states and 'quasi-states'. In *Can Institutions have responsibilities?*, ed. Toni Erskine, 19–40. Basingstoke: Palgrave Macmillan.

Fisher, Ian. 2001. At site of massacre, Polish leader asks Jews for forgiveness. *New York Times*, July 11.

French, Peter A. 1979. The corporation as a moral person. *American Philosophical Quarterly* 16: 207–215.

———. 2011. *War and moral dissonance*. New York: Cambridge University Press.

Fullinwider, Robert. 2000. The case for reparations. *Philosophy and Public Policy Quarterly* 20: 1–8.
Gall, Carlotta. 2015. In Tunisia, an ambitious mission of justice meets a moment of reckoning. *New York Times*, November 7.
Hamber, Brandon. 2009. *Transforming societies after political violence: Truth, reconciliaton, and mental health*. Dordrecht: Springer.
Huffington Post. 2015. Netanyahu: Blame Abbas For Holocaust Comments, Not Me. http://www.huffingtonpost.com, Oct 21. Accessed 6 Nov 2015.
Jelin, Elizabeth. 2003. *State repression and the labors of memory*. Minneapolis: University of Minnesota Press.
Karn, Alexander. 2015. *Amending the past: Europe's holocaust commissions and the right to history*. Madison: University of Wisconsin Press.
Kohn, Richard H. 1995. History and the culture wars: The case of the Smithsonian Institution's Enola Gay exhibition. *Journal of American History* 82: 1036–1063.
Lechtholz-Zey, Jacqueline. 2012. The laws banning Holocaust denial – revised from GPN Issue 3. *Genocide Prevention Now*, Issue 9. http://www.genocidepreventionnow.org/. Accessed 29 Nov 2015.
Lessa, Francesca. 2014. Elusive justice, changing memories and the recent past of dictatorship and violence in Uruguay: An analysis of the 2012 public act in the gelman case. *International Journal of Conflict and Violence* 8: 75–90.
Linenthal, Edward T., and Tom Engelhardt, eds. 1996. *History wars: The Enola Gay and other battles for the american past*. New York: Henry Holt and Company.
Ljunggren, David. 2009. Every G20 nation wants to be Canada, insists PM. *Reuters*, 25 September. http://www.reuters.com/. Accessed 29 Nov 2015.
Margalit, Avishai. 2002. *The ethics of memory*. Cambridge: Harvard University Press.
McCarthy, Thomas. 2002. *Vergangenheitsbewältigung* in the USA: On the politics of the memory of slavery. *Political Theory* 30: 623–648.
Rousso, Henry. 2003. Justice, history, and memory in France: Reflections on the Papon trial. In *Politics and the past: On repairing historical injustices*, ed. John Torpey, 277–293. Lanham: Rowman & Littlefield.
Smale, Alison. 2015. A burden of nazism grows bigger with time. *New York Times*, Nov 3.
Spinner-Halev, Jeff. 2012. *Enduring injustice*. New York: Cambridge University Press.
Stockwell, Jill. 2014. 'The country that doesn't want to heal itself': The burden of history, affect and women's memories in post-dictatorial Argentina. *International Journal of Conflict and Violence* 8: 30–44.
Times of Israel. 2015. Don't absolve us over holocaust, Germany says after Netanyahu comment, Oct 21. http://www.timesofisrael.com/. Accessed 6 Nov 2015.
UN Commission on Human Rights. 2005. Impunity: Report of the independent expert to update the set of principles to combat impunity, Diane Orentlicher, addendum, updated set of principles for the protection and promotion of human rights through action to combat impunity. UN Doc. E/CN.4/2005/102/Add.1, 8 Feb.
———. 2006. Study on the right to the truth: Report of the office of the United Nations high commissioner for human rights. UN Doc. E/CN.4/2006/91, 8 February.
UN General Assembly. 2006. Basic principles and guidelines on the right to a remedy and reparation for victims of gross violations of international human rights law and serious violations of international humanitarian law. UN Doc. A/RES/60/147, 21 Mar.
UN Human Rights Council. 2013. Report of the special rapporteur on the promotion of truth, justice, reparation and guarantees of non-recurrence, Pablo de Greiff. UN Doc. A/HRC/24/42, 28 Aug.
US Public Law 103–150, 103rd Congress Joint Resolution 19, November 23, 1993.
Walker, Margaret Urban. 2010. Truth telling as reparations. *Metaphilosophy* 41: 525–545.
———. 2013. *Nunca Más*: Truth commissions, prevention, and human rights culture. In *Jus post bellum and transitional justice*, ed. Larry May and Elizabeth Edenberg, 262–284. New York: Cambridge University Press.

———. 2014. Historical accountability and the virtue of civic integrity. In *Virtue and the moral life: Theological and philosophical perspectives*, ed. William Werpehowski and Kathryn Getek Soltis, 39–55. Lanham: Lexington Books.
———. 2015. Troubles with truth commissions: Putting the moral aims of truth commissions to the fore. In *The performance of memory as transitional justice*, ed. S. Elizabeth Bird and Fraser M. Ottanelli, 7–21. Cambridge: Intersentia.
Weinke, Annette. 2014. West Germany: A case of transitional justice *Avant La Lettre*? In *Transitional justice and memory in Europe (1945–2013)*, ed. Nico Wouters, 25–61. Cambridge: Intersentia.
Wouters, Nico. 2014. Transitional justice and memory development in Europe. In *Transitional justice and memory in Europe (1945–2013)*, ed. Nico Wouters, 369–412. Cambridge: Intersentia.
Zielbauer, Paul. 2000. A newspaper apologizes for slave-era Ads. *New York Times*, Jul 6.

The Ethics of Hostility

Leo Zaibert

By writing about vengeance, Peter French has turned our attention not only to a somewhat contemporarily neglected topic, but to what tends to be a very much *maligned* topic. The maligning flows from the fact that vengeance (or revenge)[1] is typically taken to be opposed to punishment, and that opposition has considerable rhetorical force. While the desire to punish is itself often maligned as well (particularly as an overreaction to the current dysfunctionality of our criminal justice system), it is at least admitted (if grudgingly, in some quarters) that punishment can, sometimes, be normatively defensible. In contrast, vengeance is taken to be essentially barbaric, cruel, and thus normatively indefensible. Punishment, that is, is often taken to be a way of civilizing vengeance. French's writings on vengeance are, thus, not merely thought provoking – they are courageous.

In the first section below I will contrast French's unabashed endorsement of the view that "the very concept of a wrong or evil action entails that it should be met with a hostile response" (French 2001, x) against the much more pious (and much more popular) views put forth by influential contemporary philosophers. In the second section I focus on French's analysis of vengeance as such, and discuss the ways in which his notion of vengeance may in fact turn out to be much more similar to the notion of punishment than on first approximation one may think. Unfortunately, the typical distinction between punishment and revenge often goes not too much farther than mere rhetoric: it is invoked in order to somehow sanitize punishment (by means of opposing it to the allegedly unredeemable vengeance),

With thanks to Zachary Goldberg.

[1]Like French, I use these terms interchangeably.

L. Zaibert (✉)
Union College, Schenectady, NY, USA
e-mail: zaibertl@union.edu

Z.J. Goldberg (ed.), *Reflections on Ethics and Responsibility*,
DOI 10.1007/978-3-319-50359-2_12

but its analytical bearings are loose at best (Zaibert 2006a, b, 69–95). While French is not afraid to praise vengeance, he may in fact share with the typical efforts to distinguish punishment from vengeance a certain emphasis on rhetorical gambits. In light of the contemporary intellectual climate described in the first section, however, even if French's treatment of vengeance may strike us as employing a suspicious rhetorical gambit here or there, the force of his *substantive* position is not thereby diminished. I conclude, in the third section by sketching a way to perhaps distinguish between punishment and revenge that is more promising than either the typical approaches, or French's own approach – and that allows me to pose an interesting question regarding French's views.

What Then? Hostility and Its Demise

French gives us an informative explanation of the origins of his interest in vengeance. The interest stems from his "favorite form of popular culture, major Western films" (French 2001, ix). These films seek to make persuasive a claim that constitutes "a dominant theme of many of the better Westerns": that "vengeance could be virtuous under certain conditions" (French 2001, ix). The connection of vengeance to Westerns is, however, not important in itself: as French himself admits "the revenge plot appeals to be very deep-rooted and, I think, very important, indeed crucial, intuitions about the foundations and point of morality" (French 2001, ix). And in fact, French insightfully discusses the various ways in which this plot plays out in other literary genres, going as far back as ancient tragedies. What is really important, as French points out, is that

> contemporary moralists tend to express great discomfort with punishment, especially capital punishment, and even responsibility, but the revenge story, not only but famously in Westerns, attracts large audiences that leave theaters or rewind videocassettes with a sense of vindication, a sense that at least in the story, the film, things came out right, morally speaking. Victimizers were killed, and their victims, at least the ones who survived, can live in a morally restored locale. (French 2001, ix)

This passage, found on the first paragraph of *The Virtues of Vengeance*, conspicuously exhibits the close proximity that exists, in French's mind, between vengeance, revenge, and punishment: French here closely connects contemporary moralists' "discomfort" with *punishment* against the attitudes of those "large audiences" who enjoy *revenge* stories. As noted at the outset, I will delay the discussion of this close proximity until the second section of the article. First I would like to further explain what exactly it is that French thinks the masses find so attractive about punishment/revenge/vengeance, and how much, and how frequently, this is indeed rejected or dismissed by contemporary moralists.

In essence, French's thesis is, "as we have seen", the following: "the very concept of a wrong or evil action entails that it should be met with a hostile response" (French 2001, x). I would rather express this not as a deontic matter, and would instead paraphrase French's formulation in the following, more axiological way:

there is value in meeting wrongdoing with hostile responses. I think my formulation is consistent with French's, perhaps being preferable merely in that it offers a more conspicuous emphasis on the foundational axiological point at hand. That is, valuable courses of action can be trumped by other courses of action with greater value: there is no need to settle the ultimate deontic consequences of the fact that there is value in punishing a wrongdoer. But French and I agree on the view that, sometimes, hostile responses are valuable. I shall henceforth refer to this as "the hostility thesis".

French is particularly concerned with a certain passivity that flows from not endorsing the hostility thesis. French points out that "most moralists and ordinary people will agree that it is wrong to torture and rape another human being". But he immediately asks us to consider the following question: "[W]hat follows from identifying those actions as wrong?" He offers the following answer: "clearly, no one should do them" (French 2001, x). This sets the stage for his addressing the problem of pious passivity. "[I]f someone does torture or rape another person, what then?", French asks, just before offering a partial response: "they should, no doubt, be rebuked or condemned or ostracized from the community of good people." But then he wonders whether this really is "all that saying the actions were wrongful involves?" (French 2001, x); that is, he wonders whether the proper moral reaction to torturers and rapists is merely one of rebuking them. And it is exactly at this point in French's train of thought that the hostility thesis proper makes its appearance: it is not enough to rebuke: for French insists that "the moral order is affronted if such responses are all that occur" (French 2001, x).

And it is precisely this sort of passivity when confronting major affronts to the moral order, that is extraordinarily popular nowadays, and regarding which French's position stands in such stark contrast. The contrast obtains if we compare French's endorsement of the hostility thesis to the sort of overly pious views that seek to abolish all punishment. But the contrast perhaps comes into sharper focus if we pay attention to the sort of passivity exhibited by thinkers who are not full-throttle abolitionists: thinkers who contend that we should respond to affronts to the moral order, but who insist that such responses should never be hostile. By "hostile" it is meant something painful, inflicted on the wrongdoers, as a response to her wrongdoing, *because* it is painful.

Consider the case of Derek Parfit, whose *On What Matters* (Parfit 2011) has been one of the most highly anticipated, and then one of the most enthusiastically celebrated philosophy books in decades.[2] Perhaps the central aim of the book is to argue for an unexpected "convergence" between Kantianism and utilitarianism – views that have traditionally been seen as, if not downright irreconcilable, at least very difficult to reconcile. Parfit is motivated by his beliefs that: "Kant is the greatest moral philosopher since the ancient Greeks" and that "Sidgwick's *Methods* [*of Ethics*] is [. . .] the best book on ethics ever written" (Parfit 2011, I, xxxiii). Parfit evocatively sees these authors (and their followers) "climbing the same mountain

[2]The enthusiasm transcended the confines of academia: see Larissa MacFarquhar "How to be Good", *The New Yorker*, (Sept 5 2011, 42–53).

on different sides" (Parfit 2011, I, 419). This constitutes a remarkable contrast with Parfit's views on punishment (revenge). Regarding this particular problem Parfit seeks no convergence whatsoever.

Parfit approvingly cites John Rawls and Thomas Nagel to the effect that our moral theories are "primitive, and have great defects" (Parfit 2011, I, 174), and that, in general, ethical theory is "in its infancy" (Parfit 2011, I, 174). This is part of what fuels his ecumenism regarding comprehensive moral doctrines, as he seeks to "learn from some existing theories, hoping to get somewhat close to the truth" (Parfit 2011, I, 174). Nowhere, perhaps, is this infancy and are these defects more noticeable than within the context of punishment. Yet, within that context Parfit is uninterested in seeing what can be learned from existing theories. Regarding punishment, Parfit disregards some central ideas by that thinker whom he deems the "greatest moral philosopher" in over 2000 years. Regarding punishment, Parfit's views are just variations on Benthamite motifs. Regarding punishment, Parfit's views are not only one-sided, but they are extraordinarily passive, in exactly the ways that French criticizes.

The last chapter of "Part Two" of *On What Matters* is explicitly titled: "Why We Cannot Deserve to Suffer". Parfit thinks that the fact that a certain wrongdoer may deserve to suffer *cannot* play any role whatsoever in the justification of punishment.[3] For, in his view, there simply is no such fact: there is no such thing as deserved suffering. If the possibility of deserving to suffer is rejected, then all we have is suffering simpliciter. And since suffering simpliciter is necessarily (at least for Benthamite utilitarians) a bad thing, we should just try to alleviate it as much as possible. Punishment, for Parfit, could only be justified if it can be expected to reduce further suffering (or to lead toward greater pleasure). This is a good restatement of Bentham's simpleminded utilitarianism, and it inherits all famous problems attendant to it.[4]

Consider Parfit's assertion in "Appendix E", towards the end of the second volume of *On What Matters*:

> We often have more reason to be sorry, not for the victim of some crime, but for the criminal. Compared with their victims, criminals have often lived more deprived and wretched lives. When we imprison such people, in order to deter future crimes, we should greatly regret what we are doing. We should regard these criminals as like people who are quarantined, because they have some dangerous and infectious disease. Any criminal's well-being matters just as much as ours. (Parfit 2011, II, 651)

Given the dysfunctional aspects exhibited by contemporary criminal justice systems, it is sadly true that sometimes we should feel sorrier for the "criminal" than for her "victim". In fact, given the proliferation of victimless, non-violent crimes, it

[3]Whatever else can be contentious about punishment, the fact that, purely as a conceptual matter, it seeks to inflict suffering is beyond dispute. See Hart (2008, 4 ff.). As we shall see, for current purposes, "suffering" can remain relatively unanalyzed, meaning something akin to "hard treatment", "pain", "unpleasantness", and even to (Parfit's) "being less happy".

[4]For these problems see above all Moore (1993, *passim*) and Smart and Williams (1973, *passim*).

is often hard to know who exactly the victim is, or why the behavior in question is considered a crime in the first place. But there are cases and there are cases. Imagine a real wrongdoer – say, like any famous villain in either Westerns or other literary genres, or indeed any famous real-life wrongdoer: it is scandalously implausible to say that when these characters get punished, we are sorrier for them than for their victims.

Since Parfit begins this paragraph cautiously, by saying that it is only "often" that we have more reason to feel sorrier for the criminal than for his victim, it could be argued that the cases I have in mind are not amongst those he has in mind. But he ends the paragraph by explicitly reminding us of his overall view: "any criminal's well-being [including, evidently, the well-being of *real* wrongdoers] matters just as much as ours" – and this is just another way of saying that that their suffering is equally bad. And this is in direct opposition to French's hostility thesis.

Like Parfit, I think that we should often regret having to punish people. (I suspect that French may agree too.) But, unlike Parfit, I do not think that this is so because no one can deserve to suffer. There are at least two independent reasons why we should regret punishing people, one contingently related to current policies and politics, and the other one intrinsically related to the nature of suffering itself. As for the first, we should regret punishing people in light of how unfair (and inefficient) criminal justice systems happen to be. Contemporary criminal justice systems punish people more than they deserve, and people who do not deserve to be punished at all. Not only is it not necessary to deny that we can deserve to suffer in order to object to these excesses of contemporary criminal justice systems, but such denial may be counterproductive. Since Parfit does deny that people can deserve to suffer, whatever *other* criticisms he may have against over-punishing and over-criminalizing criminal justice systems, he cannot join me in criticizing these systems by pointing out that they mete out so much undeserved punishment.

Second, even when someone deserves to suffer and his punishment is justified, we should regret the suffering we cause, because the badness of suffering does not just evaporate once it enters an organic whole which is made better by this suffering. Moral remainders do exist, and moral mathematics is a rather messy affair. The case of the (justified) punisher resembles the famous case of the driver who blamelessly kills a child (Nagel and Williams 1976). Just as this driver ought to feel regret, or "agent regret", the punisher who justifiably makes someone suffer ought to feel regret or "agent regret". The sight of a happy executioner walking away whistling a happy tune after *justly* punishing someone is as chilling as that of a blameless driver driving away whistling a happy tune after killing a child. What explains this chill, what explains why we want this executioner and this driver to *suffer*, has little to do with desert. Rather, it has to do with the complexity of our moral life – a complexity that, when it came to the discussion of suffering and deserved punishment, seems to have escaped Parfit's purview. In the last section below I will return to the emotional life of the punisher, and suggests ways in which it differs from the emotional life of the avenger. But for now I wish to discuss another influential author whose views, when opposed to French's views, come across as extraordinarily passive.

In a recent article Thomas Scanlon admits that he has reconciled himself with the idea of desert: he claims to thus be "departing from positions [he had] taken in earlier work, in which [he] expressed skepticism about justifications of this kind [i.e., desert-based justifications in general]" (Scanlon 2013, 102). In other words, Scanlon has come around to seeing that sometimes a certain "treatment is made appropriate *simply* by certain facts" about what someone has done (Scanlon 2013, 101). Scanlon's emphasis on "simply" is salutary: it "is intended to exclude justifications by appeal to the effects of treating the person in that way" (Scanlon 2013, 101). In other words, a desert-based justification of X, justifies wholly in terms of the fact that X is deserved. Scanlon further explains his change of heart:

> I was earlier led to reject desert altogether because I identified desert with the thesis that it is a good thing for people who have done wrong to suffer or at least that this is less bad than the comparable suffering of people who have done no wrong. It now seems to me a mistake to identify desert with these retributivist ideas. (Scanlon 2013, 104)

This is, I think, an important departure, but I wish to underscore one point. While Scanlon now accepts many desert-based justifications, he continues to believe that desert-based justifications *of punishment* are to be rejected. Scanlon continues to endorse a view that has accompanied him throughout his career: that the view that "it is good that people who have done wrong should suffer" is "morally repugnant" (Scanlon 2013, 102). A fortiori, then, Scanlon is opposed to French's hostility thesis: for retributive punishment is evidently one form of hostility, and it is precisely its being a hostile reaction that Scanlon finds morally repugnant.

Echoing some of P. F. Strawson's ideas, Scanlon admits that it is sometimes appropriate – i.e., not morally repugnant, or even bad – to respond to a wrongdoer with "withdrawals of good will" (Scanlon 2013, 107), such as, for example, when we display "a decreased tendency to hope that things go well for a person and to be sad or regretful if they do not" (Scanlon 2013, 108). But Scanlon disagrees with Strawson as to what exactly these withdrawals of good will entail. Scanlon reminds us that Strawson's view is that the withdrawal of good will can involve "modification of the general demand that another should, if possible, be spared suffering" and a "preparedness to acquiesce in that infliction of suffering on the offender which is an essential part of punishment" (Scanlon 2013, 108).

The difference then is that Strawson's "withdrawals of good will" go further than Scanlon's. Strawson recognizes that withdrawals of good will can involve the infliction of suffering on those deserving to suffer, whereas Scanlon only allows for something considerably more pious. For Scanlon, withdrawals of good will appear to at most warrant a certain tendency to stop *hoping* that a wrongdoer's life go well, or a certain condition whereby we *feel less sad* when we learn that this wrongdoer's life does not go very well.

At this point one can just stake stock and connect views such as Parfit's and Scanlon's against the background of French's poignant question.[5] We all – evidently

[5] I have here focused on these two influential authors, but there are many other authors who espouse this sort of position.

including Parfit and Scanlon – agree that it is wrong to torture and rape. But if someone tortures and rapes "then what?" Where French believes that such a rapist and torturer should be treated with hostility, Parfit and Scanlon would recommend a much more pious response: they will urge that we stop short of real hostility, and treat him with what French calls "rebuke", mere rebuke. For a variety of reasons I cannot here undertake a full explanation of why I think that French's position is more plausible than the sort of overly pious views such as Parfit's and Scanlon's. It is enough for my purposes of highlighting the significance of French's position to show how drastically it differs from this much more popular (amongst philosophers) view.

Vengeance and Punishment

There is no doubt, then, that French is in the minority when it comes to his defense of the hostility thesis. In this section I wish to suggest that perhaps the hostility thesis needs to be recognized as not directly linked to vengeance as such: vengeance is but one form of hostile response, amongst many others. Punishment (whether justified or not) is another hostile response. Very roughly, and as noted above, we can properly call a certain response "hostile" when it seeks to inflict on someone some form of suffering at least partially for its own sake.[6] (This is so because of the axiological point discussed at the outset whereby there is value in wrongdoers getting more than mere rebukes as a result of their wrongdoing.) In order to show how the hostility thesis covers punishment as well as vengeance, I shall try to suggest that French's own analysis is incapable of neatly distinguishing vengeance from punishment.

French considers Robert Nozick's famous distinctions between revenge and retribution.[7] And he unequivocally states that some of these alleged distinctions "are less than convincing" (French 2001, 67). I think that French is right about this. But to the extent that he is right, the view that he has identified virtues of *vengeance* specifically, as opposed to virtues of hostile responses more generally, loses plausibility. I think that the resemblance between French's analysis of

[6]To "force" someone to undergo a painful medical treatment is not hostile, since there is no value in that person undergoing the pain *as such*. If the effects of the treatment were attainable without the pain, then that would be preferable. Many see punishment under this exact light: the pain that punishment causes is necessary in order to diminish further pain down the road. Those who see punishment in this way may be forced that so understood punishment is in fact not hostile. But those who think that, for example, torturers and rapists ought to suffer as a consequence of having tortured and raped, independently of whatever good consequences may follow from their suffering, are perforce recognizing that punishment is a hostile response.

[7]In this context, retribution can be taken to be a synonym to punishment. "Retributive punishment" is, in a way, pleonastic – since "punishment" which does not purport to be retributive (of the guilty) can hardly be called punishment. See Zaibert (2006b, 7–37 and *passim*). See also Rawls (1955, 3–32).

someone successfully avenging someone else and standard analyses of punishment are remarkable. This is French's analysis of vengeance:

> Avenger Y succeeded in avenging X's act A (in the best-case scenario) if the following conditions held:
>
> 1. Y felt that A, an act that inflicted a harm or injury on someone, possibly Y, was, to some degree or extent, wrong,
> 2. And imposed a penalty on X,
> 3. That reflected, at the time, how strongly Y felt about the wrongness of A,
> 4. Intending that the penalty be exacted because of the wrong act A,
> 5. And in virtue of the wrongness of A,
> 6. Intending that X realize that the penalty was visited on him or her because he or she did A,
> 7. And in virtue of the wrongness of A,
> 8. By someone who intended to have the penalty fit and be executed because of the wrongness of A,
> 9. And who intended that X would understand that the penalty was inflicted on him or her so that 1–9 are satisfied. (French 2001, 70)

Now contrast it to the famous, Flew-Benn-Hart analysis of punishment (in Hart's rendering):

> So with Mr. Benn and Professor Flew I shall define the standard or central case of 'punishment' in terms of five elements:
>
> (i) It must involve pain or other consequences normally considered unpleasant.
> (ii) It must be for an offence against legal rules.
> (iii) It must be of an actual or supposed offender for his offence.
> (iv) It must be intentionally administered by human beings other than the offender.
> (v) It must be imposed and administered by an authority constituted by a legal system against which the offence is committed. (Hart 2008, 5)

And to my own analysis of a case in which A punishes B:

> (1) A believes that X is a bad thing.
> (2) A believes that X is an action of B's.
> (3) A believes that B is a moral agent.
> (4) A believes that there are no excuses, justifications or other circumstances which preclude blame.
> (5) A believes that the world would have been a better place had B not done X.
> (6) A believes that the world would be a better place if something would happen to B, something which would somehow offset B's Xing.
> (7) B's having X'ed tends to make A feel something negative, that is, a reactive emotion, like outrage, indignation or resentment.
> (8) A, as a consequence of having the beliefs and emotions listed in (1) through (7), does something to B, which A believes it is painful for B to endure, as a response to B's having X'ed. (Zaibert 2006b, 31–33)

As is immediately evident, French's analysis of vengeance is extremely similar to either the standard (widespread) account of punishment or to my own account of punishment. I wish to discuss, first of all, a couple of differences between French's account of vengeance, and the accounts of punishment with which I am comparing it. First, the standard account of punishment seems to differ in an important way from French's account of vengeance in that the former restricts punishment to legal authorities enforcing violations of legal matters, whereas French's account of vengeance is much broader than that. This would be indeed an important difference if it held without qualifications. But it does not so hold. First, consider the fact that my own account of punishment is as broad as French's account of vengeance: criminal punishment can of course be an instance of punishment but so can be cases of punishment meted out by parents, teachers, friends, and even perfect strangers. Second, the standard approach, too, admits to this possibility, albeit in a less direct way. Immediately after Hart presents the account of punishment just quoted he adds:

> In calling this the standard or central case of punishment I shall relegate to the position of sub-standard or secondary cases the following among many other possibilities:
>
> (a) Punishments for breaches of legal rules imposed or administered otherwise than by officials (decentralized sanctions).
> (b) Punishments for breaches of non-legal rules or orders (punishments in a family or school).
> (c) Vicarious or collective punishment of some member of a social group for actions done by others without the former's authorization, encouragement, control, or permission.
> (d) Punishment of persons (otherwise than under (c)) who neither are in fact nor supposed to be offenders. (Hart 2008, 5)

The fact that Hart distinguishes between "central or standard" and "sub-standard" cases of punishment does not deny that he admits that acts such as French's vengeance are to be admitted as forms of punishment, albeit sub-standard. Elsewhere I have criticized Hart's distinction between the standard and the sub-standard in this context.[8] For current purposes, however, what matters is underscoring that there is no difference in terms of hostility between the standard and the sub-standard cases, and in this regard French's vengeance (a sub-standard case of punishment under the infelicitous light of Hart's distinction) need be neither more nor less hostile than Hart's standard punishment.

The second noticeable difference between French's account of vengeance and the accounts of punishment with which I am contrasting it has to do with French's emphasis on *communication*, as visible in his condition "6" and "9". But here again the difference is less significant than it may on first approximation appear, and again for two main reasons. First, many contemporary accounts of punishment also include, sometimes even more prominently than in French's case, a concern with communication.[9] So, again, an emphasis on communication can hardly be seen as a differentiating factor separating French's vengeance from many popular and influential accounts of punishment. But there is more: even accounts such as the Flew-Benn-Hart, or mine, which do not explicitly include communicative aims in the *definition* of punishment, are quite consistent in that some communicative goals,

---

[8]In Zaibert (2006b, 41) I call it a "catch-all" and "entirely empty clause".

[9]Defenses of communicative approaches to punishment are visible in the work of leading punishment theorists, such as Joel Feinberg, Douglas Husak, Andrew von Hirsch, John Tasioulas, and above all R. A. Duff.

in some contexts, may add significant value to the infliction of punishment, and that thus may contribute to punishment's *justification*.

Elsewhere I have argued that it is worthwhile to distinguish the definition of punishment (or vengeance, etc.) from its justification (Zaibert 2006b, *passim*). Getting the wrongdoer to understand the nature of his wrongdoing, and making him further understand that the hostile reaction is in fact a fitting response to said wrongdoing is often very valuable. The only cases in which this may perhaps be of little value are those cases in which the monstrosity of the wrong is such that the sheer value of having this person suffer may eclipse the value of getting him to understand anything. Confronted with, say, Josef Mengele, one may in fact have very little interest – and see very little value – in getting *him* to understand what he did; rather, we mainly (or only) want him to suffer as a result of what he did.

Others believe that sometimes the justificatory and the definitional enterprises ought to be run together.[10] I am not sure that this is French's position. But whether the result of a deliberate decision to conflate the definitional and the justificatory enterprises in the case of vengeance, what is clear is that French analysis of vengeance does run the two enterprises together. I think that this may be somewhat problematic for him, in the sense that it is easy to imagine – and many a Western movie includes – characters seeking revenge who do not wish to communicate anything particular: they just wants the wrongdoer dead, for example.[11] And the same is true in other literary genres.

This discussion brings me to the second reason why French's emphasis on communication within the context of vengeance is not that much of a departure from typical accounts of punishment. The main reason why French emphasizes communication is that sometimes the hostile reaction can only be made to fit the wrongdoing to which it is a response by including this communicative element. In French's own eloquent words:

> vengeance cannot be complete, [. . .] it cannot truly fit the crime, if the punishment does not respond to both the crime and the guilty mind of the criminal. Taking an eye for an eye, a life for a life, might have no appreciable effect on the guilty mind of the criminal. The exquisitely devised punishments of the deeper circles of Hell are intended to demonstrate the depths of revenge to which an avenger must go to conjoin the crime and the guilty mind, the preference or disposition for wickedness, in an effective way. Achilles tells Hector why he is killing him, and, presumably, Hector has a moment or two to reflect on how he came to such an end. (French 2001, 30)

The communicative element in French's interpretation of what goes on regarding Achilles and Hector is that only by Achilles communicating something to Hector can his punishment really fit Hector's wrongdoing. In other words, Achilles's exchange with Hector serves not the purpose of getting Hector to understand the

[10]For example, see Jeffrie Murphy "Forgiveness and Resentment" in (Murphy and Hampton 1988, 23 ff.).

[11]For example, the prostitutes in *Unforgiven*, which French discusses on pp. 38 ff., just wished the cruel cowboy who disfigured one of them dead – they have no interest in communicating anything to him.

wrongness of what he did and thus be reformed (since he is just going to die right then and there) – but rather to make Hector suffer as much as he deserved to suffer. In Achilles's mind, Hector's anonymous, humdrum death would not be quite what he deserved – only if he dies at Achilles' own hands, and as he explains to him why he is killing him and that it is he who is killing him (etc.), would vengeance be "complete". Or as French makes the more general point elsewhere: "for vengeance to be successful, the target must understand that he or she is suffering injury or being killed as a penalty for his or her actions that triggered the revenge behavior of the avenger" (French 2001, 34).

This is an interesting difference between French's invocation of communication in the case of vengeance and the way other punishment theorists invoke communication. For the latter tend to turn toward communication in order to try to render our punishment practices more humane and our criminal justice systems less dysfunctional. And not without reason: the essential, original point of a "penitentiary" is evidently connected to *meaningful* repentance – and it is quite evident that modern penitentiaries do not accomplish that. Admittedly, some criminals may come to regret what they have done as a result of the horrors of life in a contemporary penitentiary – but this is not meaningful repentance in the sense that it is not caused by the realization of the wrongness of what they have done.

In French's case, in contrast, communication is important in making punishment fit the crime, as it were. But then it is clear that this difference, interesting as it is, is not going to offer a way of distinguishing between his account of vengeance from other accounts of punishment. For French's emphasis on communication can be subsumed under the extraordinarily widespread belief that the *justification* of punishment ought to include concerns with proportionality. Grossly disproportionate punishment can hardly be seen as justified. French wants avengers to communicate certain things to those upon whom they visit revenge (or to others) in order to make their punishment more fitting, more proportionate.

In the end, I think that we are entitled to conclude that French does not really offer ways to see vengeance as particularly different from punishment. This in no way detracts from the enlightening ways in which French argues for the hostility thesis. Whether we call it "vengeance" or "punishment" or "revenge", these are evidently hostile responses, and they sometimes strike us as correct. Of course, if I am right in this, one could then wonder to what extent French's book really is about *vengeance* rather than about punishment – although admittedly *The Virtues of Vengeance* is a much punchier title than *The Virtues of Punishment*. Beyond marketing decisions regarding books' titles, however, I think that exploring the topic of the differences between vengeance and punishment is worthwhile – and I will conclude this article with a brief exploration of this exact topic.

Vengeance, Punishment, and Moral Conflict

As noted above, French considers some of the alleged classical distinctions between vengeance and punishment that Nozick usefully compiled to be less than fully convincing. I agree with French. In fact, I have analyzed these famous alleged distinctions in considerable detail, and have found them wanting.[12] But I am not convinced that there is *no* difference between punishment and vengeance. I have thus suggested one possible difference between the two phenomena, and I wish here to add one additional possible – and interesting – way of distinguishing vengeance from punishment.

Before turning to these differences, I must at least mention the classical alleged differences which I, and to at least some extent French, find wanting. This is Nozick's compilation:

> (1) Retribution is done for a wrong, while revenge may be done for an injury or harm or slight and need not be for a wrong.
> (2) Retribution sets an internal limit to the amount of the punishment, according to the seriousness of the wrong, whereas revenge internally need set no limit to what is inflicted.
> (3) Revenge is personal [. . .] whereas the agent of retribution need have no special or personal tie to the victim of the wrong for which he exacts retribution.
> (4) Revenge involves a particular emotional tone, pleasure at the suffering of another, while retribution either need involve no emotional tone or involves another one, namely pleasure at justice being done.
> (5) There need be no generality in revenge . . . whereas the imposer of retribution, inflicting deserved punishment for a wrong, is committed to (the existence of some) general principles (prima facie) mandating punishment in other similar circumstances. (Nozick 1981, 366–368)

I mention these arguments only to summarily reject them.[13] While each of these arguments is to an extent compelling neither is – nor are they collectively – completely so. The idea of hostility for behaviors we do not find (however mistakenly) wrong is hard to see as a form of vengeance; completely disproportionate vengeance, similarly, seems to be rather something else; non-personal strikes me as a perfectly intelligible possibility; an avenger who simply enjoys the suffering of others, qua suffering, disconnected from the fact that it is a response to (perceived) wrongdoing, strikes me as something else: a sadist; and I also find it possible to imagine an avenger who is committed to general principles. Interestingly, I think that the sorts of literary excursions – into Westerns and into other genres as well – such as those French carries out give us plenty of reasons for skepticism. In these literary genres vengeance and punishment are often – and evidently often deliberately – confused together.

[12] See above all (Zaibert 2006, *passim*).

[13] Again, I have discussed them at length in (Zaibert 2006).

More promising, I have found, is the fact that vengeance seems to require a certain *narrative*. By this I mean the following: the stereotypical avenger schemes, plans, and carefully sets up a stage such that he can get back at the wrongdoer. A more or less instantaneous response to wrongdoing can hardly be recognized as an act of vengeance. And it is not just sheer time that seems necessary. Rather, time is necessary in order for the narrative to evolve. *Mise-en-scène* is of the essence. Not only does this explain the popular saying whereby vengeance is best served cold, but it explains the way in which French invokes the particular value of communication for avengers as well, in that to communicate their success to the wrongdoer is often the climax of the narrative of revenge. In contrast, punishment is not necessarily best served cold. Of course, punishment *can* be served cold, but it can also be served hot too. Only in revenge, the very way, the very setting, and the very means, by which the wrongdoer gets to receive his comeuppance are crucially important. This concern with a narrative may, finally, also explain the literary popularity – in Westerns and elsewhere – of vengeance.

Even more promising in terms of allowing us to distinguish vengeance form punishment, however, I now wish to suggest, is a certain difference between the sort of emotional conflict that the typical punisher – but not the typical avenger – undergoes. Insofar as punishment (like vengeance) involves a hostile reaction towards a wrongdoer, and insofar as I agree with French in that this hostility often ought to go beyond mere rebuke, punishment is revealed as necessitating an infliction of suffering. (Suffering is here understood very generally, encompassing things that are unwanted, unpleasant, painful, disagreeable, etc.) While sometimes this hostile infliction of suffering is justified, such justification does not really erase the moral disvalue that it necessarily generates. I am here thinking about the notion of moral remainders, and about notions such as Bernard Williams's "integrity" (Smart and Williams 1973). A decent punisher, a punisher with integrity, may go ahead and inflict the punishment that is deserved (or that is otherwise called for), but she will still feel a certain type of moral emotion about having had to make someone suffer. In other words, a decent punisher is not *happy* about punishing; rather, she is *conflicted*.

I cannot here explain in any detail what exactly this moral emotion I have just mentioned is, or what exactly the conflict that decent punishers experience is. But I can briefly register the relevance that notions such as "agent regret" have in our current context. Just as a completely blameless driver who kills a completely innocent child who ran under his truck ought to feel something beyond generic sadness – he ought to, given the fact that it was *he* who killed the child, feel differently from the sort of generic non-moral sadness a witness who saw what happened would feel – a punisher, too, ought to feel bad about having had to inflict suffering in another person, even though she is (ex hypothesi) completely justified (and thus completely blameless) in so doing. What I want to suggest is that it is exactly this which distinguishes punishment from vengeance, and which may explain why vengeance is so commonly assumed to be barbaric. When we think of an avenger, or when we encounter one in literature (or in movies, etc.), we do not see a conflicted person, and we do not see someone exhibiting anything resembling agent regret. What we see instead is someone "on a mission", almost monomaniacally focused on getting even. As these stereotypical avengers plan their vengeance, their focus on getting even crowds out other considerations; and as soon as they have gotten even, their satisfaction about having succeeded crowds out other emotions.

I do not think that French would disagree with my emphasis on the narrative aspect of vengeance. But I think that his views on vengeance may lead him to disagree with me regarding the importance of the sort of conflict I have just sketched. The issue is subtle, I think. For French explicitly admits that "taking revenge typically provokes extreme psychological tensions in the avenger that may be so difficult to bear that they render him or her incapable of effective action" (French 2001, 34). So he may be interpreted as endorsing the existence of the sort of conflict I have in mind. I do not think, however, that the conflict French and I are talking about the same thing. The passage just quoted is immediately followed by this: "successful avengers most likely will be persons with the emotional composure and physical stamina necessary to weather the personal pressures and losses that are likely to be endured" (French 2001, 34). And this makes it seem as if the sort of conflict of which French speaks is one that we are – or at least avengers are – better off without. "Emotional composure" and "physical stamina" are good things, and are things that while evidently hard to attain, we are better off attaining – and if we have these in sufficient degrees, then we would not be ultimately so conflicted as we carry out our vengeance. The sort of conflict I have in mind is very different: there is something intrinsically valuable about being so conflicted. The person with integrity who experiences "agent regret", for example, will *not* feel it any less as a result of greater emotional composure or physical strength. Feeling this type of agent regret, in itself, is evidence of her moral fiber and of her integrity.

I think that the difference between the sort of conflict I have in mind and the sort of conflict French has in mind is brought out nicely if we consider his treatment of Hamlet. In a very interesting passage that deserves to be quoted in full, French tells us:

> According to Jacoby, "The real greatness of Hamlet lies in its depiction of a man undone by the responsibility of carrying out a vengeful assignment unsuited to his nature". Goethe sees Hamlet, as we should see him, as overwhelmed with astonishment and trouble rather than as ready to take on the important task to which he has been assigned. He is not "a young hero, panting for revenge ... who feels himself fortunate in being called out against the usurper of his crown". The pressure of the responsibility of vengeance drives him to avoidance rather than action. Unlike Achilles, who immediately faces up to the fact that the cost of avenging Patroclus will be his own early death and carries out the task, Hamlet seems to find every way under the sun to put off the job. The differences between Achilles and Hamlet, of course, are great, and perhaps the most important is that Achilles does not face the religious prohibition against private revenge that might play on Hamlet's mind and slow his vengeful reflexes. It does, however, remain something of a mystery to me that Hamlet might think that his assignment flies in the face of the prohibition against private revenge. I am more inclined to side with Goethe who writes, "Shakespeare wished to describe the effects of a great action laid upon a soul that was unequal to it". One of the important things we learn about vengeance from Hamlet is that the responsibility of performing it can overwhelm a person unsuited to the task. (French 2001, 32)

From French's perspective, it seems to me, Hamlet's inability to act is not something good. It is the result of a certain diffidence and of slow vengeful reflexes, and it is something that shows that he is not really "suited to the task" at hand. This is quite different from the sort of conflict that I have sketched here and that I have suggested may be very important in distinguishing vengeance from punishment. In fact, it is precisely because of Hamlet's conflicts that he does not immediately stand out in our minds when one thinks of an avenger in literature. Much more immediately stands out Achilles, of course, but also Dumas' Edmond Dantès or Kleist's Michael Kohlhaas. These other characters are, essentially, conflict-free: they have but one goal – to get even. And this goal becomes a true obsession.

We have, I think, good reasons to wish punishers to be in this way unlike avengers. While I agree with French in that hostile responses are sometimes the right thing to do – and indeed the most valuable thing to do – I do believe that hostility necessarily generates remainders and conflicts that should affect any decent person. To be moved by these remainders and affected by these emotional conflicts is not a sign that one is not "suited to the task" of behaving in a hostile manner. It is, rather, an intrinsically valuable feature of a decent person who must behave in a hostile manner – and it is, further, the best assurance that hostility will be tempered and kept at check.

If I am right in that the sort of conflict that French admits is part of his notion of vengeance is not quite the one I have linked to moral remainders and emotions, it would turn out that vengeance, so understood, is importantly different from punishment. Admittedly, they would both be hostile responses to wrongdoing, but one of them would indeed seem to be much more primitive (if not quite barbaric) than the other. So, it seems to me that French faces an interesting dilemma. If he agrees that the sort of conflict I have here discussed is part of a full analysis of vengeance (either because I am wrong in thinking that the conflict he does discuss is different from the one I discuss, or because he would welcome this additional sort of conflict as also being part of a more complete analysis of vengeance), then his views on what constitutes vengeance would need to be revised. Moreover, my remark above about truth in advertising would be bolstered: French's views would be revealed as merely highlighting some virtues of punishment, not of vengeance understood as something different from punishment. But if French thinks that the sort of conflict that I have here discussed is *not* part of an analysis of vengeance as he understands it, his views would indeed be about vengeance understood as a unique form of hostility. But then it would be harder to see what is virtuous about it.

Of course, absence of conflict need not amount to obsessive behavior. One can easily imagine someone seriously committed to, say, bringing those guilty of mass atrocities or genocidal violations of human rights, to justice without being too conflicted and without thereby becoming pathologically obsessive to the point of self-sabotage, as Kohlhaas (and perhaps Dantès too) evidently did. But, in general, too much ease and steadfastness (as the result of lack of conflict) when behaving hostilely, is not an agreeable sight.

References

French, Peter A. 2001. *The virtues of vengeance*. Lawrence: University of Kansas Press.
Hart, H.L.A. 2008. *Punishment and responsibility.* (2nd ed., with an introduction by John Gardner). Oxford: Oxford University Press.
Moore, G.E. 1993. *Principia ethica*. Cambridge: Cambridge University Press.
Murphy, Jeffrie G., and Jean Hampton. 1988. *Forgiveness and mercy*. Cambridge: Cambridge University Press.
Nagel, Thomas and Bernard Williams. 1976. Moral luck. *Proceedings of the Aristotelian Society* 50: 115–135 + 137–151.
Nozick, Robert. 1981. *Philosophical explanations*. Cambridge, MA: Harvard University Press.
Parfit, Derek. 2011. *On what matters*. Vol. 2. Oxford: Oxford University Press.
Rawls, John. 1955. Two concepts of rules. *Philosophical Review* 64: 3–32.
Scanlon, Thomas M. 2013. Giving desert its due. *Philosophical Explorations* 16: 101–116.
Smart, J.J.C., and B.A.O. Williams. 1973. *Utilitarianism: For and against*. Cambridge: Cambridge University Press.
Zaibert, Leo. 2006a. Punishment and revenge. *Law and Philosophy* 25: 81–118.
———. 2006b. *Punishment and retribution*, 69–95. Aldershot: Ashgate.

(Not) Riding into the Sunset: The Significance of Endings

John Martin Fischer and Benjamin Mitchell-Yellin

Among the many areas of philosophy in which Peter French has made important contributions is the study of death and immortality. As is often the case, French has offered his insights in a bold and original way: through a fascinating book on western films (French 1997). We shall begin by laying out features of French's interpretation of westerns, as they relate to the central themes of death, immortality, and the meaningfulness of life. On French's interpretation, a key recurrent theme in westerns presents a clash of two "world views"—the eastern (roughly, Christian) and western (secular and death-embracing). In thinking critically about these world views, it is natural to wonder about a third world view—one that offers a kind of secular immortality. In this chapter we shall focus on this third possibility. In particular, we shall defend it as viable and potentially attractive against certain objections by Bernard Williams and Shelly Kagan.

French's Two World Views in Westerns

In *Cowboy Metaphysics: Ethics and Death in Westerns*, French highlights the importance of death in western films. He approvingly quotes Jane Tompkins, "Death is everywhere in this genre" (French 1997, 11; Tompkins 1992, 24). He writes,

J.M. Fischer (✉)
University of California, Riverside, Riverside, CA, USA
e-mail: john.fischer@ucr.edu

B. Mitchell-Yellin
Sam Houston State University, Huntsville, TX, USA
e-mail: bmy@shsu.edu

Z.J. Goldberg (ed.), *Reflections on Ethics and Responsibility*,
DOI 10.1007/978-3-319-50359-2_13

"Riding West is not only to ride into the unsettled frontier of mountains and valleys and deserts, especially deserts, it is to die" (French 1997, 2). French continues:

> Arguably, the dominant theme of the major Westerns is the conflict between what some philosophers might call 'world views'; the 'world view' of the westerner and that of the easterner, the cowboy/gunslinger and the settler/entrepreneur/townsperson/Christian. Death is the predominant element of the westerner's world view, death of a certain kind, that is, death understood in a certain way. And from that conception of death and the West—land of death, the ethics of the westerner both emerges and is given sense. The easterner's radically different conception of death structures the world view away from which the westerner is ridin' West, but as the plots require, the easterner is forever catching up. (French 1997, 3)

And he elaborates:

> The conceptions of death held by both 'camps' link up with other notions and are the grounds for volitional and affective dispositions that quite naturally conflict, creating the dramatic tensions of the plots that are much more than morality plays of good and evil, white hats and black hats. (French 1997, 11)

The dramatic tension tracks a deep philosophical tension. These distinct world views support very different stances toward death and, consequently, the meaning and value of life.

A crucial part of the westerner's attitude toward death, according to French, is the view that death helps to give life its meaning in a certain way. This view's association with various philosophers, including, among others, Heidegger and the contemporary analytic philosopher Bernard Williams, is familiar. French argues that it finds expression in western films as well:

> Montaigne's point, and one with which the westerner would concur, is that the temporality of life constitutes its most important feature. Montaigne quips, 'You do not die because you are sick, you die because you are alive' (Montaigne 1958: 376–7). One of the reasons the westerner says so little and detests the talkative easterner is that talk is life-wasting. Time is of the essence and not to be talked away. The Christians (the easterners in the films) act as though the temporality of life were of no special consequence; in fact, they deny that characteristic in favor of staking a claim on eternal life. In doing so, they devalue life and living, and that is to diminish their own value as persons. (French 1997, 69)

For French, the westerns contend that the way one faces death is crucial to defining one's character (and thus the value of one's life):

> Always facing death as an annihilation of yourself and still making something out of your life, whatever its span, is the moral imperative of the westerner. Death ends your life, and your life project, whenever it is 'your turn.' That is it. You will never get another chance and never get to continue after death. (French 1997, 70)

Some key elements of the western view about death are that it is the final "annihilation" of the self, and that it is necessary for shaping our lives and giving them their most important dimension of value.[1] One way of resisting this view

---

[1]Philip Kitcher and Richard Schacht argue that Wagner's *Ring* also contends that death is essential for meaningfulness in life (Kitcher and Schacht 2004). As in French's interpretation of westerns, they argue that Wagner holds that "living means dying" (Kitcher and Schacht 2004, 162) and that

would be to deny that death is the annihilation of the self; this accepts the easterner's Christianity (or another religious idea of the afterlife). But there is another way of resisting the westerner's world view: contend that robust meaningfulness could (at least in principle) be part of an immortal secular existence. This third world view expands the list of sources for value and meaning in our lives—confrontation with death is not the only way in which our characters can be formed and our lives attain value and meaning. This sets it apart from the westerners' world view. And, in contradistinction to the easterners' world view, it maintains a secular foundation for value and meaning.

Even if one thinks that confrontation with danger and overcoming serious obstacles are required for defining oneself in the way that decisively matters, it need not follow that death is required here. After all, there are many other dangers and obstacles—loneliness, poverty, physical and psychological pain, isolation, and so forth. Why wouldn't confrontation with these dangers and overcoming the related obstacles allow one to define one's character and show who one truly is, as it were? These are legitimate questions for the westerners' world view. Even if we reject the Christian conception of immortality, why would it follow that we must embrace death as inevitable and necessary for the meaningfulness of our lives? These kinds of questions should lead us to take seriously the possibility of a third world view, according to which significant life-extension or even "immortality," in a secular sense, could be choiceworthy and desirable for human beings. The dichotomy presented in the westerns—on French's interpretation—is too restrictive; it is not exhaustive insofar as it does not take seriously the possibility of secular immortality. It presumes, too abruptly (in our view), that the only alternative to the easterner's acceptance of "civilization" and religion is the embrace of the inevitability of death and annihilation.

Williams' Critique of the Third World View

The third world view is certainly a conceptual possibility. But various philosophers have been skeptical about the appeal for human beings like us of significant life-extension or even immortality (conceived of in a secular way). And their skepticism has its roots in the claim that is crucial also to the westerners' world view, namely, that death gives life meaning. Thus, their skepticism may constitute a significant obstacle to taking this third world view seriously.

---

one's confrontation with death helps to give meaningfulness to life. But whereas the inevitability of death issues in an emphasis on values such as courage in westerns, Wagner's *Ring* emphasizes (through Brunnhilde) the transforming value of love.

We shall begin by discussing a famous skeptical argument by Bernard Williams (1973; reprinted in Fischer 1993).[2] In his classic paper, "The Makropulos Case: Reflections on the Tedium of Immortality," Williams discussed EM (aka Elina Makropulos, among other names), a character in a play by Karel Capek and an opera by Janos Janacek, who had access to an elixir which would give her 300 years of additional life. The play takes place as she is considering taking the elixir for a second time (she is 337 years old at the time of the play). Although she ages chronologically, she does not deteriorate biologically (due to the effects of the elixir). In the end, she decides not to take the elixir, and helps to destroy it. Williams contends that she does not choose to live longer because she is profoundly bored with her life—a boredom that Williams views as an inevitable consequence of radical life-extension (or immortality). We shall call this claim "Williams' necessary boredom thesis." The idea is that no matter how felicitous the individual's health and surrounding circumstances, a human's life would *inevitably* become so boring that it would not be choiceworthy.

This is a slightly different, and significantly stronger, thesis than the one French attributes to Williams. French imputes this view to Williams:

> Life does not gain value in its extension. [French here refers to Williams 1973/1993.] The value of a life is in what the person has done with his or her time, no matter how long, no matter how short. (French 1997, 69)

This may well be a view to which Williams subscribes, but the view for which he argues is stronger. He argues that life *loses* value in its extension, and, indeed, life *necessarily* loses *all* value when it is extended long enough.

How does Williams argue for this thesis? We shall focus here on a famous but, in our opinion, difficult passage in which Williams diagnoses EM's plight as follows:

> Her problem lay in having been at it for too long. Her trouble was, it seems, boredom: a boredom connected with the fact that everything that could happen and make sense to one particular human being of 42 [*sic*—Williams incorrectly uses this age, rather than 37] had already happened to her. Or, rather, all the sorts of things that could make sense to one woman of a certain character; for EM has a certain character, and, indeed, except for her accumulating memories of earlier times, and no doubt some changes of style to suit the passing centuries, seems always to have been much the same sort of person. (Williams 1973/1993, 82)

This passage, together with other parts of Williams' article, suggests that he is presenting a dilemma (or, perhaps more carefully, a dilemma whose second horn is also a dilemma). On the one hand, an individual's character could remain the same, as, putatively, EM's does. In this case, at a certain point everything that could happen and make sense to the individual would have happened. Thus, further events involving her would not have any meaningful impact on her, and she would become deeply alienated and bored. On the other hand, an individual's character

[2]Williams' classic essay has elicited a large literature. There are sympathetic discussions in Kagan (2012) and Scheffler (2013). For a thoughtful critical discussion, see Rosati (2013). Also, for critical discussions, see Fischer (1994, 2013), and Fischer and Mitchell-Yellin (2014).

could change, in which case either she would not be the same person any more, or, if she were the same person, there would be no reason for her to care about her future self. This would, then, either not be immortality—the indefinitely extended existence of a single person—or not an immortality it would make sense to care about. Let us consider the horns of this dilemma in turn.

The First Horn of the Dilemma

We are to imagine that the individual's character remains the same; allegedly, given this assumption, she would inevitably become disengaged from life and bored. An initial worry about this line of reasoning comes from an ambiguity in the notion of a fixed character.

Character traits do not come with antecedently determinate criteria of individuation, and we might individuate them more narrowly or more broadly.[3] Consider, for instance, someone characterized by her love of "extreme sports," such as hang-gliding. We could consider her a lover of this particular sport, and individuate this character trait quite narrowly; on this approach, her character trait would give rise to specific projects involving hang-gliding. Perhaps we would attribute to her related, narrowly specified character traits, such as loving rock-climbing. Again, this would give rise to specific projects involving rock-climbing. Arguably, over time these projects could become boring to this individual and fail to engage her meaningfully. When character traits are specified narrowly, the thesis that any individual would inevitably become bored has some plausibility. Despite their considerable attractions to aficionados, hang-gliding and rock-climbing might eventually become boring. It is "thinkable" that they could lose their attraction.[4]

But why should we individuate character traits relatively narrowly in the context of evaluating Williams' claim that everything that could happen to an individual with a given character would have happened to EM? Why not understand the individual in question as someone who loves adventure? Engaging in extreme sports, such as hang-gliding and rock-climbing, is one way to seek adventure. But there are other

---

[3]The response to Williams that we go on to suggest in the text is distinct from, but compatible with other responses that have been offered and which also focus on contestable assumptions that seem to underlie his argument. See, for example, Bostrom and Roache (2008), where they point out the role of expected life span in shaping the projects one finds it reasonable to adopt. The fact that we can expect to live roughly 80 years makes it unrealistic to pursue the project of writing a different great novel in every major language. But if we could expect to live radically longer (perhaps indefinitely long) lives, this project may be realistic. And it is far from clear that it would be exhausted or lose its interest if one were to live for centuries. Thus, it is far from clear that radical life-extension (or immortality) entails boredom.

[4]"Nothing less will do for eternity than something that makes boredom *unthinkable*. What could that be? Something that could be guaranteed to be at every moment utterly absorbing? But if a man has and retains a character, there is no reason to suppose that there is anything that could be that" (Williams 1973/1993, 87).

forms of adventure waiting in the wings, as it were, when hang-gliding loses its appeal. Given this broader individuation of the relevant character trait, it is much less clear that eventually the individual would have experienced everything that could make sense to a person with that character trait (and thus that she would become bored). After all, there are seemingly endless opportunities for adventure of various sorts—sports, travel, relationships, research, and writing, just for starters!

Consider, similarly, an individual in love with another person. We can individuate the relevant character trait narrowly, understanding it to be loving that particular person. Thus, constancy of character would require that this individual continue loving that same person. And perhaps it is true (although this is, in our view, unclear and difficult) that, given a sufficient length of time, everything that could happen and make sense to this individual within the context of a loving relationship would eventually have happened, and thus boredom would ensue. We can grant this pessimistic conclusion for the sake of argument. (It is not that the conclusion has nothing going for it. One might worry about the prospects for marriage to a single person for eternity, given the frequent need to "spice things up," even in our finite marriages. But, then again, there are happily married octogenarians. It is not obvious that one will cease to be engaged in a loving relationship to a particular individual given a long period of time).

Our main point here is that it is not evident why we would need to individuate the relevant character trait so narrowly, in the context of considering Williams' claim. Why not individuate the character trait more broadly, so that we could understand the individual as "open to love," or "adept at love," or "adventurous in love?" Given the broader interpretation, constancy of character would require a certain orientation towards loving relationships, but not the continuation of any particular such relationship. Now it is completely unclear, or so we contend, that at some point in an extended life everything that could happen and make sense to an individual with such a character trait would indeed have happened to her, thus issuing in boredom. Why suppose that an individual who is open to, and skillful in, having loving relationships, would necessarily run out of experiences that could make sense to her? After all, one would not be limited to a relationship with one person for one's entire life; this would open possibilities for various loving relationships over the course of an extended life.

Love is magical and transforming. In our finite lives, we know people who have had various deeply rewarding loving relationships. Why think that this could not take place in a significantly extended (or even an immortal) life? That a particular relationship could not be sustained forever has some plausibility, even if it is contentious. But it is considerably more controversial that an individual could not have a series of deeply rewarding and meaningful loving relationships (or collegial relationships or friendships ...). Yet Williams' contention that boredom follows from constancy of character would appear to deny this possibility.

Consider another perplexing passage from Williams, elaborating his worries about the fixed-character horn of the dilemma:

> There are difficult questions, if one presses the issue, about this constancy of character. How is the accumulation of memories related to this character that she eternally has, and

> to the character of her existence? Are they much the same kind of events repeated? Then it is itself strange that she allows them to be repeated, accepting the same repetitions, the same limitations—indeed, *accepting* is what it later becomes, when earlier it would not, or even could not, have been that. The repeated patterns of personal relations, for instance, must take on a character of being inescapable. Or is the pattern of her experiences not repetitious in this way, but varied? Then the problem shifts, to the relation between these varied experiences, and the fixed character: how can it remain fixed, through an endless series of very various experiences? The experiences must surely happen to her without really affecting her; she must be, as EM is, detached and withdrawn. (Williams 1973/1993, 82)

As before, Williams is here presenting the proponent of life extension (or immortality) with a dilemma: either the events the individual with a fixed character remembers are repetitive, or else they are varied and, assuming they do not effect a change in character, she becomes withdrawn—either way, boredom ensues.

We wonder, as above, how finely Williams is individuating kinds of events, when he refers to "much the same kind of events." The thesis of inevitable disengagement and boredom is rather plausible on a narrower individuation. If staving off boredom requires active engagement in a fixed set of projects, narrowly construed, and one remembers (a significant proportion of) one's past projects, then it might all come to seem repetitive. Date night with the same chap every Thursday for centuries would seem altogether too much of a (good) thing. Alternatively, after a sufficient number of variations on a common theme, it may all come to seem rather inconsequential. Different fella, different restaurant, no matter.

But if we take a broader approach to individuation of kinds of events, it is unclear why the individual's character (interpreted broadly) cannot remain fixed, while she is still actively engaged with the events in question (even if there is repetition in the patterns of experiences). Suppose that the events (and associated experiences) are conceptualized as courting, falling in love, committing to the relationship, building a relationship, facing challenges, learning from those challenges, and so forth. When the events are individuated broadly in this fashion, it does not seem obvious that an individual's character cannot remain fixed while still finding the activities and associated experiences compelling. On the one hand, it is not implausible that one could fall in love with the same person all over again, and again, and again. And it is not obvious that (even if one remembers times past) each time one falls in love with this person anew cannot be an exhilarating experience. On the other hand, falling in love with different people at different times need not, it seems, lose its appeal. There is an indefinite number of ways to fall in love, so variety would not appear to pose a threat to continued interest in this experience. Why couldn't a character trait, such as "openness to love," remain in place while one has various deeply meaningful and compelling loving relationships over the course of an extended (or even immortal) life? Why would the situation be any different from a finite life? Some people do indeed have (and remember) a series of profound and rewarding loving relationships, which, though they may be varied in their nature, never lose their appeal. The hopeless romantic's problem is not that she is simply going through the motions again and again; quite the contrary.

Williams contends that everything that can happen and make sense to EM, an individual with a certain character, will eventually have happened, and thus she will inevitably become disengaged from life and bored. We have suggested that this claim gains plausibility from implicitly individuating the relevant character traits (and events) narrowly. But there is no need to do so in evaluating Williams' claim, and once we relax the individuation of the character traits (and events), his contention becomes much more difficult to establish. We do not see any strong reason to accept Williams' conclusion that if one's character remains fixed, one will inevitably become bored in a significantly longer (or even an immortal) life.

The Second Horn of the Dilemma

Here we suppose that the individual's character changes—perhaps significantly—over the course of a radically extended (or perhaps immortal) life. Hence, the projects associated with the new character will be different—perhaps even radically different—from the individual's antecedent projects. If the changes are sufficiently great, one might wonder whether we have the same person. And even if it is the same person, one might wonder why the individual who exists now should care about herself in the distant future, given that her future projects will be significantly different from her current ones.

We wish to begin by pointing out that in our finite lives we countenance changes in our characters and projects compatibly with our identities remaining the same. We know that, if we are lucky enough to live into our 90s, our preferences regarding travel and living arrangements will no doubt be very different. And yet we think of ourselves as possibly, at least, continuing into our 90s as the same individuals we now are. It makes sense to say that I might one day be 90, and that I might, at that time, no longer care to go on vacation. Further, people sometimes undergo radical and unpredictable changes in their characters and projects—sudden religious or political transformations.[5] And yet they do not take themselves to, literally, become different people.[6] The student who discards the values inculcated in him

[5]As French's work reminds us, sometimes these transformations can be, at once, physical, mental and due to events outside one's control. They may also extend to other worlds. See his 2011 discussion of a white, male Marine who is wounded by a roadside bomb, suffering loss of movement in three limbs, a disfigured face, depression and PTSD. This man, whom French calls "Bob," comes to care deeply about an African-American, female avatar he creates in the virtual world of *Second Life*. French is concerned with the question whether Bob can live a meaningful, albeit "illusionary," life by means of his avatar in this virtual world. French's concerns intersect with ours in the text, though the context of a virtual environment brings with it special complications. Bob's case requires a more thorough treatment than we can provide here.

[6]The focus on the first person case may be significant here. Strohminger and Nichols (2014) have documented the centrality of moral character traits to people's judgments about personal identity over time. If your college roommate undergoes a radical change in values, you are more likely to judge that he is no longer the same person than if he were to lose all of his memories of your

by his parents regards himself as the same person after he went off to college as before. Why apply one standard to our finite lives and another to extended (or immortal) lives? Why suppose that transformation of character—even sudden, radical transformation—is compatible with continued personal identity in our more limited, finite lives, but *not* in significantly extended (or even immortal) lives?

These reflections support the contention that personal identity (metaphysical identity of the particular person from the first-person perspective) can indeed be preserved through significant (gradual or sudden) changes of character and projects in an extended (or immortal) life. But why exactly should one care about one's future self, where that self has significantly different character traits and values? Williams offers a constraint on admissible changes of character that might be thought useful here:

> ... the state in which I survive should be one that, to me looking forward, will be adequately related, in the life it presents, to those aims I now have in wanting to survive at all. That is a vague formula, and necessarily so, for what exactly that relation will be must depend to some extent on what kind of aims and (as one might say) prospects for myself I now have. What we can say is that since I am propelled forward into longer life by categorical desires, what is promised must hold out some hopes for those desires. The limiting case of this might be that the promised life held out some hope just to that desire mentioned before, that future desires of mine will be born and satisfied; but if that were the only categorical desire that carries me forward into it, at least this seems demanded, that any image I have of those future desires should make it comprehensible to me how in terms of my character they could be my desires. (Williams 1973/1993, 83–4)

The constraint suggested by this passage is roughly this: given an individual's current character (his current categorical desires), it must be comprehensible to him, from his present perspective, how he could have some future character (some future categorical desires).

But this really does not seem to be much of a constraint at all. Our powers of comprehension are aided by our powers of imagination, which open up a wide landscape of comprehensible future possibilities indeed. All it takes for me to see myself, as I am now, as suitably related to some individual in the future, such that I should care about him in the way I care about myself, is that I can imagine getting from who I am here and now to who he is there and then. This supposed constraint on destinations for the self amounts to a mere request for a possible route

---

time on campus together. However, they note that the first personal impact of memory loss may explain why the psychological criterion of memory has been so central to philosophical discussion of personal identity. You feel less like yourself if you lose you memories than if you lose your values. Your friend, by contrast, seems less like himself if he loses his values than if he loses his memories. They note the need for future work on the apparent asymmetry between judgments of identity from the first and third person perspectives. We would like to note the relevance of this asymmetry to our argument in the text. Even if third personal judgments about personal identity over time track persistence of moral character traits, suggesting that certain radical transformations would be incompatible with persistent identity, this need not be taken to entail that these radical transformations are incompatible with first personal judgments that one is the same person. The issue that concerns Williams, and us, is whether one could see oneself as the same person given changes in character.

connecting "self-stage" A to "self-stage" B. One could presumably *comprehend* how just about any character change could occur gradually over time (and perhaps even suddenly).

Consider a case of radical political transformation. Even a progressive Democrat can presumably *comprehend* how, through gradual changes (or even an epiphany), he could become a conservative Republican. It would of course be an unattractive prospect to him, as he currently is, but he can comprehend how it might come about. He can imagine, for instance, becoming enamored with his personal wealth and wanting to shield it from the taxman, ceasing to care about the human toll of closed borders and wealth inequality, and so on. He can imagine a route from here to there. (He might even comprehend a sudden transformation caused by an epiphany). None of this requires him thinking that the transformation is at all likely; he can comprehend it even if the occurrence of the relevant events strikes him as highly unlikely. The point is that Williams' constraint seems only to require that our Democrat be capable of imagining a possible route from his current political convictions to radically different ones.

But what are we to make of Williams' remarks about the role of one's current self-prospects and categorical desires? He seems to think that the content of one's current character will restrict the future possibilities one can identify with. Perhaps he would reject our example of political conversion on the grounds that the character of a conservative Republican does not "hold out some hopes" for any of those desires associated with one's current character as a progressive Democrat.

We have a two-step response to this challenge. First, we would like to note that our earlier point about narrower and broader individuation of character traits is relevant here as well. If we individuate the character traits of a progressive Democrat narrowly, say, in terms of a desire to expand the role of the state in achieving social justice and a desire to expand access to political participation, these may seem antithetical to the political convictions of a conservative Republican. But if we individuate the character traits of a progressive Democrat more broadly, say, in terms of a desire for government to play a proper role in shaping society and a desire for just access to political participation, then it is not clear that the convictions of a conservative Republican lack hope for these desires. Rather, and this is the second step in our reply, it may be that the conservative Republican is animated by these same desires in conjunction with a *different interpretation of how best to satisfy them*. Understood in this way, the example is one of a change in one's understanding of how to pursue a stable set of projects, as opposed to a change of focus from one set of projects to another. And it does not seem all that difficult to imagine how one might arrive at a radically different understanding of the proper role of government or the requirements for political inclusion. People do, as a matter of fact, change their minds over time about these matters. This need not entail that they have become alienated from or incomprehensible to their earlier selves. One explanation why not is that they take themselves, all along, to be animated by the same concerns. It is just that they have come to a different understanding of how to pursue the aims they hold dear.

So we don't think that Williams has offered a substantive, helpful constraint on admissible changes of character—that is, changes of character that are compatible with the individual's caring about his future self in the distinctive way in which we typically care about ourselves. He admits that it is vague; but upon reflection it seems mostly without teeth. It provides this much of a constraint: in order to care about your future self, you must be able to see how you got there from *here*. Not just any route to that future character will do, but only one that begins from who one is at present. Moreover, if we take seriously Williams' comments about the prospects of one's current categorical desires, we may have to individuate our character traits more broadly than narrowly. But this is not an unreasonable requirement. And it is entirely compatible with radical transformations (be they gradual or sudden).

Perhaps there is a useful lesson here: it is doubtful that we should seek any substantive and severe constraint on which future selves we can care about in a radically extended (or infinite) life, because we *would* and *should* care (in the relevant way) about our future selves, even when we have changed our character substantially. As we have noted, in our finite lives, we *do* care about our future selves, even under the assumption of different characters and projects. And it seems that (in suitable contexts) we *should*. Why think that there is an asymmetry in this respect between our finite lives and significantly extended (or immortal) lives?

Shelly Kagan has argued for a similar position to that of Williams, with respect to the second horn of the dilemma (Kagan 2012, 165–7). It will be helpful to quote his "Methusehah Case" at some length:

> Here I am, almost sixty. I've got a set of beliefs. For example, I believe my name is 'Shelly Kagan' and I teach philosophy. I have a set of memories about growing up in Chicago, and marrying my wife, and so forth. And I have various desires—for example, I want to finish writing this book. But of course, I will get older, and my personality will change. I'll get some new beliefs, new memories; I'll have new desires and new goals. Imagine, then, that I get older and older and older. Suppose that I get very old indeed—very, very, very old. I get to be 100 years old, 200 years old, 300 years old, and more.
>
> Suppose that somewhere around 200, my friends give me a new nickname. They call me Jo-Jo. Who knows why, the call me Jo-Jo. And eventually the nickname spreads. By the time I'm 250 years old, everybody calls me Jo-Jo. Nobody calls me Shelly anymore. Indeed, by the time I'm 300, 350, 400, I've forgotten that *anybody* ever called me Shelly. I no longer remember growing up in Chicago. Of course, I do remember some things from my 'youth,' when I was a mere lad of 150. But I can't go back to what it was like in the early days, from my twenties or thirties or forties, just like you can't go back to what it was like to be three or four. And imagine that while all of this is going on, while I'm getting older and older, my personality is changing in a variety of other ways as well. Along the way I lose my interest in philosophy and take up an interest in something I've never cared about before at all, perhaps organic chemistry. I become fascinated by the details of organic chemistry.
>
> And my values change, too. Right now, today, I'm a kind, compassionate, warm individual who cares about the downtrodden. But around 300, I start to lose my compassion. At 400 I'm saying things like, 'The downtrodden, Who needs them?' And by the time I'm 500, I'm completely self-absorbed: I'm a vicious, cruel, vile person. Here I am, 800 years old, 900 years old, more.
>
> Methuselah, in the Bible, lives for 969 years. He's the oldest person in the Bible. So here I am, at the end of my life, 969 years old. (Kagan 2012, 165–6)

Kagan is willing simply to stipulate that he—the particular individual who he is—continues to exist throughout the 969 years. But he doesn't think he would care about his future self under these circumstances:

> But when I think about the Methuselah case I say, 'So what? Who cares?' ... That person is completely unlike me, as I am now. He doesn't remember being Shelly Kagan. He doesn't remember growing up in Chicago. He doesn't remember my family. He has completely different interests and tastes and values. I find myself wanting to say, 'It's me, but so what?' (Kagan 2012, 167)

Kagan's Methuselah case raises a particular difficulty for our argument against Williams. It is not clear that we can use our analogy between features of our finite lives and extended (or infinite) lives to conclude that Kagan is incorrect in supposing that he wouldn't care (in the distinctive way in which we care about ourselves) about his future self at 969 years of age. This is because in our finite lives, although we certainly lose memories and acquire new character traits, we do not typically lose *all* of our memories and character traits. An individual in a finite life may certainly forget details of earlier phases of his life or undergo changes in certain aspects of his personality, but he typically would not forget his name and his family or exhibit a completely different personality. And if the significant memory loss and personality change is due to a disease, such as Alzheimer's Disease, one might legitimately wonder if we would have the same person in the future, even in a finite life, and whether the individual in question would (or should) care about such a future individual, even if it is stipulated to be identical to him.

But even though the analogy between our finite lives and extended (or infinite) lives cannot be used straightforwardly to call into question Kagan's conclusion, it is nevertheless *suggestive*. We contend that thinking about the changes that occur in our finite lives can at least point to a basis on which one might disagree with Kagan's conclusion about the Methuselah case. And this basis can further illuminate our contention that Williams' constraint fails to do the work it is supposed to. In short, we will argue that what is required for the relevant relation to one's future self is that one can *make sense of* the changes *as connected to one's own agency*. This marks a difference between Kagan's Methuselah case and the Alzheimer's case. And it preserves the common sense lesson we took to be suggested by reflection on Williams' proposed constraint.

We can start by noting some features of our present condition. In our limited and finite lives, we often lose memories over time—even memories of significant events and people.[7] Our memories of our youths are often quite sketchy. Similarly, we often change our characters and values; typically, these changes occur gradually. We have no discomfort countenancing such changes in memory, character, and values

[7] And for good reason. We could not function well if we retained a memory of everything we experienced. For a fantastic treatment of the issue, see Borges (1962). For a clinical discussion of a woman, Jill Price, referred to as AJ, who has near perfect autobiographical memory, see Parker et al. (2006). Nietzsche's remarks about our active forgetfulness in the first aphorism of the Second Treatise of his *Genealogy of Morality* may also be relevant here; see Nietzsche (1998, 35–36).

compatibly with caring deeply about our future selves. Why can't this hold also in the Methuselah case? That is, if we are willing to countenance significant memory loss and character change in a finite life, why not even more significant memory loss and character change in an infinite life? This amounts to a request for a principled reason to distinguish between the two kinds of case.

There may indeed be good reason to treat the Methuselah case differently from the ordinary case. After all, in our finite lives, although we forget many things and change our values and dispositions, we do not forget *everything* or change *all* our values and dispositions. It might be thought that it is a presupposition of continuing to care about a future self that the future individual has at least *some* of the same memories and values. But it is just not clear to us why this should be so. It does not seem to us that we care about our future selves only on the presupposition that we will retain at least some of the same memories and values; rather, it seems that what we care about is that a certain sort of *process* take place, in which various selves or "self-stages" are linked in the right way. We care that a chain of such self-stages exists and, more specifically, that there are links of the right sort between these different self-stages. We care that the past and future self-stages are connected. But it is not clear that we require continuity between past and future self-stages.[8]

We seem to care about being related to future selves whose psychological states and associated dispositions result from certain processes, quite apart from the content of those future states and associated dispositions. Of course, it would be difficult to give a complete explanation of the relevant processes here, but they would seem to be crucially related to our self-understanding as rational agents. And this points the way to a substantive and helpful account of which future selves one might identify with and which would be unreasonable to care about.

Two features of our self-understanding seem especially relevant.[9] First, we take ourselves to do things for reasons. In particular, we conceive of ourselves as making up our minds which projects to pursue and which desires to satisfy on the basis of rational reflection. Changes in our character are attributable to us as agents when we can recognize them as justified. This holds for our finite lives, and it would seem to hold no less for radically extended (or immortal) lives as well. If one can recognize a change in one's values, even a wholesale change in values, as justified by reasons, then one can recognize it as an exercise of one's rational agency. It makes sense. Understanding the change as something one did is a means of plotting a particular kind of route from here to there. This holds both in the retrospective case and in the

[8]On the difference between continuity and connectedness, see Bratman (2007, esp. 29–30).

[9]Here we draw on the work of several philosophers. For discussion of narrative explanation and its connection to human agency, see Velleman (2003, 2009). For discussion of narrativity and the value of lives and acting freely, see Fischer (2009: chapters 9 and 10). For illuminating discussion of the role of responsiveness to reasons and identification with a future self, see Korsgaard (2009: chapter 9). For discussion of the role of responsiveness to reasons and our attitudes about the future, with special attention to our attitudes about the future loss of things we currently value, see Shiffrin (2013).

prospective case.[10] Just as one can understand why one *did* become a conservative Republican in terms of one's responding to various reasons, one can understand why one *might* do so.

The second relevant feature of our self-understanding has to do with the formation of a life-narrative. One way in which we make sense of who we are is in terms of the way our stories unfold. So long as a change in one's character fits into the narrative of one's life, it makes sense to identify with the changed individual. This holds no less for changes that result from exercises of our own agency than for changes that result from chance or circumstance. Perhaps one's transformation from Democrat to Republican had less to do with rational reflection than the influence of one's environment. Having never been that reflective about such things, one simply came to adopt the political mores of one's friends and neighbors. Having moved from a liberal coast to the conservative heartland, one's political convictions gradually changed. This is understandable in terms of the story of one's life, even if one cannot cite any justification for changing one's mind. And thus it can be made sense of. There would seem to be no barrier to caring about the life of the person one has become. After all, you fully understand how you got from who you were before to who you are today.

Our claim is that reasons-responsiveness and narrativity play a crucial role in securing agential identification over time. In addition to identifying with past or future selves whose characters are identical with ours, we also identify with those selves with whom we take ourselves to share a common narrative or whose differences in character are ones we take to be due to our own rational agency. This adds substance to the suggestion that we care about past and future selves whose psychological states and associated dispositions result from certain processes. And it suggests two noteworthy features of agential identification.

First, it suggests that identification comes in degrees. I may identify more or less with certain selves than with others. For example, consider a future self who exhibits differences in character that I can understand *both* as resulting from character development that is reasons-responsive *and* as narratively connected to my present self. It seems that I would identify more strongly with this future self than a second one, whose differences with my present self are ones I can only understand in terms of a narrative connection (they are, perhaps, understandable as the result of mere luck or chance, but not on the basis of rational reflection).[11]

[10]And it holds whether or not the reasons in terms of which one understands the change are mere confabulations. The explanation would fail if one came to realize that one was confabulating. But so long as the confabulation remains hidden to one's own understanding, it is compatible with the cited (yet false) reasons providing grounds for caring about a future self.

[11]It may be that maximal identification is secured by a future self who does not exhibit any differences in character with my present self. Perhaps we can read Williams' argument in light of this suggestion. I cannot *maximally* care about a future self unless he has an identical character to me, as I am now. But it is not so clear that it is the right way to conceive of identification with future selves. Circumstances change over time. Why not think that one's character should change

The second noteworthy feature is that *only one* of the two bonds—reasons-responsiveness or narrativity—need be present in order to secure identification with a past or future self. It is enough that I can understand a future self as a part of my story *or* as a rational development of my current self in order for it to make sense for me to care about him. Not only is it possible to identify with a past or future self more because both of these bonds are present between oneself then and now, but it is also possible to identify with a past or future self even when one of these bonds is absent.

Because of these two features, our account of identification seems to us to get the right result in a number of cases. On the one hand, it underwrites the contention that Kagan's Methuselah case can be treated in the same way as normal cases from our finite lives. Notice that reasons-responsiveness and narrativity may be no less present in Kagan's Methuselah case than in ordinary cases, such as a case of change in political convictions. Though we introduced two different versions of the change in political convictions case above, one involving reasons-responsiveness and the other involving narrative connections, there is no reason to think that both features cannot be present in a single case. One could identify with a future Republican self both because this change makes rational sense and because it makes narrative sense. And these two grounds for identification may also be present in the Methuselah case. Kagan may be able to make sense of how he became Jo-Jo in terms of responsiveness to reasons and in terms of an unfolding life story. Thus, there seems to be no barrier to Kagan robustly caring about the self-stage at age 969. Indeed, even if one thinks there may be no rational connection between present Kagan and future Jo-Jo, the intelligibility of the case suggests that, at the very least, Kagan can tell a coherent story about how he came to be Jo-Jo. Our contention is that this should be enough to secure some degree of identification with that future self. It provides Kagan grounds for caring about him, at least to some degree.

On the other hand, our account of identification supports the claim that the Methuselah case is importantly different than the Alzheimer's case. We have principled reasons to think that whatever identification there may be between a present self and a future self with Alzheimer's, it is attenuated in comparison to the identification that may hold between Kagan's present self and future Jo-Jo. The first difference between the two cases is that rational reflection may ground identification in the Methuselah case, but not in the Alzheimer's case. It is possible that the changes that result in Jo-Jo are due to exercises of an individual's rational agency, but the changes that result in an individual with Alzheimer's Disease are due solely to factors that bypass his rational agency. Thus, even if the Alzheimer's case can be made sense of in narrative terms, the changes in this person's character cannot be attributed to him as a rational agent. Yet this possibility is not ruled out, in the Methuselah case, by the mere length of his life. Hence, the two are not on a par with respect to the grounds for identification between present and future selves.

---

with them? That is, in light of the fact of changes in one's circumstances, it can come to seem strange (alien, even) to think that one's character would remain static.

Moreover, it is not even clear that the form of identification supported by narrative connections is the same in these two cases. The question is whether the individual himself can make sense of his life in narrative terms, not whether we can make sense of his life in narrative terms from the third person perspective. Even if we could connect the narrative dots in terms of chance events, this does not show that he can. This is part of what makes Alzheimer's Disease so pernicious—it results in one losing a grip on the connections between the events of one's experience. And even if the present self can make narrative sense of his life, including his coming to have Alzheimer's, there is a sense in which the narrative grasp this individual can have of his life is incomplete or attenuated in relation to the narrative grasp afforded someone like Jo-Jo. The future self, with Alzheimer's, cannot make narrative sense of his life looking back.[12] The disease is such that one becomes disconnected from the path of one's life. One cannot remember things from one's past, and, eventually, even the momentary connections between events in one's life become disjointed and unstructured in a way that precludes any narrative grasp of them. So, unlike the 969-year-old Jo-Jo, the future individual with Alzheimer's can no longer make sense of his life in narrative terms. He cannot look back at past events and fashion them into a coherent narrative. So, while a case can be made that there is some narrative connection between the present individual and the future individual in the Alzheimer's case, there is no (or much less) narrative connection between the future individual and the present individual, when looked at from the perspective of the future self. Thus, whatever narrative connection is present in the Alzheimer's case is less robust than that which is present in the Methuselah case. This further distinguishes them.

We have been arguing that our account of the processes that ground agential identification over time, such that one would care about a past or future self, support a distinction between Kagan's Methuselah case, which involves radical life extension, and a case of Alzheimer's Disease. In the former, identification between a present and future self may be grounded in both a connection through reasons-responsiveness and a narrative connection that goes both ways—from present to future and from future to past. In the latter, there may be a narrative connection from present to future self, but there will be no comparable narrative connection from future to past self and there is no apparent reason to think that the changes in character are due to rational reflection. Thus, our account supports the claim that there may be good grounds for Kagan to identify with 969-year-old Jo-Jo, even though this future self would not remember his past self. And this claim does not commit us to saying that the same must be said of one facing a future as an Alzheimer's patient.[13] We think that these are the intuitively correct things to say.

[12]Bortolotti (2010) discusses the role that confabulation can play in allowing those with Alzheimer's to form a coherent life-story from the first person perspective. Even so, there is room to doubt that a confabulated narrative provides self-understanding, or the same kind of self-understanding as a narrative based on actual events.

[13]This is not to say that there are *no* grounds for identification with a future self with (advanced) Alzheimer's Disease. As we have pointed out, there may be an attenuated narrative connection.

The upshot is that there does not seem to be an asymmetry between our finite lives and possible significantly extended (or immortal) lives. Either context may afford the connections that ground our caring about future selves.

Taking Stock

According to Peter French's illuminating analysis, the world view of the westerners posits that, not only is death inevitable, but it is necessary for a certain sort of meaningfulness in our lives. We show our true characters in how we face our inevitable deaths. Reflection on this view however might cause us to wonder whether it really is the case that we need death in order to have deeply meaningful lives. It is then worth taking seriously what we have called the "third world view," a world view "between" that of the westerners (which embraces the inevitability of death) and the easterners (which embraces immortality in an afterlife). The third world view posits the potential desirability of secular immortality.

We have considered Bernard Williams' skepticism about the possible choice-worthiness of secular immortality. Our discussion has been structured around consideration of a dilemma he offers. The first horn has it that if an individual's character remains the same in a radically extended (or immortal) life, she would necessarily become bored. The second horn claims that if one's character changes significantly, then one will either not be the same person any more or, even if one is the same person, it will not be rational for the antecedent individual to care about the resultant individual.

Williams defends the first horn by contending that at a certain point, everything that could happen to an individual with a fixed character and make sense to her would have happened. We have replied by pointing out that there is no reason to individuate the relevant character traits (and events) narrowly here, and once a more appropriate and relatively broad individuation of such traits (and events) is employed, Williams' claim becomes implausible. We have replied to both Williams' and Shelly Kagan's defenses of the second horn primarily by pushing on the analogy between our situations in our limited, finite lives and the envisaged situation of individuals in an extended (or immortal) life. Upon reflection, it can seem as though the Immortality Curmudgeons are applying a double standard.

And we hasten to add that our account of identification in terms of reasons-responsiveness and narrativity is not intended to be exhaustive. There may be other grounds for identification with future selves. And these further grounds may be present in the Alzheimer's case. Even so, our point in the text stands. There are grounds for identification with a future self in the Methuselah case that are absent in the Alzheimer's case.

References

Borges, Jorge L. 1962. Funes the memorious. In *Labyrinths*, ed. D.A. Yates and J.E. Irby, 59–66. New York: New Directions.

Bortolotti, Lisa. 2010. Agency, life extension, and the meaning of life. *The Monist* 93: 38–56.

Bostrom, Nick, and Rebecca Roache. 2008. Ethical issues in human enhancement. In *New waves in applied ethics*, ed. J. Ryberg, T. Peterson, and C. Wolf, 120–152. Basingstoke: Palgrave Macmillan.

Bratman, Michael. 2007. *Structures of agency*. New York: Oxford University Press.

Fischer, John M (ed.). 1993. The metaphysics of death. Stanford: Stanford University Press

———. 1994. Why immortality is not so bad. *International Journal of Philosophical Studies* 2: 257–270.

———. 2009. *Our stories: Essays on life, death, and free will*. New York: Oxford University Press.

———. 2013. Immortality. In *The Oxford handbook of philosophy of death*, ed. Ben Bradley, Fred Feldman, and Jens Johannson, 336–354. New York: Oxford University Press.

Fischer, John M., and Benjamin Mitchell-Yellin. 2014. Immortality and boredom. *The Journal of Ethics* 18: 353–372.

French, Peter A. 1997. *Cowboy metaphysics: Ethics and death in Westerns*. Lanham: Rowman Littlefield.

———. 2011. *War and moral dissonance*. New York: Cambridge University Press.

Kagan, Shelly. 2012. *Death*. New Haven: Yale University Press.

Kitcher, Philip, and Richard Schacht. 2004. *Finding an ending: Reflections on Wagner's ring*. New York: Oxford University Press.

Korsgaard, Christine M. 2009. *Self-constitution: Agency, identity, and integrity*. New York: Oxford University Press.

Montaigne, Michel de. 1958. *The Complete Essays of Montaigne*. Trans. D. N. Frame. Stanford: Stanford University Press.

Nietzsche, Freidrich. 1998. *The Genealogy of Morality*. Trans. Maudemarie Clark and Alan J. Swensen. Indianapolis: Hackett.

Parker, Elizabeth S., Larry Cahill, and James L. McGaugh. 2006. A case of unusual autobiographical remembering. *Neurocase* 12: 35–49.

Rosati, Connie S. 2013. The makropulos case revisited: Reflections on immortality and agency. In *The Oxford handbook of philosophy of death*, ed. Ben Bradley, Fred Feldman, and Jens Johannson, 355–390. New York: Oxford University Press.

Scheffler, Samuel. 2013. In *Death and the afterlife*, ed. N. Kolodny. New York: Oxford University Press.

Shiffrin, Seana V. 2013. Preserving the valued or preserving valuing? In *Death and the afterlife*, ed. N. Kolodny, 143–158. New York: Oxford University Press.

Strohminger, Nina, and Shaun Nichols. 2014. The essential moral self. *Cognition* 131: 159–171.

Tompkins, Jane. 1992. *West of everything: The inner life of westerns*. New York: Oxford University Press.

Velleman, J. David. 2003. Narrative explanation. The Philosophical Review 112:1–25.

———. 2009. *How we get along*. New York: Cambridge University Press.

Williams, Bernard. 1973. The makropulos case: Reflections on the tedium of immortality. In *Problems of the self*, ed. B. Williams, 82–100. Cambridge, UK: Cambridge University Press Reprinted: Fischer, John M. (ed) 1993, 73–92.

Moral Belief/Behavior Discordance and Prizing or Lessons from Huckleberry Finn and Thomas Jefferson

Peter A. French

Prelude

America's entry into the Second World War and I were virtually born twins together.[1] The war was off to a rather bad start for America and so was I. I had a rare condition that was usually fatal within a few months of birth. A doctor, a Belgium Jew, having escaped Nazi persecution, arrived in New York City within a week of my birth. He was informed of my hopeless case by one of his relatives who happened to be my mother's obstetrician. Permission was arranged for him to try a radical operative procedure on which he'd been experimenting in Europe. He conducted the surgery in a small hospital in a town up the Hudson River from New York.

No suspense, it went well, here I am 74 years later. I never met the doctor who saved my life, but about a month after my sixteenth birthday, a lawyer appeared at my house asking to see me. He had tracked me down even though I'd moved several times after my mother died when I was five. He handed me a package that he said was bequeathed to me by that doctor.

The doctor died a few years before and in his will directed that the boy whose case established his reputation in his new country was to receive the package if he turned 16. "If" not "when." I opened it and found a boxed set of two books: Franz Kafka's *The Trial* (*Der Process*) and *The Castle* (*Das Schloss*). I started to read one of the books. I think it was *The Castle* because its title sounded like it was an

[1] Apologies to Thomas Hobbes. His line in his *Autobiography* (1680) is "Fear and I were born twins together."

P.A. French (✉)
Arizona State University, Tempe, AZ, USA
e-mail: pfrench@asu.edu

Z.J. Goldberg (ed.), *Reflections on Ethics and Responsibility*,
DOI 10.1007/978-3-319-50359-2_14

adventure story with knights. I just couldn't get into it. There weren't any knights. I guessed there must be some message in those books the doctor wanted me to understand, but it was lost on me.

Casey Stengel, manager of the New York Yankees, uttered the only philosophical insights that grabbed my attention in those days. What Casey said in his humorous, inimitable fashion, was often laced with wisdom that I have relished throughout my life: "When you're young you get blamed for things you never committed and when you're old you get credit for virtues you never possessed. It evens out." "Blame is a waste of time. No matter how much fault you find with another, and regardless of how much you blame him ... you won't succeed in changing whatever it is about you that is making you unhappy." My favorite to this day: "There's three things that can happen in a ball game and in life: you can win, you can lose, or it can rain." Casey's in the Hall of Fame, Kafka isn't. Kafka is among the major literary figures of the twentieth century, Casey isn't.

I finally got around to reading *The Castle* after, as an undergraduate, I attended a lecture on Kafka given by W.H. Auden. Auden maintained that Kafka was the "Dante of the 20th century." Dante took his readers into the deepest circles of Hell. Kafka took his readers into the pit of desperation and patient suffering within the byzantine bureaucracies that we let govern our communities. As I remember it, Auden began his lecture quoting from Kafka's *Aphorisms*: "Perhaps there is only one cardinal sin: impatience. Because of impatience we were driven out of Paradise, because of impatience we cannot return." He then transitioned to a discussion of his own essay "The Guilty Vicarage" and the corruption of paradises in detective stories. Years later I used what I'd gleaned from a discussion I had with Auden to write about the import in an effective ethics of a shared conception of the "Great Good Place," (French 1992, chapter 18),[2] a place once lost, but potentially restorable, in any event, a worthy quest.

What stood out for me after I eventually read the books the doctor bequeathed me was that Kafka wrote about how human beings exploit and oppress each other without really knowing or caring about what they are doing because their actions, in the words of Mary Midgley, "flow from selective negligence" (Midgley 1984, 71). Officialdom rolls along and over those it was created to serve. I was reminded of Dickens' rant against "the system" in *Bleak House* (Dickens 1853). People often don't care that they don't care. They insulate themselves from the woes of others. People say they hold certain moral beliefs and they do, but paradoxically they act in ways that are utterly discordant with what they sincerely believe. *The Castle* is a quest story that is distorted by the fact that the hero (if he can be called that) never finds out what he is searching for. It's about the days when it rains, when you can't win, though you don't exactly lose.

---

[2]It was the last chapter in that book, despite the fact that Robert Solomon told me (and my editor) it must be the opening chapter.

In his essay on Kafka, Auden wrote that the hero of *The Castle* has an ethical problem: "how to separate what he must obey from what he must decide" (Auden 1962, 112). That is a basic ethical conundrum that now and again many of us face: Is this a situation where what my morality requires is less important to me than my personal project? That issue has dominated my reading of *The Adventures of Huckleberry Finn* (Twain 1885) and it plagues my appraisal of the life of Thomas Jefferson. I have struggled with trying to explain the behavior of people, myself included, who sincerely believe that they must obey the imperatives of their morality yet act in ways they know are inconsistent with their moral beliefs and make what they believe they morally must do unachievable by them at the relevant time.

I, of course, will never know why the doctor to whom I owe my life bequeathed the Kafka books to me. That, I suppose, puts me in somewhat of the same bind as the protagonists in both the books he left to me. Perhaps that was the doctor's intention.[3] It doesn't matter. He surely could not have imagined that I would take this occasion to explore an issue that my recollection of his giving me those books triggered. In any event, it's raining today, and that is rare in the Arizona high desert.

1.

Some years ago Jonathan Bennett wrote a provocative paper called "The Conscience of Huckleberry Finn" (Bennett 1974). It has been anthologized in many introductory philosophy and ethics textbooks. Bennett examined three cases in which sympathy does or doesn't impact a person's "bad morality" and subsequently how we are likely to morally evaluate the character of that person. On Bennett's account, "someone who acts in ways which conflict grossly with our morality may nevertheless have a morality of his own—a set of principles of action which he sincerely assents to, so that for him the problem of acting well or rightly or in obedience to conscience is the problem of conforming to those principles" (Bennett 1974, 124). For the purposes of the present paper, I will adopt Bennett's functional account of morality. A morality then is a set of believed rules and principles, typically in the imperative mode, that identifies what is right or wrong, permissible or impermissible, and for the believer in that morality the failure to conform one's actions to those rules and principles justifies public and/or personal disapprobation and penalty.

Obvious from his title, one of the exemplar characters for Bennett was Mark Twain's Huckleberry Finn the quintessential American teenager that was raised in a morally decadent social environment. Huck is "thirteen or fourteen or along there,"

[3]On those infrequent times over the last 58 years when I have thought about the doctor's possible intentions I have manufactured other reasons for his choice of a present to bequeath to me, ranging from his trying to get me to appreciate his own experience as a displaced Jew in a dangerous world to telling me that any quest I may take up is most likely to end in failure because the cards are always stacked against the quester. I tend to favor the latter motive even though it doesn't seem consistent with the doctor's life story. I won't attempt to analyze why.

an adolescent, a vagrant, "the juvenile pariah of the village."[4] He believes what Bennett calls "rotten principles" of a bad morality. Bennett defends the view that though Huck holds a bad morality that condones slavery, the treating of some human beings as property, Huck is a good person with morally commendable sentiments that motivate his actions at critical times.[5] Despite pangs of his conscience that was shaped by his beliefs in the rectitude of the bad morality of his community and thereby bearing a burden of moral guilt, Huck acts out of sympathy for the plight of the slave Jim, does the right thing that he believes to be the wrong thing, and abets Jim's escape to freedom. Having acted immorally, Huck is convinced that he will go to Hell. It might be said that what appears to be Huck's weakness of will (as Bennett describes it) when it comes to doing what he believes to be right is a moral blessing. Twain, I suspect, enjoyed the irony in his story of a character doing the right thing convinced it is the wrong thing because the motivational output of one of his mental states conflicts with and is stronger than the motivational output of his moral beliefs about slavery and thievery.

Within Huck's first-person narrative Twain stacked the rules and commands of his bad morality conscience against feelings of friendship and sympathy for the undeserved suffering of a slave.[6] Emotion, not reason or moral beliefs, according to Bennett, dominates Huck's will and consequent actions, though, on certain dramatic occasions, Twain leads the reader to believe that Huck's sympathetic support of Jim's escape will crumble under the weight of his guilt, fueled as it is by racist-laced imperatives. Huck abets the slave's escape, but his guilt is never fully placated and is a factor in driving his decision to escape the confines of civilization altogether and head out into the territories where, while reveling in adventures among savages, he might forget what he was taught to believe about morality.[7] Huck never doubts that he is behaving badly by aiding Jim's escape. He comes very close to turning Jim over to slave-hunters and to returning him to his owner. Yet, after weighing his moral beliefs against what he feels for his fellow passenger on the raft on that big muddy river that is carrying them deeper into the antebellum South, as Bennett tells the story, Huck cannot summon the willpower to do what he believes to be the right thing. Huck tells us that he hasn't the "spunk of a rabbit" to do the right thing. "I knowed very well I had done wrong," Huck says, and that made him feel "bad and low."

Bennett is mostly correct in his analysis of Huck's dilemma and his choices regarding Jim, though I will argue that what Bennett refers to as Huck's

---

[4]He compares Huckleberry Finn to Heinrich Himmler and Jonathan Edwards.

[5]Though at most times Huck is just a 13-year old boy who is more interested in play and adventure with his buddy Tom Sawyer than moral matters.

[6]Huck understood undeserved suffering first hand, having experienced it when his father mercilessly beat him. But whether that plays a role in supporting Huck's sympathy for Jim is not important for my purposes.

[7]Readers of the book will know that the entire raft journey down the Mississippi is pointless, as Jim's owner has died and emancipated him in her will. The rafters did not know that information until Tom Sawyer reveals it late in the story.

"sympathies" should be characterized somewhat differently to clarify what motivates Huck's actions and that may throw doubt on whether Huck should be described as weak of will.

What Twain exposes through Huck's internal struggle is that moral beliefs generally are motivationally feeble if they have to stand on their own or have only rationality to support them. Something other than sincerely believing them, whether or not on rational grounds, is necessary for them to move a will to actions that align with them. That is not a new revelation, of course. It is the backbone of Hume's moral theory (Hume 1739, 1978).

I think anyone reading Twain's masterpiece will agree that Huck's will is not as weak as Bennett suggests. It is not weak at all. And, as it turns out, it is a moral will, deserving our approbation, just because it is not constrained by his moral beliefs. It fends off the temptation to do what he sincerely believes to be the right thing. I would like to take a stab at outlining an account that goes further than Bennett's appeal to Huck's sympathetic emotions in explaining why, when push came to shove, Huck acted in violation of his moral principles and did the right thing (according to "our good morality"[8]). My account embraces an adage: "Believe whatever you will, it is what you will that counts morally."

Huck did the right thing as a consequence of his mismatching his behavior to his moral beliefs. There are also persons who profess and sincerely believe moral principles that have an honored place in what we regard as "our good morality," yet, like Huck they act in ways that transgress those principles. Sometimes that may be because they fail (for any number of reasons) to recognize that their moral principles are relevant to the situations in which they act. They are the morally blinded or blinkered or winkered. Sometimes it may be because they deliberately choose not to characterize their situations in moral terms and so regard their moral principles as irrelevant in the circumstances they confront, amoralists on those occasions. But sometimes their moral belief/behavior discordance may be because other factors in their mechanisms of action in those situations are more motivationally potent than the moral beliefs that they continue to espouse and assent to even as they act contrary to them. Like Huck, they do not adopt alternative moral beliefs that suit their purposes in those cases. They are not moral chameleons. Because they are steadfast with respect to their moral beliefs, they are prone to have intellectual/emotional skirmishes with their consciences that the other sorts of morality shirkers do not. They are not weak of will. They are effectively moved by other components in their neuropsychological mechanisms.

Consider a case on the flip side of the same coin from Huckleberry Finn. In his rough draft of the *Declaration of Independence* Thomas Jefferson wrote: "He has waged cruel war against human nature itself, violating its most sacred rights of life and liberty in the persons of a distant people who never offended him, captivating and carrying them into slavery in another hemisphere, or to incur miserable death in their transportation thither. This piratical warfare, the opprobrium of infidel powers, is the warfare of the CHRISTIAN king of Great Britain determined to keep open a

[8]Borrowing Bennett's term.

market where MEN should be bought and sold..." (Jefferson 1950, 426).[9] In his *Notes on the State of Virginia*, Jefferson wrote about the future of plantations, such as his Monticello, that are run on a slave labor force: "The almighty has no attribute which can take side with us ... I hope, under the auspices of heaven, for a total emancipation, and that this is disposed, in the order of events, to be with the consent of the masters, rather than by their extirpation" (Jefferson 1954).

From his writings it is fair to ascribe to Jefferson the belief that slavery is a moral wrong; that the institution is at odds with the moral principles he eloquently laid down in the *Declaration*. But throughout his entire adult life, as has been detailed in virtually every book about him, Jefferson bought, owned, worked, and sold hundreds of slaves on his two plantations, and he freed only a handful.[10] There also can be little doubt that Jefferson was a racist, as a sampling of comments he wrote in the *Notes on the State of Virginia* attests.[11] He maintained that Blacks (he used that term) were unfit by nature to participate in the American social experiment. Nonetheless, he argued that the enslavement of Blacks is immoral and must be terminated.

Jefferson's morality, we may conjecture, held that Blacks had the same natural rights as all humans and deserved to be free.[12] But he also held that Blacks lacked virtue because, for Jefferson, virtue consisted in a union of memory, reason, sentiment, moral sense, and imagination. It melded aesthetic and moral elements so that the virtuous person not only must have a well-developed sense of right and wrong, but a sensibility to beauty, an appreciation of nature, and a cultured imagination. Jefferson wrote that he was convinced that Blacks were lacking in the faculties of reason, imagination, and aesthetic sensitivity, and shortcomings in those areas precluded them from the achievement of complete virtue and made them unsuited for integration into the white society.[13] He believed that, from the moral point of view, the emancipation of Blacks was obligatory, but it must be followed by colonization at some place remote from the shores of America. He wrote to James Monroe on June 3, 1802 suggesting Sierra Leone as a "receptacle for these people."

[9]It was eliminated from the final draft after objections from South Carolina delegates. Historians claim that Jefferson was angry about its removal.

[10]Those were from the Hemmings family with whom Jefferson had a special relationship that included sexual relations with Sally Hemmings.

[11]"The blacks are inferior to the whites in the endowments both of body and mind, and that... their inferiority is not the effect merely of their condition of life... It appears to me that in memory they are equal to the whites; in reason much inferior, as I think one could scarcely be found capable of tracing and comprehending the investigations of Euclid; and that in imagination they are dull, tasteless, and anomalous."

[12]Second paragraph of the *Declaration of Independence*, as written by Jefferson contains the famous line "We hold these truths to be self-evident, that all Men are created equal, that they are endowed by their Creator with certain unalienable Rights, that among these are Life, Liberty, and the Pursuit of Happiness."

[13]Despite counterexamples in Jefferson's own experience, such as his productive correspondence with Benjamin Banneker.

Jefferson's belief that the abolition of slavery is a moral imperative is a principle we would expect to find in what we regard as "good moralities." As far as Huckleberry Finn was concerned there were no moral reasons to abolish slavery. It was not wrong; at worst it was morally permissible. Huck's morality may not have gone so far as to endorse the view of some in the antebellum American South that enslaving Blacks is morally obligatory, but Huck gets perilously close to articulating such a belief. From his moral point of view, Huck has no good reasons to abet Jim's escape. He believes that the slave-hunters pursuing Jim have moral right on their side and that when he lies to them, telling them that Jim is white, he is convinced that he has committed a number of serious moral wrongs and will be punished by eternal damnation.

Jefferson's morality provides him with no good reasons to be a slave-owner. Yet Jefferson's standard of living was utterly dependent on his participation in the institution. As far as I can tell from reading what he wrote and some of what was written about him, Jefferson never denounced himself personally for his active participation in slavery, though he obliquely condemns himself. Others explicitly reviled him. In the nineteenth century Moncure Conway, a Virginia abolitionist, "noting Jefferson's enduring reputation as a would-be emancipator, remarked scornfully, 'Never did a man achieve more fame for what he did not do'"(Wiencek 2012).

Were Jefferson and Huck hypocrites? I don't think so. Hypocrites have one set of values for public display and another that they keep to themselves. They pretend to live by a certain set of beliefs when they do not, and they calculatingly exploit for their own ends the fact that others take them to hold such beliefs, while they actually hold different beliefs that are inconsistent with the ones they publically espouse. Huck's actions mismatch his moral beliefs, but that is not because he holds a contrary set of moral beliefs and only pays lip service to those impressed on him by the Widow Douglas. If that were the case, he would have no issues with a nagging conscience. Jefferson also does not espouse as a moral belief one that is contrary to his stated moral belief that slavery should be abolished.

Some might be tempted to claim that Huck really doesn't believe that slavery isn't immoral because he never philosophically examines that belief. It is just something he was taught by Widow Douglas, his authority on things moral. How can it be one of his beliefs if he hasn't tested it? But tested it how? Against what criteria of believability? If we were to insist on such criteria before admitting that someone believes any proposition, very few people could be said to believe many propositions. People believe all sorts of things they haven't exposed to rational evaluation, even though verification of the truth or the falsification of the propositions they believe is not beyond their capabilities.[14] The unexamined belief

[14] I suspect that for many people believing a proposition may occur before the believer wonders, if the believer ever does, about whether the proposition is objectively true and if that can be established or confirmed in some demonstrable way. Surely most moral beliefs are like that, as are theological ones. Jesus's response to doubting Thomas comes to mind. "Because thou hast

is still a belief. Unexamined beliefs often are the ones people hold dearest, whether or not they actually live by them. Examined beliefs can become fraught with nuances and lose significance, death by a thousand qualifications, in the lives of believers.

Huck's moral beliefs are settled and relatively uncomplicated. Widow Douglas had seen to that. He believes what he was taught and he doesn't think any more about it: a person either acts in conformity with those moral principles and is right and good, or he acts against them and is wrong and bad, and goes to Hell. Huck's morality also allows no special pleadings, so he does not believe that there can be anything about Jim's case that exempts it from the general moral principle that theft of another's property is wrong. The right thing to do is to turn in the runaway slave, to restore him to his owner.

I propose to take both Thomas Jefferson and Huckleberry Finn at their words regarding what they believe on the moral status of slavery. Their moral belief/behavior mismatching with regard to slavery has a great deal to do with how we evaluate their characters and the quality of their wills. Because we deem Jefferson's moral belief to be a good one (slavery must be abolished) and Huck's to be a bad one (slavery is morally permissible), we regard Huck favorably and Jefferson unfavorably when we judge their characters, and their wills.[15] Perhaps some of us will concoct excuses for Jefferson's slaveholding. Despite his admirable articulation of lofty principles on which to found a country, he is morally condemnable and needs excuses. Huck is morally commendable, despite his rascally traits that were decried by the mothers of the village. But Huck is not morally laudable because Jim is ultimately a free man. As it turns out, nothing Huck does contributes to Jim's emancipation. The consequences of Huck's actions are not relevant to his deserving praise. What matters morally is what went on in Huck's and in Jefferson's internal neuropsychological mechanisms when a moral belief lost a conflict with some other mental state when it came to directing his will. Huck's behavior on the raft and Jefferson's running of Monticello are the external observables of the outcomes of their morally crucial internal battles. The point being that the misalliances of their moral beliefs with their behavior only signals what is morally intriguing. The consequences of their behavior per se are of no concern in the moral evaluation of their characters and the quality of their wills.

I think that framing Huck's journey on the raft as involving a conflict of sympathy and moral belief, as Bennett does, is on the right track, but inadequate to explain the force that motivated Huck to commit to a course of action he was convinced was his ticket to Hell. Sympathy for his slaves surely was not a motivating force for Jefferson. He seems to have shown little of it. Evidence has come to light that slaves, particularly young boys and others working in his nailery, were threated

---

seen me, thou hast believed: blessed *are* they that have not seen, and *yet* have believed." John 20:29.

[15]It doesn't matter in Jefferson's case that slavery was widely practiced in America during his lifetime and condoned in law. He condemns it by his own words. The claim that he was but a man of his times in his case does not hold water morally speaking.

harshly, often brutally. There can be little doubt that Jefferson's assessment of his monetary needs was instrumental in his keeping hundreds of Blacks in bondage on Monticello. Economics, not morality, held sway. In a letter to Washington, Jefferson extolled the annual profit to be made from slaves. He claimed to be getting a 4 % profit every year on the birth of every Black child.[16] It is of further note that in 1817, Thaddeus Kosciuszko, one of the heroes of the Revolutionary War, died and bequeathed $20,000 to Jefferson on condition that he free slaves at Monticello and set them up with farms, livestock, and equipment. Jefferson refused the bequest, preferring to monetize his slaves and use them to secure loans from European bankers.

2.

Hume famously insisted on a dualistic conception of the architecture of mental states that can provide a basis for an explanation for moral belief/behavior mismatches like Huck's and Jefferson's. He divided the mind into the cognitive, characterized by objective purport and reason, and the conative, characterized as motivational and volitional, and he maintained that all mental states fall into one or the other of those compartments, but not into both. Beliefs, residents of the world of reason, and passions (desires and emotions), the motivators, are distinct mental states. "Reason alone can never be a motive to any action of the will ... it can never oppose passion in the direction of the will" (Hume, Bk II, Sec. III, 413). The proper province of reason (and belief) is the world of ideas. The province of the will is the world of experiences and actions. For Hume, the two provinces "are totally remov'd from each other." The only thing that can counter a passion or emotion with respect to bringing about behavior is another passion or emotion. The will doesn't believe; it moves the person to action. Hume argues that the belief that x should be done and the desire to do x are modally separable in that each could exist in the other's absence. They are never a unitary or a hybrid mental state.[17]

A Humean depiction of Huck's and Jefferson's apparent moral belief/behavior discordance might be that their moral beliefs regarding slavery, no matter how laced with rationally justified moral judgments, do not align with their passions, and it is their passions that motivate their actions. Moral beliefs cannot unilaterally provoke behavior that would accord with them. Huck and Jefferson must have the desire; feel the appropriate passion that matches up with what they believe to be

[16] He wrote, "I allow nothing for losses by death, but, on the contrary, shall presently take credit four percent per annum for their increase over and above keeping up their own numbers." On another occasion he wrote, "A child raised every 2 years is of more profit then the crop of the best laboring man... it is not their labor, but their increase which is the first consideration with us." (quoted in Wiencek)

[17] There are no "besires" (half beliefs, half desires) as were proposed by John McDowell (1979). A concept that is incoherent, as Michael Smith (1994) persuasively argued.

the morally right thing if they are going to act morally. Hume writes, "reason can never immediately prevent or produce any action by contradicting or approving of it" (Bk III, Pt. I, Sec. I, 458). Jefferson's good moral beliefs are powerless to move him to act if his passion aligns with the economics and agricultural management of slaveholding.

Hume, of course, does not define a morality in terms of beliefs, as Bennett and I have. For him, morality "is more properly felt than judg'd of" (Hume, Bk III, Pt I, Sec. II, 470). It is a product of the passions. One point, however, may be worth mentioning: if Hume's account of morality as felt rather than believed were adopted, then Huck's conscience (contra-Bennett) is not comprised of what he believes is good and right, etc., but what he feels he should do in specific circumstances. His abetting Jim's escape then is not at odds with his conscience, but only with beliefs taught to him by the Widow Douglas. Also, on a Humean reading, Jefferson does come out to be a hypocrite because his abolitionist rhetoric and the business about all men having equal basic rights turns out not to reflect his morality, where his passions lie.

Tamar Gendler has proposed an alternative to Hume's characterization of the dual-process architecture of mental states that has been gaining some traction among philosophers concerned with belief/behavior discordance (Gendler 2008). According to her, one mental state behaves in accord with the rationalist model of thought and the other performs in an associative manner. The former has propositional content and syntactic structure, and the latter mostly associative content. Beliefs, within the rationalist model, have satisfaction conditions that are determined by the syntax and meanings of their contents, and they can serve as premises in inferences. A mental state that has no satisfaction conditions and no syntactic structure cannot be a premise in inferences and only can be an element in an associative chain of thought. In belief/behavior discordance cases like Huck's and Jefferson's, according to Gendler's theory, the associative mechanism fires out one mental state in an associative chain, while the rationalist system cranks out another in the form of beliefs. The associative mechanism produces affect-laden inherently motivational mental products that Gendler dubs "aliefs." Those aliefs are "associative, automatic, and arational" (Gender, 641). They occur in the brain as the result of having "undergone certain sorts of experiences—experiences that result in the creation of clusters of associations with representational-affective-behavioral content" (Gendler, 642–643).

When it comes to triggering actions, the associative mechanism, on Gendler's theory, commands the helm. Beliefs, as in Hume's account, are not inherently motivational, but they can motivate when there is an external contingent connection between them and a conative state (e.g., Gendler's aliefs). A belief-discordant alief is not a Humean passion per se. Gendler suggests it may be what Aristotle called a *hexis*, an active state or disposition that a person possesses.[18] Aliefs, as Gendler

[18] Aristotle's example is health and that it is a state acquired by habit. "There is a sense of "having" which means a disposition (diathesis), in virtue of which the thing which is disposed is disposed

describes them, have a tripartite nature of co-occurring representational, affective, and motivational elements (in varying degrees) that are activated consciously or nonconsciously by features of a person's internal or ambient environment and may be occurrent or dispositional. In an alief, the representational element of some object or concept or situation or circumstance may be, but needn't be and typically isn't, propositional, and may be conceptual or nonconceptual. Having an alief is to experience an affective or emotional state that is essentially the preliminary motivator of some motor routine. The alief generating mechanism in the neuropsychological system, as Gendler describes it, is fast and automatic and directly links to the will and so to action. The belief generating mechanism is "consciously and explicitly controllable and manipulable, but linked to action only indirectly ... A belief would be produced by more deliberate and controllable processes that have a more indirect impact on action but are often conscious" (Kriegel 2011, 10).

Most of the time in most people, on Gendler's account, aliefs and beliefs tend to align, and that can give the impression that beliefs are motivating actions though it is the aliefs that are actually doing the work. When one's aliefs are belief-discordant, however, they tend to be evident to the believer. Hence, Huck wrestles with his conscience because he is aware of the dissonance between what he believes (I ought to turn Jim over to the slave-hunters) and what he alieves (Help Jim escape).

Uriah Kriegel, following Gendler, posits moral aliefs to explain cases in which a person's behavior fails to match his or her moral beliefs. He writes, "A moral alief is produced by uncontrollable and automatized processes that are architecturally connected to motor output and inaccessible to consciousness. A moral belief is produced by usually conscious, controllable processes that generally have an indirect impact on action but are often conscious" (Kriegel, 10).

Using Kriegel's account we would describe Huck's situation as believing that morality requires him to return Jim to Miss Watson, but morally alieving, "Jim, companion on the raft. (representational or cognitive component) Friend—Good guy! (affective component) Help him escape!! (motivational component)." Huck's moral belief is weakly motivational, but persistent enough that he is convinced that "people that acts as I'd been acting about that nigger goes to everlasting fire."[19] Huck's moral alief, as aliefs according to Gendler and Kriegel are supposed to do, prevails: "All right, then, I'll GO to hell—It was awful thoughts and awful words,

well or badly, and either independently or in relation to something else. E.g., health is a state (hexis), since it is a disposition of the kind described. Further, any part of such a disposition is called a state (hexis); and hence the excellence (arête) of the parts is a kind of state (hexis)." Aristototle. Metaphysics. 5.1022b. For Aristotle a hexis is a tendency or disposition, induced by the habits, to have feelings and act (1105b25–6). Moral virtue, for Aristotle, consists of the right hexis, that is, the disposition to have appropriate feelings and act appropriately. It was a form of cognition and judgment.

[19]I'm not certain that Kriegel would call Huck's belief moral because it is a part of his "bad morality," but I will do so to continue the Bennett-based account I've adopted for present purposes. Kriegel might say that Huck has a moral alief that dominates a belief that he only thinks is moral.

but they was said .[F]or a starter I would go to work and steal Jim out of slavery again; and if I could think up anything worse, I would do that, too; as long as I was in, and in for good, I might as well go the whole hog" (Twain, chapter 31).

It is more difficult to identify the representational, affective, and motivational components of the alief(s) that motivated Jefferson to own slaves (and continue to do so throughout his life) in opposition to his moral beliefs that they were human beings with a right to liberty and that the institution of slavery is immoral. A non-moral alief he might have held, based on what he wrote in letters and in *Notes on the State of Virginia*, is "Blacks, Financial benefit. Strong backs fit for hard labor, No virtue, Inferior! Enslave them on Monticello!!" He buttressed such an alief with the belief that his slaves are better off working the fields of Monticello than were they free, but that belief had virtually no associated alief to motivate his will.[20] He certainly didn't enslave Blacks on his plantation for their own good. In fact, his calculations of the economic worth of slave children suggest another alief, lacking in moral content, that formed his will: "4 percent profit per Black child. More valuable than tobacco or other crops! Get female Black slaves to birth as many offspring as possible on Monticello!!" Either that or the earlier mentioned alief, on the theory, would have been more immediately motivational than his eloquent endorsements of his belief in the moral imperative to abolish slavery.

Gendler maintains that aliefs are incorrigible in that they are unresponsive to evidence; they do not have objective purport. They are not truth-apt for the aliever. But as Kriegel argues, they, or at least the moral ones, should be, in some sense, justified in the eyes of the aliever. They do not usually pop into minds *ex nihilo* and *se iustificari*. Kriegel, however, is unclear as to what would make aliefs justified for alievers. They cannot be objectively justified or they would not differ from beliefs. A guess is that the aliever's past experiences justify the aliefs the aliever has in specific situations. In Huck's case the most likely candidate to justify his alief is his experiences with Jim on the raft during which Jim served as a surrogate parent and dependable friend. In Huck's mind, those experiences add up to a plethora of associations with representational-affective-behavioral content regarding Jim, justification enough for Huck's alief. For Jefferson, perhaps it is either his experiences of the planter culture of pre- and post-colonial Virginia or his economic calculations that justified the slavery alief that overwhelmed his abolitionist moral belief. In any event, supporting objective evidence is seldom essential to an alief's power to motivate behavior that mismatches the aliever's moral beliefs.[21]

[20]Although it looks and sounds like a justification in his writing, I wonder if it isn't more of an excuse, an admission of having done wrong, but with mitigating circumstances.

[21]Gendler uses as a preliminary example of alieving, people who believe the glass floored skywalk bridge out over the Grand Canyon is safe, yet once out on it they panic and alieve "Really high up, long long way down. Not a safe place to be! Get off!!" Such people cannot justify their alief from past experiences on such skywalks, so they probably associate a number of past experiences, perhaps including watching movies such as *Vertigo*, if they try to formulate a justification for what triggered their belief discordant behavior.

Both Huck and Jefferson are reflective. They are aware of the discordance between what they believe and how they behave. If they were not reflective, we would not praise Huck for abetting Jim's escape or condemn Jefferson (or not so much) for practicing slavery. In fact, the defenses of or excuses for Jefferson's behavior on Monticello typically rest on the claim that he was so much a product of his times and his location that the dissonance between what he believed and what he did was opaque to him. That may seem to make him less morally blamable, but it also does Jefferson a disservice by downgrading his intellectual acumen. His own writings make clear that he could not have been unreflective regarding his belief/behavior mismatching and that makes him more to blame morally, not less. Reflective moral belief/alief misaligners, as Mark Twain must have realized, are far more interesting characters than those whose moral beliefs and motivations are insulated from each other.

The moral evaluation of a person's character in moral belief/behavior mismatch cases like those of Huck and Jefferson, Kriegel maintains, should track what the person alieves (Kriegel, 16). If we want to know the moral quality of someone's will, according to Kriegel, we should focus on their default system, and that is the associationist mechanism that Gendler identified as the producer of aliefs, not beliefs. Kriegel writes, "a person's aliefs ... constitute her real moral commitments. When aliefs and beliefs diverge, the true moral character of a person is reflected more accurately in her aliefs.... [R]eal moral commitments, reflecting true moral character, are constitutively tied to the motivational states that govern her behaviour" (16).

The account of aliefs that Gendler developed and Kriegel draws upon to deal with moral belief/behavior discordance has some serious conceptual problems that may cave in the concept. If aliefs are essentially radically different from beliefs, then a robust notion of alief is called for that identifies at least one essential property of aliefs that is not to be found in beliefs as they are standardly depicted in explications of our neuropsychological architecture. That property cannot be that they can be tokened unconsciously because beliefs, as Implicit Association Tests seem to show in cognitive dissonance cases, can be tokened unconsciously.[22] Their activation conditions ("activated by features of the subject's internal or ambient environment") are not peculiar to aliefs. Beliefs like "this movie is boring" can be and often are activated by internal and/or ambient environment cues. Beliefs can also be occurrent or dispositional, as Gendler claims that aliefs are. What's left of the descriptions of aliefs that might essentially distinguish them from beliefs? Gendler's account of the difference between a belief and an alief references their functional roles. Eric Mandelbaum characterizes those as: "The functional role of the beliefs makes them so that their existence is contingent on the status of incoming evidence; disconfirming evidence can drop one's credence in a proposition, or in the limit, destroy a belief, whereas disconfirming evidence (more or less) leaves an alief untouched" (Mandelbaum 2012, 209–10). Aliefs are not truth-apt.

[22] For information and examples see https://implicit.harvard.edu/implicit/iatdetails.html

The associative quality of aliefs seems to be the distinguishing characteristic that isolates them from beliefs and supports identifying them as an independent mental natural kind. Association chains are not truth-apt. So if the content of aliefs is purely associative, they are essentially different from beliefs. However, the representational (cognitive) elements of the suggested aliefs of Huck and Jefferson clearly have propositional content that is truth-apt, i.e., amenable to satisfaction conditions. I suspect that is true of all putative aliefs.

Consider a case suggested by one of Mandelbaum's examples. A collector will spend a considerable amount of money to own the homerun ball hit by Hank Aaron that broke Babe Ruth's record. The collector insists that it must be the exact ball, in the same condition as it left Aaron's bat and landed in the outfield stands. A dealer presents what he purports to be that ball to the collector. The collector alieves "Ball that Aaron hit to break Ruth's record, has not been doctored or otherwise modified since that momentous occasion in baseball history. Must have it for my collection! Buy it!!" But the alief that moves the collector to purchase the ball has blatant propositional content or it cannot interact in inferential ways with other things that the collector believes or knows about the value of objects of baseball memorabilia and that are crucial to his being moved to buy that particular ball. For example, if it has been varnished or has on it the signature of a previous owner or has been chewed on by a bulldog, it has lost value and is not worth the dealer's asking price. Aliefs then are not always unresponsive to evidence, as Gendler characterizes them, and they can be inferentially promiscuous. Aliefs may be stubborn when it comes to responding to contrary evidence, but they do not seem to be incorrigible. Beliefs also can be stubborn when it comes to conflicting incoming evidence, e.g., the beliefs of climate change deniers.

Incoming evidence may alter the collector's motivation to buy the purported historic baseball. In Huck's case, it seems fair to assume that Jim's continued good will toward him sustains the alief I have attributed to Huck, even though Huck never recants his anti-abolitionist moral beliefs. But, had the story gone differently, had Jim turned against Huck or mistreated him, might not Huck have taken Jim's behavior as evidence to desert his alief and do the right thing (as his morality demanded) by turning Jim over to the slave-hunters? It might take a great deal of disconcerting disconfirming evidence to overturn some aliefs, but that does not mean that aliefs are incorrigible. If Jefferson learned of Blacks that met all of his virtue criteria, would that deflate the alief that motivated his enslaving Blacks? Aliefs look more and more like a variety of beliefs.

Suppose you are out at night in my neck of the woods in the high desert foothills north of Scottsdale, Arizona and the beam of your flashlight falls upon a feline creature perched on the roof of my house. You alieve "Mountain lion. About to pounce! Run!!" Your alief, however, appears not to be much different from an ordinary perceptual belief with propositional content that is confirmable by evidence. Visitations by wild feline critters occur not infrequently on the roof of my house. I am willing to investigate whether this one is a mountain lion. I take a look. It has tufted ears and a bobbed tail. It's only a bobcat. There is no danger from which you should run. He's probably stalking a rabbit in the sage. He'll be off the roof in no time. If you persist in thinking it is a mountain lion, does that mean you are alieving, or are you doing something else, such as irrationally believing? After all, you have it on my good authority that it is a bobcat. Are you not just persisting in believing you have seen a mountain lion on my roof despite evidence to the contrary?[23]

Your mental state in the mountain lion case is propositional and truth-apt, regardless of whether, for whatever reasons, you refuse to expose its content to evidentiary confirmation. Surely your stubbornness cannot be the defining characteristic of its being an alief. If that is the case, then the believer's refusal to expose a belief to objective confirmation can transform it into an alief. The alchemy of attitude! The stance taken with respect to the incorrigibility of the content of a mental state and not that it has associative content would be the deciding factor as to whether it is an alief or a belief. Aliefs then are not a species apart from beliefs. They are beliefs shielded from objective confirmation by the believer's unwillingness to expose their propositional content to objective scrutiny.

Perhaps Huck's moral belief-behavior discordance should be described not as a conflict of a belief with an alief, but as a contest between two beliefs, one of which he exposes to confirmation and the other he does not. The, perhaps surprising, resulting account will be that Huck exposed to confirming evidence his belief (previously taken to be a moral alief) that abetting Jim's escape from slavery is a task he should undertake, but he never did the same with respect to his moral belief that slavery is not wrong and that he therefore ought to assist the slave hunters. The only thing his moral beliefs about slavery and theft have going for them is the fear of eternal damnation for trespassing them that Widow Douglas stressed in teaching them to Huck. Against hard evidence of Jim's friendship and humanity, little wonder that Huck's moral beliefs can't hold a candle to his beliefs about abetting Jim's escape when it comes to motivational power. Such an account, however, deserts the Humean position as it vests motivational power in beliefs.

Mandelbaum pointed out two additional problems that suggest that aliefs, as Gendler and Kriegel have characterized them, do not appear to be a different mental species from beliefs. Mandelbaum refers to one as "the binding problem." He extrapolates that problem from Gendler's use of examples of apparent belief/alief mismatching drawn from Paul Rozin's research (see Rozin, Markwith, and Ross 1990). In one of Rozin's experiments participants are averse to eating fudge that has been formed into the shape of dog feces though they know (believe) that it is fudge. In another they see two bottles being filled with sugar. One bottle is then labeled "Sugar," the other "Sodium Cyanide." After reading the labels, participants are more hesitant to partake from the "Sodium Cyanide" labeled bottle though they saw it filled with sugar. Gendler concludes that though the participants believe that the objects offered to them are made of fudge and that both bottles contain sugar, they alieve "Dog-feces. Disgusting! Refuse-to-eat!!" and that the

[23] I know it is a bobcat and have given you my authority to know it as well. You ought to believe it! Recall J.L. Austin, "Other Minds" in *Philosophical Papers* (1961).

bottle labeled Sodium Cyanide contains poison. Mandelbaum argues that for the putative aliefs to be motivational in the circumstances their contents must bind to the particular fudge that is proffered and the specific labeled bottle. In the sugar case, he points out that the associative content of the alief "has no way of attaching to the bottle as opposed to anything else. In order to bind in the right way, the content needs to be structured, and associative content cannot provide the right type of structure" (Mandelbaum, 205). The putative aliefs in both cases have propositional content: "Those are dog feces, don't eat them" and "That is cyanide, it will kill you, avoid it" that does the binding work. Those propositions are truth-apt. They are false.

Mandelbaum also argues that purely associative chains do not allow for inferences, yet the aliefs that Gendler provides do (as do the examples I've offered above). For example, an aliever who will not partake from the bottle marked Sodium Cyanide could infer that most people would not partake from that bottle because it is filled with poison. The participants who refuse to eat the fudge shaped like dog feces are also likely to infer that other people will also refuse the opportunity to eat that fudge. So those so-called aliefs "must be propositional, in which case these states are truth evaluative and appear to work just like beliefs. In other words, aliefs seem to be inferentially promiscuous, but if they are essentially associative then they should be inferentially dormant—after all, one cannot make inferences from associative chains" (Mandelbaum, 205).

If alief theorists insist that because of their associationistic content aliefs are novel mental states distinct from beliefs in the way that Hume held that beliefs and desires were entirely different mental states, they have to explain how inferences that appear to interact with aliefs can be explained without positing that aliefs contain propositional structure and are truth-apt. Mandelbaum's arguments set up a series of obstacles for alief theorists to hurdle. They need to show that aliefs are non-responsive to disconfirming evidence (that the bottle labeled "Sodium Cyanide" contains only sugar, that it is a bobcat and not a mountain lion, etc.) while functioning as prime motivators (refusal to partake from that bottle, running away, etc.) and they are not inferentially promiscuous. Failing that, aliefs are not likely to stand up as altogether different mental states from beliefs in the neuropsychological architecture and do not help us explain belief/behavior discordance.

Aliefs may be a variety of beliefs that though propositional and truth-apt are also associative and that alievers refuse to expose to evidentiary confirmation.[24] Aliefs may be hybrids of beliefs and impulses that in practice perform more like the latter than the former. They are typically occurrent and do not have significant durations. In effect, an alief so understood is not a *hexis*, as Aristotle used that term. It is not an acquired disposition or habit, such as the moral virtues and the intellectual

[24]Aliefs surely can be overridden by beliefs fortified by evidence or reason. To use a favored example from Gendler, people that alieve "Really high up, long long way down. Not a safe place to be! Get off!!" while they are on the Skywalk over the Grand Canyon do not run to the exit. They freeze and need to be coaxed by reassuring security personnel to complete the circuit across the structure's walkway that they believe to be perfectly safe or they wouldn't be on it in the first place. The security guards remind them of that belief and their alief usually is rendered less and less potent as they shuffle along. See, Edward Rothstein (2007).

skills are for Aristotle. An alief is an emotion-packed motivator in the moment, in the circumstances, an impetus that has doxastic elements that are typically only revealed to the aliever on reflection when their truth or falsity can be evaluated.[25]

A crucial reason why aliefs cannot be the relevant motivators in the moral belief discordant behavior of Huck and Jefferson relates to one of Gendler's characterizations of aliefs. Gendler claims that aliefs are hyperopaque to alievers and, importantly that a person cannot alieve at will. "Alief just is not reality-sensitive in the way belief is. Its content does not track (one's considered impression of) the world. At the same time, it is not reality-insensitive in the way that imagination is. For while we can (for the most part) imagine at will, we do not seem to have the same sort of freedom in alief... [I]t is practically impossible to alieve at will" (Gendler, 651). Both Huck and Jefferson clearly decide to "take up" their belief discordant behavior and willfully do so. They cannot be alieving, even if there is such a mental state as alieving that is essentially distinct from believing.

Rather than a mark of a person's character, Gendler's and Kriegel's aliefs (or mental states that act as they describe aliefs) may provide an explanation of why people sometimes do things impulsively that they cannot rationally account for later. Aliefs are neither essentially retrospective nor prospective. Therefore they cannot structure a life as do Humean passions and what Harry Frankfurt calls cares (Frankfurt 1982). In acting counter to their moral beliefs, Huck and Jefferson are both motivated by mental states that are willfully retrospective and prospective. Consequently, Huck's and Jefferson's moral belief/behavior mismatches cannot be attributed to aliefs that jumped the motivation queue. Their mismatches are character revealing because they reflect what they prize, what is embraced by their passion, not something that comes on them for an instant and can be sent packing by rational counseling that exposes them to the cold light of evidence.

3.

I agree with Frankfurt that beliefs (and I add aliefs) have no inherent persistence (Frankfurt 1982, 261). They can be momentary, aroused by features in the ambient environment, and disappear when those features change. Zachary Goldberg has argued that aliefs, as explicated by Gendler and Kriegel, are closely connected to what Frankfurt called "cares."[26] I think he is probably right, but that citing Frankfurtian cares does a rather better job than positing aliefs when it comes to explaining many cases of moral belief/behavior discordance.

---

[25]The people panicking on the Grand Canyon Skywalk are not in the habit of doing so. It is a one-off occasion for them that, no doubt, is provoked by the ambient environment. The Grand Canyon is beautiful, awesome, and can be a quite scary place when you are looking down over the rim.

[26]See Goldberg (2015). I am grateful to Zack Goldberg for the work he has done on this topic and helpful conversations I have had with him on the topic.

Frankfurt describes cares as irreducible, thick, complex cognitive, affective, and motivational mental states that constitute what are important to a person. Cares build volitional dispositions that underlie desires/intentions, and provoke the will. Frankfurt notes that caring about something and that thing's importance to the person caring are intimately interrelated (Frankfurt, 259–60). The amount a person cares about something tracks the amount of importance it has for that person. It is that characteristic of Frankfurtian cares that is critical in understanding moral belief/behavior discordance.

Frankfurt writes, "A person who cares about something is, as it were, invested in it. He identifies himself with what he cares about in a sense that he makes himself vulnerable to loses and susceptible to benefits depending upon whether what he cares about is diminished or enhanced" (Frankfurt, 260).

Aliefs, as explicated by Gendler, do not necessarily have the ability to track importance to the person alieving. They may be too momentary, too immediate, to do that. The alief Gendler attributes to the panicking patrons in her Grand Canyon Skywalk example makes no reference to what is important to them. It is a statement of impulsive fright. In fact, what seems to be important to them is exactly what their alief is vanquishing for them. That they are on the Skywalk, paid over $200 to enter the park at the West Rim and step out on the Skywalk, and either drove for nearly 3 hours from Las Vegas on some poorly maintained two-lane roads or paid "a pretty penny" for the helicopter flight from Las Vegas certainly suggests that observing the Grand Canyon from the unique perspective afforded by the Skywalk was of importance to those panicked alievers. They likely planned their trip there and cared about having the experience of looking down into the remote West Rim of the Canyon through the glass walkway or over its railing. What happened to them seems more a care/behavior mismatch situation than belief/behavior discordance. Their behavior does not reflect what they cared about, what we have reason to believe was important to them to some, not miniscule, degree. Panic spoiled their daytrip. What they cared about (a thrilling vacation at the tables in Vegas and standing over the edge of one of the seven natural wonders of the world) has been, to some extent, diminished. They may feel pained by the memory of their Skywalk experience, particularly when asked by friends and family to recount their recollections of that daytrip from Las Vegas. But, of course, their cares with respect to a vacation in the Southwest are unlikely to be as important to them as any number of other things in their lives. Caring is scaler and that trip may not have tipped their caring scales all that much, consequently they may shrug off what happened to them on the Skywalk and conceal their chagrin and embarrassment when others commiserate. They may admit that they never did look down into the Grand Canyon, but it wasn't something they really cared that much about doing. But, of course, they did care about it. In terms of money and time they invested, it had some undeniable value to them that in the aftermath of their panicking they may mendaciously deny. When things that are important to us do not turn out as we planned, denial of their importance in our grand plans for ourselves is a standard camouflaging stratagem.

Caring involves passion, and the structuring of a life in a way that merely believing and alieving do not. When an alief moves us, it acts more like an urge than a *hexis* or a disposition, albeit we may be disposed to have certain aliefs in certain circumstances. I agree with Kriegel that "real moral commitments, reflecting true moral character, are constitutively tied to the motivational states that govern ... behaviour" (Kriegel, 16). but I maintain that those moral commitments must be anchored in mental states that are inherently persistent and so not in aliefs or beliefs, but in something like Frankfurtian cares.

The particular sort of caring that seems typically to be revealed in moral belief/behavior discordant cases, like Huck's and Jefferson's, I will call prizing. Prizing involves considerably more passion, a more substantial volitional attitude, than everyday caring, like what is on the dinner menu or who won the baseball game. To prize something is to value it highly, to attach great importance to it, to regard it as very desirable for or to oneself. The term has roots in the Anglo-French verb that meant to esteem and the Late Latin *pretiare* and *pretio* for value and price. I think of prizing on a spectrum of carings that includes, loving, treasuring, cherishing, and similar emotions that express various degrees of passion or sentiment for their objects. There are, I believe, but will not attempt to sort out, distinct differences in the amount of importance one confers on, and the consequent passion one has for, or the sentiment one attaches to something when one values it, relishes it, prizes it, loves it, treasures it, and cherishes it. Some prizings may be more likely than others to drive one's desires to what Frankfurt characterized as volitional necessity, though I am not here concerned with such a radical type of caring.[27] I will use prizing as an entry-level volitional attitude of the caring sort that can dominate a person's will when it is contrary to his or her moral beliefs.

Following Frankfurt's account of cares, we are shown the true quality of a person's will when we learn what he prizes (esteems, loves, treasures, cherishes, etc.), not when we learn what he sincerely believes to be morally right, good, and proper. Prizing is cognitive, but also affective and connects to a will more directly and more potently than moral beliefs do on their own. Acting on, for, or to gain what one prizes generally is accompanied by pleasurable sensations, which echoes Hume's account of indirect passions involving complex response patterns. (See Hume, Bk. 2) Prizing something (or someone) is not to have a direct pleasurable perception. As an indirect passion it has as its object the thing (or someone) prized, in conjunction with the pleasure caused by an admirable quality the prizing person associates with the thing (or person). It involves what Hume called an indirect sensation of pleasure. Consequently it involves having certain beliefs (impressions or ideas for Hume) about the object prized. It is not raw desire; it involves propositional attitudes. It is a reflective state, but it is sentiment-laden.

[27] See Frankfurt, 263–265. Which is not to suggest that I do not think that volitional necessity is an important moral evaluative concept. I think it is and that in certain types of cases it creates a challenge to doing the right thing that is nearly insurmountable for some people, though not an excuse for doing the wrong thing. I do not thing either Huck or Jefferson are in the grips of volitional necessity, however, and leave what I have to say about it to Chap. 12 of my *War and Moral Dissonance* (2011) entitled "The Moral Challenge of Collective Memories."

Bennett identifies Huck's sympathy for the runaway slave as the affective sentiment that aligns Huck's will with abetting Jim's escape. Sympathy may well be involved, but there is evidence throughout the novel that Huck prizes Jim for his camaraderie and his kindness, and he is intellectually aware and, at some level, appreciates the impact of their fellowship and solidarity on himself, on how it shapes what he wills and how he sees himself. In effect, there is a distinct belief component in Huck's operative esteeming sentiments.

When a person contemplates what he or she takes to be moral beliefs that conflict with his or her prizings, those moral beliefs typically are associated with unpleasant sensations, fear of eternal damnation in Huck's case, and though they are still one's moral beliefs, they have less attraction when it comes to forming one's will than the pleasurable sentiments and emotions conjoined with the cognitive component of one's prizings.

In a number of papers I have argued that moral responsibility rests on a theory of control and a moderate reasons-responsiveness conception of the mechanics of action,[28] and I have adopted the internalist's position that the relation between a person's will and the consequences of that person's actions is contingent and should not be a focus of moral appraisal.[29] A person should be morally appraised only for what that person can control, and the only events or states of affairs over which a person usually exercises the relevant sort of control are internalities.[30] The moral belief/behavior discordant cases demonstrate that volitional attitudes are at the core of moral appraisals; epistemic states are not, even if they play a role in the forming of those volitional attitudes. What Huck believed was morally imperative is not operative, though what he believed about Jim, that he prized him for a number of very good reasons, is relevant to the volitions he formed. When morally assessing him we look for evidence of the quality of his will and we find it, in his narrative (as Twain wrote it), in his wrestling with his conscience and then deliberately acting contrary to what he believed to be morally correct, guided by what he prizes and the sentiment it engenders. What is essential to our moral appraisal of Huck is information regarding the workings of the internal neuropsychological mechanisms that manufacture his volitions. Learning Huck's operative esteeming sentiments, what he prizes, what he loves, what he treasures, what he cherishes in specific cases is crucial to evaluating him morally.

Prizing, like Frankfurt's caring, is in some measure under the control of the person who prizes.[31] The fact that Huck seriously considers not abetting Jim's escape makes that clear. He is not compelled. He is not just caught up in the current

---

[28]Borrowing the account from John M. Fischer and Mark Ravizza (1998).

[29]A position that, despite considerable initial resistance and after many lengthy discussions with and reading work by Andrew Khoury and others, I am persuaded is substantially the correct way to think of what we can be held morally accountable for. See French (2014).

[30]See Andrew Khoury doi: "What We Are Responsible For". In a recent paper, "The Objects of Moral Responsibility," a substantial revision of "What Are We Responsible For," that Khoury has shared with me in typescript, he uses the term "elements internal to one's mental life" rather than "internalities."

[31]A point made persuasively by Goldberg.

of that big river and inexorably floating downstream. He can adjust his course, he can guide himself with an eye on what he prizes and he does so on a number of occasions when external forces conspire to return Jim to slavery.

I think a similar account can be given to explain Jefferson's moral belief/behavior discordance. Jefferson prizes Monticello, his management of its slaves, the funds generated by the reproduction of slaves, and the like. That is where his true sentiments lie, around which he forms his volitional nature.[32] What he prizes or cherishes exposes the quality of his will.[33] Huck has a decent, kind, and, despite his bad morality, a morally good will. Jefferson had a will lacking in laudable moral quality despite his holding commendable moral beliefs.[34]

Neither Huck nor Jefferson prize (or care about) their moralities as much as they do their personal projects, though knowledge of the obligations of their moralities seems to have some impact on their thinking subsequent to the exercise of their wills. Huck condemns himself to Hell and Jefferson fears a morally justified slave uprising under divine direction and that he will be condemned by posterity for his participation in the institution. Each, however, deliberately violates what he believes to be a moral obligation, because what he prizes requires the taking of an alternative course of action rather than meeting "the demands of moral rectitude."[35] What they both do requires what they believe to be a moral sacrifice, but the sentiments that motivate their wills, that shape their "volitional natures," align with personal projects not with what their moralities require. Yitzhak Benbaji writes, "We shape our volitional nature by identifying ourselves with the desires for what we care about. In a sense, being identified with a set of desires is necessary for us as persons"(Benbaji, 420).[36]

Prizing something generates beliefs concerning the importance of what one prizes, but those beliefs may not be true. Frankfurt maintains that people generally want the things they care about to be the things that are independently important to them. But Jefferson clearly prizes the wrong thing: slavery on his plantation. It is natural for us to say that his prizing the appurtenances of Monticello blinded him to recognizing what he should be prizing, what is really independently important to him: acting on what he morally believed.

Philosophers since the time of the ancient Greeks have written about what is (or ought to be) important to people in general. But no one lives a life in general, in the abstract. We may grant that there are things that everyone needs regardless of whether or not those things are prized by anyone. But it is extremely difficult, if

[32]The term is from Yitzhak Benbaji.

[33]Antebellum and postbellum Southern Whites seem to have often used the term "cherish" when they spoke of their culture and slaveholding lifestyle.

[34]I think this is as close as I will come to Kant's statement in the *Groundwork for the Metaphysics of Morals*, "There is nothing it is possible to think of anywhere in the world, or indeed anything at all outside it, that can be held to be good without limitation, excepting only a good will."

[35]The term is owed to Frankfurt.

[36]I think Benbaji's claim about what is necessary for us to be persons is correct, but I will leave that notion for another time.

not impossible, without descending into platitude and pomposity to say what any individual person should prize or care about, what should be important in each life. Philosophers have written of reasons to care about abstract sorts of things like justice, truth, beauty, freedom, property, autonomy, and such. What they provide are directives and injunctions not unlike the maxims of Widow Douglas that we may be willing to believe, but that lack volitional potency in our lives as we live them and cast ourselves into a future.

Occasions may arise in our lives when acting on what we personally prize requires sacrificing our morality, even the beliefs of a good morality. Morality may provide a reason to undertake a certain course of action, but we cannot use our moral beliefs to settle conflicts when those moral directives damage or destroy what we prize. We can only resolve those conflicts when, like Huck, we compare the reasons that support the contesting claims. When we do that, we may sometimes discover, as Huck did, that we have stronger, more compelling reasons to act on what we prize than to do what we believe to be our moral duty. In such a case, doing the moral thing may require uncommon fortitude, but it may also be self-destructive, crushing the volitional nature that forms us as the persons we are. That is a very powerful reason not to do what one's morality requires in such conflict situations. The justification for acting counter to what one believes to be morally required, however, cannot be a moral justification.

A final point about Jefferson: No care, no prizing seems to be intrinsically irrational, but some surely are intrinsically immoral, as are Jefferson's on Monticello. Persons with a good morality but who do not act on their moral beliefs because they cannot align them with what they prize, are more morally reprehensible than those who have no good moral beliefs that are relevant to the circumstances in which they are acting. In other words, Jefferson is morally worse than the slaveholder who does not believe that "all men are created equal" and that slavery must be abolished.

Coda on Another Subject: The Supreme Court and Me

In 2010 the United States Supreme Court ruled on the case of *Citizens United v. Federal Elections Commission*. The majority opinion, written by Justice Kennedy, in the 5–4 decision was that it is a violation of the *United States Constitution* to limit communications by corporations, associations, and unions that advocate support for or opposition to political candidates, and are paid for with corporate or union funds. The majority held that the First Amendment to the *Constitution* protects associations of individuals and also protects free speech, regardless of the speaker. It argued that corporations are associations of individuals, so they have freedom of political speech, and because it takes money to broadcast opinions across an electorate, it violates the Amendment to limit the amount of money corporations spend on political campaigns.

After that decision was announced, I received an Inbox-clogging volume of emails from philosophers, legal theorists, students, and others. The majority of them conveyed the message that I should be in sackcloth and ashes doing penance for my philosophical misdeeds that contributed to such a dire legal outcome. The late Ronald Dworkin, a friend, asked me if I was willing to change my position on corporations and write an opinion piece for the *London Times*. Some philosophers, whose names I won't mention, used stronger deprecating language. Members in the audience at the Chautauqua Institution where I was making a presentation shouted at me when I mentioned *Citizens United*, "Nice going, French!" They didn't mean it as a compliment. Surprisingly, the rightwing pundits and supporters of the decision didn't bother to send me "Thank You" notes, flowers, or a bottle of Tennessee whiskey.

If my detractors understood my position and/or actually read the Court's decision, they might have noticed that the majority opinion does not reflect what I have argued regarding corporate moral personhood or agency since 1977. It articulates a diametrically opposite position to mine.

Citizens United treats corporations as mere associations of individuals. *Citizens United*, as Justice Scalia wrote in his concurring opinion, defines corporate speech in these terms: "It is the speech of many individual Americans who have associated in a common cause, giving the leadership of the corporation the right to speak on their behalf."

Setting aside the fact that many of those affiliated with an American corporation may not be Americans, if I'm right in what I've written about the mechanisms of corporate decision-making and actions, Justice Scalia's position that corporations speak on behalf of those associated with them is just false. A corporation's expressions of its opinions, beliefs, desires, plans, intentions, etc., I have long argued, are not necessarily those of the people expressing them, let alone those of all of the people affiliated with a corporation at any one time. Corporate speech, like corporate action, is speech of the corporation. It is one of the ways by which corporations express and pursue their corporate interests and express the beliefs, plans, desires, goals, etc. that motivate their corporate actions, and those actions, when expended on politics, as Justice Stevens noted, are business transactions for the purpose of enhancing the corporation's profit. To use Stevens' terms, they are "more transactional than ideological."

My point has been that there is no necessary connection between what corporate speech expresses and the beliefs, desires, interests, plans, and goals of those employed by the speaking and spending corporation, holding its stock, or otherwise affiliated with it. Hence, protecting corporate speech is not indirectly protecting the speech of corporate employees, stockholders, or other corporate affiliates. The First Amendment already protects their speech as individuals. It doesn't need additional protection. Even if Justice Scalia is right that the Constitution protects speech, not speakers, and encourages as wide a marketplace of political speech as possible, he would also have to argue that corporate speech is not just the aggregated voices of those affiliated with a corporation, but brings a perspective not already in or with access to the marketplace and protected, that corporate speech is entitled to First Amendment protection in its own right, granting, inter alia, political citizenship to corporations. For the current Supreme Court, I suspect that granting that might be a bridge too far. But had they built a bridge over that Rubicon, people might have been more justified in calling for me to make acts of contrition atoning for my metaphysical and metaethical commitments.[37]

References

Auden, W.H. 1962. *The Dyer's hand*. New York: Random House.

Austin, J.L. 1961. *Philosophical papers*. Oxford: Oxford University Press.

Benbaji, Yitzhak. 2001. The moral, the personal, and the importance of what we care about. *Philosophy* 76(297): 415–433.

Bennett, Jonathan. 1974. The conscience of Huckleberry Finn. *Philosophy* 49: 123–134.

Bratman, Michael. 1987–1999. Intention, plans, and practical reason. Stanford: CSLI Cambridge University Press.

Dickens, Charles. 1853. *Bleak house*. London: Bradbury and Evans.

Fischer, John M., and Mark Ravizza. 1998. *Responsibility and control*. Cambridge: Cambridge University Press.

[37]My first attempt to explore the concept of corporate moral responsibility was in a paper I wrote for a conference in 1977 that was published in the *American Philosophical Quarterly* under the title "The Corporation as a Moral Person" (French 1979). In that and subsequent pieces I provided a functionalist or structuralist account of corporate intentionality and responsibility at the time of an action or event. I made some modifications to my position in the ensuing years (for example: French 1995, 2005) by substituting 'actor' or 'agent' for 'person,' and clarifying that a corporate and a human agent(s) could be responsible for the same event, a position also defended by Philip Pettit (2007). I also addressed two more substantive measures by replacing my use of the traditional desire/belief model of intention with Michael Bratman's planning model (1987, 1999) in explaining corporate intentionality and by responding to the charge made by Deborah Tollefsen (2008) and Mitchell Haney (2004) that my general theory of moral responsibility requires that agents are affective, yet I cannot show how corporations can care about the moral quality of their actions by displaying appropriate self-reflective reactive attitudes. I responded to that charge in a paper I gave at Oxford a few years ago (French 2012) by arguing that the internal operational mechanisms of many corporations contain conversion rules for the redescription of certain types of utterances by appropriate employees into expressions of corporate self-reflective reactive attitudes that indicate affectivity. For example, when a corporate employee on the telephone says, "We are sorry that we double billed your credit card account," the employee does not regret the corporate act, is not ashamed or remorseful about what happened. He or she is reading from a script. You, however, are receiving an apology from the corporation because a true description of her reading from that script is "The corporation is expressing regret for what it did." It is as sincere as most apologies go. Recently a Barclays representative said, "We regret that we did not set honest Libor rates." I take it that he was saying, "Barclays is expressing shame or guilt for its falsification of its London Interbank Offered Rate reports." [I'm not sure what he expressed in his follow-up comments: "We're clean, but we're dirty-clean, rather than clean-clean."] Corporate regret or sorrow or shame is referentially opaque. When it is true that Barclays regrets, it is not necessarily true that the Barclays' spokesperson regrets, though Barclays' expression of regret and the Barclay spokesperson expressing Barclays' regret are co-referential. I also have expanded my account of corporate agency and responsibility after discussions with a number of philosophers and legal theorists, especially Andrew Khoury and Carlos Garcia-Jara, (See French 2016 and "Some Tranching of Moral Responsibility Ascriptions to Individuals in Shadow Banking During the Financial Crisis," forthcoming).

Frankfurt, Harry. 1982. The importance of what we care about. *Synthese* 53(2): 257–272. Also in Frankfurt. 1988. The importance of what we care about. Cambridge: Cambridge University Press, Ch. 7.

French, Peter A. 1979. The corporation as a moral person. *American Philosophical Quarterly* 16: 207.

———. 1992. *Responsibility matters*. Lawrence: University Press of Kansas.

———. 1995. *Corporate ethics*. Fort Worth: Harcourt, Brace.

———. 2005. Inference gaps in moral assessment: Capitalism, corporations, and individuals. *International Social Science Journal* 57: 573.

———. 2011. *War and moral dissonance*. Cambridge: Cambridge University Press.

———. 2012. *Corporate affectivity and membership in the moral community*. Oxford: Oxford University. Powerpoint presentation available at http://slideplayer.com/slide/1412408/

———. 2014. Complicity: That moral monster, troubling matters. *Criminal Law and Philosophy* 10: 575.

———. 2016. The diachronic moral responsibility of firms. In *The moral responsibility of the firm revisited*, ed. Eric Orts and Craig Smith. Oxford: Oxford University Press.

———. Forthcoming. Some tranching of moral responsibility ascriptions to individuals in shadow banking during the financial crisis. *Responsibility for the financial crisis*, eds. James Dempsey and Thomas Sorrell.

Gendler, Tamar. 2008. Alief and belief. *Journal of Philosophy*: 634–663.

Goldberg, Zachary. 2015. Aliefs, beliefs, and cares. In *Praxiology and the reasons for action*, ed. Piotr Makowski, Mateusz Bonecki, and Krysztof Nowak-Posadz. London: Transaction Publishers.

Haney, Mitchell. 2004. Corporate loss of innocence for the sake of accountability. *The Journal of Social Philosophy* 35: 391.

Hume, David. *A treatise of human nature* (1739–1978). Oxford: Oxford University Press.

Jefferson, Thomas. 1950. In *The papers of Thomas Jefferson*, ed. Julian P. Boyd, vol. 1, 1760–1776. Princeton: Princeton University Press.

———. 1954. In *Notes on the State of Virginia*, ed. William Peden. Chapel Hill: University of North Carolina Press.

Khoury, Andrew. *Moral responsibility and quality of will*. Chapter 4. What we are responsible for. 45–57 doi:http://repository.asu.edu/attachments/93155/content/tmp/package-Fs68mq/Khoury_asu_0010E_11091.pdf.

Kriegel, Uriah. 2011. Moral motivation, moral phenomenology, and the alief/belief distinction. *Australasian Journal of Philosophy* 90: 1–18.

Mandelbaum, Eric. 2012. Against alief. *Philosophical Studies* 165: 197–211.

McDowell, John. 1979. Virtue and reason. *The Monist* 62(3): 331–350.

Midgley, Mary. 1984. *Wickedness*. London: Routledge.

Pettit, Philip. 2007. Responsibility incorporated. *Ethics* 117: 171.

Rothstein, Edward. 2007. Skywalk review: Great space, glass floor-through, Canyon views. *The New York Times*, May 19.

Rozin, P., M. Markwith, and B. Ross. 1990. The sympathetic magical law of similarity, nominal realism, and neglect of negatives in response to negative labels. *Psychological Science* 1: 6.

Smith, Michael. 1994. *The moral problem*. Oxford: Blackwell.

Tollefsen, Deborah. 2008. Affectivity, moral agency, and corporate-human relations. *American Philosophical Association, Newsletter on Philosophy and Law*.

Twain, Mark. 1885. *The adventures of Huckleberry Finn*.

Wiencek, Harry. 2012. The dark side of Thomas Jefferson. *Smithsonian Magazine* October. Available online at http://www.smithsonianmag.com/history/the-dark-side-of-thomas-jefferson-35976004/?no-ist

Peter A. French: List of Publications

Books

The Scope of Morality, University of Minnesota Press, 1979. Reprinted 2009.
Ethics in Government, Prentice-Hall, 1982.
Collective and Corporate Responsibility, Columbia University Press, 1984.
The Spectrum of Responsibility, St. Martin's Press, 1991.
Corporations in the Moral Community (with J. Nesteruk and D. Risser), Harcourt, Brace, 1992.
Responsibility Matters, University Press of Kansas, 1992.
Corporate Ethics, Harcourt, Brace, 1995.
Cowboy Metaphysics: Ethics and Death in Westerns, Rowman and Littlefield, 1997.
The Virtues of Vengeance, University Press of Kansas, 2001.
Ethics and College Sports, Rowman and Littlefield, 2004.
War and Moral Dissonance, Cambridge University Press, 2011.

Edited Books

Exploring Philosophy, Schenkman Publishing, 1970, revised General Learning Press, 1972, abridged edition 1972.
Individual and Collective Responsibility, Schenkman Publishing, 1972. Revised and Enlarged Second Edition, Schenkman Books, 1995.
Conscientious Actions, General Learning Press, 1974.
Philosophers in Wonderland, Llewellyn Publications, 1975.
Philosophical Explorations, Scott Foresman, 1978.
Contemporary Perspectives in the Philosophy of Language (with H.K. Wettstein and T.E. Uehling), University of Minnesota Press, 1978. Reprinted 2009.
Corrigible Corporations and Unruly Laws (with Brent Fisse), Trinity University Press, 1985.
Puzzles, Paradoxes, and Problems (with Curtis Brown), St. Martin's Press, 1986.
Ethics When Cultures Clash, War and Border Crossings (with Jason Short), Rowman & Littlefield, 2005.

Z.J. Goldberg (ed.), *Reflections on Ethics and Responsibility*,
DOI 10.1007/978-3-319-50359-2

Journal Editor

Midwest Studies in Philosophy, a philosophical annual book, University of Minnesota Press (Volumes I–IX), University of Notre Dame Press (Volumes X–XXII), Blackwell Publishers (now Wiley/Blackwell) (Volumes XXIII – present) Founder and Senior Editor (with T.E. Uehling (retired in 1993) and H.K. Wettstein)

- Vol. I Studies in the History of Philosophy, 1976
- Vol. II Studies in the Philosophy of Language, 1977
- Vol. III Studies in Ethical Theory, 1978*
- Vol. IV Studies in Metaphysics, 1979*
- Vol. V Studies in Epistemology, 1980
- Vol. VI The Foundations of Analytic Philosophy, 1981
- Vol. VII The Social and Political Philosophy, 1982*
- Vol. VIII Contemporary Perspectives on the History of Philosophy, 1983
- Vol. IX Causation and Causal Theories, 1984
- Vol. X Studies in the Philosophy of Mind, 1985*
- Vol. XI Studies in Essentialism, 1986
- Vol. XII Realism and Anti-Realism, 1987
- Vol. XIII Ethical Theory: Character and Virtue, 1988*
- Vol. XIV Contemporary Perspectives in the Philosophy of Language, II, 1989
- Vol. XV Philosophy of the Human Sciences, 1990
- Vol. XVI Philosophy of Art, 1991
- Vol. XVII The Wittgenstein Legacy, 1992*
- Vol. VXIII Philosophy of Science, 1993
- Vol. XIX Philosophical Naturalism, 1994
- Vol. XX Moral Concepts, 1995*
- Vol. XXI Philosophy of Religion, 1996
- Vol. XXII Philosophy of the Emotions, 1997*
- Vol. XXIII New Perspectives of Philosophy, 1998
- Vol. XXIV Life and Death: Metaphysics and Ethics, 1999*
- Vol. XXV Figurative Language, 2001
- Vol. XXVI Renaissance and Early Modern Philosophy, 2002* (with Guest Editor Bruce Silver)
- Vol. XXVII Meaning and the Arts, 2003
- Vol. XXVIII The American Philosophers, 2004* (with Guest Editor Bruce Silver)
- Vol. XXIX The Metaphysics and the Ethics of Free Will, 2005
- Vol. XXX Collective Responsibility and Shared Intention, 2006*
- Vol. XXXI Philosophy and the Empirical, 2007
- Vol. XXXII Truth and Its Deformities, 2008*
- Vol. XXXIII Philosophy and Poetry, 2009
- Vol. XXXIV Film and the Emotions, 2010* (with Guest Editor Michelle Saint)
- Vol. XXXV Early Modern Philosophy Reconsidered, 2011
- Vol. XXXVI The Concept of Evil, 2012* (with Guest Editor Zachary J. Goldberg)
- Vol. XXXVII The New Atheism and Its Critics, 2013
- Vol. XXXVIII Forward-Looking Collective Responsibility, 2014*
- Vol. XXXIX Philosophy and Science Fiction, 2015 (with Guest Co-Editor Eric Schwitzgebel)
- Vol. XXXX Ethics and Global Climate Change, 2016*

---

*= Peter French is the sole editor of the volume. He also worked with a Guest Editor on four volumes as noted.

The Journal of Social Philosophy (1988–2005) Blackwell Publishers. Three issues per volume 1988–1999 – Four issues per volume 2000–2005.
Issues in Contemporary Ethics: Seven Volumes – General Learning Press.

- *Individual and Collective Responsibility*
- *The Manson Murders* (Editor D.E. Cooper)
- *Conscientious Actions*
- *Utopia/Dystopia?* (Editor P. Richter)
- *Punishment and Human Rights* (Editor M. Goldinger)
- *Abortion, Pro and Con* (Editor R. Perkins)
- *Assassination* (Editor H. Zellner)

Articles and Chapters

"Multi-Spatial Myths: Kant and the Dreamer," *Southern Journal of Philosophy*, Fall, 1973.
"On Blaming Psychopaths," *The Manson Murders: A Philosophical Inquiry*, ed. by D.E. Cooper, Cambridge, MA, 1973.
"Morally Blaming Whole Populations," *Philosophy, Morality, and International Affairs*, ed. by V. Held, S. Morganbesser, and T. Nagel, Oxford University Press, 1974. Reprinted in K. Struhl and P. Struhl, *Philosophy Now*, Random House, 1980.
"Conditional Reflexes and Mechanisms of Meaningful Behavior," (with J. Shekleton), *Philosophy*, Summer, 1974.
"Can A Man Imagine Himself Witnessing His Own Funeral," *International Journal for the Philosophy of Religion*, Vol. 5, No. 4, 1974.
"'Seeing' and 'Seeing That'; 'Observing' and 'Observing That'," *American Philosophical Quarterly*, Monograph Series #9, 1975.
"Types of Collectivities and Blame," *Personalist*, Spring, 1975.
"Wittgenstein's Limits of the World," *Midwest Studies in Philosophy*, Vol. 1, 1976.
"Senses of 'Blame'," *Southern Journal of Philosophy*, Winter, 1976.
"Institutional and Moral Obligations or Merels and Morals," *The Journal of Philosophy*, Vol. LXXXIV, No. 10, October, 1977.
"Philosophy and Psychical Research," *The Journal of Parapsychology*, Vol. 41, No. 1, 1977.
"On the Possibility of a Causal Theory of Extra-Sensory Perceptual Knowledge," *The Philosophy of Parapsychology*, ed. by B. Shapin and L. Coly, New York, 1977.
"What the Scarecrow Thought He Didn't Have," *Growing Up With Philosophy*, ed. by M. Lipman and A. Sharp, Temple University Press, 1978.
"Corporate Moral Agency," *Ethical Theory and Business*, ed. by T. Beauchamp and N. Bowie, Prentice-Hall, 1978. Reprinted in *Business Ethics*, ed. by W. Hoffman and J. Moore, McGraw-Hill, 1984, 1990 and in *Ethical Issues in Professional Life*, ed. by J. Callahan, 1988 and in numerous other anthologies.
"The Corporation as a Moral Person," *American Philosophical Quarterly*, July, 1979. Reprinted in *Ethical Issues in Business*, ed. by T. Donaldson and P. Werhane, Prentice-Hall, 1983 and subsequent editions; *Collective Responsibility*, ed. by L. May and S. Hoffman, Rowman and Littlefield, 1992; and in numerous anthologies and many languages.
"'He wos wery good to me, he wos!', Morality and Euergetics," *Essays in Honor of William Werkmeister*, ed. by E.F. Kaelin, University Presses of Florida, 1981.
"Burking a Mill," *Ethical Issues in Government*, ed. by N. Bowie, Temple University Press, Philosophical Monographs Series, 1981.

"What is Hamlet to McDonnell-Douglas, McDonnell-Douglas to Hamlet: DC-10," *Business and Professional Ethics*, Vol. 2, Spring, 1981. Reprinted in *The DC-10 Case*, ed. by J. Fielder and D. Birsch, SUNY Press, 1992 and in other anthologies.

"Collective Responsibility in the Practice of Medicine," *The Journal of Medicine and Philosophy*, Winter 1982.

"Crowds and Corporations," *American Philosophical Quarterly*, July, 1982.

"The Survival of My Counterpart," *Southern Journal of Philosophy*, Spring, 1982.

"Kinds and Persons," *Philosophy and Phenomenological Research*, 1983. Reprinted in *What Is A Person?* ed. by M. Goodman, Humana Press, 1988.

"The Principle of Responsive Adjustment in Corporate Moral Responsibility: Crash on Mt. Erebus," *The Journal of Business Ethics*, May, 1984.

"Agents and Responsible Persons," *Business and Professional Ethics*, Summer, 1984.

"A Principle of Responsive Adjustment," *Philosophy*, October 1984.

"The Hester Prynne Sanction," *Business and Professional Ethics*, Winter 1985.

"Wittgenstein and the Limits of the World," *Ludwig Wittgenstein: Critical Assessments*, ed. by S. Shanker. Croom Helm Publishers, London, 1985.

"Fishing the Red Herrings Out of the Sea of Responsibility," *Actions and Events*, ed. by E. LePore and B. McLaughlin, Blackwell's, 1985.

"Principles of Responsibility, Shame, and the Corporation," the lead essay in *Shame, Responsibility, and the Corporation*, ed. by H. Curtler, Haven Publishing, 1986.

"Publicity and the Control of Corporate Conduct," *Corrigible Corporations and Unruly Laws* (noted above). Reprinted in *Ethics and Social Concern*, ed. by A. Serafini, Paragon, 1989.

"Corporate Responses to Errant Behavior: Time's Arrow, Law's Target" (with Brent Fisse), *Corrigible Corporations and Unruly Laws* (noted above).

"A Legacy of Ignorance," *Perspectives*, Fall, 1987. "Exorcising the Demon of Cultural Relativism," *Problems of International Justice*, ed. by S. Luper-Foy, Westview Press, 1987.

"Constitutionalism and Military Justice: Making Justice From Military Justice," *Constitutionalism: The Philosophical Dimension*, ed. by A. Rosenbaum, Greenwood Press, 1988.

"What Can You Do With Art?," *Inquiries into Values*, ed. by S. Lee, Edwin Mellon Press, 1988.

"Enforced Corporate Responsive Adjustment," *Legal Studies Forum*, Fall, 1989. "It's a Damn Shame," *Freedom, Equality, and Social Change*, ed. by C. Peden and J. Sterba, Mellon Press, 1989.

"Terre Gaste," *Business, Ethics, and the Environment*, ed. by M. Hoffman, R. Frederick, and E. Petry, Greenwood Press, 1990.

"Corporate Crimes and Innovative Punishments," *Coordination of Social Values*, ed. by K. Koford and J. Miller, University of Michigan Press, 1991.

"The State of the Art of Business Ethics," (Review) *Ethics*, Spring, 1991.

"Die Korporation als moralische Person" (new German version), *Wirtschaft und Ethik*, ed. by Lenk and Maring, Reclam, 1992.

"La Responsabilita Morale Dell'Impresa," *Etica Degli Affari E DelleProffessioni*, ed. by A. Massarenti, 1992.

"Responsibility and the Moral Role of Corporate Entities," *Business as a Humanity*, ed. by T. Donaldson and E. Freeman, Oxford University Press, 1994.

"Undergraduate Research Programs: Philosophy and Accounting" (with R. Jensen and K. Robertson), *Critical Perspectives on Accounting*, 1992.

"Why Did Wittgenstein Read Tagore to the Vienna Circle?" *Proto Soziologie*, 1993. Republished in Book Form as *Protosoziologie im Kontext: "Lebenswelt" und "System" in Philosophie und Soziologie*, ed. by G. Preyer, G. Peter, and A. Ulfig, Verlag Konigshausen & Neumann, Wurzburg, 1996.

"The Practical and Ethical Costs of Corporate Reengineering," *Business and Professional Ethics Journal*, Winter 1994.

"Corporate Moral Agency," *The Blackwell Encyclopedic Dictionary of Business Ethics*, 1996.
"Action Theory, Rational-Choice Theory, and Ethics," *Business Ethics Quarterly*, Summer 1995.
"The Compensatory Opportunities of Re-engineering," *Perspectives on the Professions*, Spring, 1996.
"Rationality and Ethics," *Proto Soziologie*, Volume 8/9, 1996.
"Moral Principles, Rules, and Policies," *Ethics and Decision Making in Local Schools: Inclusion, Policy, and Reform*, ed. by J. Paul, N. Berger, P. Osnes, Y. Martinez, and W. Morse, Paul H. Brookes Publishing, 1997.
"Integrity, Intentions, and Corporations," *American Business Law Journal*, Volume 34/2, Winter 1996. Reprinted in a number of anthologies.
"Spatial and Temporal Ethics" in *Frontiers in American Philosophy*, Volume II, ed. by R. Burch and H. Saatkamp, Texas A&M University Press, 1996.
"Foreword to *Collective Responsibility*," in *Collective Responsibility* by G. Mellema, Rodopi, 1998.
"The Virtue of Shame in America," in *American Values*, ed. by K. Stewart, Angelo State University Press, 1998.
"Responsibility" in *The Philosophy of Law: An Encyclopedia*, ed. by C. Gray, Garland Publishing, 1999.
"Status" in *The Philosophy of Law: An Encyclopedia*, ed. by C. Gray, Garland Publishing, 1999.
"The Meaning of Democracy: A Western Perspective," *Proceedings of the Twentieth World Congress of Philosophy*, Volume XI, "Social and Political Philosophy," Philosophy Documentation Center, 2001.
"Unchosen Evil and Moral Responsibility," *War Crimes and Collective Wrongdoings*, ed. by A. Jokic, Blackwell Publishing, 2001.
"Unchosen Evil and the Responsibility of War Criminals," *The Leader's Imperative*, ed. by C. Ficarrotta, Purdue University Press, 2001.
"Ethics and Death in Westerns," in *Reason and Culture*, ed. by J. Arthur, A. Shapiro, and W. Throop, Prentice-Hall, 2001.
"Ethics and Special Education," (with James Paul and Ann Cranston-Gingras), *Focus on Exceptional Children*, Volume 34, Number 1, September 2001. Reprinted in *Rethinking Professional Issues in Special Education*, ed. by J. Paul, C. Lavely, A. Cranston-Gingras, and E. Taylor, Ablex Publishing, 2002.
"Honor, Shame, and Identity," *Public Affairs Quarterly*, Volume 16, Number 1, January 2002.
"Changes in Latitudes, Changes in Attitudes," (with Mitchell Haney) *Contemporary Philosophy*, Volume XXIII, Number 5 & 6, 2002.
"Ethics, Intercollegiate Sports, and the Mission of the University," *Professional Ethics*, 2001.
"Inference Gaps in Moral Assessment and the Moral Agency of Health Care Organizations," *Institutional Integrity in Health Care* ed. by A. Smith Iltis, Kluwer, 2003.
"Ethical Revenge in Westerns," in *Understanding Film Genres*, ed. by T. Pendergast, S. Pendergast, and S. Schneider, McGraw-Hill, 2003.
"Inference Gaps in Moral Assessment: Capitalism, Corporations, and Individuals," *International Social Science Journal*, 2005.
"Responsibility with No Alternatives, in Loss of Innocence, and Collective Affectivity: Responses to McKenna, Haji, and Tollefsen," *American Philosophical Association Newsletter on Philosophy and Law*, Volume 7, Number 2, ed. by S. Scalet and C. Griffin, Spring 2008, (Edition in "Tribute to Peter French")
"Worthwhile Living in Second Life," in *The Value of Time and Leisure in a World of Work*, ed. by M. Haney and A.D. Kline, Lexington Books, 2010.
"The Horror of the Weeping Angels" (with Michelle Saint) in *Dr. Who and Philosophy* ed. by P. Smithka and C. Lewis, Open Court Press, 2010.

"The Old Luddite Doctrine and the Emerging Technologies of the Twenty-First Century" in *Pacing Law And Ethics With Science And Technology*, ed. by G. Marchant, B. Allenby, and J. Herkert, Springer, 2011.

"Moral Notions, Originality, and Some Examples," in *Meaning and Morality: Essays on the Philosophy of Julius Kovesi*, ed. by A. Tapper and T.B. Mooney, Brill, 2012.

"A Critical Review of *Morality and War: Can War be Just in the Twenty-first Century?*" *Mind*, 2013.

"Complicity: That Moral Monster," *Criminal Law and Philosophy*, 2014.

"Corporate Moral Agency," *Wiley Encyclopedia of Management*, 3rd edition, 2014.

"Self-Blaming, Repentance, and Atonement," *The Journal of Value Inquiry*, Number 3, 2015.

Index

Z.J. Goldberg (ed.), *Reflections on Ethics and Responsibility*,
DOI 10.1007/978-3-319-50359-2

MIX
Papier aus verantwortungsvollen Quellen
Paper from responsible sources
FSC® C105338

If you have any concerns about our products,
you can contact us on
ProductSafety@springernature.com

In case Publisher is established outside the EU,
the EU authorized representative is:
Springer Nature Customer Service Center GmbH
Europaplatz 3, 69115 Heidelberg, Germany

Printed by Libri Plureos GmbH
in Hamburg, Germany